ROUTLEDGE HANDBO ...UL
DISABILITY LAW AND HUMAN RIGHTS

This handbook provides a comprehensive and authoritative state-of-the-art review of the current and emerging research and policy on disability law.

Bringing together a team of respected and experienced experts, the handbook offers a range of jurisdictional and multidisciplinary perspectives. The authors consider historical and contemporary, as well as comparative perspectives of disability law. Divided into three parts, the contributors provide a comprehensive reference to the theoretical underpinnings, ongoing debates and emerging fields within the subject. The study provides a strong basis for consideration of contemporary disability law, its research foundations, and progressive developments in the area. The book incorporates interdisciplinary and comparative country perspectives to capture the breadth of current discourse on disability law.

This handbook provides a valuable resource for a wide range of scholars, public and private researchers, NGOs, and practitioners working in the area of disability law, and across national and transnational disability schemes. The work will be of important interest to those in the fields of sociology, history, psychology, economics, political science, rehabilitation sciences, medicine, technology, and law, among others.

Peter Blanck is University Professor and Chairman, Burton Blatt Institute, Syracuse University, USA. He is also Honorary Professor, Centre for Disability Law & Policy, at the National University of Ireland, Galway. Blanck is Chairman of the Global Universal Design Commission (GUDC), and President of Raising the Floor (RtF) USA. He has written articles and books on the Americans with Disabilities Act (ADA) and related laws, and received grants to study disability law and policy.

Eilionóir Flynn is the Deputy Director of the Centre for Disability Law and Policy, and Senior Lecturer at the School of Law, National University of Ireland Galway. Her interest in disability law stems from a broader interest in social justice and a recognition of the invisibility of people with disabilities in broader human rights discourse. Her current research interests in this field include legal capacity, disability advocacy and access to justice, and she has published widely in national and international peer reviewed journals on these issues, as well as producing a monograph on the implementation of the CRPD for Cambridge University Press.

ROUTLEDGE HANDBOOK OF DISABILITY LAW AND HUMAN RIGHTS

Edited by Peter Blanck and Eilionóir Flynn

LONDON AND NEW YORK

First published 2017
by Routledge
2 Park Square, Milton Park, Abingdon, Oxon, OX14 4RN

and by Routledge
52 Vanderbilt Avenue, New York, NY 10017

First issued in paperback 2020

Routledge is an imprint of the Taylor & Francis Group, an informa business

British Library Cataloguing in Publication Data
A catalogue record for this book is available from the British Library

Library of Congress Cataloging-in-Publication Data
A catalog record for this title has been requested

ISBN 13: 978-0-367-58157-2 (pbk)
ISBN 13: 978-1-4724-3865-2 (hbk)

Typeset in Bembo
by Apex CoVantage, LLC

This collaborative volume is dedicated to disability advocates across the globe.

CONTENTS

FIGURES

NOTES ON CONTRIBUTORS

Anna Arstein-Kerslake is the Director of the Disability Human Rights Clinic at Melbourne Law School and the Academic Convener of the Disability Research Initiative at the University of Melbourne. Prior to her work in Australia, she worked as a Marie Curie Research Fellow at the Centre for Disability Law and Policy at the National University of Galway, Ireland. Her human rights advocacy has spanned government, civil society and academic bodies.

Peter Blanck is University Professor and Chairman of the Burton Blatt Institute (BBI) at Syracuse University. He received a Juris Doctorate from Stanford University, where he was President of the Stanford Law Review, and a PhD in Social Psychology from Harvard University. Dr Blanck is Honorary Professor, Centre for Disability Law & Policy, at the National University of Ireland, Galway. Blanck has written articles and books on the Americans with Disabilities Act (ADA) and has received grants to study the law's implementation. His recent book is *eQuality: The Struggle for Web Accessibility by Persons with Disabilities* (Cambridge University Press, 2014).

Ciara Brennan held a Marie Curie fellowship at the Centre for Disability Studies at the University of Iceland, where she is a PhD candidate. Her thesis focuses on Article 19 of the CRPD, independent living and personal assistance in Nordic countries. Prior to joining the University of Iceland, Ciara worked as a research assistant at the National Institute for Intellectual Disability at Trinity College Dublin.

Constantin Cojocariu is a freelance human rights lawyer, specializing in equality and non-discrimination. He has a rich litigation experience before the European Court of Human Rights, having acted as counsel in several major disability rights judgments, including the Centre for Legal Resources on behalf of Valentin Câmpeanu v. Romania, D.D. v. Lithuania and Đorđević v. Croatia. Constantin worked as a lawyer at international non-governmental organizations European Roma Rights Centre (2005–2007) and Interights (2007–2014). He has lectured, delivered trainings and published widely on a broad range of human rights topics across Europe and beyond. He currently acts as consultant to a number of international organizations, including the Council of Europe, the OSCE and the Open Society Foundations. He is a member for Romania of LGBT lawyers' network European Commission on Sexual Orientation Law (ECSOL) and writes his own bilingual human rights blog (www.pedreptvorbind.blogspot.com).

Theresia Degener is Professor of law and disability studies at Evangelische Fachhochschule RWL – University of Applied Sciences in Bochum, Germany and Director of the Bochum Center for Disability Studies BODYS. She is Vice–Chair of the United Nations Committee on the Rights of Persons with Disabilities. She studied law in Frankfurt am Main Germany and Berkeley, California, USA.

Aisling de Paor, BCL, LLM, PhD, Solicitor, is a Lecturer in Law at the School of Law and Government, Dublin City University. Aisling graduated from National University of Ireland, Galway with a law degree (BCL) in 2005 and graduated from University College Cork with a masters in law (LLM) in 2006. She is a qualified Solicitor (Law Society of Ireland) and trained in a large commercial law firm in Dublin (2006–9). In 2013, Aisling defended her PhD (funded by the Irish Research Council), entitled 'Advancing Science and Controlling the Misuse of Genetic Information in Employment and Insurance – Towards an Effective European Union Regulatory Framework.' From 2009 to 2014, Aisling was a part-time Lecturer in Law at the School of Law, NUI Galway, and also worked as a Research Assistant at the Centre for Disability Law and Policy, NUI Galway (2009–10). She is an honorary fellow and an affiliated researcher of the Burton Blatt Institute, Syracuse University, New York and was a visiting scholar at this Institute in October 2012 and May 2014.

Eilionóir Flynn is a Senior Lecturer at the School of Law and Acting Director of the Centre for Disability Law and Policy, National University of Ireland Galway. Her current research interests include legal capacity, advocacy, access to justice, and the intersectionality of disability, gender and ageing. She is the author of two monographs (Cambridge University Press and Ashgate Publishers), editor of four collected volumes (Intersentia and Ashgate) and several peer reviewed articles in international journals. Eilionóir is the Principal Investigator on the VOICES project, funded by a Starting Grant from the European Research Council.

Jennifer Green is an academic in the Business School at the University of Technology Sydney where she is the Program Director for Postgraduate Not-for-profit and Social Enterprise Management and the Chair of the University's Access and Inclusion Working Party. She has pursued a career in education with a focus on inclusion. This includes a previous appointment as the State Manager for Disability Service in New South Wales Technical and Further Education and current appointments as the secretary of the Australian Centre for Disability Law and the Deputy Chair of Macquarie Community College. Jenny's primary research and publications are on the inclusion of people with disability in education and employment.

Bjørn Hvinden is Professor of Sociology and Head of Research at NOVA Norwegian Social Research at the Oslo and Akershus University College. Main research interests include disability, active citizenship, comparative research on social policy, the implications of climate change for well-being and social policy, the response of social services in relation to disasters and emerging forms of social solidarity. He is scientific coordinator of the European Union FP7 research project DISCIT on active citizenship for persons with disabilities and the Horizon 2020 project NEGOTIATE on the consequences of early job insecurity and how young people's agency can mitigate the negative impact of such insecurity. He is Co-Chair of the European Social Policy Analysis Network.

Elizabeth Kamundia is a doctoral candidate as well as the Disability Rights Project Coordinator for the Centre for Human Rights of the University of Pretoria. Elizabeth has held various legal researcher positions including jobs with the Centre for Disability Law and Policy of the National University of Ireland, Galway, Kenya National Commission on Human Rights and the Committee of Experts on Constitutional Review (Kenya). Elizabeth also works as a consultant on disability rights with the Commission on the Implementation of the Constitution of Kenya, Users and Survivors of Psychiatry – Kenya and the Kenya Association of the Intellectually Handicapped. Elizabeth is an advocate of the High Court of Kenya.

Rosemary Kayess is a human rights lawyer, and currently teaches in the Faculty of Law at the University of New South Wales. Convening international law and human rights subjects, she focuses on the equality provisions within international instruments and their translation into domestic law and policy. She is also a Senior Research Fellow with Social Policy Research Centre UNSW and has extensive research experience working and advising on a variety of social research projects including access to justice, social inclusion, human rights and disability, including work on the implementation of CRPD in Australia, Asia/Pacific and Europe. Rosemary was an external expert on the Australian Government delegation to the United Nations negotiations for the Convention on the Rights of Persons with Disabilities. During the ad hoc Committee she facilitated the negotiations on Article 24 Education. She is currently a member of the Australian Department of Foreign Affairs and Trade Disability Inclusive Development Reference Group and Chairperson of the Australian Centre for Disability Law.

Mary Keogh works as Senior Advisor for Disability and Gender Equality with CBM International. She has over 15 years of experience in working with human rights and international development cooperation with a range of NGOs as well as public agencies. Her doctoral thesis explored how donor agencies mainstream disability in their international aid programs. Her research interests include gender and disability and intersectionality.

Anna Lawson is Professor of law and Director of the Centre for Disability Studies at the University of Leeds. She is also a member of the statutory Disability Committee of the Equality and Human Rights Commission for England, Scotland and Wales.

Mark Priestley is Professor of Disability Policy at the University of Leeds. He has worked for more than 25 years in the disability field, with more than 150 relevant publications. For the past 7 years he has been Scientific Director of ANED (the European Commission's Academic Network of European Disability experts), coordinating a program of evidence-based policy analysis across thirty-five countries to support the EU's policy development in the disability field.

Arie Rimmerman PhD/DSW is Richard Crossman Professor of Social Welfare and Social Planning and founder Dean of Social Welfare and Health Sciences and head of School of Social Work at University of Haifa, Israel. His research focuses on comparative disability policies, particularly in areas of employment, civic society and family support. Rimmerman is the author of two recent books, *Social Inclusion of People with Disabilities* (2013) and *Family Policy and Disability*, published by Cambridge University Press. Aside from his scientific contributions, he has served as an advisor to Ministers of Labor and Welfare in Israel and public committees on disabilities in Israel (NII, Commission on Disability Right, Committee of International Experts, and Central Bureau of Statistics) Europe and the United States. He is the recipient of the Lehman Award (1987), the William Trump Award (1998), the 1999 International Award of the American Association on Mental Retardation (AAMR) and the 2006 Burton Blatt Leadership Award.

Lisa Schur is Professor and Chair of the Department of Labor Studies and Employment Relations at Rutgers University, where she teaches employment and labor law. She received a PhD in Political Science from the University of California-Berkeley and a JD from Northeastern University. Her research focuses on the economic, political, and social inclusion of people with disabilities, particularly their political participation and employment experiences and outcomes. In addition to publishing in peer-reviewed journals, she wrote an invited White Paper on Disability and Voting for the Presidential Commission on Election Administration, and co-authored the book *People with Disabilities: Sidelined or Mainstreamed?* published by Cambridge University Press.

Lucy Series is a research associate at the School of Law and Politics, Cardiff University. Lucy's research focuses on legal capacity, deprivation of liberty, social care and disability rights. She has worked at the Centre for Disability Law and Policy at NUI Galway, and completed her PhD in law at Exeter University.

Michal Soffer, PhD, MSW, is a Senior Lecturer at the School of Social Work at University of Haifa, Israel. Her main research interests are stigma toward disability and illness as reflected in policies and social structures and processes. She has co-authored a book on women inmates in Israel and published papers on illness-related stigma, mediated images of illness and disabilities, women inmates, and disability-related policies.

Lisa Waddington holds the European Disability Forum Chair in European Disability Law. Professor Waddington's principal area of interest lies in European and comparative disability law, the UN Convention on the Rights of Persons with Disabilities, and European and comparative equality law in general. In 2000, she received an ASPASIA award from the NWO (Netherlands Organization for Scientific Research). Between 2004 and 2007 she coordinated a large EU research and education project on European non-discrimination law. She also coordinated the involvement of Maastricht University in the FP7 EuRADE project (European Research Agendas expanding Disability Equality) and the Marie Curie Initial Training Network DREAM (Disability Rights Expanding Accessible Markets, 2011–2015). Professor Waddington is a scholar of the Maastricht Centre for European Law and a member of both the Ius Commune Research School and the Human Rights Research School. Between 1993 and 2004 she was the editor of the Maastricht Journal of European and Comparative Law. She is currently a board member of a number of networks and organizations, including the European Network of Legal Experts in the Non-discrimination Field and the Academic Network of European Disability experts. Professor Waddington has been an associate professor at the University of British Columbia, Vancouver, in 2000 and was a visiting professor at the University of Melbourne in 2015.

Betul Yalcin is a PhD candidate at the University of Leeds, School of Sociology and Social Policy. She has a BSc from Middle East Technical University (METU), Psychology Department. She holds two master's degrees, one in Developmental Psychology (METU) and the other in Comparative Social Policy (University of Oxford). In total, she has 18 years of professional experience in the disability field. She was one of the fourteen ESRs at Disability Rights Expanding Accessible Markets (DREAM) Initial Training Network, funded by the EU FP7 Marie Currie Actions. Previously, she has worked as a senior expert at the Turkish Ministry of Family and Social Policy, General Directorate for Persons with Disabilities and Elderly Services.

ACKNOWLEDGEMENTS

This project was generously supported, in part, by numerous grantors and funders.

For Peter Blanck, support was provided by the U.S. Administration for Community Living, Department of Health and Human Services; the National Institute on Disability, Independent Living, and Rehabilitation Research (NIDILRR), and its Southeast ADA Center project; and the Office for Disability and Employment Policy (ODEP), in the U.S. Department of Labor. For further information on project funding and support from the Burton Blatt institute at Syracuse University, see http://bbi.syr.edu. The points of view or opinions in this volume do not necessarily represent official positions of governmental and other funders.

For Eilionóir Flynn, funding support was provided by the Atlantic Philanthropies.

Completion of this project would not have been possible without the valuable support of colleagues at the Centre for Disability Law & Policy, National University of Ireland Galway, especially Niamh Lally who coordinated the author contributions in the first instance, and Katie O'Halloran who provided valuable editing assistance. At the Burton Blatt Institute, Darlene Carelli, along with an array of research assistants, provided their usual invaluable support.

The editors thank Ashgate Publications for its commitment to the disability rights arena and the contributors to this volume for their important engagement in the area. We dedicate this volume to the next generation of disability rights advocates around the globe.

PB
EF
May 2015

INTRODUCTION

In the past 25 years, disability rights law worldwide has undergone a revolutionary transformation. Many countries started this journey by adopting equality and anti-discrimination legislation, which prohibits discrimination on the basis of disability, often inspired by the example of the Americans with Disabilities Act (ADA) of 1990 in the United States. With the entry into force of the U.N. Convention on the Rights of Persons with Disabilities (CRPD) in 2008, the landscape has changed again. The CRPD's comprehensive human rights model has refocused attention on securing the full and equal inclusion of individuals with disabilities in all aspects of society.

In light of this changing landscape, the time is right for a research companion to introduce the next generation of disability rights and other scholars to the critical ideas that have guided the development of law and policy in this field over the past several decades. In this edited collection, we have brought together a wide array of authors – from different parts of the globe and different disciplinary backgrounds – to capture the breadth of current discourse on disability rights law.

The Companion is divided into three parts: Theoretical Underpinnings of Disability Law, Ongoing Debates in Disability Law, and Emerging Fields in Disability Law. This structure provides a sound basis for consideration of contemporary disability law, its research foundations, and progressive developments in the area. In each of these parts, the chapter contributors offer a range of jurisdictional and multidisciplinary perspectives, and consider historical and contemporary, as well as comparative perspectives of disability law.

In the first part, chapter contributors Anna Lawson, Mark Priestley, Bjørn Hvinden, and Theresia Degener consider the classical theories that guide the evolution of disability rights law in different regions of the world. They examine the social model developed by disability activists and scholars in Britain, and the global approach of the human rights model of disability reflected in the CRPD. These contributions frame the remainder of the volume by providing an accessible overview of these major theoretical frameworks, their connections and distinctions, and how they shape the development of disability law in practice.

The second part of this Companion examines key conflicts and tensions in disability rights law, which continue to be debated throughout the globe. Rosemary Kayess and Jennifer Green tackle the inclusion debate in education – considering how truly inclusive education may be achieved while providing reasonable accommodation for learners with disabilities within the mainstream school setting. Lisa Waddington, Mark Priestley and Betul Yalcin address the issue of "sheltered" work. They consider how the employment rights of people with disabilities may be achieved without reinforcing outdated segregated work practices. Anna Lawson examines the elusive nature of access to justice for people with disabilities, highlighting barriers to effective participation that exist in the courtroom and beyond. Constantin Cojocariu develops this justice theme further by highlighting the difficulties of supporting people with disabilities to take their rights claims to court, using a case study of the European Court of Human Rights. Finally, Lisa Schur looks at the barriers to social and political participation of people with disabilities that continue to permeate global societies.

In the third and final part of this Companion, new and emerging fields in disability law are examined. These contributions focus on topics as diverse as legal capacity and independent living, web equality and access to culture, disability and ageing, the role of the family, genetic discrimination and inclusive development aid. Elizabeth Kamundia, Lucy Series, and Anna Arstein-Kerslake highlight new thinking about support to exercise legal capacity, while Ciara Brennan addresses the crucial issue of choice of where and with whom to live and the support required to live independently. Peter Blanck examines access to the web and its content. The intersection of disability with other identities and minority groups, such as people who experience genetic discrimination and older people, are considered by Aisling de Paor and Eilionóir Flynn. Mary Keogh delves into the argument that in order to build on the success made in disability-inclusive development we must conceptualize equality for persons with disabilities. Finally, the relationships between people with disabilities and their natural community of support – the family – is explored by Arie Rimmerman and Michal Soffer.

Given its diversity of research topics, this Companion will be of interest to a wide range of scholars, public and private researchers, NGOs, and practitioners working in the area of disability rights law, and across national and transnational disability schemes. In addition, the Companion will be of interest to those in the fields of sociology, history, psychology, economics, political science, rehabilitation sciences, medicine, technology, and law, among others. We have designed this Companion for ease of use by scholars, researchers, graduate and postgraduate students, NGOs, governmental analysts, and legal practitioners. It is intended to provide a comprehensive analysis of current and emerging research and policy in disability rights law. We hope that it will be useful to you, the reader, in your work, and in advancing the rights of persons with disabilities throughout the world.

PART I

Theoretical underpinnings of disability law

1

THE SOCIAL MODEL
OF DISABILITY

Questions for law and legal scholarship?

Anna Lawson and Mark Priestley

Introduction

The powerful influence of the social model of disability over international and regional law and policy has, in recent years, often been recognised. At the international level for instance, the committee which monitors the implementation of the United Nations Convention on the Rights of Persons with Disabilities (CRPD) has observed that the treaty 'establishes' the social model approach to disability.[1] It has also been described as the 'knowledge base which has informed'[2] the CRPD and an idea which has exercised an 'enormous influence in the development of the CRPD'.[3] At a regional level, for well over a decade the European Commission has explicitly pledged commitment to the social model of disability as a key driver of EU disability-related law and policy initiatives. Thus, in its 2003 Disability Action Plan, the Commission stated that:

> The EU . . . sees disability as a social construct. The EU social model of disability stresses the environmental barriers in society which prevent the full participation of people with disabilities in society.[4]

Claims such as these suggest that social model thinking can play a powerful role in stimulating legal reform. This chapter aims to introduce the idea of the social model and to identify the key questions it poses for law and legal scholarship. It will be divided into two main sections. In the first, we will introduce the social model, outlining its history and some of the key debates

---

1 Committee on the Rights of Persons with Disabilities, Concluding Observations on Peru, 7th session, April 2012, para 6.
2 R Traustadóttir, 'Disability Studies, the Social Model and Legal Developments' in O Arnardóttir and G Quinn (eds) *The UN Convention on the Rights of Persons with Disabilities – European and Scandinavian Perspectives* (Martinus Nijhoff, 2009) 16.
3 R Kayess and P French, 'Out of Darkness Into Light: Introducing the United Nations Convention on the Rights of Persons with Disabilities' (2008) 8 (1) *Human Rights Law Review* 1, 7.
4 'Equal Opportunities for People with Disabilities: A European Action Plan' COM/2003/650 Final, s4.

which have surrounded it. In the second, we will focus on the key questions which the social model poses for law and legal scholarship – a subject which to date has received surprisingly little attention.[5]

The social model of disability

Emergence of the model

The term 'social model of disability', which has been described as the 'big idea' of the UK disabled people's movement,[6] dates back to the writing of Mike Oliver in the early 1980s.[7] For these purposes, Oliver drew directly on the distinction between 'impairment' and 'disability', made in 1976 by the Union of Physically Impaired Against Segregation (UPIAS). According to this:

> In our view, it is society which disables physically impaired people. Disability is something imposed on top of our impairments, by the way we are unnecessarily isolated and excluded from full participation in society.[8]

This distinction, which lies at the heart of this social model,[9] was also adopted by other disabled peoples organisations, including at the international level. Thus, in 1982, Disabled People's International (DPI) defined 'impairment' as 'the functional limitation within the individual caused by physical, mental or sensory impairment' and 'disability' as the 'loss or limitation of opportunities to take part in the normal life of the community due to physical and social barriers'.[10]

In the academic setting, the implications of this distinction and the social model of disability which rests upon it were then explored in a body of work (by Oliver and others)[11] which laid the foundations of the interdisciplinary field of disability studies. Alongside the idea of the social

---

5 For important exceptions, however, see A Kanter, 'The Law: What's Disability Studies Got to Do with It, or an Introduction to Disability Legal Studies,' (2011) 42 (2) *Columbia Human Rights Law Review 403*; A Kanter, 'The Relationship between Disability Studies and Law' in A Kanter and B Ferri (eds) *Righting Educational Wrongs: Disability Studies in Law and Education* (Syracuse University Press, Syracuse, 2013); and S Mor, 'Between Charity, Welfare, and Warfare: A Disability Legal Studies Analysis of Privilege and Neglect in Israeli Disability Policy' (2006) 18 *Yale Journal of Law and Humanities* 63.

6 F Hasler, 'Developments in the Disabled People's Movement' in J Swain, V Finkelstein, S French, and M Oliver (eds) *Disabling Barriers – Enabling Environments* (Sage, 1993).

7 M Oliver, 'A New Model in the Social Work Role in Relation to Disability' in J Campling (ed) *The Handicapped Person: A New Perspective for Social Workers* (RADAR, 1981); and M Oliver, *Social Work and Disabled People* (Macmillan, 1983).

8 The Union of Physically Impaired Against Segregation and the Disability Alliance 'Fundamental Principles of Disability' (UPIAS/Disability Alliance, 1976) 3.

9 Other approaches to disability exist and are sometimes referred to as forms of 'social model'. Unlike the social model under discussion here, they do not make a distinction between impairment and disability. Because they are discussed elsewhere in this book, they will not be discussed further here. For reflection on the relationship between these different models see e.g. M Priestley, 'Disability and Social Inequalities' in M Romero and E Margolis (eds) *Blackwell Companion to Social Inequalities* (Blackwell Publishing, 2005) 372; and M Priestley, 'Constructions and Creations: Idealism, Materialism and Disability Theory' (1998) 13 (1) *Disability and Society* 75.

10 DPI, Proceedings of the First World Congress, Singapore, (Disabled People's International, 1982) 105.

11 See e.g. V Finkelstein, *Attitudes and Disabled People: Issues for Discussion* (World Rehabilitation Fund, 1980) available at: http://www.disability-archive.leeds.ac.uk; P Abberley, 'The Concept of Oppression

model of disability, a theory of disability as oppression was developed, which sought to explain 'disability' in terms of structural causes. Considerable emphasis was thus given to understanding the processes of disablement to which people with impairments are subject – particularly through the operation of disabling barriers and the operation of the material relationships of power associated with capitalism that have historically operated to exclude many people with impairments from paid work.

It is 'disability' in the sense conveyed by the quotations from UPIAS and DPI, set out above, that forms the basis of the social model of disability. Thus, it does not include the functional limitations which are inherent to a particular biological trait or 'impairment'. Disability is not caused by impairment, nor constructed by society – it is created by society. It is the exclusion and disadvantage that result from social structures and systems. In Oliver's own words:

> In the broadest sense, the social model of disability is about nothing more complicated than a clear focus on the economic, environmental and cultural barriers encountered by people who are viewed by others as having some form of impairment – whether physical, mental or intellectual. The barriers disabled people encounter include inaccessible education systems, working environments, inadequate disability benefits, discriminatory health and social support services, inaccessible transport, houses and public buildings and amenities, and the devaluing of disabled people through negative images in the media – films and television, and newspapers.[12]

The UPIAS/Oliver origination of the social model in Britain is not the only socially oriented approach to disability that has influenced the development and reform of law and public policy. Indeed, the term 'social model' has become used rather widely in recent years. As Rannveig Traustadóttir has noted, it is now often used to refer to a range of social-contextual approaches which all recognise that 'disability' is, at least to some extent, a socio-political construct.[13] Amongst these are, for example, the kinds of 'normalisation' approaches prominent in Scandinavian writing; the 'minority rights' approach strongly associated with US disability politics; as well as the social interpretation of disability that provided the basis for its origin in the British 'social model'. Although these approaches differ considerably in some respects, common to all of them is the view that people who are perceived to have some form of physical, sensory, psychosocial, cognitive or other 'impairment' are subjected to unnecessary disadvantage and marginalisation by social factors external to themselves. 'Disability', viewed through the lens of the social model, is produced by social structures and processes and is not an inevitable result of individual difference or biology. Moreover, oppressive social relations can be challenged and disabling barriers removed.

---

and the Development of a Social Theory of Disability' (1987) *Disability, Handicap and Society* 2; M Oliver, *The Politics of Disablement* (Macmillan, 1990); M Oliver, *Understanding Disability: From Theory to Practice* (Macmillan, 1996); J Campbell and M Oliver, *Disability Politics: Understanding Our Past, Changing Our Future* (Routledge, 1996); C Barnes, 'A Working Social Model? Disability, Work and Disability Politics in the 21st Century' (2000) 20 *Critical Social Policy* 441; C Barnes and G Mercer, *Disability* (Polity Press, 2003); M Priestley, 'Constructions and Creations: Idealism, Materialism and Disability Theory' (1998) 13 *Disability and Society* 75; V Finkelstein, 'Representing Disability' in J Swain, S French, C Barnes and C Thomas (eds) *Disabling Barriers – Enabling Environments* (Sage, 2004).

12 M Oliver, 'The Social Model in Action: If I had a Hammer' in C Barnes and G Mercer (eds) *Implementing the Social Model of Disability: Theory and Research* (The Disability Press, 2004) 21. See also M Oliver, *Understanding Disability: From Theory to Practice* (MacMillan, 1996) 33.

13 Above n 2.

The political power of the social model

Oliver contrasts the social model of disability with 'individual model' approaches to disability. These locate the causes of social inequality and disadvantage in the body or mind of individuals with impairments. From an individual model perspective impairments are likely to be regarded as intrinsic 'abnormalities' or 'deficits' which prevent an individual from performing everyday tasks, which in turn prevents them from fulfilling valued social roles in society. In the traditional view then, 'disability' may be seen as an inevitable consequence of embodied difference and consequently associated with personal tragedy. The natural challenge for law and public policy in this model tends towards ensuring provision for responsible care or cure. The political power of the social model of disability lies in its reorientation to the challenge of disability – turning the focus away from the limitations arising from individual biology and toward the limitations created by social structures, processes and attitudes.

By locating the source of the disadvantages experienced by disabled people in their bodies or minds, individual approaches look for responses to these inequalities which focus only on changing or treating the individual. The responsibility and authority for such treatment rests primarily with medicine and its allied professions, including biomedical research and physical therapy. Locating the source of the disadvantage in social structures and systems, by contrast, calls for responses which entail changing society. Social problems call for social and not biomedical solutions. Thus, by focusing on disadvantage that is socially created, it directs attention to avoidable disadvantage and lays the foundation for the carving out of a series of identifiable barriers which are ripe for social change. The evident basis this provides for political action is strengthened by the fact that a focus on the disadvantage created by social, economic and environmental factors has the potential to emphasise connections between people with different types of 'impairment' or biological difference and thus provides a basis for commonality and combined political action.

The political and strategic potential of the UPIAS impairment-disability distinction that inspired the social model developed by Oliver has recently been thought-provokingly explored as an 'oppositional device' by Beckett and Campbell.[14] Their analysis helps to shed light on why this model became the 'big idea' of the UK disabled people's movement and provided such a powerful basis for resistance practices and strategies. The political potency of the social model is perhaps to be expected, given that the idea was itself rooted in the activism of the 1970s, which focused on campaigns for independent living and for an end to the exclusion of disabled people from mainstream society and an end to systems in which medical and allied professionals assumed undue control over various aspects of the lives of disabled people, including issues unconnected with healthcare (such as education or employment).[15]

The social model and its terminology

This UPIAS/Oliver version of the social model of disability, unlike some other social-contextual approaches, distinguished quite categorically between notions of 'impairment' and 'disability'

---

14 A Beckett and T Campbell, 'The Social Model of Disability as an Oppositional Device' (2015) 30 (2) *Disability and Society* 270.
15 See e.g. G De Jong, 'The Movement for Independent Living: Origins, Ideology and Implications for Disability Research' in A Brecbin, P Liddiard and J Swain (eds) *Handicap in a Social World* (Hodder and Stoughton, 1981); J Campbell and M Oliver, *Disability Politics: Understanding Our Past, Changing Our Future* (Routledge, 1996); H Hahn, 'Academic Debates and Political Advocacy: The US Disability Movement' in C Barnes, M Oliver and L Barton (eds) *Disability Studies Today* (Polity Press, 2002).

and was inspired explicitly by the foundational definitions offered by UPIAS in the 1970s. Acceptance of this social model understanding of disability has implications for the terminology we use. The logical consequence is that the term 'disability' should be reserved for the collective disadvantage caused to people with impairments by externally imposed social barriers. Many of those who adopt a social model approach (particularly in the UK) therefore favour the language of 'people with impairments' and 'disabled people'. This is because in social model terms, while it makes sense to speak of people becoming 'disabled' by social barriers, it is illogical to refer to people as having 'disabilities'. The term 'people with disabilities', however, is favoured by many disability campaigners outside the United Kingdom (including those influential in the drafting of international human rights instruments) because it positions 'people' before disability or impairment.[16] In this chapter we adopt the former terminology to emphasise the significance of the original social model framing.

Impairment-based critique of the social model

The social model, based on the impairment-disability distinction, has long been the subject of lively academic debate. A significant amount of this has focused on the notion of 'impairment' and its relationship with 'disability'. It has been argued, for instance, that the external and collective focus of social model approaches has disembodied discussions of disability, with the result that the unique experiences of people with different kinds of impairments may be overlooked.[17] Feminist-inspired scholarship has often drawn attention to the importance of exploring the personal experience of having an 'impairment' as well as the experience of being excluded by socially created barriers.[18] Consequently, scholars outside the social model tradition have sometimes misinterpreted its authors as rejecting the existence of individual difference and embodiment where this was not their intention. For example, the original UPIAS definition, quoted earlier, clearly acknowledges impairment but sees social disadvantage as something imposed 'on top' of it and 'unnecessarily'.

The purpose of examining disability through a social model lens is simply to refocus attention – to focus it on the social causes of inequality rather than on its biological causes. Tom Shakespeare has drawn attention to the fact that, in the lived realities of disabled people, it is often not possible to separate the disadvantage resulting from an impairment from the disadvantage resulting from social structures and processes and argued that the impairment-disability distinction is consequently unhelpful and that 'people are disabled by society and by their bodies'.[19] Responding to concerns that embodied or impairment-sensitive approaches could not be accommodated within the framework of a social model approach, Carol Thomas has argued that 'impairment effects', as well as 'disability effects', should be considered in efforts to understand the disadvantage experienced by disabled people and that:

> . . . once the term "disability" is ring-fenced to mean forms of oppressive social reactions visited upon people with impairments, there is no need to deny that impairment

16 See e.g. G Quinn, 'The Human Rights of People with Disabilities under EU Law' in P Alston, M Bustelo and M Keenan (eds) *The EU and Human Rights* (Oxford University Press, 1999) 285.
17 B Hughes and K Paterson, 'The Social Model of Disability and the Disappearing Body: Towards a Sociology of Impairment' (1997) 12 (3) *Disability & Society* 325. See also T Shakespeare, *Disability Rights and Wrongs* (Routledge, 2006).
18 See e.g. J Morris, *Pride Against Prejudice* (Women's Press, 1991); L Crow, 'Renewing the Social Model of Disability' (July 1992) *Coalition* 5–9; and S French, 'Disability, Impairment or Something in Between' in J Swain, S French, C Barnes and C Thomas (eds) *Disabling Barriers, Enabling Environments* (Sage, 1993).
19 T Shakespeare, *Disability Rights and Wrongs* (Routledge, London, 2006) 3.

and illness cause some restrictions of activity, or that in many situations both disability and impairment effects interact to place limits on activity.[20]

Commentators have drawn attention to the socio-political nature of 'impairment' too.[21] Certain types of barriers may become manifest only for people with certain impairment characteristics in certain types of social environment. The social exclusion of people with dyslexia from employment, for instance, is less likely to arise in a society where fewer jobs require high levels of literacy and where reading difficulty is less likely to be identified as difference or 'impairment'.[22] Conversely, certain types of impairment may arise more commonly in some societies and communities than others – for example, because of a high prevalence of malnutrition or industrial injuries.[23] The same impairment characteristics that are socially normalised amongst older people in ageing societies, such as partial hearing or memory, may be regarded as aberrant amongst children and young adults.[24] Further, society's categorisation of certain characteristics (e.g. mental health conditions) as forms of illness requiring treatment continues to trigger controversy.[25] In addition, the negative connotations of the term 'impairment' problematize its adoption by people with differences which they regard as essential and positive aspects of their identity (e.g. deafness or neurodiversity).[26] For this reason, the International Disability Caucus (which coordinated the negotiating efforts of disabled people's organisations in the lead up to the CRPD) proposed that the more neutral term 'condition' be used instead of 'impairment'.[27] This proposal, however, was not accepted.

In response to critiques of the social model of disability based on the impairment-disability distinction and its exclusive focus on social structures and systems, Oliver and Barnes wrote in 2012 that:

> Almost to the point of boredom, we have constantly stated that the social model is a tool to be used to produce changes in society and is not and was never intended to be a social theory.[28]

They also reiterate the point that:

> This social model breaks the causal link between impairment and disability. The reality of impairment is not denied but is not the cause of disabled people's economic and

20 C Thomas, 'Developing the Social Relational in the Social Model of Disability: A Theoretical Agenda' in C Barnes and G Mercer (eds) *Implementing the Social Model of Disability: Theory and Research* (The Disability Press, 2004) 29. See also C Thomas, *Female Forms: Experiencing and Understanding Disability* (Open University Press, 1999).

21 See e.g. S Tremain, 'On the Subject of Impairment' in M Corker and T Shakespeare (eds) *Disability/ Postmodernity: Embodying Disability Theory* (Bloomsbury Publishing, 2002). See also LJ Davis, 'The End of Identity Politics: On Disability as an Unstable Category' in LJ Davis (ed) *Disability Studies Reader* (Routledge, 2013).

22 T Campbell, *Dyslexia: The Government of Reading* (Palgrave Macmillan, 2013).

23 P Abberley, 'The Concept of Oppression and the Development of a Social Theory of Disability' (1987) 2 (1) *Disability, Handicap & Society* 5.

24 M Priestley, *Disability: A Life Course Approach* (Polity, 2003).

25 See e.g. the Users and Survivors of Psychiatry Movement and also texts such as E Watters, *Crazy Like Us: The Globalization of the American Psyche* (Simon and Schuster Ome, 2010).

26 See generally H Dirksen, L Bauman and J Murray, 'Deaf Studies in the 21st Century: "Deaf-Gain" and the Future of Human Diversity' in LJ Davis (ed) *Disability Studies Reader* (Routledge, 2013).

27 IDC Proposal for Article 2 in the 7th Session of the Ad Hoc Committee, available at www.un.org/esa/ socdev/enable/rights/ahc7docs/ahc7idcart2.doc.

28 M Oliver and C Barnes, *New Politics of Disablement* (Palgrave Macmillan, 2012) 10.

social disadvantage. Instead, the emphasis shifts to how far, and in what ways, society restricts their opportunities to participate in mainstream economic and social activities, rendering them more or less dependent. . . . The social model therefore shifts attention to disabled people's common experiences of oppression and exclusion and those areas that might be changed by collective political action and social change.[29]

Questions for law and legal scholarship

In the previous section, we provided a brief introduction to the idea of the social model of disability originally formulated by Mike Oliver, who drew directly on thinking from disabled people's organisations. In this section, we reflect on the key questions posed by this model for law and legal scholarship. For these purposes, we have divided the discussion into three main sections, reflecting three main questions: First we address the question of law's potential as an enabler – that is as a mechanism for challenging and breaking down disabling barriers. Second, we reflect on the question of how aspects of substantive law operate to disable people with impairments. Third, we consider (briefly) the question of how the operation of law excludes and disables people with impairments. This categorisation, we suggest, offers a helpful lens through which to critique law from a social model standpoint. Our aim here is to introduce this framework and not to provide any exhaustive critique of law from a social model perspective.

Enabling law: Law as part of the solution?

As has been explained in the previous section, social model understandings of disability necessarily focus attention on social factors that operate to disadvantage and exclude disabled people. For many, the adoption of a social model perspective carries with it a desire for, and commitment to bringing about, what they believe to be the social change needed to tackle and remove the barriers experienced by disabled people. Oliver has referred to the effort to challenge and remove disabling barriers as a 'journey to Utopia' and explained that 'for me this is a society where people with impairments live and flourish alongside everyone else but where disabling barriers and disablist values and attitudes have disappeared'.[30] It should be stressed, however, that the social model is primarily a tool through which to identify problems and pose questions. It does not itself provide solutions that will address complex processes of disablement and social model thinkers may therefore not always agree on the steps needed to bring about this Utopia.

Equality and human rights law have been looked to as a potential means through which to bring about the social changes needed to tackle disabling social barriers. In the late twentieth century, efforts to secure national anti-disability-discrimination legislation took centre stage. Underpinning both the US and the UK campaigns for comprehensive national anti-disability-discrimination legislation was a social model conception of disability.[31]

---

29 Ibid. at 22.
30 M Oliver, 'A Sociology of Disability or a Disablist Sociology' in L Barton (ed) *Disability and Society: Emerging Issues and Insights* (Longman, 1996).
31 See generally H Hahn, 'Adjudication or Empowerment: Contrasting Experiences with a Social Model of Disability' in L Barton (ed) *Disability, Politics and the Struggle for Change* (David Fulton, 2001); C Barnes, *Disabled People in Britain and Discrimination: A Case for Anti-discrimination Legislation* (Hurst/BCODP, 1991). See also C Gooding, *Disabling Laws, Enabling Acts* (Pluto, 1994).

The enactment of the US Americans with Disabilities Act in 1990, and the British Disability Discrimination Act in 1995, however, did not bring about the immediate radical changes for which many social model proponents (particularly in the US) had hoped. Early experience in the US courts shook the faith previously placed by leading figures in the disability movement in seeking solutions which depended for their success on lawsuits and the courts. This is well illustrated by the following words of Harlan Hahn:

> The courts had apparently failed to read or to comprehend the extensive legislative history accompanying the ADA that contained a detailed explanation of the social model of disability. In any event, without a massive campaign to re-educate judges and lawyers, the likelihood that the disability movement can achieve significant progress through litigation now appear relatively remote. To some observers, this conclusion might seem surprising or even shocking. Bickenbach *et al.* (1999: 1180) comment on my publications by saying:
>
> > . . . Hahn puts his faith in the legal protection of rights, and in particular, the legal protection that antidiscrimination law provides. Hahn does not opt for the civil rights approaches because he believes that court and judges are somehow immune to the effects of 'disabling images' and attitudes; instead he believes that, more than any other political or social institution, the law stands the best chance of guaranteeing the basic individual rights of disabled people.
>
> Yet, this restatement of the argument does not take into account the inalienable right of any analyst, including me, to change my mind.[32]

Similar disillusionment and frustration at the pace and unpredictability of non-discrimination legislation and courtroom-dependent change is undoubtedly shared by many former campaigners for such laws. According to Oliver and Barnes:

> . . . the pursuit of a single aim or goal in disability politics was and is a mistake and was bound to lead to a dilution of the collective energy and commitment of disabled people and their organizations and would ultimately achieve relatively little.[33] Focusing on a rights route to emancipation as an end in itself rather than as a means to an end was always likely to be counterproductive. It is becoming increasingly apparent that having legal rights does not mean that they will be enforced and even if they are, that enforcement will achieve the desired aims.[34]

Disappointment in what anti-discrimination law has delivered is, to some extent, a function of (unrealistically) high initial expectations of what it can, on its own, achieve. In reality, equality and non-discrimination law, however well-crafted and carefully implemented, can never achieve meaningful social change in isolation.[35] Their effectiveness will depend on the wider policy and political context in which they operate and they can only ever be part (and not the entirety) of a solution.

---

32 H Hahn, 'Adjudication or Empowerment: Contrasting Experiences with a Social Model of Disability' in L Barton (ed) *Disability, Politics and the Struggle for Change* (David Fulton, 2001) 64–5.
33 References omitted.
34 M Oliver and C Barnes, *New Politics of Disablement* (Palgrave Macmillan, 2012) 151.
35 A point made in A Lawson, *Disability and Equality Law in Britain: The Role of Reasonable Adjustment* (Hart Publishing, 2008) 294–295. See also B Hepple, 'Have Twenty-Five Years of the Race Relations Acts in Britain been a Failure?' in B Hepple and E Szyszczak (eds) *Discrimination: The Limits of the Law* (Mansell,

More recently, and at an international level, disabled people's organisations subscribing to a broad social model approach campaigned for and contributed to the drafting of what has become the pre-eminent global law on disability – the UN Convention on the Rights of Persons with Disabilities (CRPD). Again, initial expectations for this law seem to be impossibly high. In the words of Venus Ilagan, speaking in her capacity as chair of Disabled Peoples International on the day the full draft of the CRPD was agreed to by the Ad Hoc Committee responsible for the drafting process:

> Today, August 25, 2006, is a day to celebrate! We have achieved something that has long been the dream of our membership: A UN Convention on our human rights. . . . The draft instrument accepted here today recognizes and entrenches our rights in the UN Human Rights framework, and in this way is a huge victory for us all.[36]

Kicki Nordstrom, speaking on behalf of the International Disability Caucus on the same day added that:

> The IDC and the disability community have a dream. We had a dream that started . . . years ago when the first proposal for an international convention of human rights of persons with disabilities was tabled here in the UN . . . We . . . started to think, we started to govern and we created the IDC . . . in order to support States to develop good texts for our future dream . . . The dream has come closer and today we can say that . . . [it] is fulfilled – *almost!* . . . We hope that we one day will become equal to you and to everyone and that we can enjoy all human rights and all fundamental freedoms in the world on an equal basis with you. . . . Six hundred and fifty million persons with disabilities can hopefully look forward to a better world and a better life in the future. We hold our countries accountable for ratifying and implementing the convention very soon. Please, let our dream soon come true, do not let us down again! But remember, nothing about us, without us![37]

Similar expressions of optimism about the potential impact of the CRPD are to be found in statements from UN officials and diplomats. Thus, according to Kofi Annan, then the UN Secretary-General, the UN's adoption of this 'remarkable and forward-looking document' marks 'the dawn of a new era – an era in which disabled people will no longer have to endure the discriminatory practices and attitudes that have been permitted to prevail for all too long'.[38]

1990); DA Young and R Quibell (eds) 'Why Rights Are Never Enough: Rights, Intellectual Disability and Understanding' (2000) 15 *Disability and Society* 747; M Russell, 'What Disability Civil Rights Cannot Do: Employment and Political Economy' (2002) 17 *Disability and Society* 117; AI Batavia, 'Ten Years Later: The ADA and the Future of Disability Policy' in L Pickering Francis and A Silvers (eds) *Americans with Disabilities: Exploring Implications of the Law for Individuals and Institutions* (Routledge, 2000); and M Jones and LA Basser Marks, 'The Limitations on the Use of Law to Promote Rights: An Assessment of the Disability Discrimination Act 1992' in M Hauritz, C Sampford and S Blencowe (eds) *Justice for People with Disabilities: Legal and Institutional Issues* (The Federation Press, 1998).

36 Message from the Chairperson, available at: http://v1.dpi.org/lang-en/resources/details.php?page=685 (last accessed 15 October 2006).

37 Text of a speech delivered in the closing ceremony of the Ad Hoc Committee's 8th session on 25 August 2006.

38 Secretary-General's Message on the Adoption of the CRPD, available at: http://www.un.org/apps/sg/sgstats.asp?nid=2362 (last accessed 28 December 2006).

Ambassador Don MacKay, who chaired the later sessions of the Ad Hoc Committee, also anticipated that the CRPD would effect 'a major shift' in the way disabled people across the globe are treated and 'serve to promote, protect and ensure the[ir] full enjoyment of all human rights'.[39]

Despite the clear potential for disappointment and frustration at the pace of change that can be achieved using the CRPD, this treaty does not yet appear to have triggered the type of disillusionment engendered amongst many disability activists by the early years of the US Americans with Disabilities Act or the UK's Disability Discrimination Act.[40] Several factors may account for this.

First, as an instrument of international law, it is less dependent on the interpretations of judges working with the intricate and technical arguments so often generated in adversarial legal systems. The task of interpretation and guidance is instead entrusted to the UN Committee on the Rights of Persons with Disabilities – which contains many non-lawyers and also many disabled people – and takes place through a range of mechanisms including general comments, concluding observations and views on individual communications. The latter mechanism allows individuals and groups to bring complaints to the Committee against countries which have ratified the CRPD's Optional Protocol and thus provides an important space for a form of litigation. However, general comments enable the Committee to provide interpretive guidance on particular issues of importance free of the constraints imposed by the unpredictable and arbitrary nature of the issues raised by individual litigation. Further, through its concluding observations, the Committee is able to provide guidance to States spanning the extensive range of issues dealt with in the CRPD without being confined to the particularities of the issues raised by any one specific case.

Second, whilst non-discrimination is an extremely important cross-cutting obligation, the CRPD extends well beyond the limits of an anti-discrimination instrument. It grapples with the entire range of human rights – civil, political, economic, social and cultural. It articulates the obligations stemming from these rights in new ways so as to make clear their relevance to disabled people. All of this means that the CRPD engages directly with a range of concerns that have been key to social model activists but which lie beyond the natural reach of anti-discrimination law. A good example of this is the right to live independently and be included in the community, which appears as Article 19 of the CRPD.

Third, and perhaps most importantly, the CRPD incorporates and requires States to implement principles of political and policy involvement and participation – a development which is unsurprising given the very prominent role which disabled people's organisations played in the drafting of the CRPD.[41] Thus, Article 4(3) demands that:

> In the development and implementation of legislation and policies to implement the
> present Convention, and in other decision-making processes concerning issues relating

---

39 Press Conference by Chairman of AHC on Convention on Disabled Persons' Rights 15 August 2006, available at: www.un.org/news/briefings/docs/2006/060815_disabilities.doc.htm (last accessed 15 October 2006).
40 But for a contrary view, see M Oliver and C Barnes, *New Politics of Disablement* (Palgrave Macmillan, 2012) who observe, at p 150 that 'As yet there is little sign that it has had any significant impact on securing disabled people's individual or social rights within and across nation states. Consequently initial enthusiasm amongst disabled activists and their organizations for the Convention has started to wane.'
41 See further, S Tromel, 'A Personal Perspective on the Drafting History of the United Nations Convention on the Rights of Persons with Disabilities' in G Quinn and L Waddington (eds) *European Yearbook of Disability Law* (Intersentia, 2009).

to persons with disabilities, States Parties shall closely consult with and actively involve persons with disabilities, including children with disabilities, through their representative organizations.

In addition, Article 33 requires States to ensure that 'persons with disabilities and their representative organisations are involved and participate fully in' the processes every State is required to establish to monitor its implementation of the CRPD. Also relevant is Article 29(b), which requires States to 'promote actively an environment in which persons with disabilities can effectively and fully participate in the conduct of public affairs, . . . and encourage their participation in public affairs' including by 'forming and joining organizations of persons with disabilities to represent persons with disabilities at international, national, regional and local levels'.

Considerations such as these help to make the CRPD a law which is particularly well-suited to carrying forward a social model agenda. However, as Gerard Quinn has warned, it should not be seen as a 'magic bullet'[42] which will result in a speedy and top-down imposition on States of measures which will lift disabling barriers. Instead,

> . . . we should view the Convention less as a means for coercing States and more as a powerful tool for enabling its revolutionary insights to percolate into the political process (by 'persuasion' and 'socialisation') and hence transform the political process to the point that justice and rights for persons with disabilities is seen as the primary departure point and not as an annoying distraction. The dynamics of this process will call for the emergence of new political entrepreneurial skills on the part of civil society with respect to the multiple layers of actors at the international level and especially with respect to Governments and national institutions. It calls on civil society groups to come forward not merely with considered judgments about what is wrong but also with even more considered blueprints for change.[43]

For as long as law has the potential to play even a small part in tackling disabling barriers, lawyers and legal scholars have an important role to play in crafting, critiquing and enhancing the impact and enabling potential of relevant laws. This exercise extends well beyond critiquing the definition of 'disability' which is used in anti-discrimination and other law – although this is obviously an important issue as it often constitutes a gateway to entitlement to claim the protection of equality law. In all such efforts, however, legal scholarship would be well-advised to heed the following warning from Jones and Basser-Marks:

> Lawyers have a tendency to believe that law will provide solutions to complex social and political problems. While there is clearly a place for well thought-out laws, and having appropriate law is, in fact, very important to disadvantaged or vulnerable members of the society, law is at best only part of any strategy required to provide rights for people with disabilities.[44]

---

42 G Quinn, 'Resisting the 'Temptation of Elegance': Can the Convention on the Rights of Persons with Disabilities Socialise States to Right Behaviour?' in M Arnardóttir and G Quinn (eds) *The UN Convention on the Rights of Persons with Disabilities – European and Scandinavian Perspectives* (Martinus Nijhoff, 2009) 218.
43 Ibid. at 256.
44 M Jones and L Basser-Marks, 'The Limitations on the Use of Law to Promote Rights: An Assessment of the Disability Discrimination Act 1992' in M Hauritz, C Sampford and S Blencowe (eds) *Justice for People with Disabilities – Legal and Institutional Issues* (Federation Press, 1998) 3.

Disabling law: Law as part of the problem

The preceding section has explored the link between the social model and the impetus for enabling anti-discrimination and human rights law which aims to tackle the social barriers and oppression experienced by disabled people. In other words, it was concerned with the way in which law has been looked to by social model activists to provide part of the solution. Law, however, is also part of the problem in that aspects of it undoubtedly operate to disadvantage, exclude and oppress people with impairments. The social model provides a helpful lens through which to analyse legal rules and principles with a view to identifying such effects.

In some instances, law's disablement of people with impairments will be overt and readily apparent. Guardianship and mental health laws which deprive people with impairments of rights to marry,[45] to vote,[46] to enter into employment contracts, to refuse medical treatment,[47] to protest against placement in institutional settings[48] or to see a lawyer[49] are obvious examples. There is a wealth of legal scholarship on issues such as these. Whilst an increasing body of such work is informed by the CRPD, the explicit adoption of a social model approach remains rare.

In other instances, the disabling impact of a legal rule or doctrine may be less overt but nonetheless extremely important. For example, laws which permit disabled people to claim damages in 'wrongful life' claims, on the grounds that they should not have been born, may benefit the individual disabled litigant (at least financially) but are likely to have a disabling impact on people with impairments generally because of the negative message they send out about the value of the lives of people with impairments.[50] Further, aspects of law which, at face value, might appear not to be primarily concerned with disability may have disabling effects – for instance because embedded with them is some conception of a non-disabled norm which is used to determine entitlement to some benefit. This issue was expertly analysed by Jacobus tenBroek in the context of the US law of torts as long ago as 1966 – in terms which resonate with social model thinking even though written some 15 years before that model was born.[51] Other work in the same vein has critiqued the disabling impact of aspects of English property law[52] and, it is to be hoped, many other aspects of different laws in different countries to which references are not immediately obvious.

---

45 See e.g. the facts in *Lashin v. Russia*, Application No 33117/02, 22 January 2013 (ECHR); the facts in *Kiss v. Hungary*, Application No 38832/06, 20 May 2010 (ECHR); and *Zsolt Bujdosó and Five Others v. Hungary* Communication No 4/2011, CRPD/C/10/D/4/2011.

46 See e.g. the facts in *Stanev v. Bulgaria*, Application No 36760/06, 17 January 2012 (ECHR).

47 See e.g. the facts in *Shtukaturov v. Russia*, Application No 44009/05, 27 March 2008 (ECtHR).

48 See e.g. the facts in *Stanev v. Bulgaria*, Application No 36760/06, 17 January 2012 (ECHR).

49 See e.g. the facts in *Sýkora v. Czech Republic*, Application No 23419/07, 22 November 2012 (ECHR); and *Shtukaturov v. Russia*, Application No 44009/05, 27 March 2008 (ECtHR).

50 See further A Lawson, 'Mind the Gap: Normality, Difference and the Danger of Disablement through Law' in A Lawson and C Gooding (eds) *Disability Rights in Europe: From Theory to Practice* (Hart Publishing, 2005) 271–273.

51 J tenBroek, 'The Right to Live in the World: The Disabled in the Law of Torts' (1966) 54 *Calfornia Law Review* 841.

52 See e.g. A Lawson, 'Land Law and the Creation of Disability' in A Hudson, *New Perspectives on Property Law* (Cavendish, 2003); and (for an analysis of aspects of property, contract and tort law) A Lawson, 'Mind the Gap: Normality, Difference and the Danger of Disablement through Law' in A Lawson and C Gooding (eds) *Disability Rights in Europe: From Theory to Practice* (Hart Publishing, 2005).

The operation of law in practice: A disabling system?

Thus far, the discussion has focused on the substantive content of the law itself. Barriers within the practical operation of the legal system also disable people with impairments from benefiting from law and access to justice. These are located at initial stages – when people need legal advice to inform them about a claim they might have or about their position if a claim is brought against them; or during interactions with investigative authorities such as the police. They also arise during the course of legal proceedings and in the outcomes of such proceedings or interactions with the legal system more generally. Such issues will be explored in more depth elsewhere in this book (in the chapter on access to justice). For present purposes it suffices to say that legal scholarship,[53] alongside scholarship from other disciplines,[54] has an important role to play in exposing these barriers. There is an obvious role for interdisciplinary work and collaboration.

Conclusion

The social model of disability locates disability within social structures and systems (including the law and its operation in practice) that exclude, disadvantage and oppress people with impairments. It thus poses questions about the nature of such barriers in the substance and practice of law in all areas of life. It also demands that attention be given to how those barriers can be tackled and broken down. Equality and human rights laws cannot achieve this on their own. However, they can play a useful part in the effort to challenge and tackle disabling structures, practices and attitudes.

As Arlene Kanter has observed, the discipline of law is a relatively recent newcomer to the multidisciplinary feast of disability studies.[55] There is tremendous scope for a mutually enriching relationship between law and disability studies. A greater engagement by legal scholarship with the social model of disability and the debates which surround it is one of the ways in which law stands to be enriched by disability studies, with its close connection with political activism and its wealth of literature on emancipatory and participatory research design.

53 See e.g. E Flynn, *Disabled Justice: Access to Justice and the UN Convention on the Rights of Persons with Disabilities* (Ashgate, 2015); and S Ortoleva, 'Inaccessible Justice: Human Rights, Persons with Disabilities and the Legal System' (2011) 17 *ILSA Journal of International and Comparative Law* 281.
54 See, e.g. P Swift, K Johnson, V Mason, N Shiyyab and S Porter, *What Happens When People with Learning Disabilities Need Advice about the Law?* (Nora Fry Institute, 2013); S Balderstone, A Roulstone and P Thomas, 'Between Hate and Vulnerability: Unpacking the British Criminal Justice System's Construction of Disablist Hate Crime' (2011) 26 (3) *Disability and Society* 351.
55 See e.g. A Kanter, 'The Relationship between Disability Studies and Law' in A Kanter and B Ferri (eds) *Righting Educational Wrongs: Disability Studies in Law and Education* (Syracuse University Press, 2013) 19.

2

BEYOND THE WELFARE STATE

What next for the European social model?

Bjørn Hvinden

Introduction

The future of the welfare state as we know is uncertain. Many people question its goals, costs and effectiveness, claiming that it puts too much emphasis on promoting equality, that it is too intrusive in people's private affairs, too expensive and, failing to achieve its stated aims, while having adverse consequences on economic competitiveness, individual responsibility and the motivation to work. Others argue that demographic ageing, cross-border mobility, a volatile international economy, Europeanisation and globalisation make the (national) welfare state unsustainable. So, if these claims have some validity, what future will the European Social Model have? What will follow the welfare state, as we know it? Are we moving towards the Austerity State? Can the Social Investment approach save the welfare state? What will the consequences for persons with disabilities be?

Why welfare states?

Scholars and analysts have offered a number of explanations for the origin and development of the welfare state in Europe and other regions of the world.

Handling the challenges of poverty and social order

The welfare state as we know it originated as part of efforts to solve particular social action problems. According to Abram de Swaan (1989), the process towards establishing welfare states in Europe started already by the end of the Middle Ages.[1] The process was a response to the challenge of handling unruly groups of poor people who wandered from one town or village to the next. Part of this challenge was to distinguish between the needy and others, especially those whom one suspected of being workshy or simply criminals. This led to attempts to differentiate between the deserving and the undeserving poor; the former one should try to help, the latter one should discipline and punish. However, as long as families' and local communities' capacity

---

1 Abram De Swaan, *In Care of the State: Health Care, Education and Welfare in Europe and the USA in Modern Era* (Cambridge: Polity Press, 1988).

to meet the needs of the poor tended to be limited and variable, there was often a strong impulse to try solving the problem by forcing the flocks of poor to go away and seek help elsewhere.

Over time, leaders of local communities realised that this turning away of poor people just meant a circulation of the poor that at best gave a temporary relief from the problem. The problem called for more collective and coordinated arrangements, in the form of joint approaches, agreements or regulations at higher levels of aggregation or for wider territories. De Swaan argues that such efforts helped to consolidate the powers and tasks of rulers on higher-levels social units. This consolidation contributed to the process towards the formation of what eventually became modern states. Such states were to not only defend the privileges of the ruler and the elite and protect the territorial integrity as established in the Westphalian Treaty of 1648. States were also to ensure social order by regulating or organising assistance to the poor and destitute, protecting private property, and gradually, granting the kind of individual rights we today see as part of belonging to or being citizen of a state.

Handling the social consequences
of industrialisation and urbanisation

A second social action problem emerged with the growing industrialisation and urbanisation in most European countries during the nineteenth and early twentieth century, although with different timing and speed. These processes meant a weakening of the family, kin and local community as sources of help and support in cases of loss of job, income or provider, illness, disability or high age involving reduced capacity to work or take care of one's own care needs. Obviously, some people, especially those belonging to the salaried or white-collar middle classes, tried to save money to have some means to meet such contingencies, but the vast working classes had limited possibilities to set aside any substantial amount of money. To the extent arrangements for poor help were functioning, they could offer some support in these cases. However, claiming such support tended to mean subjecting oneself to strict and degrading control over one's life, loss of ordinary citizenship rights such as rights to vote or be elected and generally, social stigmatisation and exclusion. Until this day, we have tended to talk dismissively about the cash payments one might receive from poor help – or its current equivalent, means-tested *(social) assistance* or minimum support – as 'hand-outs' of 'charity'.

Efforts to find alternatives to poor support involved establishing collective, voluntary and mutual arrangements based on joint belonging to a local community or local occupation. In practice, such arrangements ran into problems because of the challenge of collecting sufficient funds on a voluntary basis or the accumulation of bad risks; too many of the members were exposed to the same risks, for example loss of job because local factories had to close or loss of life or capacity because of a mine accident.

Disaffection with reliance on poor help and the shortcomings of voluntary mutual aid arrangements created a potential for unrest and threats to the social order among the 'lower classes'.[2] In many countries, the response to this challenge was the establishment of a wide range of arrangements of *social insurance* provision. Sometimes contributions from the employers were the main source of funding for these arrangements, while in other cases the source was a mix of contributions from employers and employees of the corporation, with or without substantial tax-based support from the state. Social insurance arrangements could be national, organised

---

2 Peter Baldwin, *The Politics of Social Solidarity: Class Bases of the European Welfare State 1975–1975* (Cambridge: Cambridge University Press, 1990).

or mandated by the state, and in principle, encompassing all employers and wage earners in the economy. Alternatively, all members of a profession or vocational groups paid contributions to a sectorial social insurance arrangement.

To avoid some of the social action problems already referred to, membership of social insurance arrangements had to be *obligatory* (e.g. for all employees of a firm, for all employers and wage earners in a country, or all members of the profession or vocational group in question). If individual employers or wage earners were free to opt out, it would undermine the funding of the provision and mean that some people would remain unprotected against the kind of risks or contingencies. This tension between the values of freedom and full coverage and equality in protection against risk has been a recurring theme and is still so in many countries.

To be effective, social insurance arrangements presuppose a form of socially structured solidarity. The more limited or selected group of citizens who are covered by a particular social insurance arrangement, the more similar this solidarity becomes the solidarity among people buying risk protection from the same private insurance company. In both cases, the right to receive payments when experiencing specific contingencies builds on the contribution or tax one has paid to the insurance provider.

Additionally, in some cases the welfare state has included various *hybrids or mixes between social assistance and social insurance* provisions. For instance, while persons who have acquired a disability during their working career might have been able to pay contribution to social insurance, this would not be the case for persons who were born with a disability or who required a disability during childhood or youth. In some countries, support from social assistance or disability-specific forms of means-tested assistance would be what the welfare state has to offer the latter group. In other countries, governments have included particular cash transfer provisions for persons without any substantial record of earnings in their social insurance system. These provisions are non-means-tested and non-contributory and give income replacement as well, other periodic or lump sum payments to cover costs related to living with a disability. While the sums of money one may receive from a disability-assistance system and from the latter kind of quasi-insurance system may not differ that much, their institutional contexts may still have symbolic significance for the person with a disability.

So far, we have only highlighted the cash transfer side of welfare states. In order to prevent that a substantial section of the population is unable to benefit from essential services, the welfare state has to a growing extent guaranteed access to or itself delivered a range of *welfare-related services*. The most important of these services have been education, health services and social care. Here there might be a scope for *substitution* or replacement between cash transfers and delivery of services. In some instances, a government has decide to reduce its direct delivery of services and instead provide citizens with more cash or give them vouchers or tax rebates to enable them to purchase services themselves.

Moreover, alongside social redistribution of public resources (through cash transfers and services), the welfare state is also involved in *social regulation*.[3] The idea here is the governments may seek to stimulate behaviour on the part of non-governmental actors that promote social or welfare policy objectives. One key objective is to diminish the social impact of lack of awareness, ignorance, customs, stereotypes and discrimination. For instance, governments try to influence employers to become more willing to interview and hire job seekers with disabilities and provide accommodation and accessible workplaces. If the government succeeds in doing this, it is likely to improve the well-being of the persons involved, promote equality in economic participation,

---

3 Giandomenico Majone, 'The European Community between Social Policy and Social Regulation' (1993) vol. 31 *JCMS: Journal of Common Market Studies* 21, 153–170.

broaden the tax base and reduce public spending. Although there may a number of potential complementarities or synergies between cash transfers, services provision and social regulation, research has not so far explored them in a systematic way.

Contributing to stabilisation and restructuring of economies

A third social action problem is that downturns in the business cycle have tended to cause sudden and strong falls in demand, resulting in a vicious circle of further fall in demand. Public provision of income maintenance and some services (especially related to improving skills and qualifications) to people who are out of work can contribute to counteracting such vicious circles and stabilisation of economies. At the same time, economic crises can also make visible the need for restructuring of an economy, in the sense of speeding up the process of labour moving from less productive and contractive branches to more productive and expansive branches. Such restructuring is likely to enhance overall productivity and stimulate economic growth. To the extent that the welfare state provides workers in contracting sectors with income maintenance benefits when they give up their old jobs and seek new jobs, combined with offers for 'active measures' like retraining and upskilling, the structuring will have less negative consequences for those affected and hence be more acceptable in terms of well-being. Experiences from restructuring processes and close-down of companies indicate the accessibility and quality of services related to upskilling, health and relocation may be essential for avoiding permanent exclusion of workers in vulnerable positions, for instance because low formal qualification, high age or disability. As we will return to later, one strand of economic thought has argued for a long time that the welfare state historically has promoted economic efficiency, by default or design.[4] 'Productivist' arguments have since the depression of the interwar period of the twentieth century complemented arguments in terms of maintaining social order and preventing destructive social unrest.

Reducing social inequality and injustice

While some of us see the promotion of social equality as a value in itself, others think that a degree of inequality stimulates aspirations and motivation to do better. However, social equality is an elusive concept and many have asked 'equality of what?'.[5] Some would argue for a version of 'equality of outcomes' (e.g. in terms of living standards, flourishing, social participation, health, longevity, etc.), while others maintain that 'equality of opportunities' (life chances, capabilities, etc.) are a more appropriate and realistic aim. One of the problems with the latter position is the problem of specification and measurement; how can we know that opportunities have been equal unless we fall back on some indicator of outcome? Behind different concepts of social equality, we find more or less explicit and elaborate theories of justice.

Interestingly, the dramatic rise of economic inequalities in recent years in many Western countries have led several economists and international organisations to argue that the trend towards more extreme inequalities in incomes and wealth can have adverse effects on economic growth and overall productivity.[6]

---

4 Robert E. Goodin, Bruce Headey, Ruud Muffels, and Henk-Jan Dirven, *The Real Worlds of Welfare Capitalism* (Cambridge: Cambridge University Press, 1999).
5 Robert E. Goodin, Bruce Headey, Ruud Muffels, and Henk-Jan Dirven, *The Real Worlds of Welfare Capitalism* (Cambridge: Cambridge University Press, 1999); A. Sen , "Equality of What?", In: Sterling M. Murrin (Ed), *Tanner Lectures on Human Values* (Salt Lake City: City of Utah Press, 1980) 195–220.
6 Federico Cingano, "Trends in Income Inequality and Its Impact on Economic Growth", *OECD Social, Employment and Migration Working Papers*, No. 163 (Paris: OECD Publishing, 2014).

Not one but many welfare states, even within Europe

Before we turn to the discussion of what will follow the European welfare state as we know it, it is worth emphasising that we are not dealing with one welfare state in Europe, but several – more or less different – welfare states. Scholars have made great efforts to identify groupings (families, models or regimes) of European welfare states (or welfare societies). They have based their groupings on various characteristics and dimensions (e.g. provisions' generosity, comprehensiveness or degree of universalism; the relative role of social insurance and social assistance; the balance between cash transfers versus services provision; the weight of redistribution versus social regulation; the relative role of public, private, voluntary and family in providing protection and support, etc.).

Prominent typologies of European welfare states (or welfare societies) have distinguished between three to six different types.[7] It is beyond the aim of this chapter to review and compare these typologies, especially as clusters of important aspects of disability policy tend to cut across them. As we will illustrate, the important points are (1) that we find great diversity in how European welfare states respond to with the situation of persons with disabilities, and (2) this diversity creates challenges for an effective and truly European disability policy. We will link our analysis of this diversity to two major frameworks for discussing what we can expect beyond the welfare state, as we know it.

What do recent trends in policy efforts suggest about the future of the European Social Model?

Towards an austerity state?

According to an important strand of thinking about the welfare state, a combination of maturing welfare provision (especially pension systems based on social insurance models), demographic ageing and the transition to service-oriented provision (health and care services in particular) has led to unsustainable levels of public deficit in many European countries. An increasingly volatile international economy and various kinds of crisis mean lower tax revenues and higher demand for income protection. These challenges force governments in these countries to make substantial and lasting cuts in public spending to consolidate public finances, for instance by tightening eligibility rules, excluding some groups and reducing levels and duration of benefits in cash and kind. The result is a state of *austerity,* and according to some analysts, even a state of 'permanent austerity' and downward retrenchment.[8] Some observers

---

7 Jonas Pontusson, *Inequality and Prosperity: Social Europe vs. Liberal America* (Ithaca: Cornell University Press, 2005); Robert E. Goodin, Bruce Headey, Ruud Muffels, and Henk-Jan Dirven, *The Real Worlds of Welfare Capitalism* (Cambridge: Cambridge University Press, 1999); Maurizio Ferrera, "The Four "Social Europes": Between Universalism and Selectivity", In: Martin Rhodes and Yves Mény (Eds), *The Future of European Welfare* (Basingstoke: Macmillan, 1998) 81–96; Gøsta Esping-Andersen, *The Three Worlds of Welfare Capitalism* (Oxford: Polity, 1990); Richard Titmuss, "Developing Social Policy in Conditions of Rapid Change: The Role of Social Welfare", In: B. Abel-Smith and K. Titmuss (Eds), *The Philosophy of Welfare: Selected Writings of Richard M. Titmuss* (London: Allen & Unwin, 1987) 254–68.
   R. M. Titmuss, "Developing Social Policy in Conditions of Rapid Change: The Role of Social Welfare", In: B. Abel-Smith and K. Titmuss (Eds), *The Philosophy of Welfare: Selected Writings of Richard M. Titmuss* (London: Allen & Unwin, 1987) 254–68; Harold L. Wilensky and Charles Nathan Lebeaux, *Industrial Society and Social Welfare* (New York: The Free Press, 1958).
8 Armin Schäfer and Woolfgang Streeck (Eds), *Politics in the Age of Austerity* (Cambridge: Policy, 2013); Paul Pierson, "Coping with Permanent Austerity: Welfare State Restructuring in Affluent Democracies", In: P. Pierson (Ed), *The New Politics of the Welfare State* (Oxford: Oxford University Press, 2011) 410–56.

have argued that the impact of the austerity state is likely to be particularly severe for persons with disabilities in Europe.[9]

Available statistical evidence about trends in spending on social benefits in general and disability-related spending in particular is limited and gives a mixed and somewhat ambiguous view. For instance, according to the Organisation for Economic Co-operation and Development (OECD), government consolidation measures have most frequently selected 'working age transfers', including benefits for persons with disabilities, for savings. Yet, in the period 2007–10, overall there had been only a minor increase in the spending on disability pensions in OECD countries.[10]

What answer one will give to whether we see a permanent austerity or not depends on exactly what period and which countries one considers and what indicators one adopts. For instance, many analysts, statistical agencies and international organisations use percentage of the gross domestic product (GDP) spent on social benefits as indicator of public policy effort. As such, it tells how much of the hypothetically 'available resources' a government allocates for a particular purpose. However, the level of GDP changes over time and to different degree between countries. For instance, we can imagine that a particular country over some years has an exceptional high growth in GDP compared to other countries, but in real terms continues to provide more or less the same purchase power or amount and quality of services. Seen in isolation, one might interpret the diminishing percentage of GDP spent on these social provisions as an indicator of retrenchment or even austerity. Conversely, if a country experiences a drastic fall in GDP over some years but still spends the roughly same in real terms on social provisions, one might interpret this as an increase in social spending.

For these reasons, it is important to complement or even replace the percentage of GDP with an indicator of what happens in real terms, for instance social spending measured in purchase power standards per inhabitant or recipient. One should also use the latter indicator with some caution, as there may be uncertainty as to whether the indicator to sufficient degree takes into account substantial fluctuation in level of prices in and between countries, whether inflation or deflation.

The recent interlinked crises in Europe starting in the first decade of the 2000s represented major challenges for European welfare states. On the one hand, the crises increased the demand for income protection and services, especially for persons who lost their jobs and their families. On the other hand, the debt crisis forced a number of governments to make substantial cuts in public welfare provisions. Yet, at the aggregate level of the EU25 countries covered in Figure 2.1, the average spending on social benefits did not show a marked decrease in terms of percentage of GDP, but rather a small increase. Evidently, the average does make visible the unequal trends in EU25 countries. Overall spending on social benefits measured in terms of purchase power standard per inhabitant indicate a marked upward trend, first of all related to increased spending on income maintenance for people hit by the unemployment crisis.

The picture was slightly different for benefits for persons with disabilities. Here there was a limited reduction in average spending in terms of percentage of GDP. Yet, in terms of spending on disability benefits measured in purchase power standards per inhabitant, we see a clear increase, although not as strong as for total spending on social benefits in purchase power standards per inhabitant. Again, it is worth reminding oneself that these averages do not say anything about

9 Harald Hauben, Michael Coucheir, Jan Spooren, Donal McAnaney, and Claude Delfosse, *Assessing the Impact of European Governments' Austerity Plans on the Rights of People with Disabilities* (Brussels: European Foundation Centre (EFC), 2012).

10 OECD, *Society at a Glance 2014: OECD Social Indicators* (Paris: OECD Publishing, 2014).

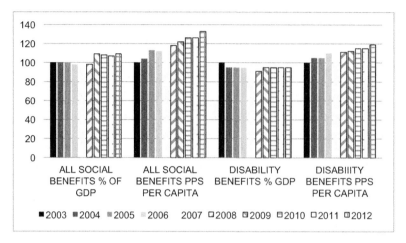

Figure 2.1 Trends in overall spending on social benefits and spending on disability benefits. Two measures of spending levels. EU25 2003–12

Notes:

PPS – purchase power standard, is a constructed currency unit. Theoretically, one PPS can buy the same amount of goods and services in each country. Because of differences in price levels, one would need different amounts of national currency to buy the same goods and services.

EU25 – The countries that were members of the EU from 1 May 2004: Austria (AT), Belgium (BE), Cyprus (CY), Czech Republic (CZ), Denmark (DK), Estonia (EE), Finland (FI), France (FR), Germany (DE), Greece (EL), Hungary (HU), Ireland (IE), Italy (IT), Latvia (LV), Lithuania (LT), Luxembourg (LU), Malta (MT), Netherlands (NL), Poland (PL), Portugal (PT), Slovakia (SK), Slovenia (SI), Spain (ES), Sweden (SE) and United Kingdom (UK). Later, Bulgaria, Romania and Croatia became members.

Source of data: http://ec.europa.eu/eurostat/data/database

differences in trends among the EU25 countries. Figure 2.2 A–B illustrates some of this variation in a subsample of eight European countries that participated in a project carried out in the DISCIT project under the European Union seventh framework programme for research 2013–16 (www.discit.eu).

Figure 2.2A–B indicates that among these countries only the United Kingdom had a clear trend towards a lower level of spending on disability benefits in terms of purchase power standards per inhabitant, while Ireland and Norway had substantial growth in their levels of spending. The other five countries had relatively stable levels or limited increases of spending. Overall, among 29 European countries, only 5 (Hungary, Malta, the Netherlands, Portugal and the United Kingdom) had lower levels of disability spending in purchase power standards per inhabitant in 2012 than in 2003.

Another possible indicator of a turn towards austerity could be that European countries to greater extent had adopted means-testing as a way to regulate and potentially limit the access to disability benefits. It turns out that in only 13 of 32 European countries did means-testing have more than a negligible role in the total spending on disability benefits in 2012. In the 10 years since 2003, 10 of these 13 countries had the share of means-tested benefits increased to any substantial extent (Belgium, Germany, Ireland, Spain, France, Malta, the Netherlands, Austria, Iceland and Switzerland). For the EU25 as a whole, we see also a certain increase in the use of means-testing (Figure 2.3). Even against the challenge of public debt, hardly any country without a historical legacy of using means-testing in disability benefits did introduce it as a rationing device in this period.

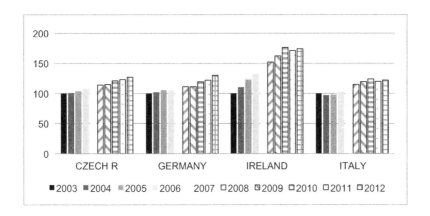

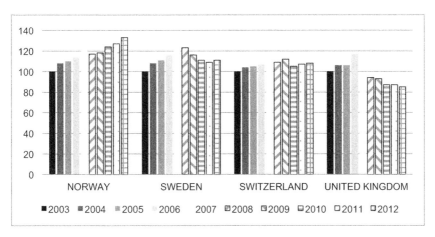

Figure 2.2A–B Trends in total spending on disability benefits (in PPS per capita) 2003–12. Per cent (2003=100)

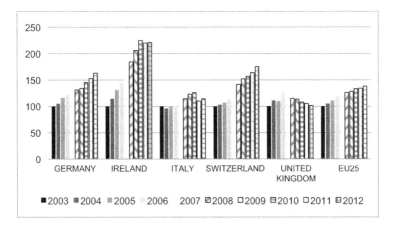

Figure 2.3 Trends in spending on means-tested disability-related benefits (in PPS per capita) 2003–12. Per cent (2003=100). European Union (EU25) and four Member States

Source of data: http://ec.europa.eu/eurostat/data/database

To conclude this section, for the countries and period considered and with macro indicators used here, we did not find evidence of a general shift toward an austerity state for persons with disabilities in Europe since the onset of the great recession in 2008. The small minority of countries that had a clear downward trend in public spending on disability benefits makes it improbable that we will see a massive shift towards austerity in the disability area in the near future.

Towards a social investment state?

Since the early 1990s, a number of social policy analysts have called for a shift towards a 'social investment' strategy in Europe. When Esping-Andersen (1996) – as one of the first – referred to the term 'social investment' in a European context, it was in cautious and rather uncommitted terms, arguing that:

> rather than draconian roll-backs, the idea is to redirect social policy from its current bias in favour of passive income maintenance towards active labour markets programmes that "put people back to work", help households harmonize work and family obligations and train the population in the kinds of skills that postindustrial society demands.
>
> *(Esping-Andersen 1996: 3)*[11]

At the same time, he expressed concern that this approach's longer-term viability was 'doubly uncertain' and, in particular, that 'very high unemployment rates seem to contradict the validity of an active "social investment"' approach.[12]

Almost two decades later, a number of scholars, including Esping-Andersen, have wholeheartedly embraced the social investment approach without such reservations, albeit on the basis of different understandings and emphasises.[13] Others scholars have are expressing a more critical stance to the approach and its practical uses.[14]

As suggested by Esping-Andersen's (1996) statement, one core meaning of social investment is a shift towards active measures to improve people's skills or 'human capital' at the expense of a one-sided focus on providing income maintenance benefits ('passive benefits'). Another and more distinct meaning is the strong orientation towards children and the consequences of current provisions towards the further life courses of children, not the least in their potential role as economically self-sufficient and highly skilled workers in the future knowledge society. Esping-Andersen's (2002) article is an important contribution to this strand of the social investment approach. This strand builds on longitudinal prospective studies of children's life courses, for instance by the prominent economist James Heckman and colleagues.

11 Gøsta Esping-Andersen, "After the Golden Age?" in Esping-Andersen (Eds), *Welfare States in Transition: National Adaptations in Global Economies* (London: Sage, 1996) 1–31.
12 Ibid. 14–15.
13 Frank Vandenbroucke, Anton Hemerijck, and Bruno Palier, "The EU needs a Social Investment Pact" (*OSE Paper Series*, No. 5, May, 2011) www.ose.be; Gøsta Esping-Andersen, "A Child-Centred Social Investment Strategy", in Esping-Andersen (with D. Gallie, A. Hemerijck and J. Myles) (Eds), *Why We Need a New Welfare State?* (Oxford: Oxford University Press, 2002) 26–67.
14 Bea Cantillon and Frank Vandenbrouck (Eds), *Reconciling Work and Poverty Reduction: How Successful Are European Welfare States?* (Oxford: Oxford University Press, 2014); Jorma Sipilä, "The Social Investment State: A New Trend in Social Expenditure or Merely a Popular Political Discourse?" In: G. B. Cohen, B. W. Ansell, R. H. Fox and J. Gingrich (Eds), *Social Policy in the Smaller European Union States* (New York: Berghahn Books, 2012) 81–104; Bea Cantillon, 'The Paradox of the Social Investment State: Growth, Employment and Poverty in the Lisbon Era' (2011) vol. 21 *Journal of European Social Policy* 5, 432–449; Jane Jenson, 'Lost in Translation: The Social Investment Perspective and Gender Equality' (2009) vol. 15 *Social Politics* 446–483.

The long-term perspectives of social investment and their uncertain pay-offs are challenging both in terms of the usually short-term horizon of policymakers, as well as in terms of the costs and complexities of following representative samples of individuals over many years. In practice, most analyses referring to a social investment framework adopt a much shorter time perspective. For instance, they focus on 'pay-offs' of improved child welfare as a result of making high-quality childcare services available and affordable for a greater number of families, as well as the gains in the form of increased employment rates and earnings of women with small children on the basis of better access to such services.

We find a lively discussion of what extent it is appropriate and relevant to interpret changes in European countries' social protection spending over the last decade or two as indicators of a turn towards social investment.[15] One challenge here is how to distinguish between spending that contributes (mainly) to "consumption" in the short term (e.g. reduced child poverty) to an investment with likely future pay-offs (e.g. in terms of educational accomplishments, labour market prospects and earnings), or both.[16] This ambiguity partly reflects the flexibility of the concept social investment, partly the lack of consensus about the precise meaning of the term.

Furthermore, some researchers have questioned whether policy changes referred as examples of social investment or introduced under the banner of social investment have actually benefitted for instance people at the risk of poverty.[17]

In October 2008 the EU Commission introduced the concept of 'active inclusion' as a multifaceted strategy to combat poverty and social exclusion for people at some distance from the labour market, combining an adequate level of income maintenance through minimum income provision, employment-promoting measures and access to necessary and high-quality social and health services. The European Union Council of Ministers endorsed the Commission's Recommendation in December the same year. The Network of Independent Experts on Social Inclusion published an assessment of the implementation the Recommendation published in 2013 and pointed to a number of limitations in the Member States implementation.[18]

Nevertheless, the Commission made an explicit link to the 2008 recommendation on active inclusion when in February 2013 it launched its Social Investment Package (European Commission 2013a, 2013b, 2013c and 2013d).[19] The Council of Europe in June 2013 endorsed this

---

15 Jorma Sipilä, "The Social Investment State: A New Trend in Social Expenditure or Merely a Popular Political Discourse?" In: G. B. Cohen, B. W. Ansell, R. H. Fox and J. Gingrich (Eds), *Social Policy in the Smaller European Union States* (New York: Berghahn Books, 2012) 81–104.

16 Anton Hemerijck, *Changing Welfare States* (Oxford: Oxford University Press, 2013).

17 Bea Cantillon and Frank Vandenbrouck (Eds), *Reconciling Work and Poverty Reduction: How Successful Are European Welfare States?* (Oxford: Oxford University Press, 2014); Bea Cantillon, 'Three Short-comings of the Social Investment Perspective' (2013) vol. 12 *Social Policy & Society* 4, 553–564; Bea Cantillon, 'The paradox of the social investment state: growth, employment and poverty in the Lisbon era' (2011) vol. 21 *Journal of European Social Policy* 5, 432–449.

18 Hugh Frazer and Eric Marlier, *Assessment of the Implementation of the European Commission Recommendation on Active Inclusion: A Study of National Policies, Synthesis Report, European Commission* (Luxembourg: Publications Office of the European Union, 2013).

19 European Commission (2013a), Communication from the Commission to the European Parliament, the Council, the European Economic and Social Committee and the Committee of the Regions – Towards Social Investment for Growth and Cohesion – including implementing the European Social Fund 2014–2020, COM (2013) 83 final.

European Commission (2013b), Commission Recommendation of 20 February 2013 – Investing in children: breaking the cycle of disadvantage, COM (2013) 778 final.

European Commission (2013c), Commission Staff Working Document – Follow-up on the implementation by the Member States of the 2008 European Commission recommendation on active inclusion of people excluded from the labour market – Towards a social investment approach, SWD (2013) 39 final.

European Commission (2013d), *Investing in Social Europe* (Luxembourg: Publications Office of the European Union).

package, including the link with active inclusion.[20] It seems fair to say that the EU in this way also relaunched the active inclusion approach.

In the spring of 2015, the Commission presented a review on "Social Investment in Europe", as reflected in national policies.[21] The report concluded that most countries had some elements of a social investment approach in their policies. Yet, the extent or nature of this element varied strongly. Thirteen countries had a well-established approach to social policies, often based on a historical legacy. Many of the national experts noted that the national strategies in many cases did not refer to 'social investment'. Another nine countries had elements of social investment and a growing awareness about social investment. Finally, in an additional thirteen countries, the overall policy agenda had few notable traces of a social investment approach.

In the experts' remit, the focus was on three issues:

- To what extent did the country's social policies facilitate early childhood development?
- To what extent did the country's social policies support parents' and especially mothers' participation in the labour market?
- To what extent did the country's social policies provide adequate, activating and enabling support to those experiencing social and labour market exclusion? The remit does not appear to have focused on the relevance of polices for persons with disabilities, although the summary report and some of the national report mention this issue.[22]

We find a relative neglect or lack of explicit attention to the situation of persons with disabilities in much of the existing literature on social investment. There are good reasons to be concerned about this neglect. Some ask whether governments and policymakers see persons with disabilities as citizens in whom it is worth investing. Still, the way in which the European Commission broadens the concept of social investment in its 2013 Package suggests that this could potentially represent a potential renewal of and boost for disability policy in Europe.

In line with the findings of the 2015 review of the progress of the EU's Social Investment package, there is hardly any explicit use of the term social investment in available comparative welfare statistics of the Eurostat or OECD. Pragmatically, we will therefore interpret a relative shift from 'pure' income protection for persons with disabilities to an emphasis on the provision of disability-related services as compatible with a turn towards 'social investment'. Based on the same kind of indicators as before, we do find indication of this kind of shift; there was a clear increase in the spending on disability-related services, but hardly any significant growth in disability cash benefit between 2003 and 2012 (Figure 2.4).

Again, there is considerable variation in the extent to which there has been a shift from spending on disability cash benefits to spending on disability services, as illustrated by the trends in the proportion of total spending on disability benefits allocated to disability services in the eight European countries involved in the DISCIT project (Figures 2.5A–B).

To conclude, in this section we have found that there is some evidence that the European countries have moved towards greater emphasis on disability services, at the expense of the

20 Council, Council conclusions – "Towards Social Investment for Growth and Cohesion", Council of the European Union, Employment, Social Policy, Health and Consumer Affairs, Council meeting, Brussels, 20–21 June, 2013, Press release (2013).
21 Denis Bouget, Hugh Frazer, Eric Marlier, Sebastiano Sabato and Bart Vanhercke, *Social Investment in Europe: A Study of National Policies* (Brussels: European Commission, Directorate-General for Employment, Social Affairs and Inclusion, 2015).
22 Ibid., 5.

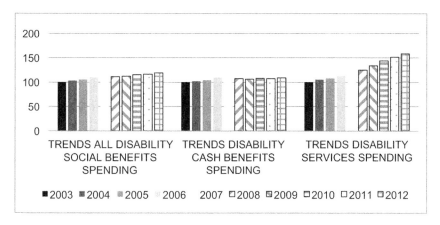

Figure 2.4 Overview – Trends in public spending on disability-related social benefits (in PPS) 2003–12. Per cent (2003=100). European Union (EU25)

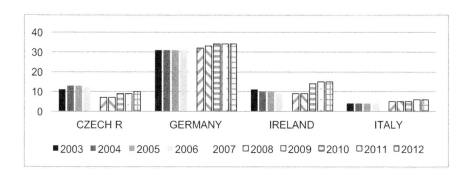

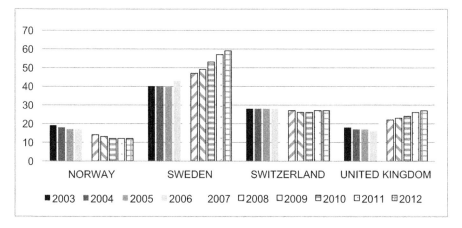

Figure 2.5A–B Trends in spending on benefits in kind (services) as share of all spending disability-related social benefits (in PPS per capita) 2003–12. Per cent (2003=100)

further growth in disability cash benefits. This finding is compatible with a turn towards de facto emphasis on a social investment approach to disability policy. We have seen, however, that there is great diversity between countries in what share spending on disability services has in the overall spending on disability benefits and in how this share has developed over time.

Conclusion: Are we moving towards a European welfare state?

In the first part of this chapter, we outlined some factors that have been significant for the development of the welfare state in Europe. We have emphasised the great cross-country variation in the characteristics of this welfare state. Next, we have focused on welfare state provisions specifically targeted at persons with disabilities in European countries. Again, we have illustrated the great diversity of European countries' approaches in this policy area. We moved on to discuss whether two prominent visions of the European welfare state and its future, the Austerity state and the Social Investment state, seem reasonable as ways to understand the developments we are currently witnessing in Europe and credible prophecies on where the welfare state in general and disability policy more specifically are moving.

Our tentative conclusions are, first, that a development towards the Austerity state does not seem very helpful in understanding what has happened in the last decade and what is likely to happen in the near future, in Europe as a whole. While some countries are struggling to sustain their policy promises to citizens, including citizens living with disabilities, this is far from the case for all countries. Evidently, many countries have restructured their welfare states and they will continue to do so. Yet, the welfare state is in most cases continuing to do what it is supposed to do, including stepping up its activity and spending in times of crisis. In this sense, it may be a bit premature to talk about '*beyond* the welfare state'.

Second, we have probably seen a silent shift towards a more service-oriented welfare state, including a more service-oriented disability provision. To the extent that there is such a shift, we can probably interpret it as compatible with a turn toward a Social Investment state. Yet, we would probably go too far if we asserted that governments or policymakers themselves have adopted the Social Investment approach or framework. There are still too many unsettled issues related to what Social Investment will mean in practice for persons with disabilities and how the Social Investment framework is going to deal with the great diversity of life situations, everyday challenges, resources and capacities among persons with disabilities.

Finally, there are many unanswered questions related to what roles European policy, legislation (e.g. related to equal treatment and full accessibility) and funding (e.g. through the Social Fund) are likely to play for future developments in the welfare state of Member States. Today, too many national governments and policymakers seem inclined to dismiss or downplay the significance that the European-level policy, legislation and funding represent in their country.

References

Baldwin, Peter, *The Politics of Social Solidarity: Class Bases of the European Welfare State 1975–1975* (Cambridge: Cambridge University Press, 1990).

Bouget, Denis, Frazer, Hugh, Marlier, Eric Sabato, Sebastiano, and Vanhercke, Bart, *Social Investment in Europe: A Study of National Policies* (Brussels: European Commission, Directorate-General for Employment, Social Affairs and Inclusion, 2015).

Cantillon, Bea, 'The paradox of the social investment state: Growth, employment and poverty in the Lisbon era' (2011), vol. 21 *Journal of European Social Policy* 5, 432–449.

Cantillon, Bea, 'Three short-comings of the social investment perspective' (2013), vol. 12 *Social Policy & Society* 4, 553–564.

Cantillon, Bea and Vandenbrouck, Frank (Eds), *Reconciling Work and Poverty Reduction: How Successful are European Welfare States?* (Oxford: Oxford University Press, 2014).

Cingano, Federico, "Trends in income inequality and its impact on economic growth", *OECD Social, Employment and Migration Working Papers*, No. 163 (Paris: OECD Publishing, 2014).

Council, Council Conclusions – "Towards social investment for growth and cohesion", Council of the European Union, Employment, Social Policy, Health and Consumer Affairs, Council Meeting, Brussels, 20–21 June, 2013, Press release (2013).

Esping-Andersen, Gøsta, *The Three Worlds of Welfare Capitalism* (Oxford: Polity, 1990).

Esping-Andersen, Gøsta, "After the Golden Age?" In: Gøsta Esping-Andersen (Ed), *Welfare States in Transition: National Adaptations in Global Economies* (London: Sage, 1996)1–31.

Esping-Andersen, Gøsta, "A child-centred social investment strategy" In: Gøsta Esping-Andersen, Duncan Gallie, Anton Hemerijck and John Myles (Eds), *Why We Need a New Welfare State?* (Oxford: Oxford University Press, 2002) 26–67.

European Commission (2013a), Communication from the Commission to the European Parliament, the Council, the European Economic and Social Committee and the Committee of the Regions – Towards Social Investment for Growth and Cohesion – including implementing the European Social Fund 2014–2020, COM(2013) 83 final.

European Commission (2013b), Commission Recommendation of 20 February 2013 – Investing in Children: Breaking the Cycle of Disadvantage, COM(2013) 778 final.

European Commission (2013c), Commission Staff Working Document – Follow-up on the Implementation by the Member States of the 2008 European Commission Recommendation on Active Inclusion of People Excluded from the Labour Market – Towards a Social Investment Approach, SWD(2013) 39 final.

European Commission, *Investing in Social Europe* (Luxembourg: Publications Office of the European Union, 2013d).

Ferrera, Maurizio, "The four social Europes: Between universalism and selectivity" In: Martin Rhodes and Yves Mény (Eds), *The Future of European Welfare* (Basingstoke: Macmillan, 1998) 81–96.

Flora, Peter and Heidenheimer, Arnold (Eds), *The Development of Welfare States in Europe and America* (Brunswick & London: Transaction Books, 1983).

Frazer, Hugh and Marlier, Eric *Assessment of the Implementation of the European Commission Recommendation on Active Inclusion: A Study of National Policies, Synthesis Report, European Commission* (Luxembourg: Publications Office of the European Union, 2013).

Goodin, Robert E., Headey, Bruce, Muffels, Ruud, and Dirven, Henk-Jan, *The Real Worlds of Welfare Capitalism* (Cambridge: Cambridge University Press, 1999).

Hall, Peter A. and Soskice, David (Eds), *Varieties of Capitalism: The Institutional Foundations of Comparative Advantage* (Oxford: Oxford University Press, 2001).

Harold, L., Wilensky, H. L., and Lebeaux, Charles Nathan, *Industrial Society and Social Welfare* (New York: The Free Press, 1958).

Hauben, Harald, Coucheir, Michael, Spooren, Jan, McAnaney, Donal, and Delfosse, Claude, *Assessing the Impact of European Governments' Austerity Plans on the Rights of People with Disabilities* (Brussels: European Foundation Centre (EFC), 2012).

Hemerijck, Anton, 'The social investment imperative beyond the financial crisis' (2011), *Social Policy in Europe: A Productive Factor? Challenge Europe* May, 11–19.

Hemerijck, Anton, *Changing Welfare States* (Oxford: Oxford University Press, 2013).

Hemerijck, Anton, Dräbing, Verena, Vis, Barbara, Nelson, Moira, and Soentken, Menno, "European welfare states in motion", *NEUJOBS Working Paper Number D5.2* (2013).

Jenson, Jane, 'Lost in translation: The social investment perspective and gender equality' (2009), vol. 15 *Social Politics*, 446–483.

Majone, Giandomenico, 'The European community between social policy and social regulation' (1993), vol. 31 *JCMS: Journal of Common Market Studies* 21, 153–170.

Morel, Nathalie, Bruno Palier, and Joakim Palme, "Beyond the welfare state as we knew it?" In: Nathalie Morel, Bruno Palier and Joakim Palme (Eds), *Towards a Social Investment State? Ideas, Policies and Challenges* (Bristol: The Policy Press, 2012) 1–30.

OECD, *Society at a Glance 2014: OECD Social Indicators* (Paris: OECD Publishing, 2014).

OECD, *In It Together: Why Less Inequality Benefits All* (Paris: OECD Publishing, 2015).

Ostry, Jonathan D., Berg, Andrew, and Tsangarides, Charalambos G., "Redistribution, Inequality, and Growth", *IMF Staff Discussion Note*, SDN/14/02 (2014).

Pierson, Paul, "Coping with permanent austerity: Welfare state restructuring in affluent democracies" In: P. Pierson (Ed), *The New Politics of the Welfare State* (Oxford: Oxford University Press, 2011) 410–456.

Pontusson, Jonas, *Inequality and Prosperity: Social Europe vs. Liberal America* (Ithaca: Cornell University Press, 2005).

Schäfer, Armin and Streeck, Woolfgang (Eds), *Politics in the Age of Austerity* (Cambridge: Policy, 2013).

Sen, Amartya, "Equality of what?" In: Sterling M. Murrin (Ed), *Tanner Lectures on Human Values* (Salt Lake City: City of Utah Press, 1980) 195–220.

Sipilä, Jorma, "The social investment state: A new trend in social expenditure or merely a popular political discourse?" In: G. B. Cohen, B. W. Ansell, R. H. Fox and J. Gingrich (Eds), *Social Policy in the Smaller European Union States* (New York: Berghahn Books, 2012) 81–104.

Swaan, Abram De, *In Care of the State: Health Care, Education and Welfare in Europe and the USA in Modern Era* (Cambridge: Polity Press, 1988).

Titmuss, Richard, "Developing social policy in conditions of rapid change: The role of social welfare" In: B. Abel-Smith and K. Titmuss (Eds), *The Philosophy of Welfare: Selected Writings of Richard M. Titmuss* (London: Allen & Unwin, 1987) 254–268.

Vandenbroucke, Frank, Anton Hemerijck, and Bruno Palier, "The EU needs a Social Investment Pact", *OSE Paper Series,* No. 5 (May, 2011) <www.ose.be>.

3

A HUMAN RIGHTS MODEL OF DISABILITY

Theresia Degener

The Convention on the Rights of Persons with Disabilities (CRPD) has been a success from the start: Its negotiation history among UN human rights treaties is the fastest;[1] its ratification record is splendid.[2] It was opened for signature in March 2007 and came into force on 3 May 2008 after the twentieth state had ratified the Convention. Only 6 years later, 151[3] states of the United Nations have become States Parties. There are several reasons why it can be called a 'first of' convention: the first human rights treaty adopted in the twenty-first century and after the 1993 Vienna Conference of human rights, the first to be acceded by a regional integration organization,[4] and the first group-focused treaty with a national monitoring mechanism.[5] Unlike its eight sister treaties, it has a stand-alone article on international cooperation.[6]

Challenges for the implementation of the Convention on the Rights of Persons with Disabilities

As a member of the CRPD Committee,[7] I am involved in reviewing States Parties' reports,[8] individual complaints[9] and other inquiries,[10] and general comments. As of 3 October 2014, we have reviewed nineteen state reports, we have decided on eight individual communications and we have adopted two general comments.[11]

Based on the status of the work of the CRPD Committee, I would argue that there are many challenges for implementing this new human rights treaty. Like any other human rights

---

1 Negotiations started in 2002.
2 As of 3 October 2014.
3 As of 3 October 2014.
4 The EU acceded to it on 23 December 2010.
5 Art. 33 CRPD.
6 Art. 32 CRPD.
7 2011–18.
8 Art. 35 CRPD.
9 Against States Parties that have ratified the Optional Protocol to the CRPD, Art. 1 OP to CRPD.
10 Art. 6 OP to CRPD.
11 GC No 1 on legal capacity (Art. 12 CRPD) and GC No 2 on accessibility (Art. 9 CRPD). All documents can be found at: http://www.ohchr.org/en/hrbodies/crpd/pages/crpdindex.aspx (last visited 5 October 2014).

treaty, the CRPD is a visionary law designed to transform society into a more just society. But visions cannot be achieved over night. Human rights implementation is a process with several agents and many hurdles to overcome. However, there are some challenges that are unique to the CRPD. Obviously, one is to establish a national monitoring mechanism that is independent from government, complies with the Paris Principles (PP) and works in collaboration with civil society organizations, notably disabled persons' organizations (DPO). National Human Rights Institutions which comply with the PP seem to be the best qualified entities to be designated as independent monitoring mechanism in accordance with Article 33 (3) CRPD. However, they often need to develop good working relations with DPOs and learn to become true 'agents of change'.[12] Further, the Convention enshrines a number of substantive provisions that bring new challenges to conventional human rights theory and jurisprudence. The most challenging being the right to be recognized as an equal person before the law (Article 12), closely followed by the right to independent and community living (Article 19). However, States Parties' obligations relating to accessibility (Article 9) and reasonable accommodation (Articles 2 and 5) are equally revolutionary, not to speak of the right to inclusive education (Article 24). Some of the dialogues with States Parties in the course of reviewing their reports showed that there is a deep misunderstanding relating to the scope and content of state obligations under these and other provisions of the CRPD. Often – so it seems – States Parties do not understand the profound change in disability policy and law that is embedded in the CRPD. The often-cited paradigm change relating to the model of disability is hard to grasp.

Disability studies provide the theoretical background for what we call the shift from the medical to the social model of disability. The social model of disability views disability as a social construct and locates the problem of disability outside the individual in discrimination policies. However, within disability studies the social model of disability has been almost as strongly criticized as the medical model of disability. Michael Oliver, one of the founding fathers of the social model of disability, has recently called for a halt to this criticism, unless someone can come up with an alternative.[13] My understanding of the CRPD is that this convention offers such an alternative: the human rights model of disability. It is by no means the only alternative to the social model of disability. Many models of disability have been developed inside and outside disability studies, among them more recently, the capability approach model[14] and the cultural model[15] of disability. My thesis is that the human rights model is an improvement of the social model of disability and that it is a tool to implement the CRPD. However, most States Parties to the CRPD are far from comprehending this new model of disability and are still stuck with the medical model of disability.

Understanding the human rights model of disability

Apparently, most States Parties have a problem in understanding the model of disability which has been adopted with the CRPD. Several States Parties reports reveal an understanding of disability which follows the traditional medical model of disability. As it has often been stated, this model

---

12 Quinn, *'Resisting the "Temptation of Elegance": Can the Convention on the Rights of Persons with Disabilities Socialise States to Right Behaviour?'*, in O. M. Arnadóttir and G. Quinn (eds), *The UN Convention on the Rights of Persons with Disabilities. European and Scandinavian Perspectives* (2009).

13 Oliver, *'The Social Model of Disability: Thirty Years On'*, 28 *Disability & Society* (2013), at 1026.

14 Mitra, *'The Capability Approach and Disability'*, 16 *Journal of Disability Policy Studies* (2006).

15 Waldschmidt, *'Brauchen die Disability Studies ein "kulturelles Modell" von Behinderung?'*, in G. Hermes and E. Rohrman (eds), *Nichts über uns – ohne uns! Disability Studies als neuer Ansatz emanzipatorischer und interdisziplinärer Forschung über Behinderung* (2006).

regards disability as an impairment that needs to be treated, cured, fixed or at least rehabilitated. Disability is seen as a deviation from the normal health status. Exclusion of disabled persons from society is regarded as an individual problem and the reasons for exclusion are seen in the impairment. For example: Because a person is deaf and blind, it is assumed that she or he cannot participate in political or cultural life. Disability according to the medical model remains the exclusive realm of helping and medical disciplines: doctors, nurses, special education teachers, rehabilitation experts, etc. Michael Oliver, one of the founding fathers of the social model of disability, has called this the ideological construction of disability through individualism and medicalization, the politics of disablement.[16] Another feature of the medical model of disability is that it is based on two assumptions that have a dangerous impact on human rights: (1) Disabled persons need to have shelter and welfare and (2) impairment can foreclose legal capacity. The first assumption legitimizes segregated facilities for disabled persons, such as special schools, living institutions or sheltered workshops. The second assumption has led to the creation of mental health and guardianship laws that take an incapacity approach to disability.[17] During the negotiations of the CRPD, the medical model served as a determent. While there was often no consensus among stakeholders which way to go in terms of drafting the text of the convention, there was overall agreement that the medical model of disability definitely was not the right path.[18] Rather the social model of disability was supposed to be the philosophical basis for the treaty. The paradigm shift from the medical to the social model has often been stated as the main achievement of the CRPD. However, while it is true that the social model of disability has been the prevalent reference paradigm during the negotiation process, my understanding of the CRPD is that it goes beyond the social model of disability and codifies the human rights model of disability.

The social model of disability explains disability as a social construct through discrimination and oppression. Its focus is on society rather than on the individual. Disability is regarded as a mere difference within the continuum of human variations. The social model differentiates between impairment and disability. While the first relates to a condition of the body or the mind, the second is the result of the way environment and society respond to that impairment. Exclusion of disabled persons from society is politically analysed as the result of barriers and discrimination. For example: Because voting material is not produced in Braille or information on candidates is not provided in sign language or through alternative communication, a person who is deaf-blind is excluded from political participation. Because deaf-blind persons are denied the right to interpreters outside employment in theatre plays, cinemas and other places of cultural life, they are excluded from cultural participation in society. Because deaf-blind persons are never accepted as actors or actresses in television, theatre or the film industry, they are invisible in cultural life.

Thus far, the social model of disability is the heuristic venture of a rights-based approach to disability that focuses on anti-discrimination law rather than on welfare programmes. The scientific context and theoretical framework of this model is disability studies – an interdisciplinary school of thought that breaks away from the traditional disciplines of the disability industry such as special education or rehabilitation science.

16 M. Oliver, *The Politics of Disablement* (1990).
17 Dhanda, '*Legal Capacity in the Disability Rights Convention*', 34 *Syracuse Journal of International Law and Commerce* (2007).
18 Kayess and French, '*Out of Darkness Into Light?*', 1 *Human Rights Law Review* (2008); Trömel, '*A Personal Perspective on the Drafting History of the United Nations Convention on the Rights of Persons with Disabilities*', in G. Quinn and L. Waddington (eds), *European Yearbook of Disability Law* (2009).

Now, what is the difference between the social and the human rights model of disability and why is the CRPD a manifestation of the latter?

While I do not claim ownership of the terminology, the human rights model of disability appeared in an article on international and comparative disability law reform that I wrote together with Gerard Quinn in 1999/2000[19] and in the background study to the CRPD that we undertook in 2001. In a chapter called 'Moral Authority for Change', we wrote:

> Human dignity is the anchor norm of human rights. Each individual is deemed to be of inestimable value and nobody is insignificant. People are to be valued not just because they are economically or otherwise useful but because of their inherent self-worth. . . . The human rights model focuses on the inherent dignity of the human being and subsequently, but only if necessary, on the person's medical characteristics. It places the individual centre stage in all decisions affecting him/her and, most importantly, locates the main 'problem' outside the person and in society.[20]

However, in that study we did not expressly distinguish the human rights model from the social model. I do so now and provide six arguments to substantiate.

The difference between the social and the human rights model

Impairment does not hinder human rights capacity

First, whereas the social model merely explains disability, the human rights model encompasses the values for disability policy that acknowledges the human dignity of disabled persons. Only the human rights model can explain why human rights do not require absence of impairment.

The social model of disability was created as one explanation[21] of exclusion of disabled people from society. It has been developed as a powerful tool to analyse discriminatory and oppressive structures of society. To use Michael Oliver's words:

> Hence, disability according to the social model, is all the things that impose restrictions on disabled people; ranging from individual prejudice to institutional discrimination, from inaccessible public buildings to unusable transport systems, from segregated education to excluding work arrangements, and so on. Further, the consequences of this failure do not simply and randomly fall on individuals but systematically upon disabled people as a group who experience this failure to discrimination institutionalised throughout society.[22]

This sociological explanation of disability may lay the foundation for a social theory of disability. But the social model does not seek to provide moral principles or values as a foundation of

19 Degener and Quinn, '*A Survey of International, Comparative and Regional Disability Law Reform*', in M. L. Breslin and S. Yee (eds), *Disability Rights Law and Policy* (2002), at 13.
20 G. Quinn and T. Degener, *Human Rights and Disability* (2002), at 14.
21 Other models are e.g. the normalization principle, the minority model, or the Nordic relational model, Traustadóttir, '*Disability Studies, the Social Model and Legal Developments*', in O. M. Arnardóttir and G. Quinn (eds), *The UN Convention on the Rights of Persons with Disabilities* (2009).
22 M. Oliver, *Understanding Disability* (1996), at 33.

disability policy. The CRPD, however, seeks exactly that. The purpose of the treaty is 'to promote, protect and ensure the full and equal enjoyment of all human rights and fundamental freedoms by all persons with disabilities, and to promote respect for their inherent dignity'.[23] In order to achieve this purpose, eight guiding principles of the treaty are laid down in Article 3 CRPD and the following articles tailor the existing human rights catalogue of the International Bill of Human Rights[24] to the context of disability. Human rights are fundamental rights. They cannot be gained or taken away from an individual or a group. They are acquired qua birth and are universal, that is every human being is a human rights subject. Neither social status, nor identity category, nor national origin or any other status can prevent a person from being a human rights subject. Therefore, human rights can be called unconditional rights. It does not mean that they cannot be restricted but it means that they do not require a certain health status or a condition of functioning. Thus, human rights do not require the absence of impairment. The CRPD reflects this message in its preamble and in the language of its articles, for example when the universality of all human rights for all disabled persons is reaffirmed,[25] or when it is recognized that the human rights of all disabled persons, including those with more intensive supports needs, have to be protected.[26] The article on the rights to equal recognition as a person before the law with equal legal capacity[27] is of course another example of this assumption.

Thus, the human rights model of disability defies the presumption that impairment may hinder human rights capacity. The social model of disability also acknowledges the importance of rights[28] and has often been associated with the rights-based approach to disability as opposed to needs-based or welfare approach to disability policy.[29] However, non-legal scholars of disability studies have emphasized that the social model of disability is foremost not a rights-based approach to disability but extends beyond rights to social relations in society, to the system of inequality.[30] They do, however, concede that social model advocates have supported struggles for civil rights and anti-discrimination legislation.[31]

The human rights model includes first- and second-generation human rights

Secondly, while the social model supports anti-discrimination policy civil rights reforms, the human rights model of disability is more comprehensive in that it encompasses both sets of human rights, civil and political as well as economic, social and cultural rights.

---

23 Art. 1 CRPD.
24 Consisting of three human rights instruments: Universal Declaration of Human Rights, Human Rights Committee, Committee on Economic, Social and Cultural Rights.
25 Preamble para c) CRPD.
26 Preamble para j) CRPD.
27 Art. 12(1) and (2) CRPD.
28 M. Oliver, *supra* note 22, at 63.
29 L. Waddington, *From Rome to Nice in a Wheelchair* (2006); Degener and Quinn, *supra* note 19; A. Lawson, *Disability and Equality Law in Britain: The Role of Reasonable Adjustment* (2008); A. Lawson and C. Gooding, *Disability Rights in Europe: From Theory to Practice* (2005).
30 V. Finkelstein, *The 'Social Model of Disability' and the Disability Movement* (2007), at: http://www.leeds.ac.uk/disability-studies/archiveuk/finkelstein/The%20Social%20Model%20of%20Disability%20and%20the%20Disability%20Movement.pdf; Priestley, *We're All Europeans Now! The Social Model of Disability and European Social Policy*', in C. Barnes and G. Mercer (eds), *The Social Model of Disability* (2005), at 23.
31 Priestley, *supra* note 30, at 23; M. Oliver, *supra* note 22, at 152–156.

The social model of disability served as a stepping-stone in struggles for civil rights reform and anti-discrimination laws in many countries.[32] Meanwhile, the social model of disability has become officially recognized by the European Union as the basis for its disability policy.[33] Within disability studies, this rights-based approach in disability was characterized as a tool for stipulating citizenship and equality.[34] To demand anti-discrimination legislation was a logical consequence of analysing disability as the product of inequality and discrimination. In the United States where the social model of disability was conceptualized as the minority model,[35] the fight for civil rights was similarly seen as a way to disclose the true situation of disabled persons as members of an oppressed minority. The focus on rights was perceived as an alternative to needs-based social policy, which portrayed disabled persons as dependent welfare recipients. The ideology of dependency was coined by Michael Oliver as an essential tool of social construction of disability.[36] Thus, anti-discrimination legislation was seen as a remedy to a welfare approach to disability. Disabled persons could thus be described as citizens with equal rights. Architectural barriers could be defined as a form of discrimination. Segregated schools could be described as apartheid. The shift from welfare legislation to civil rights legislation in disability policy became the focus of disability movements in many countries.[37] 'We want rights not charity' was and still is a slogan to be heard around the world from disability rights activists.

However, anti-discrimination law can only be seen as a partial solution to the problem. Even in a society without barriers and other forms of discrimination, people need social, economic and cultural rights. People need shelter, education, employment or cultural participation. This is true for all human beings, and thus for disabled persons. However, because impairment often leads to needs for assistance, it is especially true that disabled persons need more than civil and political rights. While welfare policies and laws in the past have failed to acknowledge and empower disabled persons as citizens,[38] laws on personal assistance services or personal budgets proved that even classical social laws can give choice and control to disabled persons.[39] It is thus illustrative that the global independent living movement has always phrased their demands in terms of broader human rights, rather than in terms of pure anti-discrimination rights. The human rights model of disability includes both sets of human rights: political and civil, and economic, social and cultural rights. These two baskets of human rights, which have been adopted as distinct categories of human rights during the Cold War era for political reasons,[40] are fully incorporated in the CRPD as they are in the Universal Declaration of Human Rights (UDHR) of 1948. The legal hierarchy of

---

32 Degener and Quinn, *supra* note 19, at 6; C. Gooding, *Disabling Laws, Enabling Acts* (1994), at 10–13; C. Barnes, *Disabled People in Britain and Discrimination* (1991).

33 European Disability Strategy 2010–2020, at: http://eur-lex.europa.eu/LexUriServ/LexUriServ. do?uri=CELEX:52010DC0636:en:NOT (last visited 14 March 2013).

34 M. Oliver, *supra* note 22, at 112.

35 L. J. Davis, *The Disability Studies Reader* (1997).

36 M. Oliver, *supra* note 22, at 83.

37 M. L. Breslin and S. Yee, *Disability Rights Law and Policy* (2002); A. Lawson and C. Gooding, *supra* note 29.

38 Hvinden, 'Redistributive and Regulatory Disability Provision: Incompatibility or Synergy?', in G. Quinn and L. Waddington (eds), *European Yearbook of Disability Law* (2009).

39 Degener, 'Personal Assistance Services and Laws: A Commentary', in Rehabilitation International/World Institute on Disability (eds), *International Symposium on Personal Assistance Models* (1991); A. Power, J. E. Lord and A. S. DeFranco, *Active Citizenship and Disability* (2013); R. Townsley, *The Implementation of Policies Supporting Independent Living for Disabled People in Europe* (2010).

40 For an illustrative account of the political history of human rights, see R. Normand and S. Zaidi, *Human Rights at the UN* (2008).

civil and political rights over economic, social and cultural rights is slowly but steadily decreasing through international jurisprudence and the strengthening of monitoring and implementation of the International Covenant on Economic, Social and Cultural Rights (ICESCR).

A major milestone was the coming into force of an individual complaints procedure for economic, social and cultural rights in 2012 enabling the United Nations 'to come full circle on the normative architecture envisaged by the Universal Declaration of Human Rights'.[41] The universality, indivisibility and interdependence of all human rights were firmly established as a principle of international human rights law on the World Conference of Human Rights two decades earlier in Vienna.[42] The CRPD is a good example of the indivisibility and interdependence of both sets of human rights. It not only contains both sets of human rights, the text itself is evidence of the interdependence and interrelatedness of these rights. Some provisions on rights cannot be clearly allocated to one category only. For instance, the right to be regarded as a person before the law[43] is a right commonly regarded as a civil right.[44] However, Article 12 (3) CRPD speaks of support measures disabled persons might need to exercise their legal capacity. Are these support measures realized by social services which fall into the economic, social and cultural rights sphere? Another example would be the right to independent living.[45] It is one of the few rights of the CRPD which has no clear equivalent in binding pre-treaty law. The right to independent living and being included in the community is an answer to human rights violations against disabled persons through institutionalization and other methods of exclusion, such as hiding in the home or colonizing at distant places. The concepts of independent living and community living do not root in mainstream human rights philosophy, which is why the terms cannot be found in the International Bill of Human Rights but in international soft law related to disability that preceded the CRPD. The concept derives from the disability rights movement and other social movements such as the deinstitutionalization movement,[46] which came into being in the 1960s and 1970s in the United States, Scandinavia, Italy and many other countries.[47] The common catalogue of human rights of the UDHR does not contain a right to independent or community living. If at all, the right to independent living can be traced back to the freedom to choose one's residence, which in other treaties is usually linked to the freedom of movement and designed as a pure civil right.[48] However, independent living requires – among others – personal assistance services, which are measures to realize social rights. Thus, the CESCR Committee has interpreted the right to an adequate standard of living[49] to include a right to independent living for disabled persons. But it has also linked the issue to anti-discrimination measures. Its General Comment No 5 interprets Article 11 ICESCR as a right to 'accessible housing' and to 'support

---

41 Statement by Mr. Ivan Simonovic, Assistant Secretary-General. Deposit of the 10th instrument of ratification of the OP-IESR New York, 5 February 2013, at: www2.ohchr.org/english/bodies/cescr/index.htm (last visited 4 March 2013).
42 Vienna Declaration and Programme of Action, A/CONF.157/23, 12 July 1993, at: http://www.unhcr.org/refworld/docid/3ae6b39ec.html (last visited 14 March 2013).
43 Art. 12 CRPD.
44 Art. 16 ICCPR, Art. 6 UDHR.
45 Art. 19 CRPD.
46 Which in some countries was part of the disability rights movement, in other countries it was not.
47 T. Degener and Y. Koster-Dreese, *Human Rights and Disabled Persons: Essays and Relevant Human Rights Instruments* (1995); C. Parker, *A Community for All: Implementing Article 19* (2011); G. Quinn and S. Doyle, *Getting a Life* (2012).
48 Art. 13(1) UDHR: 'Everyone has the Right to Freedom of Movement and Residence within the Border of Each State'. See also Art. 12(1) ICCPR, Art. 5(d), (i) CERD, Art. 15(4) CEDAW.
49 Art. 11 ICESCR.

services including assistive devices' which enable disabled persons 'to increase their level of independence in their daily living and to exercise their rights'.[50] During the last 15 years, there has been an influx of publications on deinstitutionalization, the right to independent and community living and the member state obligations under Article 19 CRPD.[51] Most legal publications characterized this article as a social right with strong freedom and autonomy components.[52] In the words of the Council of Europe Commissioner of Human Rights, Thomas Hammarberg, who has published an issue paper on Article 19:

> The core of the right . . . is about neutralising the devastating isolation and loss of control over one's life, wrought on people with disabilities because of their need for support against the background of an inaccessible society. 'Neutralising' is understood as both removing the barriers to community access in housing and other domains, and providing access to individualized disability-related supports on which enjoyment of the right depends for many individuals.[53]

The CRPD Committee has not qualified the right to independent living yet as either a civil or social human right. While the CRPD contains the progressive realization clause usually applied to state responsibility regarding social, economic and cultural rights, it also includes a reminder that even economic, social and cultural rights are immediately applicable under some circumstances in public international law.[54]

The human rights model values impairment as part of human diversity

As a third argument, I would state: whereas the social model of disability neglects the fact that disabled persons might have to deal with pain, deterioration of quality of life and early death due to impairment, and dependency, the human rights model of disability acknowledges these life circumstances and demands them to be considered when social justice theories are developed.

The social model of disability has been criticized for neglecting the experience of impairment and pain for disabled people and how it affects their knowledge and their identity. Both the dichotomy of impairment and disability, as well as the materialist focus of the social model, have been criticized, especially by feminist disabled writers such as Jenny Morris. In her famous book *Pride Against Prejudice*, she claims:

> However, there is a tendency within the social model of disability to deny the experience of our own bodies, insisting that our physical differences and restrictions are *entirely*

---

50 CESCR General Comment No 5 para 33.
51 For example: R. Townsley, *supra* note 39; G. Quinn and S. Doyle, *supra* note 47; C. Parker, *supra* note 47; J. Mansell *et al.*, *Deinstitutionalization and Community Living* (2007); FRA European Union Agency for Fundamental Rights, *Choice and Control: The Right to Independent Living* (2012).
52 C. Parker, *supra* note 47; G. Quinn and S. Doyle, *supra* note 47.
53 T. Hammarberg, *The Right of People with Disabilities to Live Independently and be Included in the Community* (June 2012), at 11.
54 Art. 4(2) CRPD reads: 'With regard to economic, social and cultural rights, each State Party undertakes to take measures to the maximum of its available resources and, where needed, within the framework of international cooperation, with a view to achieving progressively the full realization of these rights, without prejudice to those obligations contained in the present Convention that are immediately applicable according to international law.'

socially created. While environmental barriers and social attitudes are a crucial part of our experience of disability – and do indeed disable us – to suggest that this is all there is to it is to deny the personal experience of physical or intellectual restrictions, of illness, of the fear of dying. A feminist perspective can help to redress this, and in so doing give voice to the experience of both disabled men and disabled women.[55]

In a later publication, she writes:

> If we clearly separate out disability and impairment, then we campaign against the disabling barriers and attitudes which so influence our lives and the opportunities which we have. This does not justify, however, ignoring the experience of our bodies, even though the pressures to do this are considerable because of the way that our bodies have been considered as abnormal, as pitiful, as the cause of our lives not being worth living. . . . In the face of this prejudice it is very important to assert that autonomy is not destiny and that it is instead the disabling barriers 'out there' which determine the quality of lives. However, in doing this, we have sometimes colluded with the idea that the 'typical' disabled person is a young man in a wheelchair who is fit, never ill, and whose only needs concern a physically accessible environment.[56]

Other writers followed this path of criticism. Marian Corker and Sally French who brought discourse analysis to disability studies added that besides neglecting the importance of impairment, the social model fails to 'conceptualize a mutually constitutive relationship between impairment and disability which is both materially and discursively (socially) produced'.[57] Many other disability studies scholars have shared this critique. Bill Hughes and Kevin Paterson proposed to develop a sociology of impairment based on post-structuralism and phenomenology as a response to this dilemma of impairment/disability dichotomy.[58] Tom Shakespeare has challenged the dichotomy on the basis that both are socially constructed and inextricably interconnected.[59] The founders and advocates of the social model have emphasized that the social model of disability was never meant to ignore impairment. Michael Oliver states: 'This denial of the pain of impairment has not, in reality, been a denial at all. Rather it has been a pragmatic attempt to identify and address issues that can be changed through collective action rather than professional and medical treatment.'[60]

However, he also contends that the social model is not a social theory of disability, which when developed should contain a theory of impairment.[61]

The human rights model of disability has not been brought into this debate yet, which is why my claim is hard to defend. The CRPD does not make any statement regarding impairment as a potential negative impact on the quality of life of disabled persons because the drafters were very determined not to make any negative judgement on impairment. However, persons with

55 J. Morris, *Pride against Prejudice* (1991), at 10 (emphasis in the original).
56 Morris, '*Impairment and Disability: Constructing an Ethics of Care which Promotes Human Rights*', 4 *Hypatia* (2001), at 17.
57 M. Corker and S. French, *Disability Discourse* (1999), at 6.
58 Hughes and Paterson, '*The Social Model of Disability and the Disappearing Body: Towards a Sociology of Impairment*', 3 *Disability & Society* (1997).
59 T. Shakespeare, *Disability Rights and Wrongs Revisited* (2014), at 72–91.
60 M. Oliver, *supra* note 22, at 38.
61 M. Oliver, *supra* note 22, at 42.

higher support needs are mentioned in the preamble,[62] as a reminder that they must not be left behind and that the CRPD is meant to protect all disabled persons not only those who are 'fit' for mainstreaming. Impairment as an important life factor is also recognized in two of the principles of the treaty, though both principles do not mention impairment explicitly. Article 3 (a) introduces 'respect for the inherent dignity . . . of persons' and paragraph (d) refers to 'respect for difference and acceptance of persons with disabilities as part of human diversity and humanity.' Respect for human dignity is one of the cornerstones of international human rights and domestic constitutional law today. It was introduced in many human rights catalogues after World War II as a response to the atrocities of the Nazi Regime and today is recognized as a core value of the United Nations.[63] However, it needs to be recognized that the CRPD relates to the concept of human dignity more often than other human rights treaties. Respect for the human dignity of disabled persons is the purpose and one of the eight guiding principles of the treaty.[64] In addition, it is referred to five times in such various contexts such as discrimination,[65] awareness raising,[66] recovery from violence,[67] inclusive education[68] and care delivery by health professionals.[69] Further, recognition of the 'inherent dignity and worth and the equal and inalienable rights of all members of the human family' are regarded as the 'foundation of freedom, justice and peace in the world'.[70]

The diversity principle of Article 3 CRPD is a valuable contribution to human rights theory in that it clarifies that impairment is not to be regarded as a deficit or as a factor that can be detrimental to human dignity. Thus, the CRPD is not only build on the premise that disability is a social construct, but it also values impairment as part of human diversity and human dignity. At this point, I think the human rights model goes beyond the social model of disability. This recognition is important as a fundamental premise for answering ethical questions which are triggered by the way society treats impairment, such as euthanasia, prenatal diagnosis, or medical normalization treatment. As we have stated in our background study:

> The human rights model focuses on the inherent dignity of the human being and subsequently, but only if necessary, on the person's medical characteristics. It places the individual centre stage in all decisions affecting him/her and, most importantly, locates the main 'problem' outside the person and in society. The 'problem' of disability under this model stems from a lack of responsiveness by the State and civil society to the difference that disability represents. It follows that the State has a responsibility to tackle socially created obstacles in order to ensure full respect for the dignity and equal rights of all persons.[71]

Another important aspect of the principle of human dignity is that it reaffirms that all human beings are right-bearers. As Lee Ann Basser has pointed out, this is particularly important for

62 Preamble para j) CRPD.
63 Petersen, '*Human Dignity, International Protection*', in R. Wolfrum (ed), *The Max Planck Encyclopaedia of Public International Law* (2012).
64 Art. (1), (3)(a) CRPD.
65 Preamble para h) CRPD.
66 Art. 8(1) (a) CRPD.
67 Art. 16(4) CRPD.
68 Art. 24(1)(a) CRPD.
69 Art. 25(d) CRPD.
70 Preamble para a) CRPD.
71 G. Quinn and T. Degener, *supra* note 20, at 14.

disabled people who have long been denied this status. She refers to Dworkin's conceptualization of rights as special entitlements as 'trumps',[72] and says if rights are trumps 'then dignity is the key that turns the lock and allows entry into society and require that each person be treated with equal concern and respect in that society'.[73] The international disability rights movement has fought for the CRPD for more than two decades. I think the long-time struggle for a human rights treaty was not only a fight of DPOs for political change but also an individual struggle of disabled people for recognition and respect in the sense of Axel Honneth's recognition theory.[74] According to Honneth, political struggles of social movements always have a collective and an individual dimension. The individual dimension relates to the struggle as a process of identity formation which needs to be facilitated by self-respect, self-confidence and self-esteem. The struggle for human rights of disabled persons is thus a struggle for the global collective of disabled people but also a fight for respect and recognition of the disabled individual by society. The human rights model of disability clarifies that impairment does not derogate human dignity nor does it encroach upon the disabled person's status as rights-bearer. Therefore I think, the human rights model of disability is more appropriate than the social model to encompass the experience of impairment, which might not always be bad but certainly can be. It also allows us to analyse politics of disablement as the denial of social and cultural recognition, which is an aspect of the critique of the social model of disability.[75] The human rights model of disability demands that impairment is recognized in theories of justice. Whether these are social contract theories, take a capability approach or take an ethics of care as their basis is another matter.[76]

The human rights model acknowledges identity issues

Fourth, the social model of disability neglects identity politics as a valuable component of disability policy whereas the human rights model offers room for minority and cultural identification.

The social model also has been criticized for neglecting identity politics as a valuable component of emancipation. Identity politics can be defined as politics which values and cares for differences among human beings and allows persons to identify positively with features which are disrespected in society. Gay pride, black pride, feminism, or disability culture are manifestations of these identity politics. The social model of disability does not provide much room for these issues because its focus is not on personal emancipation but on social power relations. Identity politics in the context of disability can have several meanings. The term might relate to impairment categories or impairment causes. Deaf people have created their own culture and deaf studies have become an important strand of disability studies in which deaf identity plays an important role.[77] Like deaf or hard of hearing persons, blind and deaf-blind people were among the first

---

72 R. Dworkin, *Taking Rights Seriously* (1978).
73 Basser, '*Human Dignity*', in M. H. Rioux, L. A. Basser and M. Jones (eds), *Critical Perspectives on Human Rights and Disability Law* (2011), at 21.
74 A. Honneth, *The Struggle for Recognition* (1996).
75 Watson, '*The Dialectics of Disability: A Social Model for the 21st Century?*', in C. Barnes and G. Mercer (eds), *Implementing the Social Model of Disability* (2004), at 101–117; Danermark and Gellerstedt, '*Social Justice: Redistribution and Recognition – A Non-Reductionist Perspective on Disability*', 19 *Disability & Society* (2004).
76 For a combination of capabilities and other approaches see: M. A. Stein, '*Disability Human Rights*', 95 *California Law Review* (2007).
77 P. Ladd, *Understanding Deaf Culture* (2003); M. Corker, *Deaf Transitions* (1996).

groups who created their own organizations, which are still operative today[78] and so are many other impairment-related organizations.

Another identity factor in the context of disability might be the difference between acquired and congenital impairment. To be born blind or deaf or physically or intellectually impaired is very different from becoming disabled through illness, accident, violence or poverty. Further, some impairments or 'disorders' may come along with unique experiences of exclusion and identity. For example, Peter Beresford, who identifies as a mental health user, argued for a social model of madness, way before the CRPD came into being.[79] Finally, identity may be shaped by more than impairment, but by gender, 'race', sexual orientation and identity, age or religion. Disabled women were among the first to criticize the disability rights movement (and the women's movement) for neglecting other identity features.[80] Disabled people of colour followed[81] and others such as Ayesha Vernon raised the issue of intersectional discrimination and multidimensional oppression.[82]

Impairment-related identity policy has been seen with suspicion by social model proponents because these organizations were either seen as apolitical self-help groups or as another example of the medicalization of disability. Anita Silvers found identity politics unsuitable for disabled persons because of the heterogeneous constituency of the disability community or because other identity constructs such as women's roles as caretakers or child-bearers are commonly denied to disabled individuals.[83] Tom Shakespeare has offered a helpful summary of further criticism against identity politics and the harm it might do to disability politics.[84]

Other systems of oppression such as sexism and racism have been acknowledged as an important factor in constructing identity and social status from the beginning of the social model of disability,[85] but it has been admitted that the social model of disability was not intended to cover all the different experiences of oppression.[86]

Human rights instruments are at least partly the political response to collective experiences of injustice. The history of human rights law as it developed after World War II shows that identity-based social movements were strong players in the making of international law.[87] The current core human rights treaties are a manifestation of this process. The International Convention on the Elimination of All Forms of Racial Discrimination (CERD) of 1965 as well as the

78 World Blind Union (http://www.worldblindunion.org/English/Pages/default.aspx), World Federation of the Deaf (http://wfdeaf.org/).

79 Beresford, '*Madness, Distress, Research and a Social Model*', in C. Barnes and G. Mercer (eds), *Implementing the Social Model of Disability* (2004).

80 Asch and Fine, '*Nurturance, Sexuality, and Women with Disabilities*', in L. J. Davis (eds), *The Disability Studies Reader* (1997); Wendell, '*Toward a Feminist Theory of Disability*', in L. J. Davis (eds), *The Disability Studies Reader* (1997); Garland Thomson, '*Feminist Theory, the Body, and the Disabled Figure*', in L. J. Davis (ed), *The Disability Studies Reader* (1997); J. Morris, *supra* note 55.

81 C. M. Bell, *Blackness and Disability* (2011).

82 Vernon, '*Multiple Oppression and the Disabled People's Movement*', in T. Shakespeare (ed), *The Disability Reader* (1998).

83 Silvers, '*Triple Difference: Disability, Race, Gender and the Politics of Recognition*', in L. A. B. Marks and M. Jones (eds), *Disability, Divers-ability and Legal Change* (1999).

84 T. Shakespeare, *supra* note 59, at 92–110.

85 M. Oliver, *supra* note 22, at 70–78.

86 M. Oliver, *supra* note 22, at 39.

87 R. Burke, *Decolonization and the Evolution of International Human Rights* (2010); C. Bob, *The International Struggle for New Human Rights* (2009).

International Convention on the Protection of the Rights of All Migrant Workers and Members of Their Families (CRMW) of 1990 are responses to colonization and racism, the Convention on the Elimination of All Forms of Discrimination Against Women (CEDAW) of 1979 is the response to sexism, the Convention on the Rights of the Child (CRC) of 1989 is the answer to adultism and the CRPD is the answer to ableism. The development of these thematic human rights treaties have been called the personification[88] and the pluralization[89] of human rights. These treaties were adopted because human rights politics and theory as developed on the basis of the International Bill of Human Rights were based predominantly on the experiences of western, white, male, non-disabled adults and ignored the experiences of other individuals. This ignorance was and is a reflection of different systems of subordination that run alongside axes of inequality such as 'race', gender, sexuality, body and mind functioning. The emergence of social movements that opposed these systems of subordination brought with it the birth of critical studies such as gender studies, critical race studies and disability studies. Human rights law as moral law and as ideology is not only a reflection of political conflict among states or a reflection of global and domestic power relations, it is also a tool for social transformation. Whether successful or not may be debated, but it is important to acknowledge these different functions of human rights law. The current human rights treaties may be the outcome of World War II and Cold War conflicts, but they also reflect emancipation and democratic gains of social movements. Feminism for example did have a major impact on international public law in theory and practice during the last decades. The artificial distinction between private and public spheres of life and the assumption that states only hold responsibility for violations in the public sphere were successfully challenged by feminist international lawyers. The public/private distinction in international law is the result of the hegemony of male experiences of human rights violations. Human rights violence taking place in the private sphere, such as domestic violence, was ignored within the first four decades of international human rights law. Feminist legal scholars such as Hilary Charlesworth, Christine Chinkin[90] and Catherine MacKinnon[91] have successfully argued that this artificial distinction not only ignores women's experiences but that it also serves to hide state complicity with the perpetrators and that this legal doctrine stabilizes patriarchal subordination. Feminist critical race lawyers such as Mari Matsuda[92] and Angela Harris[93] have taken feminist legal theory a step further by introducing anti-essentialist approaches to civil rights law. Thus, I would argue that current human rights law is the result of human rights law becoming truly universal rather than seeing these group-specific human rights instruments as testimony 'that there is something specific about these groups . . . which . . . *cannot* be taken adequately into account by human rights instruments that have the ambition to covering the whole human genre'.[94]

The human rights model of disability as based on the existing canon of core human rights treaties gives consideration to different layers of identity. It acknowledges that disabled persons may be male or female, non-whites, disabled, children or migrants. It is clear that there are more

---

88 Mégret, *The Disabilities Convention'*, 494 *Human Rights Quarterly: A Comparative and International Journal of the Social Sciences, Humanities, and Law* (2008), at 495.
89 C. C. Gould, *Globalizing Democracy and Human Rights* (2004), at 77.
90 C. Chinkin and H. Charlesworth, *Feminist Analysis of International Law* (1998).
91 C. A. MacKinnon, *Toward a Feminist Theory of the State* (1989).
92 M. J. Matsuda, *Where Is Your Body?* (1996).
93 Harris, *'Race and Essentialism in Feminist Legal Theory'*, 3 *Stanford Law Review* (1990).
94 Mégret, *supra* note 88, at 497 (emphasis in the original).

layers of identity to be considered in international human rights law[95] and that the issue of inter-sectionality of discrimination has yet to be solved.[96]

In addition to human rights law in general, the CRPD also acknowledges different layers of identity within the context of disability and human rights. For instance, disabled children and disabled women have their own stand-alone articles.[97] The women's article even acknowledges 'that women and girls with disabilities are subject to multiple discrimination', which is the first binding intersectionality clause in a human rights treaty. Further recognition of gender and age can be found throughout the treaty.[98] Other grounds, such as 'race', colour, language, religion, political or other opinion, national, ethnic, indigenous or social origin, property, or birth and age are, however, only recognized in the preamble.[99] For these and other layers of identity – such as age or sexual orientation – lobbying was not strong enough during the negotiations.

A few impairment-related groups are recognized though. These are deaf, blind and deaf-blind persons. Article 30 CRPD on cultural participation demands that states recognize and support their 'specific culture and cultural identity, including sign languages and deaf culture'.[100] The other context in which deaf, blind and deaf-blind persons are specifically mentioned is the right to education. Article 24 CRPD demands that persons who belong to these impairment groups are provided with the tools to education that are adequate to their identity, such as Braille and sign language,[101] and that they are provided with role models and qualified teachers; the most disputed paragraph reads:

(1) . . . States Parties shall ensure an inclusive education system at all levels and lifelong learning directed to:

. . .

(c) Ensuring that the education of persons, and in particular children, who are blind, deaf or deafblind, is delivered in the most appropriate languages and modes and means of communication for the individual, and in environments which maximize academic and social development.

. . .

I remember very well the long nights we fought over the wording of this paragraph in the Ad Hoc Committee. The World Blind Union, the World Federation of the Deaf and the World

95 Intersex or transgender people as well as gay and lesbians are yet to be included in international human rights law. See Report of the United Nations High Commissioner for Human Rights: Discriminatory laws and practices and acts of violence against individuals based on their sexual orientation and gender identity, UN Doc A/HRC/19/41, 17 November 2011.
96 Degener, '*Intersections between Disability, Race and Gender in Discrimination Law*', in D. Schiek and A. Lawson (eds), *European Union Non-discrimination Law and Intersectionality* (2011); Bond, '*International Intersectionality: A Theoretical and Pragmatic Exploration of Women's International Human Rights Violations*', 52 *Emory Law Journal* (2003).
97 Art. 6 and Art. 7 CRPD.
98 Preamble para p), q), r), s); Art. 3(g), (h); Art. 4(3); Art. 8(2)(b); Art. 13; Art. 16(2), (3), (5); Art. 18; Art. 23(1)(b), (c), (3), (5); Art. 25 (b); Art. 28; Art. 29; Art. 34 CRPD.
99 Preamble para p) CRPD.
100 Art. 30(4) CRPD.
101 Art. 24(3)(a) and (b).

Federation of the Deafblind were all represented with superb experts. We had long debates about whether or not there should be a human right to special education or at least a right to choose between mainstream and special education. The opinions oscillated between 'segregation is always and inherently unequal' and 'mainstream education means assimilation which means for many bad education'. These debates were loaded with identity issues, showing us that it was important to make room for them.

The final text is a true compromise and in my opinion a masterpiece. The credit for it goes to a large extent to Rosemary Kayess – an eminent international lawyer and disability rights activist from Australia, who acted as a facilitator to the article on the right to education.

The human rights model allows for assessment of prevention policy

My fifth argument is that while the social model of disability is critical of prevention policy, the human rights model offers a basis for assessment when prevention policy can be claimed as human rights protection for disabled persons.

Prevention of impairment is an element of public health policy which has long been criticized by disability rights activists as being stigmatizing or discriminatory. The object of critique can be the mode of implementation of public health policy or the goals. While prevention of traffic accidents or polio is not seen as problematic, the ways these policies are proclaimed can be stigmatizing towards disabled persons. For instance, if an advertisement for safe driving is accompanied by a poster of a quadriplegic person titled: 'Being crippled for the rest of your life is worse than death', disabled persons are abused as deterrents. Another example are vaccination campaigns against polio which utilize slogans such as 'Oral vaccination is sweet, polio is cruel!' Public health campaigns like these led to fierce protest from the disability rights movement in the 1970s and 1980s in several countries. The goals of medical prevention programmes can be the target of protest if they have to do with life or death issues such as selective abortion or assisted suicide. The message that some see conveyed with these programmes is that a life with a disability is not worth living. What is claimed as a prevention of impairment policy is in fact a policy that aims at eliminating disabled persons. Michael Oliver has characterized these programmes as the core of ideological construction of disability.[102] Feminist disability studies scholars have written widely on the conflicts between women's right to reproductive autonomy and disabled people's right to non-discrimination.[103] This particular difficult subject also came up during the negotiations of the CRPD, but was dropped due to time pressure and the unlikelihood to achieve a compromise on this matter with pro-life advocates[104] and many feminists in the room.

Unlike the UN World Programme of Action Concerning Disabled Persons (WPA) of 1982[105] and the UN Standard Rules on the Equalization of Opportunities for Persons with Disabilities of 1993 (StRE), the CRPD does not refer to impairment prevention as a matter of disability policy. These two declarations are the most important human rights instruments preceding the CRPD.

---

102 M. Oliver, *supra* note 22, at 54–59.
103 T. Degener and S. Köbsell, *Hauptsache es ist gesund?* (1992); E. Parens and A. Asch, *Prenatal Testing and Disability Rights* (2000); A. Silvers, D. T. Wasserman and M. B. Mahowald, *Disability, Difference, Discrimination* (1998); Saxton, '*Why Members of the Disability Community Oppose Prenatal Diagnosis and Selective Abortion*', in E. Parens and A. Asch (eds), *Prenatal Testing and Disability Rights* (2000); J. Morris, *supra* note 55.
104 The Vatican is a UN member state and the delegation took a very active role in this matter.
105 WPA A/37/351/Add.1 and Add.1/Corr.1, annex .

At the time of their adoption, they marked a milestone in the eventual recognition of human rights of disabled persons because they added a human rights component to traditional disability policy. The latter consisted of a three-tiered approach to disability: definition, prevention and rehabilitation. The WPA and the StRE added a fourth element to disability policy: equality of opportunities. However, both instruments refer to prevention of impairment as an element of disability policy and include prenatal care as an important measure.[106] Especially the WPA has been influenced not only by an upcoming international disability rights movement[107] but also by health professionals. This is revealed by the fact that the Leeds Castle Declaration on the Prevention of Disablement of 12 November 1981 is cited almost in full length in the WPA text.[108] This declaration, which was written by a group of scientists, doctors, health administrators and politicians, praises biomedical research as 'revolutionary new tools which should greatly strengthen all interventions'.[109] The WPA even includes a paragraph on the cost-effectiveness of prevention programmes: 'It is becoming increasingly recognized that programmes to prevent impairment or to ensure that impairments do not escalate into more limiting disabilities are less costly to society in the long run *than having to care later for disabled persons*.'[110]

The WPA has been criticized for perpetuating the medical model of disability.[111] While the WPA and StRE are both referenced in the preamble of the CRPD,[112] prevention does not appear prominently in the text of the treaty. This was a deliberate decision taken during and before the negotiations.[113] The purpose of the CRPD is to promote and to protect the rights of persons who have a disability. It was argued that it was incoherent to deal with prevention of disability in the same instrument. Thus, with the adoption of the CRPD, it was made clear that primary prevention of impairment might be an important aspect of the right to health[114] as enshrined in the ICESCR, but that it is certainly not an appropriate measure to protect the human rights of people living with a disability. This is an important message to member states who claim that they spend a lot of money for disabled persons and then submit reports which show that a large part of the budget is spent on impairment prevention policy.

However, as Tom Shakespeare has pointed out,[115] not all impairment prevention policy is bad, and most disabled persons actually are in need of this kind of public health policy. In fact, the 2011 WHO World Report on Disability gives evidence that disabled persons experience poorer level of health due to a variety of factors, such as inaccessible health care services, risk of developing secondary conditions, higher risk of being exposed to violence, and increased rates of health risk behaviour.[116] This is also recognized in the CRPD in the context of the rights to health. There prevention is addressed not with relation to primary prevention but to secondary prevention programmes to 'prevent further disabilities including among children and older

---

106 WPA para 13 and 52–56; StRE para 22.
107 D. Driedger, *The Last Civil Rights Movement* (1989), at 97–99.
108 WPA para 54.
109 WPA para 54.
110 WPA para 55 (emphasis added).
111 Degener, '*Disabled Women and International Human Rights*', in K. D. Askin and D. M. Koenig (eds), *Women and International Human Rights Law* (2001), at 278; O. Nagase, *Difference, Equality and Disabled People* (1995).
112 Preamble para f) CRPD.
113 Trömel, *supra* note 18, at 120.
114 Art. 12 ICESCR.
115 T. Shakespeare, *supra* note 59.
116 World Health Organisation/World Bank, *World Report on Disability* (2011), at 57–60.

persons'.[117] Article 25 CRPD is an example of framing the right of health of disabled persons in a human rights context. It demands equal access to general and specialized health care services for disabled persons. Services must be community based and sensitive to freedom rights and to the dignity of disabled persons. Discrimination through provision or denial of health care must be prohibited and prevented. As the WHO Report underlines:

> Viewing disability as a human rights issue is not incompatible with prevention of health conditions as long as prevention respects the rights and dignity of people with disabilities, for example in the use of language and imagery. . . . Preventing disability should be regarded as a multidimensional strategy that includes prevention of disabling barriers as well as prevention and treatment of underlying health conditions.[118]

The human rights model strives for social justice

As a sixth argument, I opine: Whereas the social model of disability can explain why two-thirds of the one billion disabled persons in this world live in relative poverty, the human rights model offers a roadmap for change.

From early on, social model proponents and critics acknowledged the close link between poverty and disability.[119] Indeed, the interrelatedness of poverty and disability was put forward as evidence that not only disability but also impairment is a social construct.[120] There is now abundance of evidence that impairment and poverty are mutually reinforcing.[121] Impairment may increase the risk of poverty and poverty may increase the risk of impairment. Lack of resources, lack of education, and dearth of access to fundamental services are among the factors to be considered when trying to understand why two-thirds of the world population of disabled people live in the developing world. The social model has helped to understand that disability is a development issue. Social model advocates and disability studies researchers have had a significant impact on empowerment policies that address these issues.[122] The United Nations, the World Bank and other development agents have long acknowledged that disability is a development issue,[123] however, disability was not mainstreamed in development policies. Thus, disability was initially not recognized as one of the issues in the Millennium Development Goals. Only after the adoption of the CRPD did this change dramatically, and disability became a central subject of international cooperation policy.

The CRPD is the first human rights treaty with a standalone provision on development. Article 32 CRPD on international cooperation was one of the major controversial provisions from the beginning to the end of the negotiations.[124] Together with Article 11 CRPD on situations of

117 Art. 25(b) CRPD.
118 World Health Organisation/World Bank, *supra* note 116, at 8.
119 M. Oliver, *supra* note 22, at 12–13.
120 T. Shakespeare, *supra* note 59, at 34–35.
121 World Health Organisation/World Bank, *supra* note 116, at 10–11.
122 C. Barnes and G. Mercer, *The Social Model of Disability* (2005), at 15; D. Driedger, *supra* note 107; B. Watermeyer, *Disability and Social Change* (2006), at 206–259; M. Priestley, *Disability and the Life Course* (2001); E. Stone, *Disability and Development* (1999); B. Albert, *In or Out of the Mainstream? Lessons from Research on Disability and Development Cooperation* (2006).
123 J. Braithwaite and D. Mont, *Disability and Poverty: A Survey of World Bank Poverty Assessments and Implications* (February 2008).
124 Trömel, *supra* note 18, at 132.

risk and humanitarian emergencies, it provides a solid roadmap for disability policy in international humanitarian and development cooperation. Article 32 CRPD demands that international cooperation is inclusive and accessible to disabled people, that disability is mainstreamed in all development programmes and that DPOs are involved in the monitoring of these activities. Article 11 CRPD demands that states take adequate actions to protect disabled persons in situations of natural disaster or humanitarian emergencies. This latter article was introduced after the tsunami of 2004 in the Indian Ocean, which led to the death of several hundred thousand human beings, among them many disabled individuals who were excluded from rescue. By the time of the end of the negotiations, the Lebanon war had started in July 2006, which increased the already politicized nature of the article. Under these circumstances, it was amazing to reach consensus on the text of these articles.[125] Both these articles bring at least three important aspects to the development and humanitarian policy: (1) a human-rights-based approach to development and humanitarian aid; (2) disability mainstreaming as a leitmotif of international cooperation and (3) the importance of DPO involvement. These aspects are not new – they have been raised before – but with the CRPD, they have become binding international law.

A human rights approach in development means that people living in poverty are not objects of welfare and charity but rights holders who have a say in the distribution of resources and needs assessment. Participation is a means, and a goal and strategies need to be empowering. Development projects need to target disadvantaged, marginalized and excluded groups. These are some of the principles that make up the UN common understanding of the human-rights-based approach to development cooperation which was adopted in 2003.[126] While the new rights-based approach in development is not without shortcomings,[127] it is an important step into the direction of achieving social justice in times of globalization. Disability mainstreaming is an important strategy to overcome segregation structures implemented and maintained by traditional disability policies. Without active and equal participation of disabled people and their representative organizations, development strategies and programmes will perpetuate and exacerbate discrimination against disabled persons.[128]

Developing the social model into a human rights model of disability

My intention is not to abandon the social model of disability, but to develop it further. The social model of disability was the most successful dictum during the negotiations of the CRPD. If there is one single phrase which summarizes the success story of the CRPD, it is that it manifests the paradigm shift from the medical to the social model of disability in international disability policy. Not everyone who used the term during the negotiation process was knowledgeable about disability studies. Indeed, I concur with Rosemary Kayess and Phillip French in their analysis that the enormous influence the social model had during the negotiations has come from a 'populist conceptualization of the social model as a disability rights manifesto and its tendency towards a

125 Actually, because there could not be reached consensus on a reference to foreign occupation in the treaty – initially in Article 11, later in the preamble – , this issue was the only part of the treaty which could not be approved by consensus. For details see Trömel, *supra* note 18, at 125.

126 UN Common Understanding on Human Rights-Based Approaches to development cooperation and programming, at: http://www.undg.org/archive_docs/6959-The_Human_Rights_Based_Approach_to_Development_Cooperation_Towards_a_Common_Understanding_among_UN.pdf (visited 5 March 2013).

127 Cornwall and Nyamy-Musembi, *'Putting the 'Rights-Based' Approach to Development Into Perspective'*, 8 *Third World Quarterly* (2004).

128 *Global Thematic Consultation on the Post-2015 Development Agenda* (February 2013).

radical social constructionist view of disability, rather than from its contemporary expression as a critical theory of disability'.[129] But given that the drafting of international human rights norms is always a highly political undertaking, the reductionism in the use of the social model is comprehensible. The social model of disability had become the motto of the international disability movement and it served as a powerful tool to demand legal reform. As Rannveig Traustadóttir, Mark Priestley and Tom Shakespeare[130] have illustrated, there is a variety of different social theories and models of disability in disability studies and other science fields. The British social model has been distinguished from the US minority group approach and from the Nordic relational approach.[131] In addition to social, cultural[132] and individual models of disability, theories of disability have been divided into materialist and idealist typologies.[133] My intention is not to denounce the social model but to carry it further. Like many other human rights projects, the CRPD once planted into this world through adoption by the General Assembly took on a life of its own. The impact has been enormous so far in many areas, such as human rights monitoring, international cooperation, accessibility and legal capacity discourse, or inclusive education, to name but a few. In the context of the background study, we found that the disability rights movement had embraced the idea of human rights but many disability rights organizations had not become human rights organizations in terms of agents in the system, comparable to mainstream human rights organizations like Amnesty International or Human Rights Watch.[134] Nevertheless, DPOs have quickly learned and some of the organizations such as the International Disability Alliance have become some of the most influential agents in the UN human rights system. Thus, it could be concluded that political activism has turned to human rights and the CRPD is a codification of the human rights model of disability. The Committee has embraced the term human rights model of disability in its more recent concluding observations.[135] Most of the state party reports, however, do not reflect a clear understanding of the human rights model of disability. While it has become unfashionable to rely on the medical model of disability, the paradigm shift to the human rights model has yet to be reflected in implementation.

---

129 Kayess and French, *supra* note 18, at 7.
130 T. Shakespeare, *supra* note 59, at 9–92.
131 Traustadóttir, *supra* note 21.
132 Waldschmidt, '*Disability Studies: Individuelles, soziales und/oder kulturelles Modell von Behinderung?*', 1 *Psychologie und Gesellschaftskritik* (2005).
133 Priestley, '*Constructions and Creations: Idealism, Materialism and Disability Theory*', 1 *Disability & Society* (1998).
134 G. Quinn and T. Degener, *supra* note 20, at 256–270.
135 Concluding Observations on the initial report of Argentina as approved by the Committee at its eighth session (17–28 September 2012), CRPD/C/ARG/CO/1, 8 October 2012, para 7–8; Concluding Observations on the initial report of China, adopted by the Committee at its eighth session (17–28 September 2012), CRPD/C/CHN/CO/1, 15 October 2012, para 9–10, 16, 54.

PART II

Ongoing debates in disability law

Introduction

In this section, the contributors address a number of key debates regarding the substantive rights of people with disabilities in contemporary societies. To frame this discussion, Theresia Degener provides an overview of the human rights model of disability – outlining how this draws on and expands upon existing theories such as the social and relational models of disability, discussed in further detail in Part I.

In terms of the substantive rights of people with disabilities, this section examines some key areas of concern – considering both socio-economic rights, such as the rights to education and employment, and civil and political rights, such as the rights to access justice and to political participation.

While the prohibition on discrimination in education and employment is a long-standing fundamental right in many jurisdictions, the authors consider how far laws and policies have developed to proactively and meaningfully include people with disabilities in mainstream activities – through inclusive education (Rosemary Kayess and Jennifer Green) and employment on the open labour market (Lisa Waddington, Mark Priestley and Betul Yalcin). In both contexts, segregated provision (in the form of special schools and sheltered workshops) remain the norm in many countries, and the authors consider how human rights frameworks can advance educational attainment and labour market activation for people with disabilities.

Turning next to the civil and political rights of people with disabilities, Anna Lawson examines the barriers and opportunities in achieving access to justice for people with disabilities, considering a broad human rights framework encompassing substantive, procedural, symbolic and participatory justice. Lisa Schur's contribution further highlights the links between social participation, political activity and economic empowerment – demonstrating the interlinked and interdependent nature of all human rights – civil, political, economic, social and cultural.

Constantin Cojocariu provides a practical illustration of the barriers faced by people with disabilities in asserting and enforcing their human rights – using a case study of the European Court of Human Rights' approach to applicants with mental disabilities. Taken together, these contributions illustrate the ongoing substantive human rights concerns of people with disabilities, as well as the procedural challenges and opportunities in making these human rights claims, and working towards changing law and policy at a national and regional level.

4

TODAY'S LESSON IS ON DIVERSITY

Rosemary Kayess and Jennifer Green

Introduction

Inclusive education is education for all in one system. Its focus is not disability, but the recognition of human diversity and the benefits to all when that diversity is valued and difference is accommodated in practice.

From the beginning, what constitutes an education has been at the core of pedagogical theorising. As Aristotle said, 'educating the mind without educating the heart is no education at all.' This underscores the importance of a holistic approach to education – one that considers not only what is taught in a curriculum but how, where and with whom. It acknowledges that education is made up of formal, informal, incidental and vicarious learning that goes beyond facts to attitudes and values that inherently shape an individual's understanding and expectations of life. The school is one of the first role models of our communities and society. If the school values, embraces and caters for pluralism and human diversity then those will be the civic and citizenship understanding and expectations of its community. Inclusive education, by its very nature, underscores the universality of human rights and the inherent dignity and worth of all members of the human family.

So what would an inclusive education experience look like? In some respects it is best illustrated by the experience of the non-disabled student.

As a non-disabled peer you would learn that there is no question about where your sibling, friend and neighbour will go to school. They will go to school with you. They are part of your community and your world. You will observe and participate in their learning as they will in yours. You will see adaptions enable students' participation and performance. You will watch teachers move seamlessly between the needs of students, aware of the value of including everyone in the classroom. You won't remember when or how you learnt sign language as it is just part of the immersion programme, but signing behind the teacher's back and across crowded noisy rooms is one of your great pleasures. As is singing in the Deaf and Hearing Choir. You will learn Braille because of the enormous benefits in being able to continue to read at night after 'lights out'.

As a typical student you will detect perceived weaknesses in your peers, identify injustices largely to yourself (like why does she get extra time or a reader or a computer in exams). At best you will witness bullying and at worst you may participate in it, the consequence of which will be a strong response from the school that reinforces its general safe school policies and the importance and value of diversity and respect.

By the time you finish your education and commence your working life, some of your friends and peers will be people with a diverse range of abilities. Consequently your assumptions of life will be of mixing with people with a diverse range of abilities. You will imagine and expect to work in places that are gender, age, culture, race, religion and ability diverse. As a result of your education experience you will know how this is meant to look and what is required. It will leave you with an incomprehensible view of today's unemployment statistics for people with disability.

Persons with disability have been consistently denied equal access to education and the opportunity for life-long learning. The right to education is recognised as a central pillar of human rights which is enshrined in international law. In all parts of the world, including in developed societies, persons with disability are frequently excluded from education on the basis of disability, or are afforded greatly inferior education experiences to those of their non-disabled peers. In particular, too often those education opportunities that are provided to children and young persons with disability are provided in environments where students are segregated and congregated away from their non-disabled peers. This greatly diminishes the social development of all students, disabled and non-disabled alike. It is common that these environments provide very poor quality curricula and instructional methods, greatly curtailing students' academic development and achievement.

The Convention on the Rights of Persons with Disabilities (CRPD) is based on the premise that disability is but one aspect of human diversity. The convention tailors and applies human rights to the specific human rights problems experienced by persons with disability and is as such regarded as an implementation treaty. One of the key objectives of the convention is to build capacity in human rights implementation efforts so that they effectively respond to the human rights of persons with disability.

This chapter posits that CRPD provides an implementation framework for building inclusive education systems based on two central tenets. The first is the default position that all children are educated together in their local neighbourhood school. The second is that the policy architecture and resourcing of the education system is based on that default position and consequently prepares for and caters to staff, students and school community across the range of diverse abilities.

The chapter is developed in three parts. The first examines briefly the history of inclusive education, taking the Australian experience as an example. The second part addresses CRPD and human diversity by examining the case for the convention and how the convention frames the right to education. Finally the third part looks at a conceptual framework from the perspective of macro, meso and micro level implementation.

Inclusive education: A brief history

Since the International Year of Disabled Persons (IYDP) in 1981 with its theme of 'full participation and equality', there has been a revolution in the education of students with disability throughout the world from comprehensive exclusion to progressive inclusion.[1] Taking New South Wales (NSW), Australia's most populous state as an example, this revolution is briefly

1 Tracey, D., "Self-concepts of preadolescents with mild intellectual disability: Multidimensionality, measurement, and support for the big fish little pond effect" (2002) University of Western Sydney – Dissertations.

reviewed, illustrating the developments and issues commonly faced by education systems in the developed world during this period.

For the better part of the twentieth century, students with disability who received an education in NSW did so in segregated settings ranging from residential institutions to special schools and special classes. For children and youth with physical and/or sensory disability, their education took place alongside the treatment of their 'medical' needs. In the segregated settings the student teacher ratios were low (1:12), the curriculum was developed for the students' needs and abilities and the teachers were trained and experienced in special education. Moreover, according to one of the strong arguments of the day, the students with disability were not exposed to the rejection and bullying likely to occur in mainstream education settings.[2]

With the progression of the American civil rights movement of the 1960s the disability rights movement took form and framed the issue of disability as one of social justice not welfare or care.[3] IYDP placed social justice issues of disability on the agenda of the United Nations member states. In NSW it raised awareness and consciousness about community inclusion and exclusion. The deinstitutionalization of large congregate care facilities commenced, assisted by government support for the placement of people with disability in the community. Community-based and in-home supports increased and parents' expectations for their sons and daughters with disability exploded. The principles of segregated education were challenged and the beginnings of inclusion in mainstream schools commenced. Special education teacher training included classroom strategies for teaching mixed ability groups and regular teacher education degrees commenced offering electives in special education subjects.

In 1981 and 1982, the NSW Anti Discrimination Act was extended to include disability; in 1992, the Commonwealth Government passed the Commonwealth Disability Discrimination Act. Inclusion was promoted to the extent that it did not incur 'unjustifiable hardship'. Mainstream enrolments of students with disability steadily increased. The NSW government commenced the process of moving to inclusion with segregated classes attached to mainstream schools. Classes were categorized accordingly:

Mild Intellectual Disability (IM)
Moderate Intellectual Disability (IO)
Severe Intellectual Disability (S)
Language Disability (L)
Emotionally Disturbed (ED)
Conduct/Behaviourally Disordered (BD)
Autism (A)
Hearing (H)

For those students in mainstream classes, support teachers and teachers' aides were recruited and provided on a limited budget.

In 1993, the NSW State Government released the Special Education Policy, which stated that every 'child with a disability, learning difficulty, or behaviour disorder has the right to attend the

2 See Johnson, G., "A study of the social position of mentally handicapped children in regular grades" (1950) 55 *American Journal of Mental Deficiency* 60; Madden, N., and Slavin, R., "Mainstreaming students with mild handicaps: Academic and social outcomes" (1983) 53(4) *Review of Educational Research* 519.
3 Vaughan Switzer, J., *Disabled Rights: American Disability Policy and the Fight for Equality* (Washington, DC, Georgetown University Press, 2003).

regular neighbourhood school where this is possible and practicable and in the best interest of the child'.[4] However the implementation of the policy varied considerably from school to school, region to region and system to system. There were widely differing views on what constituted 'possible, practicable and the best interest of the child'.

Some schools simply refused to enrol students with disability. There were many more seg-regated classes than in-class inclusion and the resourcing of support for students with disability and their teachers was poor.[5] Moreover, far from Universal Design for Learning (UDL) that provides 'accessible, flexible, usable and customisable curriculum for all students',[6] there was little curriculum adaptation beyond tacked-on adaptations.[7]

With a desire to understand and improve inclusion, the NSW State Minister for Schools com-missioned a study into the costs and benefits of further inclusion of students with disability in 1996. The report was unequivocal in its finding that anti-discrimination law and educational pol-icy were not being followed or implemented in policy or practice. It recommended the abolition of special enrolment procedures for students with disability and an individualised funding model that attached funding to the student with disability regardless of his or her educational placement.

Considerable resistance to the reports recommendations came from the industrial union, the NSW Teachers' Federation. It had espoused a reasonably balanced position towards inclusion but commenced an ideological debate supporting the status quo.[8] It was clear that a reduction in special schools would impact on the career paths of special education teachers.[9]

Nonetheless, parents were not discouraged. Three significant cases have been brought before the Australian Human Rights and Equal Opportunity Commission, as it was then. Each of these cases demonstrated critical areas for reform.

The first case was *Hills Grammar School v. Human Rights And Equal Opportunity Commission N794 Of 1999*, in which the Federal Court decided that the Hills Grammar School had unlaw-fully discriminated against a 6-year-old student with spina bifida by refusing her enrolment on the basis that its assessment of retrofitting the physical environment would constitute 'unjustifi-able hardship'. The Court found that the School had failed to undertake a proper assessment of the student's needs, instead relying on stereotypical assumptions and general information about spina bifida, which affects children differently. This case established clear standards for all schools in assessing applications on behalf of children with disability, taking into account their individual abilities and needs with expert assessments. Moreover, it highlights that an accessible physical environment and retrofitting does not and in itself constitute unjustifiable hardship. This high-lighted the need for reform whereby the school environment, policies and practices are planned, informed and reflect diversity.

4 New South Wales Department of School Education, *Special Education Policy* (1993) 4.
5 McRae, D., *The integration/inclusion feasibility study: A summary of the findings and recommendations* (Sydney, Ministry of Education and Training, 1996).
6 Van Krayenoord, C. E., Moni, K. B., Jobling, A., Koppenhaver, D., and Elkins, J. (2007). Teacher atti-tudes, knowledge and practices of writing in the context of instruction for students with special needs in inclusive classrooms. In: *11th Biennial Conference of the European Association for Research on Learning and Instruction*, Nicosia, Cyprus, 23–27 August 2005.
7 McRae, D., *The integration/inclusion feasibility study: A summary of the findings and recommendations* (Sydney, Ministry of Education and Training, 1996).
8 Clear, M. (ed), *Promises Promises: Disability and Terms of Inclusion* (Sydney, Federation Press, 2000).
9 Dempsey, I., "Ideology and ideologues: The influence of a teacher union on integration and inclusion in schools" (1997) 3 *Australian Disability Review* 29; Davis, L. and Green, J., "Workers rights, human rights: One and the same in education?" (SDRN and AHRC Human Rights and Disability and Education Conference, Sydney, September 1999).

The second case was *Purvis v. New South Wales*,[10] in which a first-year secondary student with mild intellectual disability who as a result of his disability had intermittent aggressive outbursts when frustrated was regularly suspended due to these outbursts and finally expelled from his school. His guardians claimed discrimination on the basis of the school's failure to provide reasonable accommodation to address the triggers that caused frustration. At the time the definition of direct discrimination did not include a duty to accommodate. Consequently the Court found that the school had not discriminated. Subsequently the provisions in the act were amended to ensure that the failure to provide reasonable accommodation is a ground for discrimination. This case demonstrated that successful inclusion was not possible without individual education plans that ensured the needs of the student with disability were met and the school was a safe environment for all.

Finally in the case of *Clarke v. Catholic Education Office*,[11] (Clarke) the Federal Court decided that the Catholic Education Office had unlawfully discriminated against a secondary student with profound deafness by failing to provide communication in Australian Sign Language (Auslan). The respondents had proposed note-taking as the main source of classroom communication. However, it was claimed that the applicant would not have been able to adequately participate and benefit from his classroom education without Auslan. This case illustrated the fundamental importance of reform required for inclusion whereby teacher education and professional development includes sign language.

Since 1996 in NSW there has been a substantial increase in the number of students identified with one or more disability in both mainstream and in-support classes. However, there has not been a corresponding decrease in the enrolments in special schools and segregated classes.[12] The probable explanation is that increased awareness of disability and diagnostic characteristics along with increased funding that has lead to a greater identification of students requiring support. It suggests that these students were probably always included in mainstream education settings.[13]

An increase in the numbers of students identified for support in mainstream education without a decrease in the number of enrolments in special schools and segregated classes in not unique to NSW. It appears that Finland has experienced similar identification and enrolments,[14] but with the difference that it has an international reputation for education excellence. This is largely based on its high Programme for International Student Assessment (PISA) scores. PISA is 'a triennial international survey which aims to evaluate education systems worldwide by testing the skills and knowledge of 15-year-old students'.[15]

---

10 *Purvis v. New South Wales* [2003] HCA 62; 217 CLR 92; 202 ALR 133; 78 ALJR 1.
11 *Clarke v. Catholic Education Office* [2003] FCA 1085.
12 Forlin, C., Chambers, D., Loreman, T., Deppeler, J., and Sharma, U., "Inclusive education for students with disability: A review of the best evidence in relation to theory and practice" (2013) Report to the Australian Government Department of Foreign Affairs & Trade and Australian Research Alliance for Children and Youth, Canberra. Available at: http://www.aracy.org.au/publications-resources/command/download_file/id/246/filename/Inclusive_education_for_students_with_disability_-_A_review_of_the_best_evidence_in_relation_to_theory_and_practice.pdf (last accessed 14 May 2015).
13 Dempsey, I., "Trends in the proportion of students with a disability in Australian schools, 2000–2009" (2011) 36(2) *Journal of Intellectual & Developmental Disability* 144.
14 Saloviita, T., "Inclusive education in Finland: A thwarted development" (2009) *Zeitschrift für Inklusion*. Available at: http://www.inklusion-online.net/index.php/inklusion-online/article/view/172/172 (last accessed 14 May 2015).
15 Organisation for Economic Co-Operation and Development (OECD), *About PISA* (2015). Available at: http://www.oecd.org/pisa/aboutpisa/ (last accessed 14 May 2015).

Finland's does not have an inclusive education system as defined in the introduction to this chapter. Its education system is based on the principles of equality, equity and building 'education for all'.[16] Approximately 8 per cent of children in Finland are identified as having special needs.[17] Half of them are educated in mainstream schools and the other half are educated in special schools.[18] Finland's emphasis for students with mild and/or temporary problems and low support needs in the mainstream is preventative. Students do not require a disability diagnosis (disability model) to be eligible for support, only an observed difficulty is sufficient (difficulty model).[19] Initially, support was provided through a resource-room withdrawal model. However, now there are many variations in support including collaborative and consultative teaching.[20] Nonetheless, there is no hard evidence that links their 'difficulty' model to the success they have achieved internationally in comparative assessments such as PISA.[21]

Timo Salovitta, a Finnish professor in special education, attributes the continuation of special schools to three factors: the models of financing, teacher professionalism and the teachers union and the Finnish set of values.[22] Students with disability who have high support needs receive individually defined extra funding from pools other than normal education base funding resources.[23] Teaching in Finland is high status and carries with it considerable community trust.[24] The teachers' union is strong and from the outset it took a very negative stance on inclusion.[25] Finally, the Finnish set of values stress overall conformity and tend to reject people who would be

16 Itkonen, T., and Jahnukainen, M., "Disability or learning difficulty? Politicians or educators? Constructing special education in Finland and the United States" (2010) 9(2) *Comparative Sociology* 182.
17 Organisation for Economic Co-Operation and Development (OECD), Chapter 5 Finland: Slow and steady reform for consistently high results. In: *Strong Performers and Successful Reformers in Education: Lessons for PISA for the United States* (2010). Available at: http://www.oecd.org/pisa/pisaproducts/46581035.pdf (last accessed 14 May 2015).
18 Ibid.
19 Itkonen, T., and Jahnukainen, M., "Disability or learning difficulty? Politicians or educators? Constructing special education in Finland and the United States" (2010) 9(2) *Comparative Sociology* 182.
20 Jahnukainen, M., "Different strategies, different outcomes? The history and trends of the inclusive and special education in Alberta (Canada) and in Finland" (2011) 55(5) *Scandinavian Journal of Educational Research* 489.
21 Forlin, C., Chambers, D., Loreman, T., Deppeler, J., and Sharma, U., "Inclusive education for students with disability: A review of the best evidence in relation to theory and practice" (2013) Report to the Australian Government Department of Foreign Affairs & Trade and Australian Research Alliance for Children and Youth, Canberra. Available at: http://www.aracy.org.au/publications-resources/command/download_file/id/246/filename/Inclusive_education_for_students_with_disability_-_A_review_of_the_best_evidence_in_relation_to_theory_and_practice.pdf (last accessed 14 May 2015).
22 Saloviita, T., "Inclusive education in Finland: A thwarted development" (2009) *Zeitschrift für Inklusion*. Available at: http://www.inklusion-online.net/index.php/inklusion-online/article/view/172/172 (last accessed 14 May 2015).
23 Kirjavainen, T. (2010). Esiselvitysraportti: Erityisopetuksen vaikuttavuus perusopetuksessa [Report of the preliminary study: The effectiveness of special education in compulsory education]. Helsinki: National Audit Office of Finland.
24 Forlin, C., Chambers, D., Loreman, T., Deppeler, J., and Sharma, U., "Inclusive education for students with disability: A review of the best evidence in relation to theory and practice" (2013) Report to the Australian Government Department of Foreign Affairs & Trade and Australian Research Alliance for Children and Youth, Canberra. Available at: http://www.aracy.org.au/publications-resources/command/download_file/id/246/filename/Inclusive_education_for_students_with_disability_-_A_review_of_the_best_evidence_in_relation_to_theory_and_practice.pdf (last accessed 14 May 2015).
25 Saloviita, T., "Inclusive education in Finland: A thwarted development" (2009) *Zeitschrift für Inklusion*. Available at: http://www.inklusion-online.net/index.php/inklusion-online/article/view/172/172 (last accessed 14 May 2015).

considered socially deviant. This has been evident in 'the internationally high proportions of past sterilization of people with disabilities, high proportion of disabled people in institutions (and) in the exceptionally high frequency of fetal screening'.[26]

The New South Wales and Finnish examples illustrate that the right to education for all is accepted and practiced but with riders that determine where and how that education is delivered such as 'possible, practicable and in the best interest of the child' and the 'least restrictive environment' which is 'the maximum extent appropriate, that children with disabilities are educated with children who are not disabled'.[27] Such riders continue the assumption that there are and always will be students with disability that cannot be accommodated in an inclusive local neighbourhood school. Consequently, they allow for the continuation and growth of segregated special schools designed to meet the needs of students with 'types' or categories of disability where the support needs are deemed to be too high to be met in the local school. The principle of inclusive education as stated in CRPD is based on the assumption that first and foremost every child can be accommodated in its neighbourhood school. This places the onus on the education system to meet the needs of all students irrespective of the level of support required. It is only when this assumption is the 'default' position in an education system that policy, procedures, resourcing and teacher education and promotion criteria will line up to realise inclusive education.

The principle of inclusive education has been widely accepted in academia and law even if it is less evident in practice. It is this acceptance that is shifting international norms and standards. The adoption of the CRPD in and of itself is a significant shift in the recognition of inclusive education.

Convention on the Rights of Persons with Disabilities

A core pillar of human rights is equality for all members of the human family. To effectively address equality, societies' systems and structures must recognise human diversity in all its forms and develop policies to reflect that diversity. Existing international human rights standards had a strong focus on race and gender with little guidance for States on disability. Calls for a thematic convention identified the failure of both binding and non-binding instruments to have a significant impact on the situation of many of the world's people with disability.[28] The various developments in soft law had provided a significant framework of principles, but had not necessarily delivered reform and social change.[29] Earlier human rights instruments were framed around formal equality that promoted gender and race neutral approaches.[30] This narrow approach failed

---

26 See Emerson, E., Hatton, C., Bauer, I., Bjorgvinsdottir, S., Brak, W., Firkowska-Mankiewcz, A., Haroardottir, H., Kavaliunaite, A., Kebbon, L., Kristoffersen, E., Saloviita, T., Schippers, H., Timmons, B., Timcev, L., Tossebro, J., and Witt, U., "Patterns of institutionalisation in 15 European countries" (1996) 3 *European Journal on Mental Disability* 29; Meskus, M., "Eugenics and the new genetics as technologies of governing reproduction: The Finnish case. Vital politics: Health, medicine and bioeconomics into the 21st Century" (2003) *London School of Economics* 5.
27 The Individuals with Disabilities Education Improvement Act 2004.
28 Degener, T., and Quinn, G., "The moral authority for change: Human rights values and the worldwide process of disability reform" In: *Human Rights and Disability: The Current Use and Future Potential of United Nations Human Rights Instruments in the Context of Disability* (New York and Geneva, United Nations, 2002).
29 Kayess, R., and French, P., "Out of darkness into light? Introducing the convention on the rights of persons with disabilities" (2008) 8(1) *Human Rights Law Review* 1.
30 Ibid.

to achieve substantive equality and address the structural normative change required to achieve equality in practice. This was especially true in meeting the needs of persons with disability.[31]

The adoption of the CRPD is a significant legal and policy advance, moving from non-binding international standards to formally binding legal obligations for those States that become party to the Convention. The Convention was intended to build on existing human rights standards and apply them within a disability context to ensure that persons with disability can exercise and enjoy all of the human rights and fundamental freedoms. Some of the rights are simply restated in the form in which they appear in other documents, for example the right to life, but most contain detailed content to provide a clearer understanding of the obligations with which it is necessary to comply in order to fulfil the right. It is effectively an international charter of rights for persons with disability. The CRPD provides a framework for policy analysis, design and implementation and is a tool for disabled persons' organisations in advocating for the rights of persons with disability. Article 24 is one such example in detailing obligations and illustrating implementation.

Without access to adequate education, persons with disability have greatly diminished prospects of gaining employment and of achieving economic independence. Education builds resilience to, and pathways out of, poverty and disadvantage. It also provides persons with disability with the means of gaining the knowledge and skills necessary for civic participation and to effect social change. Education plays an important role in social development and interaction as well as often being the avenue for lifelong friendships and support networks. On this basis education is recognised as a cornerstone of social inclusion, and as such Article 24 was an acutely contentious article during the Convention negotiations. It was extensively debated throughout the negotiations and intensively over 3 days at the Sixth Session with more than 110 interventions from Member States and NGO delegations. The underlying tensions in the education debate were around the principle of inclusive education, the right to choose and ensuring equality of education for all persons with disability through reasonable accommodation and individualised support.

The CRPD addresses the macro, meso and micro levels of the education system.

1   Macro (government and state)

The macro level in an inclusive education system is the overarching level. It includes government policy, national and state curriculum, education budgets, university teacher education programmes and ongoing professional development.

2   Meso (schools and communities)

The meso level includes the physical school environment, digital and technological resources, staffing, whole of school policy implementation (e.g. anti-bullying, diversity celebrations, sports) and community relations.

3   Micro (individual classrooms and people)

The micro level includes curriculum adaptations, in-classroom support, classroom management, mixed ability teaching strategies and reasonable accommodations.

Article 24 establishes the right to education for persons with disability without discrimination based on the principle of inclusive education and promotes reasonable accommodation of an

---

31 Ibid.

individual's requirements. The article requires States Parties to take effective measures to support people with disability in the general education system at all levels and requires that all support measures are provided in environments that maximise academic and social development of people with disability.[32] The emphasis is on establishing an inclusive education system that effectively supports the full participation of persons with disability.

To date there has been little guidance for State implementation from the jurisprudence of the *Committee on the Rights of Persons with Disabilities* but the *travaux prepetoires* of the Ad Hoc Committee negotiations does provide an understanding of the right. The Ad Hoc Committee established a Working Group (WG) to develop draft text. This formed the basis of the Ad Hoc Committee's negotiations. The text incorporates many elements that were maintained in the final version such as the goals that education should be directed to,[33] the provision of support[34] and a prohibition on excluding children with disability from compulsory education.[35] The WG text very much reflected the existing approach many governments have taken to the education for persons with disability where there are small pockets of integration in mainstream education and separate 'special education' system for most persons with disability. The text was not based on a principle of inclusive education and emphasised a principle of choice whereby people could choose segregated education.[36] It also had limited focus on vocational training and further education.

The General Assembly mandate under which the *CRPD* was developed stipulated that the negotiating Committee was not to develop any new human rights, but was to apply existing human rights to the particular circumstances of persons with disability.[37] Accordingly, the Chairman of the negotiating Committee has referred to the *CRPD* as an 'implementation convention', one that 'sets out a detailed code [for how existing rights] should be put into practice' with respect to persons with disability.[38] This indicates that the *CRPD* should be informed by existing norms and standards as a basis for prescriptive interpretation and as such, rights contained in *CRPD* should not derogate from or apply a lower standard to that of existing norms and standards.

It was noted during the negotiations that the WG text failed to meet this criteria, especially on the issue of Article 24 enshrining the principle of inclusive education. First, delegates raised that the developing jurisprudence in relation to the UN Convention on the Rights of the Child (CRC) 1989, was increasingly focused on the inclusion of children in mainstream education rather than in segregated 'special' education.[39] The Committee on the Rights of the Child following a day of General Discussion in 1997 on the rights of children with disabilities concluded

32 UN Convention on the Rights of Persons with Disabilities, 2006.
33 UNGA Ad Hoc Committee on a Comprehensive and Integral International Convention on the Protection and Promotion of the Rights and Dignity of Persons with Disabilities, Working Group (UNGA Ad Hoc Committee Working Group), Draft Article 17 Education 1(a)(b)(c) (January 2003).
34 Ibid. 2(b) and 5.
35 Ibid. 2(c).
36 Ibid. 2(a) and 3(c).
37 This point was made repeatedly in the course of negotiations, was a feature of the rhetoric associated with its adoption and opening for signature, and now also permeates formative implementation dialogue and planning: see for example Jean-Pierre Gonnot.
38 United Nations Media Release Chairman says *draft convention sets out 'detailed code of implementation and spells out how individual rights should be put into practice,* United Nations General Assembly SOC/4680 (12 August 2005).
39 UNGA Ad Hoc Committee Working Group (January 2003).

that the segregation of children with disabilities 'for care, treatment or education' represented a breach of the Convention.[40]

Second, it was also acknowledged that current international norms, in particular the *UN Standard Rules on the Equalization of Opportunities for Persons with Disabilities* (1993) (Standard Rules), clearly indicate that the existence of separate 'special' educational provision is only acceptable insofar as mainstream education has not yet developed sufficiently to accommodate all children (United Nations 1993).[41] The Standard Rules provide:

> In situations where the general school system does not *yet* adequately meet the needs of all persons with disabilities, special education may be considered. . . . States should aim for the gradual integration of special education services into mainstream education. It is acknowledged that in some instances special education *may currently* be considered to be the most appropriate form of education for some students with disabilities.[42]
>
> *(emphasis added)*

It is clear from the construction of Rule 7(8) that segregated special education is considered as part of the progressive realisation of the goal of inclusive education within the general education system. It does not endorse maintenance of parallel education systems due to a failure of the general education system to establish inclusive practices and supports. Whilst the WG text imported Standard Rules wording, it critically leaves out the word '*yet*'. This omission dramatically changes the nature of the provision. Instead of recognising that the maintenance of segregated special education is only considered appropriate if measures are taken to progressively realise inclusive education, it establishes the maintenance of segregated special education as an exception with no emphasis on realising the goal of inclusion.

Third, the *UNESCO Salamanca Statement and Framework for Action on Special Needs Education* (1994) (Salamanca Statement) unequivocally calls on all governments to 'adopt as a matter of law or policy the principle of inclusive education'.[43] The CRC jurisprudence and existing international norms provided a compelling argument for Article 24 Education to be based on the principle of inclusive education as an aspirational right. There was significant support for this position and it was incorporated into the first *Facilitator's Text*.[44]

The incorporation of the principle of inclusive education still left language that established segregated special education as a valid exception to inclusive education. Several variations

40 Committee on the Rights of the Child, Day of General Discussion: Children with Disabilities 1997 Document ref CRC/C/66, Annex V, para. 338(d). Available at: http://www.ohchr.org/EN/HRBodies/ CRC/Pages/DiscussionDays.aspx (last accessed 7 August 2015).
41 Standard Rules on the Equalization of Opportunities for Persons with Disabilities A/RES48/96 of 20 December 1993. Available at: http://www.unhchr.ch/huridocda/huridoca.nsf/(Symbol)/A.RES.48. 96.En?Opendocument (last accessed 14 May 2015).
42 Ibid., Rule 7(8).
43 UNESCO Salamanca Statement and Framework for Action on Special Needs Education (1994) 3(b).
44 Australia provided an alternate text incorporating 'inclusive education' into the text which drew strong support from delegates during the plenary session upon which the Chair referred the changes to the facilitator, see UNGA Ad-Hoc Committee on a Comprehensive and Integral International Convention on the Protection and Promotion of the Rights and Dignity of Persons with Disabilities (UNGA Ad Hoc Committee), Daily Summaries of Discussions, (August 2005). Available at: http://www.un.org/ esa/socdev/enable/rights/ahc6sum2aug.htm (last accessed 14 May 2015).

were proposed, including one from the European Union (EU), that retained a variation of the WG text:

> Where exceptionally the general education system does not adequately meet the needs of persons with disabilities, States Parties shall take appropriate measures to ensure effective alternative forms of education, bearing in mind the goal of full inclusion.[45]

The proposal had some support but was seen as establishing an exception and not strongly emphasising progressive realisation of inclusive education. The concept was incorporated into the first draft by the facilitator:

> (d) persons with disabilities receive the support required, within the general education system, to facilitate their effective education. In exceptional circumstances where the general education system **can not** adequately meet the support needs of persons with disabilities, States Parties shall ensure that effective alternative support measures are provided, **consistent** with the goal of full inclusion.
>
> (emphasis added)

The facilitator's text made some specific changes to the EU text to reflect the 'progressive realisation' context. The use of the words '*can not*' and '*consistent with*' instead of '*does not*' and '*bearing in mind*' establishes a higher threshold and emphasises that the obligation on the state is to ensure inclusive education to the maximum extent possible. The structure of the sub-paragraph focuses on educational support measures rather than justifying alternative forms of education. The facilitator's text was seen as an improvement[46] and adopted by the Chair in the Chair's Text.[47] This text formed the basis of negotiations during the final two sessions. At the seventh session, both Canada and Australia proposed removing the exception language and strengthening the non-discrimination focus and the duty to accommodate an individual's support needs. Canada's proposal was to replace the last sentence of 2(d) of the facilitator's text with the following:

> [I]n order to meet adequately the individual support needs of persons with disabilities, States Parties shall ensure that effective individualized support measures are provided in environments which maximize academic and social development, consistent with the goal of full inclusion.[48]

The Australian position emphasised the standard of non-discrimination, arguing that there was no need to build in exceptions, 'but rather what was needed is a clear statement that persons with disability receive the support required to facilitate their education within the general education

---

45 UNGA Ad Hoc Committee – Sixth Session – Contributions by Governments (August, 2005) EU proposal Draft Article 17 Education. Available at: http://www.un.org/esa/socdev/enable/rights/ahc6eu.htm (last accessed 14 May 2015).

46 UNGA Ad-Hoc Committee on a Comprehensive and Integral International Convention on the Protection and Promotion of the Rights and Dignity of Persons with Disabilities *Chair's Text* covering letter. Available at: http://www.un.org/esa/socdev/enable/rights/ahc7.htm (last accessed 14 May 2015).

47 Ibid., *Chair's Text*.

48 UNGA Ad-Hoc Committee, Daily Summaries of Discussions (2006) Canada Seventh Session. Available at: http://www.un.org/esa/socdev/enable/rights/ahc7sum24jan.htm (last accessed 14 May 2015).

system and the communities in which they live'.[49] However, to address the resource impact question, reasonable accommodation means that it is necessary to cater to the needs of the people with disability, and accepting that there are some persons who cannot be educated at the present time in the general education system within existing resources, measures should be taken to include all students in the general education system to the maximum extent possible. The overall concept outlined by Canada and Australia of reinforcing the non-discrimination framework as opposed to creating an exception was very well supported by governments and strongly pushed by civil society.[50] This approach formed the basis for the final wording.

Underlying the central point of inclusive education was that education for persons with disability should be governed by the same legislation and departmental responsibility as the rest of the community. Experience had demonstrated that giving responsibility for education of children with disability to community or human service/welfare departments had meant that academic outcomes were in many cases secondary to therapeutic and vocational endeavours. This approach to education for persons with disability continually left students with an academic disadvantage and ultimately a vocational disadvantage. Existing international norms had addressed this issue with the Standard Rules providing that:

> [g]eneral educational authorities are responsible for the education of persons with disabilities in integrated settings. Education for persons with disabilities should form an integral part of national educational planning, curriculum development and school organization.[51]

This is a valid point of equality but also raises strong operational arguments. A single portfolio responsibility is an instrumental element of meeting the objectives of the Salamanca Statement. In particular, developing an inclusive education system through giving policy and budgetary priority to improving the education system as well as establishing mechanisms for planning, monitoring and evaluating educational provision.[52]

This was an issue in relation to inclusive education that was raised on several occasions by delegates and civil society.[53] The point is not overtly referred to within the text of Article 24 but is the concept behind the language of 'general education system' and it is within this context that it should be interpreted.

The right to choose

The WG text included incorporated provisions whereby States ensure individuals can choose inclusive education systems.[54] It can bee seen from the footnotes of the WG text that there was not consensus on this approach. Respect of the liberty to choose different educational setting is

49 Ibid., Australia.
50 Ibid.
51 Standard Rules on the Equalization of Opportunities for Persons with Disabilities A/RES48/96 of 20 December 1993. Available at: http://www.unhchr.ch/huridocda/huridoca.nsf/(Symbol)/A.RES.48.96.En?Opendocument (last accessed 14 May 2015).
52 UNESCO Salamanca Statement and Framework for Action on Special Needs Education (1994).
53 In particular Canada, Centre for Studies on Inclusive Education and Canadian Community Living Association. See UNGA Ad-Hoc Committee, Daily Summaries of Discussions. Available at: http://www.un.org/esa/socdev/enable/rights (last accessed 14 May 2015).
54 UNGA Ad Hoc Committee Working Group 2003, Draft Article 17 2(a), 3(c). Available at: http://www.un.org/esa/socdev/enable/rights/ahcwgreportax1.htm (last accessed 7 August 2015).

established in International Covenant on Economic Social and Cultural Rights (ICESCR) which provides that:

> The States Parties to the present Covenant undertake to have respect for the liberty of parents and, when applicable, legal guardians to choose for their children schools, other than those established by the public authorities, which conform to such minimum educational standards as may be laid down or approved by the State and to ensure the religious and moral education of their children in conformity with their own conviction.[55]

It is directed at accommodating religious plurality and is support for the development of 'private' schools catering to particular religious beliefs. The WG text[56] provided that:

2 In realising this right, States Parties shall ensure:
  a) that all persons with disabilities can choose inclusive and accessible education in their own community (including access to early childhood and preschool education);
3 States Parties shall ensure that where the general education system does not adequately meet the needs of persons with disabilities special and alternative forms of learning should be made available. Any such special and alternative forms of learning should
  c) allow a free and informed choice between general and special systems;

This construction essentially established a choice between two State provided options creating the basis for a parallel segregated education system for persons with disability. This would have endorsed an approach similar to the 'separate but equal' doctrine[57] which was found by the United States Supreme Court to be discriminatory 50 years earlier. Such a provision would justify the exclusion of persons with disability from the general education system based on this separate but equal doctrine in direct contravention of United Nations treaty body jurisprudence.[58]

It was noted during the negotiations that this issue went to the heart of the sought 'paradigm shift' whereby the education system accommodates the person as opposed to the person accommodating the education system. The emphasis is on the education system to provide the necessary infrastructure and supports for persons with disability to ensure equality of education as opposed to persons with disability accommodating the education system by travelling to centralised facilities, being separated from siblings and non-disabled peers. The arguments for advocating the maintenance of both inclusive and segregated education are economic as well as conceptual.[59]

---

55 United Nations, International Covenant on Economic Social and Cultural Rights, Article 13(3).
56 UNGA Ad Hoc Committee Working Group 2003. Available at: http://www.un.org/esa/socdev/enable/rights/ahcwgreportax1.htm (last accessed 7 August 2015).
57 In *Brown v. Board of Education of Topeka*, 347 U.S. 483 (1954) the US Supreme Court declared that laws establishing separate education for black children was unconstitutional finding that that 'separate educational facilities are inherently unequal.' Overturning earlier rulings going back to *Plessy v. Ferguson* 163 U.S. 537 1896, which endorsed the policy of 'separate but equal'.
58 Committee on Economic, Social and Cultural Rights, General Comment 13. Available at: http://tbinternet.ohchr.org/_layouts/treatybodyexternal/Download.aspx?symbolno=E%2fC.12%2f1999%2f10&Lang=en (last accessed 14 May 2015).
59 Centre for Studies on Inclusive Education (CSIE), Ad Hoc Committee 2005, 6. Available at: http://www.un.org/esa/socdev/enable/rights/ahc6contngos.htm (last accessed 7 August 2015).

Most often resource implications are cited as the main reason for the failure to fully implement inclusive education.[60] It was argued by civil society delegations that while resources (human and financial) are used to develop inclusive education *and* to support exclusion through maintaining segregated education, most obviously by maintaining a dual system of education, inclusive education will not be developed to maximum effect.[61] Economically, it is far more efficient to target resources towards a single inclusive education system from the outset than to develop a dual-system-based segregated education for persons with disability and then have to work towards bringing about inclusive education. Where dual systems of education already exist, 'special' education should be only maintained as part of an overall strategy to progress to inclusive education. The focus should be on building a restructured and appropriately resourced and supported general education system that aims to meet the needs of the full diversity of students in their local areas.

Conceptually it was argued by Deaf, Deaf/Blind and Blind representatives that segregated education was essential to ensure equality in language and literacy instruction.[62] They also sought recognition of the need for life skills that people with disability need to acquire to interact both with other persons with similar impairments and with the community as a whole, such as Braille, sign language and orientation and mobility skills. The learning of such skills may be most effectively obtained in segregated environments rather than inclusive settings. Although, it was noted that such life skills may be acquired through a formal education system but also at any stage of life. It is important that it is recognised that these activities are fundamental but relevant more broadly than just in the context of education.[63]

Further representative organisations for people who are Blind, Deaf and Deaf/Blind suggested that the choice of special education settings is not only important for language and literacy instruction, but also for establishing peer group support, which typically lasts throughout the person's life. It was also suggested that segregated education environments for Deaf persons had a further important cultural dimension. Additionally, concerns were expressed that in less wealthy countries there was insufficient resources to provide Braille education in mainstream schools, and therefore the only setting in which children and young people who are Blind or Deaf/Blind were likely to receive Braille education was in centralised special schools.

As it was with the Working Group there was no clear consensus within the Ad Hoc Committee on the issue of choice and importantly it was noted that there is a diversity of views, even among persons with sensory disability on the issue of inclusive versus special educational environments for Deaf, Blind and Deaf/Blind persons. It was argued that effective sign language and Braille instruction can and should be provided in inclusive settings, and that it is important that children and young people with sensory disability establish relationships with a broad range of peers if they are going to function effectively within the general community as adults. The need for the peer support of other children and young people with sensory disability was acknowledged, but it was suggested that this could be facilitated through extracurricular activities.

60 UNESCO Economic and Social Council, Inclusive Dimensions of the Right to Education: Normative Bases. A Concept Paper. Eighth and Ninth Meetings of the Joint Expert Group UNESCO (CR) ECOSOC (CESCR) on the Monitoring of the Right to Education – 2008.
61 CSIE, Ad Hoc Committee 2005, 6. Available at: http://www.un.org/esa/socdev/enable/rights/ahc6 contngos.htm (last accessed 7 August 2015).
62 UNGA Ad-Hoc Committee, Daily Summaries of Discussions, 2005. Available at: http://www.un.org/esa/socdev/enable/rights (last accessed 14 May 2015).
63 UNGA Ad-Hoc Committee, Daily Summaries of Discussions 2005. See Australia. Available at: http://www.un.org/esa/socdev/enable/rights/ahc6sum2aug.htm (last accessed 14 May 2015).

In many countries it will never be possible to establish special schools for children and young people with sensory disability at the local level. As a consequence the choice of a special school will also typically mean living away from family and community, which is viewed as being detrimental to the emotional needs and development of children and young people.[64] It was suggested that bilingual schools[65] may be a way to address these issues. Such education would be open to siblings and non-disabled peers, providing social development in a more diverse setting and addressing economies of scale. It could also provide an avenue to promote the use of sign language and address the chronic shortage of interpreters.

Enshrining choice within the text of the convention would have been diametrically opposed to the realisation of inclusive education and the standard of non-discrimination enshrined at international law. It would place an obligation on States to maintain a parallel education system catering for persons with disability to provide the basis for choice. Utilising budgetary resources across two systems would essentially mean that neither system would be adequately resourced. In all likelihood, the general education system would fail to adequately meet the needs of persons with disability due to a lack of resources to implement the necessary structural and programmatic changes. So, whilst 3 (c) of the WG text provided for 'free and informed' choice between general and segregated education, the resource dilemma would mean few would choose the general education option, further pushing resources into segregated education. As noted by delegates, this is in fact a false choice enforced by a lack of resources and access to support.[66]

Finally, and perhaps most fundamentally, it could be argued that enshrining choice within the CRPD would be in contravention of the standard of non-discrimination established in Article 5 of CRPD and in international law more broadly. As noted earlier, the obligation on States to provide a choice for persons with disability in selecting inclusive or segregated education by default forces States to maintain a dual system of education incorporating both a general education system and segregated education for persons with disability. The maintenance of a parallel system of segregated education would establish a 'separate but equal' principle for the education of persons with disability.

In the end, the convention is silent on the liberty to choose between the general education system and segregated 'special' education. The final wording leaves an obligation for States to ensure an inclusive education system without discrimination. Within this context, flexibility is given to States to ensure that persons with disability – giving attention to the specific requirements of persons who are Deaf, Blind or Deaf/Blind – are not disadvantaged in their access to inclusive education. This does not provide States with a justification for maintaining segregated education as the overall obligation is to realise an inclusive system not maintain a dual 'separate but equal' segregated system. The Committee on Economic Social and Cultural Rights (CESCR) concluded in General Comment 13:

> . . . measures intended to bring about de facto equality for men and women, and disadvantaged groups, is not a violation of the right to non-discrimination with regard to education, so long as such measures do not lead to the maintenance of unequal or separate standards for different groups.[67]

---

64 Ibid.

65 UNGA Ad-Hoc Committee 2005, Informal Facilitator Discussions – Draft Article 17 Education.

66 UNGA Ad Hoc Committee 2005, See for example New Zealand, Available: http://www.un.org/esa/ socdev/enable/rights/ahc6sum2aug.htm (last accessed 14 May 2015).

67 Committee on Economic, Social and Cultural Rights, General Comment 13. Available at: http://tbinternet. ohchr.org/_layouts/treatybodyexternal/Download.aspx?symbolno=E%2fC.12%2f1999%2f10&Lang= en (last accessed 14 May 2015).

The Convention was negotiated with groundbreaking civil society participation, particularly disabled persons' organisations. It brought together people from all parts of the world who had had quite different experiences of education. This made the development of the article highly contentious. For example, there were people whose generation were educated in segregated schools with full augmentative communication and access to alternative scripts. Their advocacy organisations were aware of students with similar disability in mainstream schools receiving inadequate support that impacted significantly on their education and life opportunities. There were members of a younger generation who had mainstream education with adequate support and who valued the experience of attending the local neighbourhood school. This underscored the importance of support which starts with the education and training of the teaching profession. Article 24 (4) addressed this issue, stating that States Parties train and employ teachers, including teachers with disabilities, who are qualified in augmentative and alternative modes, means and formats of communication, educational techniques and materials to support persons with disabilities. This was one of the few paragraphs that received universal agreement.

CRPD implementation

The principle that all children regardless of disability have a right to education has been broadly accepted throughout the world. Whilst it has been explicitly enshrined in international law, this shift can be seen in the following two significant cases.

The first was in the European Committee of Social Rights *Mental Disability Advocacy Centre v. Bulgaria.*[68] In this case the Committee unanimously concluded that there was a violation of Article 17 section 2 of the Revised Charter because children with moderate, severe or profound intellectual disabilities who were residing in homes for intellectually disabled children were being discriminated against as they were not receiving any type of education because of their disability.

The second case was in the South African Constitutional Court, *Western Cape Forum for Intellectual Disability v. Government of the Republic of South African, Government of the Province of the Western Cape.*[69] The Court found that the Western Cape Government had failed to take reasonable measures to provide educational support to children with intellectual disability and high support needs in the Western Cape, breaching the children's right to basic education, protection from neglect or degradation, equality and human dignity. The Western Cape Government was directed to take reasonable steps in order to ensure the rights of the affected children. The steps include providing funds to organisations that support children with intellectual disability and high support needs, providing affordable access to basic education, providing transportation to and from special care centres and ensuring that staff members at special care centres are properly trained.

The Western Cape case demonstrates that to bring practice into line with law there needs to be an investment in building an inclusive education system. These investments need to occur within the macro, meso and micro levels of the education system. Until recently there has been little direction for States on ways to build an inclusive education system. The adoption of the CRPD changes that by providing the architecture.

For many countries CRPD marks the beginning of their road to implementing inclusive education. The following framework explores the critical elements that are the building blocks for such a system.

---

68 *Mental Disability Advocacy Centre (MDAC) v. Bulgaria,* Complaint No. 41/2007.
69 *Western Cape Forum for Intellectual Disability v. Government of the Republic of South African* [2010] ZAWCHC 544.

Conceptual framework for reform for inclusive education

In order to conceptualise a framework for inclusive education it is important to define what it means. This is not a simple task. It is a highly contentious issue and the variety of definitions and interpretations is increasing.[70] For the purposes of this chapter 'inclusion' is a single education system in which all students are educated together.[71] Inclusion is premised on the principle that educating students in physically separate environments is inherently discriminatory and unequal because the site of educational instruction is the most important issue of equality.[72]

Notwithstanding and for the purposes of a framework, the features of inclusive education identified by Loreman[73] are used. These features include:

- All children attend their neighbourhood school.
- Schools and districts have a 'zero-rejection' policy when it comes to registering and teaching children in their region.
- All children are welcomed and valued.
- All children learn in regular, heterogeneous classrooms with same-age peers.
- All children follow substantively similar programmes of study, with curriculum that can be adapted and modified if needed.
- Modes of instruction are varied and responsive to the needs of all.
- All children contribute to regular school and classroom learning activities and events.
- All children are supported to make friends and to be socially successful with their peers.
- Adequate resources and staff training are provided within the school and district to support inclusion.[74]

These features can be further categorised into macro, meso and micro levels of implementation.

Macro

The macro level starts with the overarching principles that inform the education system's pedagogy including but not limited to human rights, the value of diversity and universal design for learning. The principles of inclusive education are important to disabled and nondisabled students alike. Not only does it embed diversity in the notion of 'us', but it values difference with aspects such as sign language and Braille.

---

70 Forlin, C., Chambers, D., Loreman, T., Deppeler, J., and Sharma, U., "Inclusive Education for students with disability: A review of the best evidence in relation to theory and practice" (2013) Report to the Australian Government Department of Foreign Affairs & Trade and Australian Research Alliance for Children and Youth, Canberra. Available at: http://www.aracy.org.au/publications-resources/command/download_file/id/246/filename/Inclusive_education_for_students_with_disability_-_A_review_of_the_best_evidence_in_relation_to_theory_and_practice.pdf (last accessed 14 May 2015).
71 Sage, D. (ed), 'It means more than mainstreaming . . .' (1993) 1(1) *Inclusion Times* 2.
72 See Gartner A., and Lipsky D. K., "Beyond special education: Toward a quality system for all students" (1987) 57(4) *Harvard Educational Review* 367; Stainback W., and Stainback S., "A rationale for the merger of special and regular education" (1984) 51(2) *Exceptional Children* 102; Kauffman J., "How we might achieve the radical reform of special education" In: Kauffman J. and Hallahan D. (eds), *The Illusion of Full Inclusion: A Comprehensive Critique of a Current Special Education Bandwagon* (Austin, Prod-Ed, 2005).
73 Loreman T., *Straight Talk about Inclusive Education* (CASS Connections, Spring, 2009).
74 Ibid., 43.

For successful inclusion to be readily available to all, the principles and practices required need to be a fundamental part of national educational planning and curriculum development.

Policy, funding and procurement need to ensure accessibility and adaptability by enabling access to augmentative and alternative modes, means and formats of communication and ensuring that students with disability can participate on an equal basis with others.

The key to successful inclusion is the classroom teacher. Teacher knowledge, skills, attitudes and expectations determine the success of a mixed ability class. There are three core aspects to achieving such a skilled and resourceful teaching workforce. The first is to ensure that mixed ability teaching and classroom management is included in the core of teacher education programmes. The second is to provide ongoing staff development to the existing workforce to increase mixed ability teaching skills. Finally, the third is to include the following in promotion criteria: respect for diversity; skills and knowledge in mixed ability teaching; and positive, proactive attitudes towards inclusive education.

Meso

The meso level relates to the school, institute and district level. This means that from the outset schools, institutes and districts have no basis to refuse the enrolment and teaching of any students in their area. The built environment is retrofitted and new buildings are fully accessible. All of a school needs to be accessible for students, parents and teachers with disability. An accessible built environment means the possibility of employing teachers with disability, presenting invaluable role modeling to the whole school community.

For successful inclusion and the valuing of diversity the school or institute organisation needs to ensure that inclusive practices are optimally implemented. This means that resources are used flexibly to meet classroom diversity and ensure that all students are learning together. Teachers' attitudes to diversity and inclusion are central to the recruitment and promotion processes. Support and development is provided to teachers to continually improve their teaching and classroom management. Finally, whole school extracurricular activities celebrate diversity such as a deaf and hearing choir.

Of increasing importance is information technology and the use of interactive multimedia in learning and teaching. It is essential that the production of materials for multimedia and information sharing websites are accessible to all members of the school community.

Micro

The importance of inclusive education being demonstrated effectively can't be underestimated. Inclusive education which is well implemented and maintained demonstrates capability and achievement seamlessly. Poor attempts at inclusion can reinforce negative assumptions.

It is essential that all students follow substantively similar programmes of study, with curriculum that can be adapted and modified if needed. Modes of instruction should be varied and responsive to the needs of all. All children should contribute to regular school and classroom learning activities and events. All children should be supported to make friends and to be socially successful with their peers. Diversity should be recognized, respected, understood and celebrated in the classroom and in the school.

Learning sign language, the use of alternative script such as Braille, augmentative and alternative modes, means and formats of communication must be available to all students, disabled and non-disabled. Moreover, the learning is facilitated with peer support and mentoring.

Conclusion

There is no question about the significance of the change that the CRPD enshrines. It requires the dismantling of existing segregated school systems and corresponding professional career paths. Consequently, for meaningful inclusion to be achieved the first step is for States to commit to the principle of education for all in one system – following with clear overarching inclusion policy, resourcing at all three levels of implementation and the education, preparation and ongoing development of the teaching profession. With this in place there will be generations for whom the spectrum of human diversity is part of their everyday experience and embedded in their community life.

5

EQUALITY OF OPPORTUNITY IN EMPLOYMENT?

Disability rights and active labour market policies

Lisa Waddington, Mark Priestley and Betul Yalcin[1]

The past 50 years have seen significant change with regard to understanding disability as a form of social and economic exclusion and, in particular, the role that environmental and social barriers play in disabling people with impairment (as illuminated in the early chapters in this volume). This, in turn, has impacted on the response of policymakers to the challenges that disabled people face, including the challenge of securing equality of opportunity in employment. New ways of conceptualising disability have led to a reorientation of policies designed to support the employment of disabled people, including the emergence of a more rights-based approach designed to combat disability discrimination.[2] At the same time there has been a move away from segregated active labour market programmes, in the form of sheltered employment institutions, towards inclusive active labour market policies that facilitate greater integration of disabled people in the open labour market. Such policies include both push and pull mechanisms, focusing, respectively, on equipping disabled people for employment opportunities in the open labour market and encouraging or obliging employers to take them on. This chapter introduces the challenge of achieving full participation and equality in employment by disabled people and examines the different approaches taken in law and policy to address this challenge. It shows that while clear and enforceable non-discrimination provisions are a prerequisite, there is also a need for active interventions to counter the unequal employment opportunities faced by disabled people and to structure the labour market accordingly.

---

1 Acknowledgement: the authors are grateful to Kate O'Reilly and Maastricht University for providing editorial assistance.
2 Brian Doyle, *Disability Discrimination and Equal Opportunities: A Comparative Study of the Employment Rights of Disabled Persons* (Mansell 1995); Mike Floyd and John Curtis, 'An Examination of Changes in Disability and Employment Policy in the United Kingdom' (2000) 2 *European Journal of Social Security* 303; Susan Lonsdale and Alan Walker, *A Right to Work: Disability and Employment* (Disability Allowance and Low Pay Unit 1984).

Employment as a right

The International Labour Organisation (ILO) estimate that a majority of disabled people in the world are of working age – some 470 million – yet the extent of their collective exclusion from full participation and equality in employment is marked.[3] Data from around the world show that a large number of disabled people remain unemployed or economically inactive, more than 80 per cent in some countries, and even in economically developed countries a substantial proportion of this group remain without work.[4] Unequal access to education and training, negative attitudes of employers and colleagues, inaccessible transport systems and workplaces and a lack of flexible work practices and employment support schemes present significant barriers to equality of opportunity in the labour market for disabled people. The potential for law and policy reform to address such inequality is contingent not only on framing and enforcing (new) legislation, but on understanding the social causes and consequences of labour market marginalisation.

In this context, Article 27 of the United Nations Convention on the Rights of Persons with Disabilities (CRPD) addressing work and employment lays down a bold challenge to policymakers and raises complex issues. It requires that:

> States Parties recognize the right of persons with disabilities to work, on an equal basis with others; this includes the right to the opportunity to gain a living by work freely chosen or accepted in a labour market and work environment that is open, inclusive and accessible to persons with disabilities.

Of particular note here is the concept of an equal right to work and the principle of free choice, at least to the extent that anyone is free to choose the work that they do. At the same time, this bold commitment hints at some of the enablers that are prerequisite to the realisation of employment choices and rights for disabled people in a competitive labour market – notably the inclusivity and accessibility of that market to people with diverse capabilities and resources. The challenge for law and policymakers is not only to create and enforce equal employment rights but also to facilitate the kinds of labour market conditions that will enable such rights to be exercised in practice. Eradicating employment discrimination on grounds of disability is a significant challenge; building a 'work environment that is open, inclusive and accessible' is even more challenging.

As discussed in this chapter, the development of public policies to advance employment opportunities for disabled people reveals a historic shift from 'compensatory' approaches, towards those based on equal rights, greater accessibility and support in the workplace. In many ways these are positive developments, responding to the claims and activism of the disability rights movement, but disabled people have also been the targets of more punitive policy reforms to reduce welfare spending by requiring more of those out of work to search for employment in unequal labour market conditions.

Work and employment is undoubtedly important to the general functioning of modern societies, but the way we think about work has been an important factor too in defining what we

---

3 International Labour Organization, *Employment for Social Justice and a Fair Globalization: overview of ILO programmes* (ILO 2012). Available at http://www.ilo.org/wcmsp5/groups/public/—-ed_emp/documents/publication/wcms_140958.pdf
4 World Health Organization and World Bank, *World Report on Disability* (WHO 2011) 237–8.

understand as 'disability' and its governance through social policies. Indeed, in some countries, legal definitions of what it means to be 'disabled' (for the purposes of social policy and administration) are based quite explicitly on measures of a person's work capacity or 'ability to work'.

Early proponents of the social model of disability, like Oliver (see chapter 1 in this volume), viewed the social relations of competitive labour markets as formative to the emergence of disability as a policy category in capitalist economies.[5] Indeed, Stone argued that the definition of who is included in the policy category of disabled people flows directly from state interventions to control labour supply.[6] This thesis suggests that, while many people with impairments have been excluded from labour market opportunities, the exact definition of who should be exempt from employment obligations changes in response to economic cycles and market demands. This means that laws and policies which define people as 'unable to work' at times of low demand (e.g. during an economic recession) may redefine them as able to work at times of labour shortage (e.g. during rapid economic growth). Legal definitions of disabled people's rights and responsibilities to work are, in this sense, rather 'elastic'[7] and vary between different countries and at different points in time. Yet research evidence from countries across the world shows that disabled adults, and disabled women in particular, remain disproportionately unemployed, underemployed and underpaid compared to their non-disabled peers.[8] Moreover, despite the adoption of non-discrimination laws over the past 25 years, there has been little evidence of any dramatic improvement in this disparity.[9]

The centrality of work to our historic understanding of what disability means is underlined by the extent to which exclusion from the labour market affects people's opportunities across the life course.[10] For example, in framing the 'fundamental principles' that would be later transposed into the social model of disability, the Union of Physically Impaired Against Segregation argued in the 1970s that:

> . . . the struggle to achieve integration into ordinary employment is the most vital part
> of the struggle to change the organisation of society so that physically impaired people
> are no longer impoverished through exclusion from full participation. Only when all
> physically impaired people of working age are as a matter of course helped to make

5 Vic Finkelstein, 'More on Phase 2' (1975) XXVII *The Magic Carpet* 16; Mike Oliver, *The Politics of Disablement* (Macmillan 1990); Mike Oliver and Colin Barnes, *The New Politics of Disablement* (Macmillan 2012); Joanna Ryan and Frank Thomas, *The Politics of Mental Handicap* (Penguin 1980).

6 Deborah Stone, *The Disabled State* (Temple University Press 1984). See also Mark Priestley, 'The Origins of a Legislative Disability Category in England: A Speculative History' (1997) 17 *Disability Studies Quarterly* 87.

7 Jonathan Gruber, 'Disability Insurance Benefits and Labor Supply' (2000) 108 *Journal of Political Economy* 1162.

8 OECD, *Sickness, Disability and Work: Breaking the Barriers: A Synthesis of Findings across OECD Countries*, (OECD Publishing 2000). Available at http://www.oecd-ilibrary.org/social-issues-migration-health/sickness-disability-and-work-breaking-the-barriers_9789264088856-en, accessed 27 February 2015; APPLICA, CESEP and European Centre Study of Compilation of Disability Statistical Data from the Administrative Registers of the Member States (European Commision 2008).

9 See for example, Daron Acemoglu and Joshua Angrist, *Consequences of Employment Protection? The Case of the Americans with Disabilities Act* (National Bureau of Economic Research Working Paper No. 6670 1998); Clare Bambra and Daniel Pope, 'Evidenced Based Public Health Policy and Practice: What Are the Effects of Anti-Discriminatory Legislation on Socioeconomic Inequalities in the Employment Consequences of Ill Health and Disability?' (2007) 61 *Journal of Epidemiology and Community Health* 421.

10 Mark Priestley, *Disability: A Life Course Approach* (Polity 2003).

whatever contribution they can in ordinary work situations, will secure foundations for full integration in society as a whole be laid. All the other situations from which physically impaired people are excluded are linked, in the final analysis, with the basic exclusion from employment.[11]

This strong emphasis placed on paid employment underlines the importance that is attached to socially valued work in modern constructions of adult citizenship. The opportunity for employment is increasingly presented as a key social right, as a means to the realisation of other economic rights, and as a route to social inclusion more widely. For governments there are also economic benefits in tapping the labour potential of historically excluded groups, particularly in times of labour shortage or when there are fiscal constraints on welfare spending, as in a period of austerity. As a consequence both policymakers and disability activists have made economic, social and moral arguments for public policy reform to expand the opportunities, and the expectations, for disabled adults to find employment.[12]

Different policy approaches

Broadly speaking, a liberal approach to rights-based labour law might suggest that enforcement of the negative right to non-discrimination in a free and open labour market would be sufficient to protect disabled people's opportunity for employment 'on an equal basis with others'. By contrast, an approach to employment policy based on positive rights and countering discrimination might suggest that active intervention in the labour market is needed to reshape the opportunities within that market. The evolution of public intervention to promote the employment of disabled people in contemporary welfare states is strongly associated with the emergence of 'active labour market policies' (ALMPs). The rationale for a more active intervention approach to employment policy assumes that market forces alone will not deliver optimum employment or social outcomes, even with legislative protection for employment rights in place. The different emphases given to the role of the market and the state (and the family) in varying national welfare regimes was initially characterised in the work of Esping-Andersen.[13]

Broadly speaking, ALMPs fall into three categories – the provision of public employment services that help people look for and find work, employment training that helps people to increase their employment skills, and subsidies (either for the employer or the employee) to incentivise recruitment and work experience opportunities for people unable to find work easily in the open market.[14] ALMPs are by no means solely targeted towards disabled people, and often focus on young people entering the labour market, older workers who have fallen out of the labour market, and other long-term unemployed people. Although interventionist in approach, the aim of ALMP programmes is very often stated as encouraging people who are marginal to the labour market to assume greater independence and responsibility for themselves and their families

11 Union of Physically Impaired Against Segregation/Disability Alliance, *Fundamental Principles of Disability* (UPIAS / Disability Alliance 1976) 15.
12 Colin Barnes, 'A Working Social Model? Disability, Work and Disability Politics in the 21st Century' (2000) 20 *Critical Social Policy* 441.
13 Gøsta Esping-Andersen, *The Three Worlds of Welfare Capitalism* (Polity 1990).
14 Lars Calmfors, *Active Labour Market Policy and Unemployment: A Framework for the Analysis of Crucial Design Features* (Organisation for Economic Co-operation and Development 1994).

through routes into paid employment.[15] Disabled people without work have been a key target group for such policies in recent years. However this led some within the disability movement, like Abberley, to caution against the 'over-enthusiastic espousal of work-based programmes of overcoming the exclusion of disabled people'.[16]

ALMPs thus play an important role in defining the relationship between individuals and (welfare) states, and in structuring the relationship between the market and the state.[17] ALMPs may be defined as 'measures taken in order to improve the functioning of the labour market that are directed towards the unemployed'.[18] Calmfors suggests that such improvements include the efficiency of matching job vacancies with job-seekers, upgrading and adapting the skills of job applicants, and job creation. Gilbert and Besharov identify four categories of active labour market policies: (a) measures that raise the cost of non-work (such as sanctions and penalties for non-participation, job search programmes, lowering of replacement rate and duration of benefit, and narrowing the eligibility criteria or conditionality for benefits); (b) measures that increase the benefits of work (such as increasing work-pay through tax credits and tax relief and restricting eligibility for benefits); (c) measures to increase the availability of work (such as creating jobs in the public sector, subsidising employment costs to employers, providing flexible working conditions, sheltered employment or micro credits to start-up businesses); and (d) measures that increase readiness to work (such as providing education and training, opportunities to learn social and therapeutic skills for people with lower qualifications to increase their employability).[19]

ALMPs have been widely targeted at supporting disabled people to enter and remain in employment,[20] and this trend has been accentuated by the increasing numbers of people claiming long-term out-of-work welfare benefits on grounds of disability and by the downturn in employment arising from the widespread economic recession after the financial crisis of 2008. At the launch of its 2010 *Sickness, Disability and Work Report*, the General Secretary of the Organization for Economic Cooperation and Development (OECD) stressed the importance of economic integration of disabled people, urging governments 'to speed up their welfare reforms to help people with disabilities find a job' and that 'the mantra of making work pay must become central to all welfare schemes'.[21]

As applied to disabled people, the most commonly targeted intervention policies can be categorised as follows. 'Sheltered employment' involves the funding or operation of segregated

15 Peter Dwyer, P Welfare Rights and Responsibilities: Contesting Social Citizenship (Policy Press 2000); Peter Dwyer, *Understanding Social Citizenship: Themes and Perspectives for Policy and Practice* (Policy Press 2010).
16 Paul Abberley, 'The Significance of Work for the Citizenship of Disabled People', Paper Presented at University College Dublin 15 April 1999. Available at http://disability-studies.leeds.ac.uk/files/library/Abberley-sigofwork.rtf. 15.
17 Janet Newman, 'The "Double Dynamics" of Activation: Institutions, Citizens and the Remaking of Welfare Governance' (2007) 27 *International Journal of Sociology and Social Policy* 364, 2.
18 Calmfors (n 14) 8.
19 Neil Gilbert and Douglas Besharov 'Welfare States amid Economic Turmoil: Adjusting Work-oriented Policy' (2011) 39 *Policy and Politics* 295.
20 Bent Greve, *The Labour Market Situation of Disabled People in European Countries and Implementation of Employment Policies: A Summary of Evidence from Country Reports and Research Studies* (ANED 2009); EIM Business and Policy Research, *Active Labour Market Programmes for People with Disabilities: Facts and Figures on Use and Impact*, 2002.
21 Organisation for Economic Co-operation and Development, *Sickness, Disability and Work: Breaking the Barriers: A Synthesis of Findings Across OECD Countries* (OECD 2010) 1.

workshops or work centres designated for the employment of disabled people, often at or below the minimum wage, as a form of training or therapeutic activity. While sheltered employment is typically included in policy typologies of labour activation, the difficulty with this approach is that it depends, by definition, on work outside the mainstream labour market and is thus at odds with an equality and non-discrimination approach.[22] 'Supported employment' by contrast involves the provision of support on-the-job in the open labour market. 'Subsidised employment' refers to investments and incentives that reduce the cost of employing disabled people, for example through wage subsidies or tax subsidies for the employer. 'Vocational rehabilitation and training' aims to increase the job skills and productivity levels of disabled people and may also feature in either sheltered or supported employment schemes. 'Quota schemes' place obligations or expectations on employers to employ a specified minimum proportion of disabled people in their workforce, often accompanied by a tax penalty or levy for failing to meet the target. These approaches are all common within the active labour market policy approach. The most prominent types of ALMP are supported employment, vocational rehabilitation, work placement, employment quotas and incentives.

'Non-discrimination' policies, as discussed, involve stipulating and enforcing rights to equal opportunities in any aspect of job seeking and employment but may exist independently from, or do not necessarily rely upon, active policy measures to promote or create employment.[23] It is in this area that there have been the rapid and positive advances in law and policy development in recent years.[24] At the same time, however, there has been increasing attention to more negative social policy measures designed to channel disabled people into job search activity in the open labour market simply by removing or narrowing their eligibility criteria for out-of-work disability benefit schemes.[25] In this way, the promotion of a stronger rights-based policy discourse has been accompanied by the promotion of a stronger responsibility-based policy discourse in the disability employment field.

In addition, the promotion of 'social enterprises' as a new category of business[26] has produced outcomes somewhere between sheltered and supported employment, in that companies may be formed specifically to employ disabled people, and with primarily social objectives, but with exposure to the open market when selling their products or services. There are also policy examples of incentive and grant schemes targeting disabled people wishing to establish their

---

22 Laura Hoffman, 'Employment Opportunity or a Discrimination Dilemma: Sheltered Workshops and the Employment of the Disabled' (2013) 16 *University of Pennsylvania Journal of Law and Social Change* 151.

23 EIM (n 20); Patricia Thornton and Neil Lunt, *Employment Policies for Disabled People in Eighteen Countries: A Review* (University of York Research Unit 1997); Greve (n 20); Chon-Kyun Kim, 'Comparative Perspectives on Disability and Employment Policy' (2010) 15 *International Review of Public Administration* 27.

24 Gerard Quinn and Eilionóir Flynn 'Transatlantic Borrowings: The Past and Future of EU Non-Discrimination Law and Policy on the Ground of Disability' (2012) 60 *American Journal of Comparative Law* 23.

25 David Etherington and Jo Ingold, 'Welfare to Work and the Inclusive Labour Market: A Comparative Study of Activation Policies for Disability and Long Term Sickness Benefit Claimants in the UK and Denmark' (2012) 22 *Journal of European Social Policy* 30; Sarah Parker Harris, Randall Owen and Robert Gould, 'Parity of Participation in Liberal Welfare States: Human Rights, Neoliberalism, Disability and Employment' (2012) 27 *Disability and Society* 823; Chris Grover, 'Disability, Benefits and Welfare Reform and Employment Policy' (2014) 29 *Disability and Society* 1168.

26 Rory Ridley-Duff and Mike Bull, *Understanding Social Enterprise: Theory and Practice* (Sage Publishing 2011); Simon Teasdale, *What's in a Name? Making Sense of Social Enterprise Discourses* (Sage Publishing 2011).

own independent businesses as entrepreneurs.[27] As Walls, Dowler, Cordingly, Orslene and Greer argue, the experience of micro-enterprise has enabled many disabled people to 'redefine success' in employment, not simply in terms of income generation, but also in achieving control over the day-to-day management of workloads and workplace environments.[28]

The development of international law and policy

As outlined earlier, Article 27 CRPD provides a context for thinking about the state of the art in disability and international employment law. Beyond an assertive recognition of equal rights, choices and opportunities, it sets out eleven steps states should take to safeguard and promote these employment-related rights. For example, the article requires the prohibition of discrimination on the basis of disability in all aspects of recruitment, working conditions and relationships, remuneration and labour rights. It highlights the need for good access to training, support for job searching or help in starting a business. It points to the significance of reasonable accommodation and appropriate vocational rehabilitation (also highlighted in Article 26). It also outlaws slavery and other forms of forced labour of disabled people on an equal basis with others. These provisions are intended to apply both to public and private sector employment and are supported by other articles of the Convention, and particularly by Article 9, which requires that barriers to accessibility should be removed from workplaces (as well as from other buildings, roads, forms of transport and information technologies).

The CRPD was preceded by a number of other instruments of international law, which addressed the employment of disabled people. One of the earliest international instruments specifically addressing the employment of disabled people was Recommendation No. 99 of the International Labour Organisation (ILO) on Vocational Rehabilitation (Disabled). This dates from 1955 and was quite forward-looking for its time and prefigured the spirit of the CRPD in some respects. It stressed that the goal of vocational training was to prepare the disabled person 'for working normally on an equal basis with non-disabled workers if he is capable of doing so',[29] and noted that measures designed to widen employment opportunities for disabled persons should be based on the following three principles:

(a) disabled persons should be afforded an equal opportunity with the non-disabled to perform work for which they are qualified;
(b) disabled persons should have full opportunity to accept suitable work with employers of their own choice;
(c) emphasis should be placed on the abilities and work capacities of disabled persons and not on their disabilities.[30]

The Recommendation made reference to both employment promotion measures and to sheltered employment, but the latter was to be reserved only for those 'who cannot be made fit for ordinary

---

27 Sarah Parker Harris, Maija Renko and Kate Caldwell, 'Social Entrepeneurship as an Employment Pathway for People with Disabilities: Exploring Political-Economic and Socio-Cultural Factors (2014) 29 *Disability and Society* 1275.
28 Richard Walls, Denetta Dowler, Kimberly Cordingly, Louis Orslene and John Greer, 'Microenterprising and People with Disabilities: Strategies for Success and Failure' (2001) 67 *The Journal of Rehabilitation* 29.
29 Convention of the Rights of Persons with Disabilities 2007, Article 6(c).
30 Ibid., Article 29.

competitive employment'.[31] Sheltered workshops were to provide both 'useful and remunerative work' and 'opportunities for vocational adjustment and advancements' with the opportunity to transfer to open employment wherever possible.[32] Disabled workers employed in sheltered workshops should enjoy the same protection in terms of employment conditions and statutory wage regulation as other workers.[33] Sheltered workshops were therefore seen as an important element of disability employment policy under this Recommendation, with certain safeguards recommended to ensure that only those regarded as unable to work in the open labour market would be placed in sheltered employment, and that they would continue to benefit from the general protection of labour law. Disability employment policy in the 1950s was, however, still largely framed by a discourse of rehabilitation rather than one of rights.

The 1955 ILO Recommendation did refer to measures to promote the employment of disabled people in the open labour market. The recommended measures included the 'engagement by employers of a percentage of disabled persons' (i.e. a quota system, reserving certain designated occupations for disabled people, and 'arranging that seriously disabled persons are given opportunities for employment or preference in certain occupations considered suitable for them' (i.e. reserving some types of jobs for disabled people).[34] Such approaches were widely implemented in numerous countries, but seen from the perspective of today it is questionable both how effective such measures are and the extent to which they result in stigmatizing the beneficiaries.[35]

Following the UN International Year of Disabled Persons in 1981, the ILO adopted Convention No. 159 in 1983, with an accompanying Recommendation No. 167 on international standards to promote greater equality of opportunity and treatment in employment. This instrument was still framed within a discourse of rehabilitation and adopted an individual impairment-related definition of disability, rather than a social model definition, such that 'the term disabled person means an individual whose prospects of securing, retaining and advancing in suitable employment are substantially reduced as a result of a duly recognized physical or mental impairment' (Article 1). Nonetheless, it was also founded on the principle of equal opportunity, couched in the following terms:

> The said policy shall be based on the principle of equal opportunity between disabled workers and workers generally. Equality of opportunity and treatment for disabled men and women workers shall be respected. Special positive measures aimed at effective equality of opportunity and treatment between disabled workers and other workers shall not be regarded as discriminating against other workers.
>
> *(Article 4)*

Both the Convention and the Recommendation note that, since the adoption of Recommendation No. 99 in 1955, 'significant developments have occurred in the understanding of rehabilitation

---

31 Ibid., Article 32(1).
32 Ibid., Article 33.
33 Ibid., Article 35.
34 Ibid., Article 31.
35 For critical reflections on the functioning of quota systems see Lisa Waddington, 'Legislating to Employ People with Disabilities: The European and American Way' (1994) 1 *Maastricht Journal of European and Comparative Law* 367; and see also Lisa Waddington, 'Reassessing the Employment of People with Disabilities in Europe: From Quotas to Anti-Discrimination Laws' (1996) 18 *Comparative Labor Law Journal* 62.

needs'.[36] Convention No. 159, which is binding on those States that have ratified it, is relatively brief and does not refer to any specific employment activation strategies or to sheltered employment. Instead it requires ratifying States to promote *inter alia* employment opportunities for disabled persons in the open labour market.[37]

In contrast to the Convention, Recommendation No. 168 is more detailed as to the kind of steps States should be taking. Sheltered employment is once again seen as needed for 'disabled persons for whom access to open employment is not practicable'[38] and governments are to provide appropriate support for various types of sheltered employment.[39] In addition, a wide variety of measures to stimulate employment in the open labour market are recommended, including 'financial incentives to employers to encourage them to provide training and subsequent employment for disabled persons, as well as to make reasonable adaptation to workplaces, job design, tools, machinery and work organisation to facilitate such training and employment'[40] and 'elimination, by stages if necessary, of physical, communication and architectural barriers and obstacles affecting transport and access to and free movement in premises for the training and employment of disabled persons'.[41] The 1983 Recommendation still reveals the perceived importance of sheltered employment as an element of disability employment policy, although with a less prominent position than it had in the 1955 Recommendation. The 1983 Recommendation also reflects, to some degree, recognition of the socially created barriers that hinder open employment for disabled people, and the need to address those barriers as part of a labour activation strategy.

A change in the prominence given to sheltered employment as an element of disability employment policy is also reflected at the European level in the European Social Charter (ESC). The ESC is a treaty of the Council of Europe which guarantees social and economic rights. It was first adopted in 1961 and then revised in 1996 (the original ESC remains in force for those States which have not ratified the latter). Both versions of the Charter address the rights of disabled people in Article 15. The relevant article is entitled 'The right of physically or mentally disabled persons to vocational training, rehabilitation and social settlement' in the original Charter and calls on the Contracting Parties to 'take adequate measures for the placing of disabled persons in employment, such as specialised placing services, facilities for sheltered employment and measures to encourage employers to admit disabled persons to employment'.[42] Segregated measures, including sheltered employment, are therefore seen as a key element of disability employment policy under this article.

The revised ESC, of 1996, entitles Article 15 'The right of persons with disabilities to independence, social integration and participation in the life of the community'. It is clear from section one of the article that measures to support persons with disabilities should be provided through 'general schemes' wherever possible. Integration and participation in the mainstream, as reflected in the title of the article, had become the key goal. With regard to employment, section 2 provides that the Parties are 'to promote their access to employment through all measures tending to encourage employers to hire and keep in employment persons with disabilities in the ordinary working environment and to adjust the working conditions to the needs of the

---

36 Preamble Convention Concerning Vocational Rehabilitation and Employment (Disabled Persons) 1985.
37 Ibid., Article 3.
38 Ibid., Article 11 (b).
39 Ibid.
40 Ibid., Article 11(a).
41 Ibid., Article 11(g).
42 Ibid., Article 15(2).

disabled or, where this is not possible by reason of disability, by arranging or creating sheltered employment according to the level of disability . . . '. In comparison with the original ESC, the desirability of segregated and sheltered employment services is reversed: under the 1961 ESC specialised or segregated services, including sheltered employment, were listed first in terms of the obligations on States, whilst the revised ESC only sees such measures as the exception, to be provided when open employment is not an option. This change of emphasis marks a generalised shift of thinking about disability and employment and the emergence of a more rights-based approach in international law.

The change in approach to sheltered employment as an element of disability employment policy is revealed most dramatically through a comparison of the UN Standard Rules on the Equalization of Opportunities of Persons with Disabilities, adopted by the UN General Assembly in 1993 and the UN Convention on the Rights of Persons with Disabilities (CRPD), adopted in 2006. Rule 7 of the Standard Rules specifies that 'States should actively support the integration of persons with disabilities into open employment'. The measures which States should take in this respect include 'vocational training, incentive-oriented quota schemes, reserved or designated employment, loans or grants for small business, exclusive contracts or priority production rights, tax concessions, contract compliance or other technical or financial assistance to enterprises employing workers with disabilities'. Attention should also be paid to designing and adapting workplaces so that they are accessible, providing reasonable accommodations by employers, training and placement and public awareness. The emphasis is very clearly placed on inclusion in the open labour market and addressing the wide variety of barriers which hamper this. Nevertheless, a place remains for sheltered employment: whilst 'the aim should always be for persons with disabilities to obtain employment in the open labour market . . . [f]or persons with disabilities whose needs cannot be met in open employment, small units of sheltered or supported employment may be an alternative'.

However, even this modest role for sheltered employment is not recognised in Article 27 CRPD on work and employment. The emphasis throughout this article is on equality and promoting employment in the open labour market. There is no reference whatsoever to sheltered employment or to any other segregated or specialised employment measure. Anna Bruce has noted with regard to this article that '[t]he current largely segregated state of affairs is not mentioned and instead the goal is emphasized by calling for "a labour market and work environment that is open, inclusive and accessible to persons with disabilities"'.[43] The decision not to refer to sheltered employment was not undisputed by the negotiating parties. Bruce argues that consensus was agreed following the inclusion of section 1(a) of the article, which provides that discrimination on the basis of disability is to be prohibited 'with regard to all matters concerning all forms of employment'.[44] As a result, segregated settings which qualify as employment must comply with the requirements of Article 27. Sheltered employment is not explicitly prohibited, but the article poses real challenges to its continuation in certain circumstances and the emphasis is firmly on equality of opportunity in the mainstream labour market. Bruce concludes 'through the prominence of choice and inclusion in Article 27 as well as in the remainder of the CRPD it can be concluded that segregated employment opportunities as the only alternative for an individual, particularly one who wishes otherwise, is highly questionable'.[45]

---

43 Anna Bruce, *Which Entitlements and for Whom? The Convention on the Rights of Persons with Disabilities and Its Ideological Antecedents* (PhD Thesis, Lund University 2014) 203.
44 Ibid., 204.
45 Ibid., 204.

This brief review has revealed the declining importance attached to sheltered employment as an element of disability employment policy in modern international and European human rights instruments. Instead, the focus has been placed more and more on full participation and equality in the open labour market on an equal basis with others, and on measures which can facilitate mainstream employment. Nevertheless, with the exception of the CRPD, these instruments still indicate a place for sheltered employment for individuals who are deemed to be unable to fulfil the conditions for employment opportunity in the open labour market. This view of the role of sheltered employment may have been thrown into doubt by the CRPD. In order to understand the tensions between segregated and inclusive approaches it is useful to learn more about the development of disability employment policies more generally.

Action on employment opportunities

The preceding sections indicate the key legal developments at the international level. State responses to the challenge of achieving full participation and equality in employment by disabled people have taken a number of different forms. The 1990s saw a rapid expansion of active labour market policies, involving a mixture of compulsory and voluntary measures and the proliferation of schemes for employment support and training.[46] Such initiatives emphasized the need for increased flexibility in responding to the employment needs of disabled people, and the economic benefits of bringing them into paid work.[47] A number of comparative studies on policies to support and retain disabled people in employment chart developments during this period – following the adoption of ILO Convention No. 159 but prior to adoption of the UN CRPD.

For example, in 1997 Thornton and Lunt reviewed disability employment policies in eighteen countries, building on earlier work in Europe, North American and Australia.[48] Their study suggested an apparently universal commitment to the aims of participation and equality. It also indicated that legislation which sought to support these goals was becoming more common. In reviewing the legislation, they identified two broad trends. First, they identified a general policy approach based on broad anti-discriminatory legislation, in which employment appears amongst several fields addressed within a common legislative framework (although often a dominant field). Examples of this approach are the Americans with Disabilities Act 1989 (ADA) and the Disability Discrimination Act 1995 (DDA – since incorporated in the Equality Act 2010) in the United Kingdom. Second, they identified the division of disability policy into departmental concerns, in which employment rights and/or support measures are addressed in specific legislation, separate from other policy areas. At the time of the report, such employment policies mostly sought to compensate, facilitate or encourage the employment of disabled people (e.g. via employment quotas, subsidies and services) rather than to ensure and enforce equal rights or to make the labour market more accessible and inclusive. Hybrid approaches merging both non–discrimination legislation and employment specific measures have subsequently become evident. For example, the EU Employment Equality Directive 2000/78/EC[49] reflects

---

46 John Martin and David Grubb, 'What Works and for Whom: A Review of OECD Countries' Experiences with Active Labour Market Policies' (2001) 8 *Swedish Economic Policy Review* 9.
47 Ruth O'Brien, *Crippled Justice; The History of Modern Disability Policy in the Workplace* (University of Chicago Press 2001).
48 Thornton and Lunt (n 23).
49 Council Directive 2000/78/EC of 27 November 2000 Establishing a General Framework for Equal Treatment in Employment and Occupation [2002] O.J. L 303/ 16. 8.

the non-discrimination principle of the first approach but is limited to the field of occupation, employment and vocational training as in the second type of policy.

Goss, Goss and Adam-Smith also identified two distinct approaches to promoting the employment of disabled people in more developed economies during the 1990s.[50] Thus, they identify an American tradition, based on anti-discrimination measures and civil rights, and a European tradition, based on compulsory employment quotas and state intervention. This binary distinction is somewhat problematised by the EU Framework Directive and the proliferation of national non-discrimination laws in European countries which occurred subsequently. Gooding linked the differences in policies to different models of disability, equating quota systems with medical and compensatory models of disability, and rights-based approaches with social models:

> The different approaches are reflected in the contrasting rationales of the two policies. The quota is fundamentally a collective compensation to individuals for loss of capacity. The impetus for this derives from the state. In contrast impetus for the rights approach derives from the movement of disabled people themselves, and it does not seek to compensate the individual but to change society by opening it up to disabled people as a whole.[51]

Within the compensatory model, the provision of 'sheltered' employment in segregated workshops or 'training centres' was commonplace in Europe after World War II (sometimes in the form of compulsory work placement for the purposes of therapeutic intervention or rehabilitation programme rather than employment opportunity, or as a precondition for receiving disability-related income benefits). Sheltered employment persisted as a policy approach for some decades, and continues today in the repertoire of several advanced welfare economies, but as the post-war rehabilitation paradigm was transcended by the equal opportunities paradigm there was a notable shift from sheltered employment policies towards 'supported' placements in mainstream employment settings. Great optimism surrounded the development of supported employment and there was rapid growth in this form of employment from the mid 1980s, particularly in North America.[52] Although supported employment and training were not always seen as 'real work',[53] as 'socially valid',[54] or as 'cost-effective',[55] there were positive outcomes for disabled people.[56]

---

50 David Goss, Fiona Goss and Derek Adam-Smith, 'Disability and employment: A Comparative Critique of UK Legislation' (2000) 11 *International Journal of Human Resource Management* 807.

51 Caroline Gooding, 'Employment and Disabled People: Equal Rights or Positive Action' in Gerry Zarb (ed), *Removing Disabling Barriers* (Policy Studies Institute 1996) 65.

52 Paul Wehman, Grant Revell and John Kregel, 'Supported Employment: A Decade of Rapid Growth and Impact' in Paul Wehman, Grant Revell, John Kregel and Michael West (eds), *Supported Employment Research: Expanding Competitive Employment Opportunities for Persons with Significant Disabilities* (Rehabilitation Research and Training Center on Supported Employment, Virginia Commonwealth University 1997).

53 James Black and Luanna Meyer, 'But . . . Is It Really Work – Social Validity of Employment Training for Persons with Very Severe Disabilities' (1992) 96 *American Journal on Mental Retardation* 463.

54 David Test 'Supported employment and social validity' (1994) 19 *Research and Practice for Persons with Severe Disabilities* 116.

55 Robert Cimera, 'Are Individuals With Severe Mental Retardation And Multiple Disabilities Cost Efficient to Serve via Supported Employment Programs?' (1998) 36 *Mental Retardation* 280.

56 Lyke Thompson, Greg Powers and Bernice Houchard, 'The Wage Effects of Supported Employment' (1992) 17 *Journal of the Association for Persons with Severe Handicaps* 87; Ruth Crowther, Max Marshall, Gary Bond and Peter Huxley, 'Helping People with Severe Mental Illness to Obtain Work: Systematic Review' (2001) 322 *British Medical Journal* 204.

While policy evaluations tended to focus on the technical merits of sheltered versus supported employment, the wider policy shift from segregated to mainstream employment was a significant force for change in thinking and practice. At the same time, there were some concerns that a shift of emphasis towards rights-based legislation and mainstream jobs might not be sufficient to ensure the realisation of equal rights in practice. For example, reviewing the British Government's Supported Employment Programme in 1998, Hyde concluded that new policies adopted during the 1980s and 1990s were more a response to employer interests than to the interests of disabled people and that market deregulation risked abandoning disabled people to the disabling social relations of a competitive capitalist labour market.[57]

Hodges-Aeberhard and Raskin, writing in 1997, advocated affirmative action to promote the employment of disabled people, and suggested that the exclusion of disabled people from employment was a product of deeply institutionalised discrimination and that:

> prohibiting discrimination is often insufficient to eliminate the *de facto* practice. Positive measures, then, may be seen as steps which are set out to eliminate and make good any *de facto* inequalities, thereby enabling members of groups suffering from discrimination or disadvantage to work in all sectors of activity and at all levels of responsibility.[58]

Within the emergent rights-based model, epitomised by the ADA, the emphasis is on anti-discrimination legislation and the transformative potential of the open labour market. However, just as non-discrimination legislation failed to deliver equal employment opportunities or outcomes for women,[59] this approach alone is insufficient to ensure equal opportunities for disabled people. For example, in 1997 Yelin noted that the raised expectations of disabled people following the adoption of the ADA had to be balanced against job insecurity in US labour markets, where disabled women were likely to be particularly disadvantaged.[60] Much concern was also evident in the early years of implementation of the ADA, from 1990 in the United States, that neither employers nor the courts were well versed in what 'reasonable accommodation' really meant in the context of the workplace, and that they would focus more on technical adjustments than on the social context of workplaces and work groups.[61]

To summarise, despite differing political origins and policy traditions, there are some important parallels in the development of compensatory and rights-based approaches to supporting the employment of disabled people. There is a sense in which both take a somewhat unquestioning view of the positive role attributed to paid employment as a social status in capitalist economies (and the social devaluation of those who do not or cannot work on an equal basis with others). For example, echoing the themes outlined at the beginning of this chapter, Burkhauser argues that there is unlikely to be any real progress towards independence in any sphere until there is a

---

57 Mark Hyde, 'Sheltered and Supported Employment in the 1990s: The Experiences of Disabled Workers in the UK' (1998) 13 *Disability & Society* 199.

58 Jane Hodges-Aeberhard and Carl Raskin (eds), *Affirmative Action in the Employment of Ethnic Minorities and Persons with Disabilities* (International Labour Organization 1997) 1.

59 Gillian Whitehouse, 'Legislation and Labour Market Gender Inequality: An Analysis of OECD Countries' (1992) 6 *Work, Employment & Society* 65.

60 Edward Yelin, 'The Employment of People with and without Disabilities in an Age of Insecurity' (1997) 549 *Annals of the American Academy of Political and Social Science*117; Justin Schneider, Ken Simons and Greg Everatt, 'Impact of the National Minimum Wage on Disabled People' (2001) 16 *Disability & Society* 723.

61 See for example Paul Grossman, 'Employment Discrimination Law for the Learning-Disabled Community' (1992) 15 *Learning Disability Quarterly* 287.

culture shift in accepting that disabled people 'can and should be expected to work'.[62] This raises some difficult questions about whether public policy should ever assume that everyone must seek work without a corresponding revision of what valued work means.[63]

Factors affecting employment

As noted earlier and at the beginning of this chapter, political discourse often conveys employment as a precondition for successful participation in adult society, and as a means to both social status and security.[64] Increasing the employment participation of disabled people has been credited also with bringing benefits to wider society, since disabled people's cost to the economy may be lower and their economic contribution greater when they have paid work.[65] However, it is also clear that the long-standing marginalisation of disabled people from full participation and equality in working life has deep roots in societal attitudes, institutionalised discrimination and environmental barriers.[66]

A number of social and physical barriers have been identified that affect disabled people's opportunity to obtain employment. For example, the willingness of employers to hire disabled employees is often cited as a key factor hampering equality of opportunity, particularly in relation to direct recruitment discrimination in small private sector firms, and this may indicate a need for public policies that promote equality through public education and positive information messages. Access to an effective employment support system, previous experience of having disabled employees, or personal interaction with disabled people have been shown to increase the willingness of employers to hire a disabled person.[67] From the perspective of disabled workers, the existence of negative societal attitudes, fear of stigmatisation, low expectations, fears of rejection or being labelled as unproductive are amongst the factors which can hinder employment.[68] The attitudes of employers and co-workers are clearly important in shaping social barriers to equality employment opportunities, but there are physical barriers too. The accessibility of the built environment, transport systems and information technologies is also of critical importance for employment. The availability of reasonable accommodations in the work place, vocational rehabilitation and training, transition programmes, flexible working conditions, on-the-job support and job quality are amongst the factors that influence employment rates of disabled persons.[69]

---

62 Richard Burkhauser, 'Post-ADA: Are People with Disabilities Expected to Work?' (1997) 549 *Annals of the American Academy of Political and Social Science* 71.

63 See Barnes, 2000 (n 12); 2003; Bammer Gleeson, *Geographies of Disability* (Routledge 1999).

64 See Barnes, 2000 (n 12); Abberley, 1999 (n 16).

65 Ibid.

66 Barnes, 2000 (n 12); Hodges-Aeberhard and Raskin (n 58).

67 House of Commons, *Employer Attitudes and Discrimination: Education and Employment* (House of Commons Report No. 9, 1999); Darlene Unger, 'Employers' Attitudes towards Persons with Disabilities in the Work Force: Myths or Realities' (2002) 17 *Focus on Autism and Other Developmental Disabilities* 2; Frances Hannon, *Literature Review on Attitudes Towards Disability: Disability Research Series* (National Disability Authority 2007).

68 John Kitching, 'Can Small Businesses Help Reduce Employment Exclusion?' (2006) 24 *Environment and Planning C: Government and Policy* 869; Marilyn Howard, 'An Interactionist Perspective on Barriers and Bridges to Work for Disabled People' (2003) *IPPR Research Paper, Institute for Public Policy Research*; Arthur Crisps, 'Tendency to Stigmatize' (2001) 178 *British Journal of Psychiatry* 197; Liz Sayce, *Getting in, Staying in and Getting On: Disability Employment Support Fit for the Future* (The Stationery Office 2011).

69 Carol Goldstone, *Barriers to Employment for Disabled People. In-House Report 95* (Department of Work and Pension Report 95, 2002), Equality North East, *Barriers to Employment 2004–2005 Report* (The European Social Fund Report of 2004/2005, 2005); Sayce (n 68).

In his writings on the social model of disability, Oliver highlighted how disability, and our responses to it, are shaped by interactions between the mode of production and social values attached to the impaired body.[70] Thus, the industrial revolution and factory production methods gave rise to new ways of working and new types of worker, whereby mechanised manufacture became more common than agricultural work and the requirements imposed on workers, such as the ability to operate new machines, became more standardised. In this way, Oliver and others argued that the impaired body became increasingly devalued in a competitive and routinised labour market geared to employer expectations of an average productive worker. The globalisation of industrial capital has disseminated such assumptions widely[71] and Kemp argues that technological developments have intensified the importance of higher level qualifications and skills, while the demand for low-skilled workers has declined, further impacting on disabled people, who are more likely to be educationally marginalised.[72]

Changes in future markets may offer new opportunities for disabled adults to participate in economically productive labour. For example, much hope has been placed on the potential impact of technology and flexible working in post-Fordist modes of production.[73] However, technologies are not isolated from the prevailing relations of production, and technology alone can be no guarantor of successful employment. As, Michailakis notes, 'technological optimism' often overlooks the embeddedness of technologies within economic, social and cultural contexts.[74] Similarly, Light questions uncritical approaches to the role of technology in achieving the employment goals of the Americans with Disabilities Act, expressing concern that technological developments in the information age may actually subvert progressive policies.[75] Thus, Levine and Nourse show how an increased reliance on information technology within competitive US labour markets works against the provision of job opportunities for young people with learning difficulties.[76] Rapid economic change therefore brings with it both new opportunities and new forms of exclusion.[77]

---

70 Oliver (n 5).
71 Michael Davidson 'The Work of Disability in an Age of Globalization' in Lennard Davis (ed), *The Disability Studies Reader* (Taylor & Francis 2006).
72 Peter Kemp, 'Comparing Trends in Disability Benefit Receipt' in Peter Kemp, Annika Sunden and Bernhard Bakker – Tauritz (eds), *Sick Societies: Trends in Disability Benefits in Post Industrial Welfare States* (International Social Security Association 2006).
73 Colin Barnes 'Disability and Paid Employment' 13 *Work, Employment and Society* (1999) 147.
74 Dimitris Michailakis, ' Information and Communication Technologies and the Opportunities of Disabled Persons in the Swedish Labour Market' (2001) 16 *Disability & Society* 477.
75 Jennifer Light, 'Separate but Equal? Reasonable Accommodation in the Information Age' (2001) 67 *Journal of the American Planning Association* 263; See also Katherine Seelman, 'Science and Technology Policy: Is Disability a Missing Factor?' (2000) 12 *Assistive Technology* 144.
76 Phyllis Levine and Steven Nourse, 'What Follow-Up Studies Say About Postschool Life for Young Men and Women with Learning Disabilities: A Critical Look at the Literature' (1998) 31 *Journal of Learning Disabilities* 212.
77 See Denison Jayasooria, Bathmavathi Krishnan and Godfrey Ooi, 'Disabled People in a Newly Industrialising Economy: Opportunities and Challenges in Malaysia' (1997) 12 *Disability & Society* 455; Cathy Lysack, 'Modernity, Postmodernity and Disability in Developing Countries' (1997) 20 *International Journal of Rehabilitation Research* 121; Colins Barnes and Alison Sheldon, 'Disability, Politics and Poverty in a Majority World Context' (2010) 25 *Disability & Society* 771.

Conclusion

The policy discourse on disability and employment has clearly shifted, from traditional narratives of paternalism and compensation towards arguments based on social inclusion and employment rights. Yet the challenge of achieving full participation and equality in employment by disabled people remains very great for policymakers. Despite the widespread implementation of non-discrimination provisions in law, there has been relatively little demonstrable improvement in overall levels of employment for disabled people.[78] The same is true for the operation of employment quota schemes over a much longer period.[79] There is some evidence that various combinations of ALMPs create better employment outcomes than any single approach,[80] and that there is a need to address both social and physical barriers to employment. More widely there is still a concern amongst disability advocates that the way in which we conceptualise work expectation in relation to disability also needs to change – or that a more fundamental reassessment of what work means is required in order to achieve an inclusive labour market.

78 OECD (n 21); Chon-Kyun Kim 'Comparative Perspectives on Disability Employment Policy' (2010) 15 *International Review of Public Administration* 27.
79 See Lisa Waddington (1994) 1 (n 35); and Lisa Waddington (1996) 18 (n 35).
80 APPLICA, CESEP and European Centre (n 8); Kim (n 78).

6

DISABLED PEOPLE AND ACCESS TO JUSTICE

From disablement to enablement?

Anna Lawson

Introduction

This chapter focuses on the (non)interaction between justice systems and people who have, or who are perceived to have, 'impairments'. It will reflect on how such people are disadvantaged and excluded, or 'disabled', by the justice system and also on the potential afforded by the UN Convention on the Rights of Persons with Disabilities (CRPD) to address these problems and thereby contribute to processes of 'enablement'. It will thus engage with the questions for law and legal scholarship posed by the social model of disability, outlined elsewhere in this book.[1]

In an attempt to ensure clarity, the first main section of this chapter will be devoted to the meaning of the term 'access to justice'. Several different usages of the term will be identified and the associated differences in meaning explained. The second main section will address the disabling potential of the justice system. A range of barriers which commonly obstruct disabled people's access to justice will be explored. Barriers created directly by legal rules will be integrated into this discussion rather than being made the subject of a separate discrete section.[2] In the third and final main section attention will turn to the enabling potential of Article 13 of the CRPD, and UN human rights law more generally, to address the problems outlined in the second section.

Access to justice – usages and meanings

The term 'access to justice' is used in a variety of contexts to convey a range of different meanings. Three broad contexts in which the term is used are particularly relevant for present purposes. In the first two of these, the meaning conveyed is essentially the same. In the third, however, it is slightly different. Each of these three contexts will be explained in turn at the outset of this chapter in order to facilitate the subsequent discussion.

---

1 See A Lawson and M Priestley, 'The Social Model of Disability: Questions for Law and Legal Scholarship', Chapter 1, this volume.
2 The question of how substantive law 'disables' people with impairments was treated as a separate question from how the operation of the justice system disables them in the chapter referred to in n1 above. However, as noted there, the questions overlap and addressing both of them in one section works well for present purposes.

First, 'access to justice' is used to connect a body of academic work which addresses this topic. The academic study of access to justice is rooted in the extensive work carried out by Cappelletti and his colleagues in the 1970s.[3] According to Cappelletti and Garth:

> The words 'access to justice' are admittedly not easily defined, but they serve to focus on two basic purposes of the legal system. . . . First, the system must be equally accessible to all; second, it must lead to results that are individually and socially just.[4]

Since that time, writings on the subject have continued apace.[5]

Like disability studies, access to justice scholarship has tended to be action-orientated, with an ambition to facilitate social change. It, too, has enjoyed a strong focus on exposing and addressing social inequality. It is slightly surprising therefore that disability has emerged only relatively recently as an explicit focus of access to justice literature.[6]

Second, the term 'access to justice' is also used as a focus of campaigns and other calls for justice to be made available to all. In England and Wales, dramatic cuts in legal aid funding[7] and increases in court and tribunal fees[8] have recently triggered a number of energetic campaigns under this banner (including ones led by the Law Society of England and Wales, the Citizens Advice Bureau and the Access to Justice Group). Used in this sense, 'access to justice'

---

3 See e.g. M Cappelletti, J Gordley and E Johnson, *Toward Equal Justice: A Comparative Study of Legal Aid in Modern Societies* (Oceana, 1975); and M Cappelletti and J Jolowicz, *Public Interest Parties and the Active Role of the Judge in Civil Litigation* (Oceana, 1975); B Garth and M Cappelletti, 'Access to Justice: The Newest Wave in the Worldwide Movement to Make Rights Effective' (1978) 27(2) *Buffalo Law Review* 181; and the four volume set, consisting of M Cappelletti and B Garth (eds), *Volume I – Access to Justice: A World Survey* (Sijthoff & Noordhoff, 1978); M Cappelletti and J Weisner (eds), *Volume II – Access to Justice: Studies of Promising Institutions* (Sijthoff & Noordhoff, 1978); M Cappelletti and B Garth (eds), *Volume III – Access to Justice: Emerging Perspectives and Issues* (Sijthoff & Noordhoff, 1979); and K Koch (ed), *Volume IV – Patterns in Conflict Management: Essays in the Ethnography of Law. Access to Justice in an Anthropological Perspective* (Sijthoff & Noordhoff, 1979).
4 M Cappelletti and B Garth, 'Access to Justice: The Newest Wave in the Worldwide Movement to Make Rights Effective' (1978) 27(2) *Buffalo Law Review* 181.
5 See e.g. Y Ghai and J Cottrell (eds), *Marginalised Communities and Access to Justice* (Routledge, 2010); I Van de Meene and B Van Rooij, *Access to Justice and Legal Empowerment: Making the Poor Central in Legal Development Co-operation* (Leiden University Press, 2008); F Francioni (ed), *Access to Justice as a Human Right* (Open University Press, 2007); H Genn, *Judging Civil Justice* (Cambridge University Press, 2010); JM Jacobs, *Civil Justice in the Age of Human Rights* (Ashgate, 2007); D Rhode, *Access to Justice* (Open University Press, 2005).
6 See e.g. S Ortoleva, 'Inaccessible Justice: Human Rights, Persons with Disabilities and the Legal System', (2011) 17 *ILSA Journal of International and Comparative Law* 281; P Swift, K Johnson, V Mason, N Shiyyab and S Porter, *What Happens When People with Learning Disabilities Need Advice about the Law?* (Nora Fry Institute, 2013); E Flynn, 'Making Human Rights Meaningful for People with Disabilities: Advocacy, Access to Justice and Equality before the Law' (2013) 17(4) *International Journal of Human Rights* 491; E Flynn and A Lawson, 'Disability and Access to Justice in the European Union: Implications of the UN Convention on the Rights of Persons with Disabilities' (2013) 4 *European Yearbook of Disability Law* 7; D Larson, 'Access to Justice for Persons with Disabilities: An Emerging Strategy' (2014) 3 *Laws* 220; E Flynn, *Disabled Justice: Access to Justice and the UN Convention on the Rights of Persons with Disabilities* (Ashgate, 2015). There is also a growing body of closely related literature focusing on particular issues which have direct implications for access to justice (such as legal capacity, participation in legal proceedings and disability hate crime and victimisation).
7 Following, in particular, the Legal Aid Sentencing and Punishment of Offenders Act 2012.
8 See e.g. Civil Proceedings and Family Proceedings Fees (Amendment) Order 2015.

becomes a political claim for an inclusive, affordable and impartial justice system – a claim which is often presented as inseparable from a claim to a functioning and fair democracy. Thus, according to Liberty:

> Access to justice and the right to a fair hearing are fundamental to the rule of law and any just society which values dignity and fairness.[9]

and in the words of the Lord Chief Justice:

> Some would say that with such dramatic reduction, our system will break. But that cannot be permitted. If it breaks we lose more than courts, tribunals, lawyers, and judges. We lose our ability to function as a liberal democracy capable of prospering on the world stage, whilst securing the rule of law and prosperity at home.[10]

Alongside these uses of the term 'access to justice' is a third which, although closely linked, has a different function. The term is increasingly being used to describe the bundle of rights relating to the justice system which are recognised in human rights law. For example, it is the title given to Article 13 of the CRPD. When used to refer to entitlements conferred by existing law, the right to 'access to justice' means something more precise and more rooted in legal provisions than the more expansive and aspirational meanings often attached to it for purposes of campaigning or academic study. In this chapter, the term will be used in both senses but an attempt will be made to ensure clarity about which is being used at any particular time.

Disablement: Examples of disabling factors at work in justice systems

Although space constraints prevent a detailed analysis of all the factors that disadvantage or exclude people with impairments in connection with the justice system, an attempt will be made to draw attention to some of them. This discussion will include consideration of factors which impede access to the justice system both for disabled people who have claims they might be able to bring against others and also for disabled people who face claims (civil or criminal) brought against them. Examples will be drawn predominantly from the UK simply because they are the ones to which I have easiest access. However, this should not be understood as suggesting that the situation is more problematic in the UK than in other countries. The discussion will be organised by reference to the timeframe of a person's engagement with the system – but it should be noted that many of the barriers identified will operate at more than one of the three broad stages identified and that connections between them are multiple and complex.

---

9 https://www.liberty-human-rights.org.uk/campaigning/justice-within-reach, last accessed 2 April 2015.

10 Lord Thomas of Cwmgiedd, 'Reshaping Justice' (3 March 2014), available at http://www.judiciary.gov. uk/announcements/lcj-speech-reshaping-justice/, last accessed 6 April 2015. See also, *Access to Justice: Practice Note*, United Nations Development Programme (Sept. 3, 2004), 3, available at http://www.undp. org/governance/docs/Justice_PN_English.pdf, last accessed 6 April 2015.

Before legal proceedings

A multitude of factors combine with the result that disabled people surprisingly seldom appear to resort to legal proceedings to challenge wrongs done to them.[11] However, it is difficult to begin any account of the barriers which prevent disabled people accessing justice with anything other than a discussion of laws restricting legal capacity.[12] As illustrated by a range of cases that have come before the European Court of Human Rights,[13] laws on plenary or partial guardianship may transfer to a guardian, and away from a disabled person, all powers to enter into legal acts and all ability to engage with a lawyer or the legal system. Thus, the person concerned may find themselves in the Kafkaesque position of being unable to bring legal claims independently of their guardian – even if those claims relate to the decision to place them under guardianship or concern decisions made by their guardian with which they disagree and which have profound implications for their lives (e.g. that they should have invasive medical treatment or live in a social care institution or hospital).

As Flynn eloquently explains, even where legal capacity is restricted on the basis of a functional test, serious access to justice barriers arise where a person judged to lack capacity to litigate is denied the chance to choose their own legal adviser.[14] This is well illustrated by the English case of *Stokes City Council v. Maddocks*,[15] in which a daughter took her father, who was judged to lack litigation capacity and therefore was represented by the Official Solicitor, out of his care home to see a lawyer. The Court of Protection ruled that the daughter was in contempt of court, because she had contravened a court order that her father should not be removed from the care home. More importantly for present purposes, it warned that the lawyer would have risked being in contempt of court had she provided legal advice to the father.

Another important factor underlying the relatively low number of cases brought by disabled people, particularly people with intellectual disabilities, is lack of awareness of entitlement to claim or even of having been the victim of some kind of wrong-doing.[16] Research conducted

---

11 See e.g. L Clements and J Read, 'The Dog that Didn't Bark: The Issue of Access to Rights Under the ECHR by Disabled People', in A Lawson and C Gooding (eds), *Disability Rights in Europe: From Theory to Practice* (Hart Publishing, 2005); M Jones and LA Basser-Marks, 'The Limitations on the Use of Law to Promote Rights: An Assessment of the Disability Discrimination Act 1992', in M Hauritz, C Sampford, and S Blencowe (eds), *Justice for People with Disabilities – Legal and Institutional Issues* (Federation Press, 1998); Foundation for Law and Justice, *Access to Justice and Legal Need* (Foundation for Law and Justice, 2003).

12 See generally Mental Disability Advocacy Center, 'Guardianship and Human Rights in Bulgaria', 'Guardianship and Human Rights in Czech Republic', and 'Guardianship and Human Rights in Hungary', (2008), available at www.mdac.info. See also EU Agency for Fundamental Rights, 'Legal Capacity of Persons with Intellectual Disabilities and Persons with Mental Health Problems' (2013).

13 See e.g. *Shtukaturov v. Russia*, Application No 44009/05, judgment 27 March 2008, (2008 54 EHRR 27; *Salontaji-Drobnjak v. Serbia*, Application No 36500/05, judgment 13 October 2009; *Stanev v. Bulgaria*, Application No 36760/06, judgment 17 January 2012; and *DD v. Lithuania*, Application No 13469/06, judgment 14 February 2012. For discussion of the European Court of Human Rights approach to these cases, see L Series, 'Legal Capacity and Participation in Litigation: Recent Developments in the European Court of Human Rights' in G Quinn, L Waddington and E Flynn (eds), *European Yearbook on Disability Law* (Intersentia, 2015).

14 E Flynn, *Disabled Justice: Access to Justice and the UN Convention on the Rights of Persons with Disabilities* (Ashgate, 2015) ch 3.

15 *See v. LM & Ors* [2013] EWHC 1137 (COP) 12 April 2012.

16 See e.g. J Lerpiniere and K Stalker, 'Taking Service Providers to Court: People with Learning Disabilities and Part III of the Disability Discrimination Act 1995' (2009) 38 *British Journal of Learning Disabilities* 245; and J Lord, KN Guernsey, JM Balfe, VL Karr and N Flowers (eds), *Human Rights: Yes! Action and Advocacy on the Rights of Persons with Disabilities* (Human Rights Resource Center, 2009), ch 12, para 12.1.

by Hollomotz on sexual assaults revealed that such lack of awareness was often underpinned by inadequate support and education about identifying and responding to inappropriate behaviour.[17]

Even where disabled people are aware of an entitlement to make a claim and have access to information about how to do so, there may be strong disability-related disincentives against initiating legal proceedings.[18] There may be fear of reprisals or the withdrawal of care if the complaint concerns a caregiver in either the community or institutional context.[19] In domestic violence cases, disabled women risk losing their packages of care if they leave the home and may struggle to find an accessible alternative place to go – a problem intensified by the fact that disability services and domestic services tend to be developed separately.[20] For some disabled people, there is also a concern that the outcome of legal proceedings might have negative consequences for them – a factor which will be considered further later in this chapter. The potential inhibiting effect of factors such as these emerges clearly from the responses of several of the people with intellectual disabilities interviewed as part of the EU Agency for Fundamental Rights' study on independent living.[21] In their words

> Well, to complain is to . . . It just means things will be worse for me.
>
> *(Woman, 31, Latvia)*

> I would be too afraid.
>
> *(Woman, 32, Romania)*

> I know lots [of places to lodge a complaint] . . . but I'm always scared they'll find out and then not stand by me.
>
> *(Germany)*

> The manager of the guy who was running the residential home came and gave me a talk and told me that complaints were a threat, and they warned me not to do that again.
>
> *(Man, 54, United Kingdom)*

> What is the use in complaining? He [the director of an institution] would just say it is your own fault!
>
> *(Woman, 41, Latvia)*

. . .

17 See e.g. A Hollomotz, *Learning Difficulties and Sexual Vulnerability: A Social Approach* (Jessica Kingsley Publishers, 2011); and A Hollomotz, '"A Lad Tried to Get Hold of My Boobs, So I Kicked Him": An Examination of Attempts by Adults with Learning Difficulties to Initiate their Own Safeguarding' (2012) 27(1) *Disability & Society* 117.
18 See e.g. Equality and Human Rights Commission, *Hidden in Plain Sight: Inquiry Into Disability-Related Harassment* (Equality and Human Rights Commission, 2011).
19 See e.g. the discussion of these sorts of considerations in P Swift, K Johnson, V Mason, N Shiyyab and S Porter, *What Happens When People with Learning Disabilities Need Advice about the Law?* (Nora Fry Institute, 2013) section 4.4.3.
20 See further e.g. R Thiara, G Hague and A Mullender, 'Losing Out on Both Counts: Disabled Women and Domestic Violence' (2011) 26(6) *Disability & Society* 757; and K Howe, *Violence against Women with Disabilities* (Women with Disabilities Australia, 1999).
21 EU Agency for Fundamental Rights, *Choice and Control: The Right to Independent Living* (Publications Office of the EU, 2012) pp 40–41, available at http://fra.europa.eu/sites/default/files/choice_and_control_en_13.pdf

Respondents also reported bad experiences when trying to secure help from law enforcement officials and the justice system. A young man from a small town in Latvia went to the police after a dispute with his relatives, but felt the police made no effort to help him. When he returned to the police station to sign the necessary documents, an officer made him sign without letting him first read them or his brother, his support person, take part in the conversation. Later, the policeman warned him not to return to the police station. The policeman, the man said, 'threatened to take me to the psychiatric hospital.'

> *[The policeman said] 'Did you not do it?' 'Did you not break your own window? Or chuck paint and eggs at your window?' You must be joking! And that's how they treat you, because you have a learning difficulty. They have no respect for us. And sometimes some police say: 'You shouldn't be out here. You should still be locked up.'*
>
> *(Man, 63, United Kingdom)*[22]

In addition, the potential financial cost of bringing a case may prove prohibitive.[23] Access to financial assistance is likely to be of considerable importance to many disabled people, given the link between poverty and disability and the fact that a disproportionate number of the world's poor are disabled.[24] Alternative dispute resolution mechanisms may be available to disabled people in place of court processes and may reduce some of the barriers associated with cost. However, these alternative systems may be unavailable because of non-financial forms of disabling barrier. Larson has recently drawn attention to the fact that, in the growing trend to solving legal disputes through Online Dispute Resolution mechanisms, ensuring accessibility of those systems for disabled people does not appear to have been given a high priority.[25]

Where disabled people or their supporters do make complaints, responses may be affected by disability-related considerations.[26] This is particularly likely for people with intellectual or psychosocial disabilities, whose credibility may not be regarded as convincing. There is thus evidence, for example, that a disproportionately high number of cases in which complaints of rape are made by women with psychosocial disabilities in England do not proceed to prosecution.[27]

Finally, the quality and accessibility of communications with lawyers and legal advisers emerges as an important factor in the engagement of disabled people in the legal process. This is illustrated

---

22 Ibid., at p 41.
23 See e.g. P Swift, K Johnson, V Mason, N Shiyyab and S Porter, *What Happens When People with Learning Disabilities Need Advice about the Law?* (Nora Fry Institute, 2013) 4.4.5.
24 See e.g. United Nations Economic and Social Council, *Mainstreaming Disability in the Development Agenda, Report for the Commission for Social Development* (46th session 6–15 February 2008).
25 D Larson, 'Access to Justice for Persons with Disabilities: An Emerging Strategy' (2014) 3 *Laws* 220 at 226.
26 See e.g. S J Modell and M Suzanna, 'A Preliminary Assessment of Police Officers' Knowledge and Perceptions of Persons with Disabilities' (2008) 46(3) *Intellectual and Developmental Disabilities* 183; J R Petersilia, 'Crime Victims with Developmental Disabilities: A Review Essay' (2001) 28(6) *Criminal Justice and Behaviour* 655; J McBrien and G Murphy, 'Police and Carers' Views on Reporting Alleged Offences by People with Intellectual Disabilities' (2006) 12(2) *Psychology, Crime & Law* 127.
27 L Ellison et al, 'Challenging Criminal Justice? Psychosocial Disability and Rape Victimisation', (2015) 15(2) *Criminology and Criminal Justice* 225.

by the following observations by participants with intellectual disabilities in research conducted by the Nora Fry Centre in 2013:

> For a start they need a lot of training for people with learning difficulties and disability, not to be rude and arrogant and just sort of pass you to one side. No jargon words and have patience.
>
> *(London)*

> Solicitors are a bit like doctors, they have so much time allotted to a client and they have quite a lot of clients and all I am saying is where they would normally give somebody say half an hour to three quarters of an hour they should give us an hour because sometimes it's very hard for us, we stammer over some of the words that we want to say, some of the words don't come out the way we want them to come out, and I think if they gave us just that little bit more time we would eventually be able to say what we want to say without having to rely on our support.
>
> *(West Midlands)*

> Very patient with me . . . he wrote everything down . . . and also he sat there and he listened to me.
>
> *(London)*

> He more or less he explained a lot of it to me without some of the jargon that you would get with most. Some solicitors they go through all this jargon and you think 'what are they on about' you know and he did explain a lot of it to me as well.
>
> *(London)*[28]

. . .

In light of the importance of adjustments such as these, evidence about the first year of the Civil Legal Advice Telephone Gateway in England and Wales is worrying. This is a telephone help line, introduced in 2013 under the Legal Aid Sentencing and Punishment of Offenders Act 2012, which determines prima face eligibility for legal aid in discrimination, debt and special educational need cases. Legal aid cannot be awarded to anybody who has not passed through this telephone gateway. However, initial evidence suggests that requests for adjustments by disabled callers are not being met. For instance, the review refers to a case in which the request of a man with a hearing impairment to speak to the CLA operator without the call centre's background noise was refused and alternatives such as type talk or webcam chat were not offered.[29]

---

28 P Swift, K Johnson, V Mason, N Shiyyab and S Porter, What Happens When People with Learning Disabilities Need Advice about the Law? (Nora Fry Institute, 2013) sections 4.5.1 and 4.5.2.

29 C Paskell et al, *CLA Mandatory Gateway: Findings from Interviews with Users, MoJ Analytical Series*, December 2014, available at https://www.gov.uk/government/uploads/system/uploads/attachment_data/file/384308/cla-gateway-users-interviews.pdf, p 16, last accessed 6 April 2015.

During legal proceedings[30]

Lack of accessibility of courtrooms and other facilities in which justice is administered is an obvious barrier to access to justice for disabled people. Lack of physical accessibility of court buildings has been the focus of cases in a number of different countries – e.g. the UK,[31] Hungary,[32] the United States,[33] South Africa[34] and Poland.[35] In addition, as Blanck and Larson have stressed, attention needs to be given to the accessibility of technologies and the potential that technology within courtrooms has to overcome traditional access barriers.[36]

Another form of barrier to access to justice which is particularly evident in the course of legal proceedings occurs where legal systems provide for disabled people (e.g. those who are deemed to lack litigation capacity) to be represented by somebody who is advocating for what is considered to be in their 'best interests' even if that is contrary to their expressed wishes. This situation is illustrated by the European Court of Human Rights case of *RP v. UK*,[37] which concerned the State's attempt to remove a child from the care of a mother who had intellectual disabilities. Because she was deemed to lack litigation capacity, the Official Solicitor advised her solicitor on her behalf. The Official Solicitor considered that it was in her best interests not to contest the removal of her child, and consequently her legal representative did not advance the argument she wanted – that she should be permitted to keep her child.

A third form of barrier is also worthy of mention here. This is the failure to provide reasonable accommodations or adjustments to disabled people involved in court proceedings. Whilst there are examples of excellent practice in this regard, problems undoubtedly persist. It is not uncommon, for example, for disability-related adjustments and supports to be made available to victims and witnesses in criminal proceedings, but not to the accused.[38] This is because such adjustments and supports tend to be characterised as 'special measures' which are rooted in efforts to protect people who are 'vulnerable' (e.g. because of fear of reprisals from the accused) and thus are more oriented to protecting victims than those accused. This, however, overlooks the equality-driven requirement for adjustments to be made to court and other processes in order to ensure that disabled people (whether they are the accused or the victim) are able to participate on an equal basis with others. The importance of this point is perhaps reinforced by the fact that estimates suggest that between 20–30 per cent of 'offenders' in England have intellectual disabilities[39] – a figure which seems likely to be replicated elsewhere.

---

30 For a much fuller consideration of the types of barriers that arise during legal proceedings, see E Flynn, *Disabled Justice: Access to Justice and the UN Convention on the Rights of Persons with Disabilities* (Ashgate, 2015) ch 4.

31 See e.g. *Malone v. UK,* Application No 25290/94, admissibility decision 28 February 1996.

32 See e.g. Equal Treatment Authority, Case 13/2006, available at www.egyenlobanasmod.hu, last accessed 6 April 2015.

33 See e.g. *Tennessee v. Lane*, 541 US 509, 512–14 (2004) at para 7.

34 See e.g. *Esthe Muller v. the Justice Department and the Department of Public Works*, 2003, (Equality Court, Germiston Magistrates Court, 01/03).

35 *Monica O v. Prosecutors Office in L*, Polish Supreme Court, 12 April 2012 (II PK 218/11).

36 See e.g. D Larson, 'Access to Justice for Persons with Disabilities: An Emerging Strategy (2014) 3 *Laws* 220; and P Blanck, A Wilichowski and J Schmeling, 'Disability Civil Rights Law and Policy: Accessible Courtroom Technology' (2004) 12 *William and Mary Bill of Rights Journal* 825.

37 (App no 38245/08) [2012] ECHR 1796.

38 See e.g. the Youth Justice and Criminal Evidence Act 1999 (in England and Wales) and the fact that registered intermediaries are not available as of right to 'vulnerable' defendants whereas they are to 'vulnerable' victims.

39 N Loucks, *No One Knows: Offenders with Learning Difficulties and Learning Disabilities – Review of Prevalence and Associated Needs* (Prison Reform Trust, 2007).

After legal proceedings

As mentioned earlier, fear of potentially adverse outcomes might well deter disabled people from making complaints or initiating legal proceedings. Some of these potentially negative outcomes may follow the making of a complaint rather than a court decision or settlement.

Where crimes against disabled people are reported, there is some evidence that outcomes may focus on safeguarding the disabled victim through measures which may be perceived to be intrusive and to reduce independence. Thus, the Equality and Human Rights Commission for England and Wales, in its investigation into disability-related harassment, reported that: 'There is often a focus on the victim, questioning their behaviour and "vulnerability", rather than dealing with the perpetrators.'[40] This is illustrated by the following words of an interviewee quoted in this report:

> I was talking to a woman who basically said that she wouldn't report something like that to the police again because it ended up with teams of safeguarding people and social workers . . . questioning whether she was able to live independently. And she said 'I'm never going to do that again' and 'I felt that the process was completely taken out of my control and essentially somebody had just nicked some money from me, and if that happened to anybody else their capacity to live in their own home would not have been the first question everybody asked'.[41]

In the civil context too, a successful claim for damages brought by a disabled person (particularly if he or she has intellectual or psychosocial disabilities) may be accompanied by curtailments on independence and autonomy. These sometimes take the form of guardianship or wardship arrangements, designed to ensure that the disabled person is able to manage the money they have acquired by way of damages. Too often, however, such schemes take the form of subjecting the disabled person to the wishes of another instead of supporting and enabling them to follow their own life paths.

Another negative outcome of making a complaint, particularly for mothers with intellectual disabilities, is the loss of parental care of children. According to a 2012 study on women with intellectual disabilities who had experienced domestic abuse within intimate relationships:

> Some of the women who had children disclosed the domestic abuse to Social Services in desperation to leave the relationship. Their pleas for help were dismissed; family work was implemented; when this failed and the abuse escalated, Social Services removed the children.[42]

Finally, a word should be said about the outcomes of legal proceedings in which disabled people are accused of criminal acts. Particularly relevant to access to justice are schemes which divert

---

40 Equality and Human Rights Commission, *Hidden in Plain Sight: Investigation Into Disability-Related Harassment* (EHRC, 2011) p 130.
41 Ibid. at p 150.
42 A Walter-Brice, R Cox, H Priest and F Thompson 'What Do Women with Learning Disabilities Say about their Experiences of Domestic Abuse within the Context of their Intimate Partner Relationships?' (2012) 27(4) *Disability & Society*, 503 at 510.

people deemed 'unfit to plead' (e.g. on the basis of psychosocial or intellectual disability) into forms of detention without an opportunity to stand trial. As Tina Minkowitz has observed:

> In most cases, insanity acquittals and declarations of unfitness to plead result not in release from custody and supervision but in transfer to the forensic mental health system, which, like its civil counterpart, is characterised by indefinite detention according to the judgment of medical professionals and by the administration of mind-altering drugs and other psychiatric interventions as a security measure and as non-consensual treatment.[43]

In addition, disabled people accused of crimes may be detained for long periods of time before trial because of the difficulties of finding an accessible or appropriate court in which to try them.[44] All too often it is the court that is unfit to try the person rather than the person who is not fit to be tried by the court.

Enablement: The potential of Article 13 of the Convention on the Rights of Persons with Disabilities?

The text

Article 13 of the CRPD is entitled 'Access to Justice' and is the first article in a UN human rights treaty to use this phrase. It reads as follows:

> (1) States Parties shall ensure effective access to justice for persons with disabilities on an equal basis with others, including through the provision of procedural and age-appropriate accommodations, in order to facilitate their effective role as direct and indirect participants, including as witnesses, in all legal proceedings, including at investigative and other preliminary stages.
>   (2) In order to help to ensure effective access to justice for persons with disabilities, States Parties shall promote appropriate training for those working in the field of administration of justice, including police and prison staff.

This articulation of a right to access justice is thus highly innovative. It includes explicit reference to the need for 'procedural and age-appropriate accommodations' and also for disability-related training. However, there is much that is left unstated and which requires regard to be had to other human rights treaty provisions and their interpretation. For current purposes, these additional human rights treaty provisions can helpfully be divided into two categories – first, those from other treaties which concern rights relevant to the justice system; and, second, other provisions of the CRPD which underpin and give shape to Article 13.

---

43 T Minkowitz, 'Rethinking Criminal Responsibility from a Critical Disability Perspective: The Abolition of Insanity/Incapacity Acquittals and Unfitness to Plead, and Beyond' (2015) 23 (3) *Griffith Law Review* 434 at 435.
44 See e.g. Open Society Foundations, *Presumption of Guilt: The Global Over Use of Pre-Trial Detention* (OSF, 2014) – which draws attention to the disproportionate numbers of people with mental health conditions and intellectual disabilities held in pre-trial detention.

Pre-existing UN human rights treaty provisions on the justice system

Article 13(1) of the CRPD opens by imposing on States Parties the obligation to provide 'effective access to justice for persons with disabilities on an equal basis with other'. In order to understand what this entails, it is therefore essential to identify what the 'others', to whom reference is made, are entitled. Clearly this will vary from country to country and Article 13 demands that steps are taken by each State Party to ensure that disability-related disadvantage in their justice systems is identified and tackled. Regional human rights treaties also contain a range of provisions relating to the functioning of the justice system but a detailed consideration of these lies beyond the scope of this chapter.[45] What will be outlined briefly here are the provisions of UN human rights law which lay down a baseline for access to justice rights. These are clustered around the right to a fair hearing and the right to an effective remedy, each of which will now be discussed in turn.

Turning first to the right to a fair hearing, Article 10 of the Universal Declaration of Human Rights 1948 (UDHR) recognises the right to a 'fair and public hearing by an independent and impartial tribunal'. The right to a fair hearing also finds expression in Article 14 of the International Covenant on Civil and Political Rights (ICCPR). Whilst the emphasis of this Article is on criminal proceedings and includes, for example, the right to legal aid in that context, Article 14(1) is framed in terms broad enough to include other types of proceeding. According to it:

> In the determination of any criminal charge against him, or of his rights and obligations in a suit at law, everyone shall be entitled to a fair and public hearing by a competent, independent and impartial tribunal established by law.

As early as 1984, in its General Comment 13, the Human Rights Committee drew attention to the fact that this extended to civil and constitutional as well as criminal proceedings.[46] This point was reiterated in its 2007 General Comment 32 (which replaced General Comment 13).[47]

General Comment 32 is also of interest because of its recognition that the right to 'equality before courts and tribunals' guarantees 'equality of arms' as well as non-discrimination. This entails consideration of a range of issues including those concerning finances and interpretation. As regards finances, the Comment notes the potential inconsistency with Article 14(1) of 'the imposition of fees on the parties to proceedings that would de facto prevent their access to justice',[48] and that the 'availability or absence of legal assistance often determines whether or not a person can access the relevant proceedings or participate in them in a meaningful way'.[49] As regards interpretation, the Comment suggests that

> In exceptional cases, it also might require that the free assistance of an interpreter be provided where otherwise an indigent party could not participate in the proceedings on equal terms or witnesses produced by it be examined.[50]

---

45 See, for an excellent discussion, E Flynn, *Disabled Justice: Access to Justice and the UN Convention on the Rights of Persons with Disabilities* (Ashgate, 2015) 25–31.

46 Human Rights Committee, General Comment No 13 – Equality Before the Courts and the Right to a Fair and Public Hearing by an Independent Court Established by Law, (1984) para 2.

47 Human Rights Committee, General Comment No 32 – Article 14: Right to Equality Before Courts and Tribunals and to a Fair Trial, (2007) CCPR/C/GC/32 paras 8–9.

48 Ibid., para 11.

49 Ibid., para 10.

50 Ibid., para 13.

Although there is no explicit mention of disability, the relevance of the interpreter-duty to for example people with hearing or intellectual impairments which prevent them from following proceedings is evident. General Comment 32 also suggested that, read in conjunction with Article 2(3) (on the right to an effective remedy), the need for the State to provide legal assistance in a broad range of cases can be inferred from Article 14.[51]

Turning now to the right to an effective remedy, Article 8 of the UDHR provides that everyone has the right to an 'effective remedy by the competent national tribunals for acts violating the fundamental rights granted him by the constitution or by law'. This is elaborated more fully in Article 2(3) of the ICCPR as follows:

3.   Each State Party to the present Covenant undertakes:

(a)   To ensure that any person whose rights or freedoms as herein recognized are violated shall have an effective remedy, notwithstanding that the violation has been committed by persons acting in an official capacity;

(b)   To ensure that any person claiming such a remedy shall have his right thereto determined by competent judicial, administrative or legislative authorities, or by any other competent authority provided for by the legal system of the State, and to develop the possibilities of judicial remedy;

(c)   To ensure that the competent authorities shall enforce such remedies when granted.

Guidance on this right is provided in General Comment 31 of the Human Rights Committee.[52] This explains that the obligation concerns remedies for breach of rights created by domestic law as well as rights recognised by the ICCPR and stresses that the remedies must be 'appropriately adapted so as to take account of the special vulnerability of certain categories of person'.[53] The right includes entitlement to the investigation of a potential violation and cessation of a violation, to reparation, which might involve 'restitution, rehabilitation and measures of satisfaction, such as public apologies, public memorials, guarantees of non-repetition and changes in relevant laws and practices, as well as bringing to justice the perpetrators'.[54]

There is no explicit right to an effective remedy in the International Covenant on Economic Social and Cultural Rights (ICESCR). However, in its General Comment 9,[55] the Committee on Economic, Social and Cultural Rights (CESCR) recognised that such a right was implicitly incorporated into the Covenant.

In attempting to understand the nature of the obligations imposed by Article 13 of the CRPD then, these provisions (together with their associated guidance and jurisprudence) form an essential reference point. They help to throw light on what UN human rights law requires of States Parties as regards ensuring the existence and effectiveness of fair hearings and access to effective remedies. Whilst the principle of equality is enshrined in these more general human rights treaty provisions, Article 13 of the CRPD provides an important mechanism for ensuring that there is full engagement with what this will entail for disabled people.

---

51 Ibid., para 10.
52 Human Rights Committee, General Comment No 31 – The Nature of the General Legal Obligation Imposed on States Parties to the Covenant, (2004) CCPR/C/GC/31 paras 15–20.
53 Ibid., para 15.
54 Ibid., para 16.
55 Committee on Economic, Social and Cultural Rights, General Comment No 9 – The Domestic Application of the Covenant, (1998) E/C.12/1998/24.

Associated provisions of the Convention on the Rights of Persons with Disabilities

In addition to justice-related provisions in other UN human rights treaties, any attempt to understand the obligations imposed by Article 13 of the CRPD must look to other provisions of the CRPD itself. Foremost amongst these are the cross-cutting provisions on non-discrimination and accessibility. However, the allied rights to equality before the law and to freedom from violence, exploitation and abuse are also of particular significance. A few words will therefore be devoted to each of these issues here. Before doing this, however, it should be noted that the Convention explicitly requires attention to be given to the situation of disabled women and disabled children throughout.[56]

Article 5 of the CRPD addresses equality and non-discrimination – concepts which are also acknowledged to be general principles and obligations of the Convention by Articles 3 and 4 respectively. It therefore plays an important role in explaining the reference in Article 13 to ensuring that access to justice is provided to disabled people 'on an equal basis with others'.

A point that merits particular note is that the obligations not to discriminate extend to all participants including witnesses and jury members. Thus, the Reporting Guidelines of the Committee on the Rights of Persons with Disabilities request States to report on the 'availability of reasonable accommodations . . . that are made in the legal process to ensure effective participation of all types of persons with disabilities in the justice system, whatever the role in which they find themselves (for example as victims, perpetrators, witnesses or jury members and others)'.[57] The reach of this non-discrimination duty is therefore wider in scope than that of the duties emanating from the rights to a fair hearing and an effective remedy –the emphasis of the latter duties being on the person bringing a claim or against whom a claim is made rather than on all participants in the process.

Article 5 makes it clear that action which is discriminatory in purpose or effect must be prohibited. It also makes it clear that a failure to provide a reasonable accommodation will also amount to discrimination[58] and therefore falls within the scope of what must be prohibited. A reasonable accommodation, in this context, requires an adjustment to standard practice or procedure in order to remove a particular disadvantage at which a specific disabled person would otherwise be placed in their attempt to access justice.[59] Examples might include the timetabling of a case (for instance by avoiding an early morning start for a person taking certain types of medication); allowing more frequent breaks for a person with a physical impairment which requires this; allowing a sign language interpreter or reader to accompany a person with sensory impairments; or communicating with a deaf person who has visited a police station in writing rather than orally.

Article 13(1) does not explicitly mention reasonable accommodation, but it does require States to ensure that 'procedural and age appropriate accommodations' are carried out. The relationship between such accommodations and 'reasonable accommodation' is not explained. It seems, however, that these procedural and age-related accommodations may be more generic and less individualised in nature. Further, it seems likely that the obligation to provide them cannot be mitigated by arguments about reasonableness and the extent of the burden they would place on the duty-bearer. If such a distinction is made, then it would only be those failures to make

---

56 Articles 6 and 7 respectively.
57 United Nations Committee on the Rights of Persons with Disabilities, *Reporting Guidelines on Treaty Specific Document to be Submitted by States Parties under Article 35(1) of the UN Convention on the Rights of Persons with Disabilities*, (United Nations, 2009).
58 See Article 2, UN CRPD, for a definition of 'discrimination' which includes a failure to provide a reasonable accommodation.
59 Article 2, CRPD, (2006).

individualised adjustments that would have been reasonable, and not imposed an undue or disproportionate burden, that could found claims for discrimination – but States would be under more programmatic duties to ensure that accommodations are integrated into the design and delivery of the justice system.

Article 9 and Article 21 of the CRPD require accessibility considerations to be factored into the justice system as well as elsewhere. Article 21 focuses on the accessibility of information and communication, whereas Article 9 is broader in scope – requiring States to ensure the physical accessibility of buildings and spaces open to the public;[60] the provision of live assistance and intermediaries such as sign-language interpreters;[61] accessible signage, including in Braille and easy-to-read formats;[62] accessible information and communication technologies;[63] and other forms of assistance and support needed to ensure access to information.[64] Guidance on Article 9 is set out in General Comment 2 of the Committee on the Rights of Persons with Disabilities, which includes an acknowledgement that:

> There can be no effective access to justice if the buildings in which law-enforcement agencies and the judiciary are located are not physically accessible, or if the services, information and communication they provide are not accessible to persons with disabilities.[65]

There is clearly considerable potential for overlap in the operation of requirements for reasonable accommodation, procedural and age-sensitive accommodation and accessibility. However, this overlap need not lead to a duplication of the effort required to discharge the various duties. It is beyond doubt that the greater the degree of accessibility that can be incorporated into the justice system, the lower will be the likelihood of individual reasonable accommodations being required.[66]

Article 12 of the CRPD is entitled 'equal recognition before the law' and acknowledges that disabled people are persons before the law and have rights to exercise their legal capacity on an equal basis with everybody else. It therefore constitutes a head-on challenge to traditional wardship and guardianship laws which deprive disabled people of their legal capacity. The connection between Articles 12 and 13 is extremely close and readily apparent – as demonstrated by the fact that in the early drafts of the Convention, what is now Article 13 spent time within the boundaries of what has become Article 12.[67] Without the recognition of legal personality, there can be no access to justice and, without access to justice, the right to be recognised as an equal before the law is worthless.

Article 16 of the CRPD guarantees a right to be free from exploitation violence and abuse, and thus has a particular relevance to cases in which disabled people are actual (or potential)

---

60 Article 9(1)(a), CRPD, (2006).
61 Ibid., Article 9(2)(e).
62 Ibid., Article 9(2)(d).
63 Ibid., Article 9(2)(g)–(h).
64 Ibid., Article 9(2)(f).
65 Committee on the Rights of Persons with Disabilities, General Comment No 2 – Article 9: Accessibility, (2014) crpd/c/gc/2, para 37.
66 See further A Lawson, Disability Equality, 'Reasonable Accommodation and the Avoidance of Ill-Treatment in Places of Detention: What Role for Monitoring and Inspection Bodies?' (2012) *International Journal of Human Rights* 845.
67 For further discussion of this, see e.g. E Flynn, *Disabled Justice: Access to Justice and the UN Convention on the Rights of Persons with Disabilities* (Ashgate, 2015) 31–35; and E Flynn and A Lawson, 'Disability and Access to Justice in the European Union: Implications of the UN Convention on the UN Convention on the Rights of Persons with Disabilities' (2013) 4 *European Yearbook of Disability Law* 7.

victims of crime. It imposes a range of obligations on States Parties which, if effectively executed, would certainly go some way to addressing the access to justice barriers facing disabled crime victims identified in the previous section of this chapter. For this reason, it is worth setting out the Article in full here. It reads as follows:

(1) States Parties shall take all appropriate legislative, administrative, social, educational and other measures to protect persons with disabilities, both within and outside the home, from all forms of exploitation, violence and abuse, including their gender-based aspects.

(2) States Parties shall also take all appropriate measures to prevent all forms of exploitation, violence and abuse by ensuring, inter alia, appropriate forms of gender- and age-sensitive assistance and support for persons with disabilities and their families and caregivers, including through the provision of information and education on how to avoid, recognise and report instances of exploitation, violence and abuse. States Parties shall ensure that protection services are age-, gender- and disability-sensitive.

(3) In order to prevent the occurrence of all forms of exploitation, violence and abuse, States Parties shall ensure that all facilities and programmes designed to serve persons with disabilities are effectively monitored by independent authorities.

(4) States Parties shall take all appropriate measures to promote the physical, cognitive and psychological recovery, rehabilitation and social reintegration of persons with disabilities who become victims of any form of exploitation, violence or abuse, including through the provision of protection services. Such recovery and reintegration shall take place in an environment that fosters the health, welfare, self-respect, dignity and autonomy of the person and takes into account gender- and age-specific needs.

(5) States Parties shall put in place effective legislation and policies, including women- and child-focused legislation and policies, to ensure that instances of exploitation, violence and abuse against persons with disabilities are identified, investigated and, where appropriate, prosecuted.

Conclusion

In this chapter I have sought to introduce the idea of 'access to justice' as a subject of academic study and the focus of campaigning activity as well as a human right. It is clear from the second main section in this chapter that disabled people may encounter a wide range of disadvantages or barriers to accessing justice through legal proceedings. Thus, the justice system itself contributes to the disablement of people with impairments. The extent of this disablement and of any progress in efforts to reduce it is, however, impossible to gauge. There is very little relevant data on the participation of disabled people in the justice system. This is a key finding of the 2015 ten-country EU-funded project on access to justice for children with intellectual and psychosocial impairments.[68] It is also reflected in the following words of the Equality and Human Rights Commission of England and Wales in its 2011 report on disability-related harassment:

> We found major gaps in evidence gathering by public authorities relating to disability harassment across all sectors. Schools don't know how many disabled pupils are bullied; local authorities and registered social landlords don't know how many antisocial

---

68 See further A Lawson, 'Access to Justice for Children with 'Mental Disabilities': The Collection and Dissemination of Data' (March 2015), available at http://www.mdac.info/en/access-to-justice-for-children, last accessed 6 April 2015.

behaviour victims are disabled; health services don't know how many assault victims are disabled; police don't know how many victims of crime are disabled; the courts don't know how many disabled victims have access to special measures, what proportion of offences against disabled victims result in conviction or how many of these offences result in a sentence uplift; and the prisons don't know how many offenders are serving sentences for crimes motivated by hostility to disabled people.

This lack of data compounds public authorities' lack of understanding of disability-related harassment. Without such data it is impossible for authorities to understand disability-related harassment in their area, assess the effectiveness of their responses to it and develop interventions to prevent it.[69]

One of the purposes of the CRPD was to raise the visibility of the human rights violations experienced by disabled people by heightening the profile of duties on States to collect data on the situation on the ground. Thus, in addition to the obligations on States Parties to report to the CRPD Committee on a regular basis, Article 31 of the Convention imposes obligations to collect and disseminate data relevant to the lives of disabled people and their participation in society. It is to be hoped that this Article, and the CRPD generally, can be used to boost efforts to collect relevant data about the inclusiveness and accessibility of the justice system and about what happens to disabled people within it.

The final main section of the chapter was devoted to outlining the broad scope and content of Article 13 of the CRPD. This is the first human rights treaty provision to be entitled 'access to justice' and the first to focus explicitly on the engagement of disabled people in the justice system. Its implications can be understood only in light of analysis of the development of pre-existing justice-related rights – which make up the constituent elements of Article 13 – and also of related provisions in the CRPD. When given this contextual reading, Article 13 clearly promises significant potential as a lever to squeeze out disabling barriers and create space for inclusive and enabling structures and practices in the justice system. The extent to which this promise will be realised will depend partly on issues of participation by disabled people and their organisations:

The first type of participation which is important for current purposes is the participation of disabled people and their representative organisations in the process of CRPD implementation and monitoring. The foundations for this are laid by Article 4(3) of the Convention, according to which:

> In the development and implementation of legislation and policies to implement the present Convention, and in other decision-making processes concerning issues relating to persons with disabilities, States Parties shall closely consult with and actively involve persons with disabilities, including children with disabilities, through their representative organizations.[70]

In the specific context of access to justice, the participation of disabled people in the operation of the justice system itself is also of crucial significance – as Eilionóir Flynn and I have argued elsewhere.[71] Article 29 of the CRPD can be interpreted as requiring States Parties to take steps

---

69 Equality and Human Rights Commission, *Hidden in Plain Sight: Inquiry into Disability-Related Harassment* (Equality and Human Rights Commission, 2011) p 95.
70 See also Article 33(3).
71 E Flynn and A Lawson, 'Disability and Access to Justice in the European Union: Implications of the UN Convention on the Rights of Persons with Disabilities' (2013) 4 *European Yearbook of Disability Law* 7.

to ensure that disabled people are encouraged and supported to take on public roles in the justice system – including as jurors (in countries in which the jury system is used), as judges and members of lay tribunals or panels. Article 29(b) requires States to '[p]romote actively an environment in which persons with disabilities can effectively and fully participate in the conduct of public affairs, without discrimination and on an equal basis with others, and encourage their participation in public affairs'.

As Genn has stressed, there is considerable social value in ensuring that opportunities to participate in the judiciary are not confined to a narrow sector of society. In her words:

> It is simply no longer acceptable for an institution of such power and influence to appear to exclude well-qualified candidates who are neither male nor white. . . . The shortage of women and minority ethnic judges, in particular in more senior positions, is and should be interpreted as exclusion from power. The diversity issue is about participation in powerful practices. It is about participation in the small and large decisions that shape the society in which we live.[72]

Entitlement to participate on an equal basis with others in the justice system, not simply as litigant or judge, but also in capacities such as witness, juror,[73] lawyer or magistrate is an essential element of citizenship, failure to address which will condemn to failure attempts to enhance access to justice for disabled people in other respects.

In conclusion, it is fitting to close with some reflections on the importance of access to justice to individuals from marginalised communities, including disabled people, who are frequently subjected to a range of rights violations. In the words of the Director of the EU Agency for Fundamental Rights:

> The possibility of enforcing a right is central to making fundamental rights a reality. Access to justice is not just a right in itself but also an enabling and empowering right in so far as it allows individuals to enforce their rights and obtain redress. In this sense, it transforms fundamental rights from theory into practice.[74]

Similarly, according to Cappelletti himself,

> The human rights philosophy has been the most important contribution not only of the West, but of humankind generally, to political science and moral philosophy. What is new in our epoch, however, is the full recognition of the insufficiency of a mere philosophy of human rights – the recognition, that is, that adequate machinery and processes are needed to make those rights effective.[75]

---

72 H Genn, *Judging Civil Justice* (Cambridge University Press, 2010), 153. See also S Ortoleva, 'Inaccessible Justice: Human Rights, Persons with Disabilities and the Legal System', (2011) 17 *ILSA Journal of International and Comparative Law* 281.

73 See V D Amar, 'Jury Service as Political Participation Akin to Voting', (1994–1995) 80 *Cornell Law Review* 203.

74 EU Agency for Fundamental Rights, *Access to Justice: An Overview of Challenges and Opportunities* (EU Agency for Fundamental Rights, 2011).

75 M Cappelletti, 'Human Rights and the Proceduralist's Role', in Scott (ed), *International Perspectives on Civil Justice* (Sweet and Maxwell, 1990) p 2.

7

HIT AND MISS

Procedural accommodations ensuring the effective access of people with mental disabilities to the European Court of Human Rights

Constantin Cojocariu

Introduction

Persons with mental disabilities[1] in Eastern Europe suffer from high and well-documented rates of discrimination and abuse, which are often embedded in the law. Phenomena such as large-scale institutionalization or denial of legal capacity are frequently described as benevolent measures aimed at ensuring the welfare of those concerned. The advent of the UN Convention on the Rights of Persons with Disabilities (hereinafter referred to as the 'CRPD'), widely ratified across Europe, highlighted these structural inequities and framed them as violations of basic human rights. The European Court of Human Rights (hereinafter referred to as 'the Court'), as the pre-eminent regional mechanism for human rights protection, would appear to hold great potential for those seeking to challenge the status quo and achieve systemic change. However, its output on disability rights to date has been quite limited and rather disappointing. The physical, social and economic barriers that hinder access to justice at all levels of the judicial system may at least partially explain this dearth of jurisprudence. At the same time, many disability cases that do reach the Court are dismissed on admissibility grounds, revealing a lack of comprehension on the part of the Strasbourg judges of the specificity of disability rights claims, or result in judgments that often replicate and legitimize the oppressive narratives and structural discrimination that are prevalent at the national level.[2] A close inspection of the Court's jurisprudence reveals how procedural devices such as 'standing', 'material scope', 'legal representation', 'margin of appreciation', 'exhaustion of domestic remedies' have been used to render disability claims non-justiciable under the European Convention on Human Rights (hereinafter 'the Convention').

---

1 While acknowledging the variety of terminology in use, the term 'mental disabilities' as used in this article is understood to comprise people with psychosocial disabilities and those with intellectual disabilities.
2 See further L. Clements, *Disability, Dignity and the Cri de Coeur*, [2011] E.H.R.L.R., Issue 6, pp. 675–685, and L. Clements, J. Read, *The Dog that Didn't Bark: The Issue of Access to Rights under the European Convention on Human Rights by Disabled People*, in A. Lawson, C. Gooding (eds.), *Disability Rights in Europe: From Theory to Practice* (Oxford/Portland, Oregon: Hart Publishing, 2005), pp. 21–34.

This chapter examines recent jurisprudential developments on disability rights in an attempt to decipher whether disabled people benefit from 'practical and effective'[3] access to the Court. The relevant reference point is Article 13 of the CRPD on access to justice, which requires States Parties to 'ensure effective access to justice for persons with disabilities on an equal basis with others, including through the provision of procedural . . . accommodations, in order to facilitate their effective role . . . in all legal proceedings'. For its part, the Court has also emphasized that 'special procedural safeguards may prove called for in order to protect the interests of persons who, on account of their mental disabilities, are not fully capable of acting for themselves'.[4] This chapter offers a practitioner's perspective, based on the author's 10-year experience of litigating high profile disability cases before the Court.[5]

The first part of the chapter examines the concept of 'de facto representation' introduced for the first time recently in the case *Câmpeanu v. Romania*, and its potential implications for proxies seeking to introduce complaints on behalf of people with disabilities suffering from abuse, lacking relatives or other guardians and who are unable to instruct a lawyer. The second part of the chapter explores the manner in which the Court deals with disabled applicants unable to secure adequate legal representation. The Court's practice in this respect has been quite diverse, revealing a deeper ambivalence in its jurisprudence towards measures that interfere with a person's legal capacity in the form of partial or plenary guardianship. Finally, the last part looks more closely at some of the recent changes in the Court's procedure, and in particular the ongoing move to tighten as well as enforce more strictly the admissibility criteria for individual petitions, likely to have a disproportionate impact on disabled applicants.

The concept of de facto representation after *Câmpeanu*

Valentin Câmpeanu was an HIV-positive intellectually disabled young man, who lived all his life in state institutions and who lacked any known relatives or a designated guardian. Upon reaching majority age in 2003, the authorities decided to transfer him to an adults' institution. After several mishandled transfers between a social care home and a psychiatric hospital, either of which refused to take responsibility for him, Câmpeanu died in brutal circumstances, having been withheld basic medical treatment, and in extremely substandard living conditions. The Centre for Legal Resources (hereinafter referred to as 'the CLR'), a Romanian non-governmental organization, witnessed his plight just before he died during a routine monitoring visit to the psychiatric hospital in question, and immediately started campaigning on his behalf. After failing to secure accountability at the national level, the CLR lodged an application with the Court in 2008. Although the main purpose of the case was to shed light on the blatant abuses that take place in closed institutions in Romania, it also tested the manner in which the Court construed the notion of standing in cases brought by third parties seeking to complain of abuses taking place in closed institutions against persons with disabilities lacking a legal guardian and who are unable to instruct a lawyer for various reasons.

---

3 The Court stated that 'the Convention is intended to guarantee not rights that are theoretical or illusory but rights that are practical and effective', *Artico v. Italy*, 13 May 1980, §33, Series A no. 37.
4 *Winterwerp v. the Netherlands*, 24 October 1979, §60, Series A no. 33.
5 Including *Centre for Legal Resources on behalf of Valentin Câmpeanu v. Romania* [GC], no. 47848/08, ECHR 2014 (hereinafter referred to as *Câmpeanu v. Romania*); *Đorđević v. Croatia*, no. 41526/10, ECHR 2012; *D.D. v. Lithuania*, no. 13469/06, 14 February 2012 and *Farcaş v. Romania* (dec.), no. 32596/04, 14 September 2010.

In a long-awaited judgment, on 17 July 2014 the Grand Chamber declared the case admissible and ruled that there had been a breach of Article 2 of the Convention on the right to life and of Article 13 on the right to an effective remedy.[6] The Court also determined that the facts revealed a 'wider problem' and called on the Romanian Government to 'envisage the necessary general measures to ensure that mentally disabled persons in a situation comparable to that of Mr. Câmpeanu, are afforded independent representation, enabling them to have Convention complaints relating to their health and treatment examined before a court or other independent body'.[7] Notably, Judge de Albuquerque issued a hard-hitting concurring opinion, in which it criticized the majority for its 'casuistic and restricted' approach, and proposed an 'alternative principled reasoning' on the concept of 'de facto representation'.[8]

The requirements for individual access to proceedings before the Court, in particular those related to standing and victim status, have generated a rather convoluted jurisprudence.[9] In principle, only living individuals may validly lodge an application, either in person or through a proxy possessing the requisite authority to act. The Court exceptionally allows close relatives of those who died or disappeared, acting as 'indirect victims', to initiate proceedings concerning the violation of Article 2 on the right to life. If the direct victim died after the events giving rise to the complaint took place, standing depends on a number of factors, including the timing of the death (before or after the Court was seized) and the nature of the rights involved. In relation to the latter criterion, relatives are as a rule only able to take over cases regarding transferrable or pecuniary rights, such as the right to property, but not cases regarding non-transferrable or personal rights, such as the right to liberty. The Convention does not provide for the institution of an *actio popularis*. On rare occasions, the Court departed from these rules in consideration of various circumstances, including the vulnerability of the victims, or in 'the interest of human rights', a notion defined in a discretionary manner.

In its admissibility ruling in *Câmpeanu*, the Court set out by emphasizing that the case did not fall easily within any pre-existing categories and that therefore it 'raised a difficult question of interpretation of the Convention relating to the standing of CLR'.[10] After ruling out the possibility of granting the CLR status as 'indirect victim' due to a lack of a personal interest or of a sufficiently close link with the victim,[11] the Court decided to grant it the status of 'de facto representative', even in the absence of a duly signed power of attorney, bearing in mind the 'exceptional circumstances of the case', as well as 'the serious nature of the allegations'.[12] In order to reach this decision, the Court noted that even during his lifetime, Câmpeanu was in a 'wholly different and less favorable position than that [of applicants] in previous cases', considering that he was de facto denied his legal capacity, and because of his state of 'extreme vulnerability'. This in turn meant that 'he was not capable of initiating any . . . proceedings by himself, without proper legal support and advice'.[13] The Court placed substantial weight on the fact that the CLR had enjoyed *locus standi* to act on Câmpeanu's behalf during proceedings at the national level,[14] and

---

6 *Centre for Legal Resources on behalf of Valentin Câmpeanu v. Romania* [GC], no. 47848/08, ECHR 2014.
7 §160–161.
8 Concurring opinion of Judge Pinto de Albuquerque.
9 This jurisprudence is summarized in *Câmpeanu v. Romania*, §96–102.
10 §105.
11 §107.
12 §112, 114.
13 §108.
14 §110.

on the absence of any next of kin or legal guardians entitled to take care of his interests.[15] The CLR had to have standing, as otherwise serious allegations of human rights violations would not be examined at the international level. The State could not be allowed to escape liability based on its own culpable failure to appoint a legal representative in line with national law, which, the Court strikingly suggested, represented a breach of its obligation under Article 34 of the Convention not to hinder the right to individual petition.[16] Finally, the Court stated that this approach was consonant with the Contracting States' obligations under the Convention to provide people with mental disabilities with 'special procedural safeguards' in order to ensure effective access to justice.[17]

The importance of this ruling cannot be overstated. The Court's repertoire on admissibility has been enriched to include the new notion of 'de facto representation'. In reaching its verdict, the Court acknowledged the special circumstances of people with mental disabilities, opening the way for litigation that seeks to secure accountability for a wider range of serious violations of human rights that previously would have foundered on admissibility grounds. Furthermore, the Court recognized the special role of NGOs in defending vulnerable individuals, based on their public interest mandate. This breakthrough is all the more remarkable as it has been achieved at a time when, as discussed later, access to the Court is being restricted to better control its burgeoning caseload.

However, the Court's momentous admissibility ruling is weakened by its insistence that this outcome represented an exceptional departure from its jurisprudence, justified by the 'unique' circumstances of the case. In doing so, the Court ignored abundant evidence to the effect that far from being unique, Câmpeanu's case was fairly representative of institutional life in the region. Thus, the CLR presented evidence that hundreds of patients died in similar circumstances at the same psychiatric hospital, that many also lacked relatives, and that their deaths had not been properly investigated.[18] The Bulgarian Helsinki Committee noted in its third-party intervention that the official investigations into the suspicious deaths of hundreds of abandoned or orphaned children in Bulgarian institutions had not led to any indictments.[19] For his part, the Council of Europe Commissioner for Human Rights, acting as third-party intervener, presented information collected during his country visits suggesting that serious abuses taking place in institutions frequently remained un-investigated, due to structural barriers blocking the victims' access to justice.[20] Additionally, Judge de Albuquerque aptly criticized the majority's reasoning as contradictory, as on the one hand it described Câmpeanu's circumstances as exceptional, and on the other hand decided that the case revealed a more systemic access to justice problem. The Court's approach somewhat stunts the judgment of its potential, rendering its extrapolation to other scenarios difficult, particularly considering Câmpeanu's tragic but admittedly singular set of afflictions. In the end, the ruling appears to rest on a compromise between the imperative of ensuring effective protection to a particularly vulnerable segment of society, and a concern

---

15 §110–111.
16 §112.
17 §113.
18 §43–44, 47, 74–78.
19 Written comments submitted by the Bulgarian Helsinki Committee, 30 September 2011, available here: http://www.bghelsinki.org/en/news/press/single/written-comments-submitted-bulgarian-helsinki-committee/ (last accessed on 1 February 2015).
20 Third-party intervention by the Council of Europe Commissioner for Human Rights, 14 October 2011, available here: https://wcd.coe.int/ViewDoc.jsp?id=1851457 (last accessed on 1 February 2015).

that any relaxation of rules on access might open the floodgates to NGO-driven public interest litigation.

Nor should the procedural position of the CLR at the national level take decisive importance, considering the Court's avowed objective of ensuring effective access to justice for serious breaches of human rights. Other countries may lack the relatively permissive rules on standing available in Romania, or may even move to deny NGO standing in order to avoid external scrutiny. The presence of a state-appointed guardian theoretically entitled to take action on the victim's behalf is equally inconclusive, in view of research suggesting that unreformed guardianship systems often facilitate abuse against persons with mental disabilities,[21] also reflected in the Court's own jurisprudence.[22] It can therefore be said that far from characterizing a whole class of claims, the elements grounding the Court's admissibility ruling are more or less case-specific, seriously undermining its potential.

A judgment on similar facts, in the case *Nencheva and other v Bulgaria*,[23] illustrates the ambiguousness of the Court's admissibility holding in *Câmpeanu*, which it predated by several weeks. *Nencheva* concerned the deaths from hunger and cold of fifteen severely disabled children in a social care home, having been lodged by several parents and by an NGO acting on behalf of some children whose parents had not come forth during domestic proceedings. The Court declared the complaint admissible insofar as it had been lodged by parents, and inadmissible for the rest. In denying the applicant organization *locus standi*, the Court accepted that in cases of 'conflicts of interest, the interest of justice and the necessity to ensure that the victims' individual rights and liberties are effectively protected, may require exceptional measures with a view to ensure the participation of the public and the representation of victims who are not able to act in order to defend themselves'.[24] However, the Court also noted that the applicant association had not brought the same claims to the attention of domestic authorities, before turning to Strasbourg. Therefore, it in effect appeared to demand recognition of 'authority to act on behalf of deceased individuals whose legitimate heirs were unknown or who did not manifest interest to participate in proceedings at the national level', which in itself did not justify a departure from existing jurisprudence.[25]

However, in *Nencheva*, the Court did not attach sufficient significance to the fact that domestic criminal proceedings, which ended with the acquittal of all those charged, concerned all fifteen victims, including those whose parents remained inactive. The domestic authorities had therefore been adequately seized of the matter, which should be the main consideration for the purpose of determining standing before the Court. The applicant association's lack of involvement was

---

21 See L. Series, *Legal Capacity and Participation in Litigation: Recent Developments in the European Court of Human Rights*, in L. Waddington, G. Quinn, E. Flynn (eds.), *European Yearbook of Disability Law Volume 5* (Cambridge: Intersentia, 2015), pp. 107–108 and the sources cited therein.

22 See for example *Shtukaturov v. Russia*, no. 44009/05, ECHR 2008, *X v. Croatia*, no. 11223/04, 17 July 2008, *Kruškovć v. Croatia*, no. 46185/08, 21 June 2011, *X and Y v. Croatia*, no. 5193/09, 3 November 2011, *Stanev v. Bulgaria* [GC], no. 36760/06, ECHR 2012, *D.D. v. Lithuania*, no. 13469/06, 14 February 2012, *Kędzior v. Poland*, no. 45026/07, 16 October 2012, *Sýkora v. the Czech Republic*, no. 23419/07, 22 November 2012, *A.K. v. Croatia*, no. 37956/11, 8 January 2013, *Lashin v. Russia*, no. 33117/02, 22 January 2013, *Mihailovs v. Latvia*, no. 35939/10, 22 January 2013, *M.S. v. Croatia*, no. 36337/10, 25 April 2013, *Nataliya Mikhaylenko v. Ukraine*, no. 49069/11, 30 May 2013, *Ivinović v. Croatia*, no. 13006/13, 18 September 2014.

23 *Nencheva and Others v. Bulgaria*, no. 48609/06, 18 June 2013.

24 §93.

25 §93.

not a material consideration in this respect, particularly as it did not assert an independent right. Instead, it brought before the Court serious human rights violations on behalf of victims who were not able to do so on their own, in line with its public interest mandate. The position of the parents whose standing was acknowledged is also worth examining. It transpires from the Court's ruling that many of the victims had been placed in state care upon their parents' request or with their agreement,[26] that most parents had never visited their children, that they did not provide them with food or clothes during the winter when they died,[27] that they did not attend their funerals,[28] and that they only became formally involved in the national proceedings 8 years after their children died.[29] While we do not intend to pass judgment on their behaviour, these details nevertheless call into question the relevance of generalizations on the position of would-be representatives to the detriment of an intensive inquiry on a case-by-case basis, aimed at ensuring effective access to justice. We also note that while presumably the children had a State-appointed guardian, this did not prevent their tragic deaths, or ensure their access to justice.

In *Câmpeanu*, the Court focused its scrutiny on the Article 2 claim, repeatedly described as the 'main complaint' in the case.[30] The Court also declared the Article 3 claim admissible, but it incorporated it in its Article 2 analysis, as it did not give rise to any 'separate issues'.[31] Although Câmpeanu's representatives also made voluminous submissions under Articles 5, 8 and 14 of the Convention, the Court dismissed them summarily, considering that the Article 2 ruling sufficiently encompassed them.[32] Dissenting judges variously disagreed with the majority's parsimonious approach, criticizing it as unjustified and for being in breach of previous jurisprudence.[33] Additionally, this approach makes it difficult to draw any conclusions regarding the standing of a proxy to lodge a complaint on behalf of a living person unable to complain independently or to provide written authorization, or on behalf of a dead victim in relation to abuses suffered while they were alive. The Article 3 admissibility finding does not enlighten us, as it is not clear if it encompassed facts related to Câmpeanu's death, which could therefore conceivably be incorporated in the analysis under Article 2, or on the contrary, if it referred to separate incidents unrelated to his death. The Court's reluctance to fully engage with the facts is regrettable, particularly seeing its acknowledgment that Câmpeanu was not able to initiate legal proceedings on his own while he was alive.[34]

In the absence of clear guidance from the Court regarding the situation of (living) people locked in institutions lacking support to complain, the old *Skjoldager v. Sweden* decision should be considered valid authority.[35] The applicant in *Skjoldager* was a State-employed psychologist who noticed three nursing home residents locked up in their rooms while carrying out an inspection and complained that they had been unlawfully detained. He argued that he should be allowed to act on their behalf, since they were not able to complain independently and the authorities refused to disclose their names or otherwise facilitate contact between the applicant and the

26 §7.
27 §54.
28 §9.
29 §49.
30 *Câmpeanu v. Romania*, §111, 106.
31 §154.
32 §155–156.
33 See the partly dissenting opinions of Judges Spielmann, Bianku and Nußberger, and of Judges Ziemele and Bianku respectively.
34 §108.
35 *Skjoldager v. Sweden*, (dec.), Application no. 22504/93, 17 May 1995.

victims or their guardians in order to obtain powers of attorney. The former Commission rejected the complaint for lack of *locus standi*, as the applicant lacked valid authority to act on the victims' behalf, and at the same time he failed to show that they were unable to lodge an application in their own names. By restricting the scope of 'de facto representation' to cases in which the direct victim died, the Court leaves the hurdles preventing access to justice of victims of abuse occurring inside institutions intact. In other words, had the CLR made contact days and not hours before Câmpeanu died, they would presumably lack standing to represent him.

In these circumstances, we rally to Judge De Albuquerque's critique in that it would have been preferable to institutionalize the concept of 'de facto representation', at the very least for violations of Articles 2, 3, 4 and 5 of the Convention. Any request for the recognition of standing based on de facto representation should include an intensive scrutiny of the personal circumstances of the direct victims, including with respect to the existence of alternative sources of representation. As opposed to Judge de Albuquerque, we suggest that it is necessary to also look at the quality of the representation available, as frequently relatives or guardians are themselves complicit in the abuse in question. In that respect, the underlying objective of the Court's scrutiny should be to ensure effective protection against serious human rights abuses, as opposed to administrative expedience or procedural formalism, which sometimes appears to take primary importance in Strasbourg. It is also important to note that although 'de facto representation' can be a valuable tool for shedding light on the dark corners of the institutional system, it cannot be a substitute for deinstitutionalization, personal autonomy, or supported decision-making. In order to prevent it from becoming another instrument for abuse, when applying in cases concerning living victims, de facto representation should be a temporary measure, until contact can be established and a proper mandate secured.

Representation of applicants with mental disabilities in proceedings before the court

People with mental disabilities, particularly those who are institutionalized, often find it difficult to secure reliable legal representation, a crucial component of access to justice. Applicants, including those with disabilities, are theoretically entitled to initiate proceedings before the Court in person. However, the ongoing trend of tightening and strictly enforcing admissibility criteria renders legal representation from the onset of the proceedings more or less indispensable. In any event, legal representation becomes in principle obligatory from the moment when the Court notifies the respondent Government of an application, although applicants may also seek leave to continue on their own. The applicant is in principle responsible for securing representation, and failure to do so may lead to the case being dismissed. Although the Court operates a legal aid scheme, that usually benefits indigent applicants who already are represented. The purpose of this section is to review the Court's practice on dealing with unrepresented applicants with mental disabilities, which ranges from dismissing cases for failure to secure representation to instructing the national authorities to identify and provide representation.

Several inadmissible cases have been reported which involved applicants with mental disabilities who were not able to secure legal representation. The applicant in *Drăguşin v. Romania* was a woman deprived of her legal capacity, who complained among others about her inability to challenge her guardian. The Court's request to the Bucharest Bar that a lawyer be appointed to represent the applicant was ignored. The case was ultimately struck out ostensibly because the applicant stopped communicating with the Court, although this happened after 5 years during which she had been in touch (from 2002, when she lodged her application, until 2007, the date of the last communication received from her). In another case, *Tatu v. Romania*, the applicant complained of a whole range of abuses, including ill treatment, forced hospitalization, forced medical treatment and incapacitation.[36] The applicant was not able to find a lawyer willing to represent her, and the Court's appeals to the local bar association remained unanswered. In these circumstances, the Court decided to strike the application out of its list of cases, noting that the applicant failed to provide any explanation for not complying with her procedural obligations. The inflexible application of the legal representation requirement even to applicants who are clearly unable to secure the services of a lawyer risks perpetuating structural disadvantage present at the national level, with the result that certain vulnerable groups are clearly denied access to justice.

In another category of cases, the Court moved to take a decision on the merits even if the applicants were not represented. For example, in *B. v. Romania*[37] and *B. v. Romania (No. 2)*,[38] concerning the same applicant (a woman diagnosed with a 'severe mental disorder'), the Court ultimately ruled that her Convention rights had been breached. *B. v. Romania (No. 2)* in particular is very problematic in at least two respects. First, although the applicant complained that she had been involuntarily committed to a psychiatric hospital, the Court decided to examine her claim from the standpoint of the right to respect for private life under Article 8, instead of the right to liberty under Article 5, as per its usual practice. It then found a procedural violation in that the applicant lacked a legal representative at the time of her hospitalization, in breach of national legal provisions on the 'legal protection' of people with mental disabilities. The Court's approach breaks away from a fundamental tenet in its jurisprudence that any deprivation of liberty has to be justified by reference to the closed list of grounds provided for under Article 5§1, including 'unsoundness of mind', interpreted narrowly. By examining the validity of the applicant's psychiatric confinement under Article 8, which contains a much broader range of public interest restrictions justifying interference with the right in question, the Court impermissibly dilutes the guarantees against unlawful detention. An additional two psychiatric commitment cases have recently been communicated to the Romanian Government under Article 8, suggesting that *B. v. Romania (No. 2)* may have signaled a more significant turn in the Court's jurisprudence.[39]

Second, the Court's reasoning under Article 8 to the effect that the authorities failed to ensure that the applicant's rights were adequately protected, by appointing a 'full or partial' guardian to represent her, in accordance with national law, is erroneous and unfortunate. Without going into detail, it suffices for the time being to state that Romania shares with other countries in Europe an all-or-nothing approach to legal capacity whereby an individual either has intact legal capacity or is fully incapacitated without any intermediate possibilities.[40] In that respect, it is not apparent what the Court referred to when mentioning 'partial' guardianship. More importantly, by basing the finding of a violation on the lack of compliance with national law, the Court unwittingly imported into its jurisprudence, and thus legitimized, the institution of guardianship, which is

---

36 *Tatu v. Romania* (dec.), Application no. 1282/05, 13 March 2012.

37 *B. v. Romania*, no. 42390/07, 10 January 2012.

38 *B. v. Romania (no. 2)*, no. 1285/03, 19 February 2013.

39 *N. v. Romania*, Application no. 59152/08, communicated on 11 September 2013 and *Ivaşcu v. Romania*, Application no. 41719/12, communicated on 23 October 2014.

40 In addition to plenary guardianship ('*punere sub interdicţie*'), the Romanian law also provides for a form of guardianship ad litem ('*curatelă specială*'), which applies during proceedings for placement under plenary guardianship. In *B. v. Romania (No. 2)*, the Court apparently designated 'curatorship' ('*curatelă*') to be a type of 'partial guardianship'. Curatorship is in fact a form of assistance available only to people with full mental capacity, thus excluding those subject to compulsory psychiatric hospitalization on account of impaired mental capacity.

outdated, and in breach of the Respondent State's obligations under the CRPD. The Article 8 holding also has the potential to victimize the applicant further since she faces the risk of being incapacitated, a paradoxical outcome after proceedings in which she nominally prevailed.[41] It is also worth noting that similarly ambiguous language around the notion of 'representation' also threatens to destabilize the *Câmpeanu* ruling. Thus, although throughout the judgment the Court insisted that Câmpeanu, like the applicant in *B. (No. 2)* lacked a legal guardian, at the end it used more positive language in framing its recommendation to the Romanian Government, to ensure people with mental disabilities are afforded 'independent representation' enabling their access to justice.[42] Whether substituted decision-making in the form of plenary guardianship may be construed as such 'independent representation', with the consequence that institutionalized people with mental disabilities in Romania will have to be incapacitated in order to 'enjoy' access to justice, remains an open question.

The Court's approach in *B. v. Romania (No. 2)* resembles that of a best interests decision maker, in that it reclassified, of its own motion, the applicant's unlawful detention claim as one concerning the absence of protection in the form of guardianship. Under the best interests doctrine, substitute decision makers are entitled to take decisions based on what they believe to be in the objective 'best interests' of the person concerned, as opposed to being based on the their own will and preferences. The CRPD Committee has clarified that the 'best interests doctrine' is in breach of Article 12 of the CRPD on the right to equal recognition before the law.[43] This approach is even more evident in *Gheorghe Predescu v. Romania,* which concerned an unrepresented prisoner with mental disabilities who complained of ill treatment at the hands of other inmates.[44] The Court dismissed the applicant's claim, which it apparently took as a symptom of mental illness, and instead found a violation of Article 3 on account of the authorities' failure to provide him with 'effective' psychiatric treatment, which he had not in fact asked for. In doing so, the Court criticized the authorities for discharging the applicant from psychiatric wards after he 'refused to acknowledge his illness or to be treated',[45] as well as their conclusion that 'he could look after himself' as unwarranted, in the absence of an 'expert [medical] evaluation'.[46] This outcome is in direct contradiction with the Court's jurisprudence on consent to medical treatment,[47] and with the provisions of the CRPD on equal legal capacity and freedom from non-consensual medical treatment. Waiving the legal representation requirements and examining the merits is clearly preferable to dismissing the case for failure to comply with procedural rules as discussed earlier. However, the lack of involvement of a party to the proceedings, if need be through representation, is incompatible with the key fair trial principles of adversarial justice and equality of

---

41 During the execution procedure before the Committee of Ministers, the Romanian Government reported that it was looking to initiate proceedings with a view to applying a 'measure of protection', which can only mean her placement under plenary guardianship, *Communication from Romania concerning the case of B. No. 2 against Romania,* Application no. 1285/03, 13 December 2013, available here: https://wcd.coe.int/ViewDoc.jsp?Ref=DH-DD(2013)1340&Language=lanEnglish&Site=CM (last accessed on 1 February 2015).

42 *Câmpeanu v. Romania,* §161; although also note that *Câmpeanu* has already been relied once as authority to support the position that an individual should benefit from 'obligatory representation . . . by an independent lawyer' during proceedings aimed at placing him under guardianship, see *Ivinović v. Croatia,* no. 13006/13, §45, 18 September 2014.

43 The CRPD Committee, General Comment No. 1(2014), 19 May 2014, §27.

44 *Gheorghe Predescu v. Romania,* no. 19696/10, 25 February 2014.

45 §49.

46 §53.

47 See for example *Plesó v. Hungary,* no. 41242/08, §67, 2 October 2012.

arms. Furthermore, it may also lead to a decrease in the quality of the adjudicatory process, which may at least partially explain the unsatisfactory outcomes in *B. v. Romania (No. 2)* and *Gheorghe Predescu v. Romania*.

The *B. v. Romania (No. 2)* ruling also had ramifications on the manner in which the Court deals with unrepresented applicants. Thus, in a pending case involving an unrepresented man diagnosed with schizophrenia, who claimed that his 14-year detention in high security psychiatric hospitals has been unlawful, the Court instructed the State to provide the identification details of the applicant's legal representative.[48] This request was based on Rule 54§2(a) of the rules of procedure, whereby the Court may 'request the parties to submit any [relevant] factual information, documents or other material'. The Court justified it on the basis that the applicant lacked litigation capacity and that he had been detained in a psychiatric hospital, relying on *B v. Romania (No. 2)* as precedent. As a result, the Romanian authorities initiated proceedings before national courts to place the applicant under plenary guardianship, which in all likelihood will be successful. From a disability rights standpoint, this is an alarming new development. This order renders placement under guardianship a procedural obligation to be implemented immediately, notwithstanding its deleterious consequences. Once appointed, the guardian may conceivably choose to withdraw the application in Strasbourg, remove the applicant's chosen counsel or consent to the applicant's *sine die* hospitalization or to forced medical treatment, even against his stated wishes and preferences.

The Court's inconsistent approach to unrepresented applicants reflects its ambivalence more broadly regarding the scope and nature of the obligations incumbent on Contracting States to facilitate access to justice of persons with mental disabilities. States are duty bound, under Article 6, as well as under other articles with a procedural component such as Articles 3 or 8, to ensure that persons with mental disabilities enjoy effective access to justice. However, within the scope of that duty, States maintain a wide degree of discretion to choose the measures that are appropriate in the circumstances of each case. The Court has validated a wide range of procedural accommodations in its jurisprudence, including, insofar as relevant to our purposes, legal aid,[49] trusteeship or guardianship ad litem, and even partial or plenary guardianship.[50] This stance may be contrasted with a different line of jurisprudence, where the Court criticized guardianship for its breadth, considering that it interferes needlessly and radically with a person's rights;[51] its lack of flexibility, in that it does not take into account the particular circumstances of the person concerned;[52] and the lack of safeguards against abuse, for example in the form of conflict of interest.[53] Thus, the

---

48 *N. v. Romania*; the author acts as the applicant's counsel in this case and holds all case records mentioned in this chapter.

49 *Megyeri v. Germany*, 12 May 1992, §23, Series A no. 237-A, *Magalhães Pereira v. Portugal*, no. 44872/98, §43–63, ECHR 2002-I, *A.K. v. Croatia*, no. 37956/11, 8 January 2013. On the jurisprudence concerning the rights of persons with mental disabilities to have access to and participate in litigation see L. Series, *Legal Capacity and Participation in Litigation: Recent Developments in the European Court of Human Rights*, supra fn 21.

50 *R.P. and Others v. the United Kingdom*, no. 38245/08, 9 October 2012, *B. v. Romania (No. 2)*, §93–101, *Ümit Bilgiç v. Turkey*, no. 22398/05, §113–114, 3 September 2013, *Nataliya Mikhaylenko v. Ukraine*, no. 49069/11, §28, 30 May 2013.

51 *Ivinović v. Croatia*, §38; *Shtukaturov v. Russia*, no. 44009/05, §71, 90, ECHR 2008; *X and Y v. Croatia*, no. 5193/09, §90, 3 November 2011.

52 See for example *Shtukaturov v. Russia*, §95; *Lashin v. Russia*, no. 33117/02, §92, 22 January 2013; *Alajos Kiss v. Hungary*, no. 38832/06, 20 May 2010.

53 See for example *Shtukaturov v. Russia*, §74; *D.D. v. Lithuania*, no. 13469/06, 14 February 2012; *Antonyuk v. Russia*, no. 47721/10, 1 August 2013.

Court effectively suggests that plenary guardianship regimes are in breach of the Convention, at least insofar as persons retaining de facto mental capacity are concerned. Guardianship therefore lives a double life in the Court's jurisprudence – as an excessive interference with a person's rights, to be subjected to strict scrutiny, and as the embodiment of a positive obligation aimed at ensuring the protection and fair treatment of persons with disabilities. As evidenced by the cases presented in this section, the confusion spreads to terminology, where the Court is unable or unwilling to distinguish substitute decision-making within the broader scope of the notion of 'legal representation', which thus encompasses the services provided by a lawyer as well as full substitution in the form of plenary guardianship.

Ultimately, the approach of providing the applicant with assistance to identify suitable representation appears to be the best solution in terms of creating the best chances for achieving true equality of arms between the parties and fair treatment more broadly. However, in order to be effective, any such intervention has to go beyond writing supplicating letters to Bar Associations or expecting highly vulnerable applicants to find a lawyer on their own, and might necessitate the cooperation of the national authorities. *X. v. Croatia* is the only example of a case in which the Court relied on Rule 39 to instruct the Government to appoint a lawyer to represent a mentally disabled applicant.[54] Rule 39, entitling the Court to indicate binding measures to the parties, is possibly the most effective procedural tool available in that respect. However, the Court appears reluctant to repeat the experience in *X. v. Croatia*.

The impact of recent procedural changes within the scope of the reform of the Court

The Court has undergone over the past two decades an ongoing process of reform driven primarily by the need to address the steady increase of its case law to almost unmanageable levels. Several high-level conferences have taken place over the past several years aimed at considering the measures required to reduce the Court's caseload, as well as its long-term future. While formally emphasizing their continued adherence to the right to individual petition, the Contracting States also sought to curtail the Court's ability to construe the Convention more expansively, through a continued emphasis on the margin of appreciation and on subsidiarity.[55]

Insofar as relevant for our purposes, the Court has adopted various measures designed to increase efficiency and streamline case-management procedures. Significantly, Rule 47 governing the institution of individual proceedings was amended in 2013, consistent with the Court's announced intention to 'take a stricter, more formal approach than previously'.[56] Thus, the Court introduced a new application form that applicants normally have to type into on a computer, and issued exhaustive instructions for its completion. As a rule, failure to observe these formalities is sanctioned with the application being struck out from the Court's list. This procedure is considerably more exacting than that previously in place. In addition the Court Registry polices

---

54 *X v. Croatia*, no. 11223/04, §61, 17 July 2008.

55 See for example the recommendations by the Contracting States addressed to the Court included in the *Izmir Declaration*, 27 April 2011, available here: https://wcd.coe.int/com.instranet.InstraServlet?command=com.instranet.CmdBlobGet&InstranetImage=2074588&SecMode=1&DocId=1733590&Usage=2 (last accessed on 2 February 2015).

56 Rule 47 of the Rules of Court, 1 July 2014, available here: http://echr.coe.int/Documents/Rules_Court_ENG.pdf (last accessed on 2 February 2015). The changes to Rule 47 were explained in the Court's document Interlaken process and the Court (2013 report), 28 August 2013, available here: http://echr.coe.int/Documents/2013_Interlaken_Process_ENG.pdf (last accessed on 2 February 2015).

compliance with procedural rules much more closely than in the past. Also significant is the fact that the Court eliminated the possibility that applicants used to have, allowing them to complete their application at a later date, as long as they submitted an initial letter setting out briefly the facts and their claims within 6 months after exhaustion. Currently, applicants have to submit the completed application and all annexes in good order within the 6-month time limit. To pave the way for these changes, the Court provided a range of multilingual informative materials on its website. Also relevant are the changes foreseen by Protocol no. 15, opened for signature in 2013, and yet to come into force, which reduces the time limit for filing a new application from 6 to 4 months from the date when domestic remedies had been exhausted.

Although the double thrust of tightening and strictly enforcing the admissibility criteria makes life more difficult for all applicants, certain vulnerable groups are particularly hard-hit. This in fact was one of the primary concerns that civil society constantly expressed throughout the reform process. For example, in a submission by several prominent international NGOs responding to a draft version of Protocol no. 15, it was stated that the proposal to reduce the time limit for lodging new applications from 6 to 4 months 'would greatly risk the exclusion of individuals who live in geographically remote areas, those without access to communications technology such as the internet, those with complicated cases or lawyers who are not adequately experienced in preparing or lodging claims before the Court, and those with limited access to sufficiently qualified lawyers'.[57] Persons with mental disabilities, particularly those in institutions, are especially affected by these changes, considering that many do not have access to information or the Internet, do not have access to a lawyer, usually lack any outside support, are under the control and supervision of the very institutions and people perpetrating the abuse, etc.

The Court has frequently deployed the principle that admissibility rules should be applied flexibly to the benefit of applicants with disabilities, taking into account any extenuating personal circumstances.[58] At the same time, the Court has occasionally used various procedural tools at its disposal to facilitate access and participation by persons with mental disabilities in its proceedings in a variety of contexts.[59] Although the Court's rules of procedure do not contain special provisions regarding persons with disabilities or for that matter any other vulnerable group, they constantly leave room for exceptional treatment based on a determination made on a case-by-case basis. For example, Rule 47 mentioned earlier provides among others that an application would be struck out from the case list for failure to abide by the formal requirements set therewith, unless the applicant has provided an adequate explanation for the failure to comply, or unless the Court otherwise directs. The problem with this type of clauses is that they are discretionary. Similar clauses in domestic law would run afoul of the principle of legal certainty if brought to the attention of the Court, particularly where fundamental rights are at stake such as the right to liberty. The Court has actually held in various contexts that institutions and individuals holding discretionary powers to act in order to safeguard the rights of people with disabilities do not

---

57 Joint NGO comments on the drafting of Protocols 15 and 16 to the European Convention for the Protection of Human Rights and Fundamental Freedoms, 4 October 2012, p. 2, available here: http://www.coe.int/t/dghl/standardsetting/cddh/reformechr/DH_GDR/DH-GDR(2012)008_Joint%20preliminary%20comments%20on%20the%20drafting%20of%20Protocols%2015%20and%2016.pdf (last accessed on 2 February 2015).

58 See for example *B. v. Romania (No. 2)*, §76–80, or *X v. Croatia*, §32–33.

59 See further C. Cojocariu, *Handicapping Rules: The Overly Restrictive Application of Admissibility Criteria by the European Court of Human Rights to Complaints Concerning Disabled People*, [2011] E.H.R.L.R., Issue 6, pp. 691–693.

provide the requisite standard of protection, leading to violations of the Convention.[60] In fact, the Court's practice on unrepresented applicants described earlier provides a neat illustration of the considerable risk of arbitrariness engendered by a lack of clear rules.

Conclusion

This chapter examined recent developments before the European Court of Human Rights with a view to determining if disabled applicants benefit from effective access to its proceedings. It hypothesized that the dearth of jurisprudence on disability rights is also due to the lack of procedural accommodations designed to facilitate disabled people's access. In the landmark *Câmpeanu v. Romania* judgment, the Court took the major step of recognizing the concept of 'de facto representation', enabling NGOs to act on behalf of people with disabilities in certain circumstances, even without specific authorization, justified by the imperative of securing accountability for gross human rights abuses. At the same time, the notion of 'de facto representation' is defined in relation to circumstances that are more or less case-specific, rendering any generalization with a view to determining its exact scope quite difficult. Additional litigation will now be necessary to clarify the exact contours of the *Câmpeanu* admissibility finding. The approach in *Câmpeanu* is a recurrent trope in the Court's disability jurisprudence, where cases are frequently described as exceptional or one-off, despite abundant evidence of systemic abuse and discrimination. This also helps explain why certain judgments hailed as a breakthrough at the time when they were delivered remained isolated and did not command more lasting authority across the Court's jurisprudence.[61]

The Court's highly inconsistent approach towards unrepresented disabled applicants highlights the lack of procedural accommodations designed to facilitate their access to justice, and is in breach of the legal certainty principle, engendering arbitrariness, a grievous harm in cases involving fundamental rights such as the right to liberty. At the same time, this practice illustrates the lack of substantive guidance on a range of issues critical to persons with disabilities, including legal capacity. Without a clear substantive stand, the Court largely defers to national jurisdictions to decide how best to ensure that people with disabilities enjoy their rights, with the result that plenary guardianship sits happily on a continuum of measures that also includes legal representation, all coming within the scope of the States' margin of appreciation. This helps explain the Court's preference for procedural violations in legal capacity cases or for finding violations based on a lack of compliance with national law, as well as the fraught relationship of the Court with the CRPD. Finally, the situation of disabled applicants may get even worse as a result of current changes undermining the right to individual petition within the scope of the ongoing process of reform of the Court.

---

60 See for example *M.H. v. the United Kingdom*, no. 11577/06, §58, 22 October 2013.
61 See for example *Alajos Kiss v. Hungary*, no. 38832/06, 20 May 2010 or *Stanev v. Bulgaria* [GC], no. 36760/06, ECHR 2012.

8

TOWARD INCLUSION

Political and social participation of people with disabilities

Lisa Schur

Introduction

People with disabilities have historically had low levels of political and social participation, frequently as a result of stigma, discrimination, and inaccessible environments. Over the past several decades, however, the disability rights movement has made major gains worldwide in civil rights and legal protections. The struggle for disability rights is itself a political movement and its efforts have also increased other opportunities for political and social participation among people with disabilities.

A major achievement of the disability rights movement is the adoption of the UN Convention on the Rights of Persons with Disabilities (CRPD) in 2006. The Convention "adopts a broad categorization of persons with disabilities and reaffirms that all persons with all types of disabilities must enjoy all human rights and fundamental freedoms."[1] It emphasizes respect for the inherent dignity of individuals with disabilities, and espouses the principles of "full and effective participation and inclusion in society on an equal basis with others" (Article 1). Among other provisions, the Convention states that people with disabilities have the right to participate fully in cultural, public, and political life (Articles 29 and 30). Article 29 specifies the right to "effectively and fully participate" in "political and public life" and "the conduct of public affairs." This includes the right to voting procedures, facilities, and material that are accessible and easy to understand and use, and the right to vote by secret ballot. Article 30 specifies that people with disabilities are entitled to "take part on an equal basis with others in cultural life," "to have the opportunity to develop and utilize their creative, artistic and intellectual potential," and "participate on an equal basis with others in recreational, leisure and sporting activities." Following its adoption, the UN Convention has helped stimulate disability legislation in many of its member countries.[2] The Convention has helped stimulate and shape national disability strategies in a number of countries.[3]

---

1 http://www.un.org/disabilities/default.asp?navid=14&pid=150.
2 See "Compilation of Legislative Measures Undertaken in the Implementation of the Convention on the Rights of Persons with Disabilities: 2011 Update" at www.un.org/disabilities/documents/COP/crpd_csp_2011_crp.5.doc, accessed December 2015.
3 Flynn E, *From rhetoric to action: Implementing the UN convention on the rights of persons with disabilities* (Cambridge University Press, 2011).

This chapter focuses on social and political participation as defined by Articles 29 and 30 of the Convention, reviewing evidence on the nature and extent of participation among people with disabilities. Clearly participation in activities is only one aspect of full equality and inclusion, which also encompasses the right to receive an education, live independently in the community, receive adequate and appropriate support services, and obtain accessible technology and transportation, along with more intangible factors such as being treated with dignity and respect, being able to form and maintain friendships and intimate relationships, and generally being able to live as equals in the broader community.[4]

Disability activism

Achievements such as the Convention are the result of sustained, concerted action by disability activists across multiple countries. Involvement of disability activists in the development of the Convention was both rewarding for the participants and resulted in more relevant language.[5]

The disability rights movement, however, should not be viewed as having a single agenda or goal. There are a variety of different disability organizations with different goals, strategies and approaches. For example, Kelly discusses the "multiple disability movements" in Canada.[6] Based on work developed by Oliver, Barnes and Mercer construct a typology divided into organizations primarily *for* and those primarily *of* disabled people.[7] The former include partnership/patronage organizations focused on charity and the provision of disability services, and economic/parliamentarian organizations that focus on a single issue and conduct lobbying, research and/or legal work. The latter include self-help groups, populist organizations focused on empowerment, collective action and consciousness raising, and umbrella organizations made up of disability groups.[8]

No comprehensive data exist on how many people with disabilities are politically active on disability issues. A U.S. survey in 2010 found that one-sixth (17%) of people with disabilities said they had participated in a group or organized activity that advocates for rights of people with disabilities, while earlier U.S. data from surveys in 1998 and 2000 found that a similar figure (15%) had either taken political action or taken action against a private organization on a disability issue in the past year.[9] One interesting finding is that disability activism in the United States is highest among young people with disabilities.[10] This may reflect generational differences, as older Americans were socialized in a time when disability had greater stigma, while younger

4 Rimmerman A, *Social inclusion of people with disabilities: National and international perspectives* (Cambridge University Press, 2013). Bates P, and Davis F A, "Social capital, social inclusion and services for people with learning disabilities" (2004) *Disability & Society* 19(3).

5 Moriarity L, and Dew K, "The united nations convention on the rights of persons with disabilities and participation in aotearoa new Zealand" (2011) *Disability & Society* 26(6).

6 Kelly C, "Towards renewed descriptions of Canadian disability movements: Disability activism outside of the non-profit sector" (2013) *Canadian Journal of Disability Studies* 2(1).

7 Oliver M, *The politics of disablement* (MacMillan, 1990). Barnes C, and Mercer C, *Exploring disability* (2nd ed., Polity Press, 2010).

8 Ibid. Barnes.

9 Schur L, and Adya M, "Sidelined or mainstreamed? Political participation and attitudes of people with disabilities in the united states" (2013) *Social Science Quarterly* 94(3).

10 Schur L, Shields T, and Schrine K, "Generational cohorts, group membership, and political participation by people with disabilities" (2005) *Political Research Quarterly* 58(3).

people have been socialized in an era of disability rights and greater access to education, which would suggest that disability activism may increase in the coming decades.

While there are no systematic data available on the number of disability activists outside of the United States, there are comparative data on disability protests around the world. An extensive search of news sources identified a total of 1,936 disability protests over the 1970–2005 period, defined as protests that included people with disabilities and concerned an issue with relevance to people with disabilities.[11] Almost two-thirds (1,247) of these protests occurred in the United States, which Barnartt attributes largely to the U.S. organization ADAPT, which commonly uses public protests in its advocacy efforts. The non-U.S. protests were most likely to occur in Canada (179) and the UK (148), with 100 in Asia, 70 in Russia and Eastern Europe, and 60 in Western Europe. There were only 16 non-U.S. protests in the 1970s, which increased to 325 in the 2000–2005 period. Just over half of the protests in both the United States and other countries were focused on cross-disability issues, while the remainder were most likely to focus on demands regarding mobility impairments, deafness, or blindness. About half of the non-U.S. protests (49%) were classified as having gotten a response, compared to only two-fifths (39%) of the U.S. protests.

The Internet has become a tremendous tool for disability activists in mobilization for protests and other political efforts such as the adoption of the UN Convention. While people with disabilities in general are less likely than non-disabled people to have computer and Internet access (U.S. Department of Commerce, 2011), those who do have access have found it to be highly valuable for political action, particularly among those with mobility impairments and financial constraints that limit their ability to travel.[12] The Internet has been used extensively by UK disability groups to influence disability policy development.[13] Other examples include the organization Women with Disabilities Australia, which uses the Internet to connect members across a large geographical area (Meekosha, 2002), and the Disabled Women's Network in Ontario, which describes its mission as "fostering virtual activism and individual empowerment" by using the Internet to educate and organize members and allies.[14]

Early political protests often focus on increasing government benefits for people with disabilities; for example, Rimmerman and Herr found that the main goal of the 1999 disability strike in Israel was to improve disability benefits for people with severe disabilities, while in Japan, the first disability groups in the early 1960s were motivated by the goal of increasing the Welfare Pension for people with disabilities.[15]

Similarly, efforts in former Communist countries in Eastern Europe remain primarily focused on improving services for people with disabilities.[16] Gayle and Palmer contend the demand for

---

11 Barnartt notes that there are methodological problems in international comparisons; for example, the search for disability protests was based primarily on English-language news reports, although some were obtained from non-English sources. Barnartt S, "The globalization of disability protests, 1970–2005: Pushing the limits of cross-cultural research?" (2010) *Comparative Sociology* 9(2).

12 U.S. Department of Commerce, *Exploring the digital nation: Computer and internet use at home* (U.S. Department of Commerce, 2011).

13 Power D, and Power M, "The internet and government disability policy development in the United Kingdom" (Internet, Politics, Policy 2010: An Impact Assessment, 2010).

14 www.dawn.thot.net/what.html

15 Rimmerman A, and Herr S S, "The power of the powerless: A study on the Israeli disability strike of 1999" (2004) *Journal of Disability Policy Studies* 15(1). Hayashi R, and Okuhira M, "The disability rights movement in Japan: Past, present and future" (2001) *Disability & Society* 16(6).

16 Holland D, "The current status of disability activism and non-governmental organizations in post-communist Europe: Preliminary findings based on reports from the field" (2008) *Disability & Society* 23(6).

services may be based on the premise that people with disabilities feel they have a right to the services, which will in turn enhance their development and participation in society.[17] In other words, disability activists and organizations may often begin with service-based agendas and gradually develop more overtly "political" focus as their members gain political efficacy and a broader conception of discrimination through their political efforts. Disability scholars such as Barnes and Mercer maintain there is a risk, however, that once disability organizations gain more widespread acceptance their priorities tend to shift and their radicalism diminishes in terms of both political aspirations and activities.[18]

It would be a mistake to overgeneralize regarding patterns in disability activism. First, even in developing countries where people with disabilities receive few services, disability activists sometimes focus on specifically "political" goals. For example, in Lebanon disability rights organizations conducted a non-partisan nation-wide campaign to safeguard and promote voting rights of citizens with disabilities on the eve of the 2005 governmental elections.[19] Furthermore, it is a mistake to separate "non-political" disability issues (such as the receipt of government benefits and services) from overtly "political" issues (such as access to voting). As noted, a fundamental aspect of the disability rights movement is the recognition that many disability-related problems that are traditionally viewed as private, personal problems are in fact caused by "disabling" social and political environments and need to be addressed through public action.

It is unclear what leads some people to view disability-related problems as political rather than purely private problems. Studies of psychological responses to disability find that some people respond to disability-related problems with a sense of fatalism, feeling a loss of efficacy and control over their lives that discourages all action.[20] Other people respond with "role distance" and "normalization," seeking to avoid other people with disabilities and ignore or minimize the role of disability in their lives, which clearly discourages activism on disability issues.

Psychological factors can also encourage political activism among people with disabilities. Anspach describes disability activists as individuals who identify strongly with others who have disabilities and maintain a positive self-concept while rejecting society's devaluation of people with disabilities.[21] They view most or all disability-related problems not as an inherent part of living with a disability, but are socially constructed issues that can be eradicated by political action. Blaming the environment rather than the individual for disability-related problems is a basic part of the social model of disability, which Scotch claims is a "prerequisite to activism."[22] The focus on the environment leads activists to see disability problems as widely shared, which helps create and sustain a sense of identification with others who have disabilities. They also perceive that many disability-related problems require political, rather than purely individual, solutions. They emphasize changing policies, practices, and laws, rather than relying on self-help strategies such as developing a "positive attitude" or learning how to put non-disabled people at ease.

17 Gayle A, and Palmer D, "The activism of persons with disabilities in Jamaica: An evaluation of the impact" (2005) *Social and Economic Studies* 54(4).
18 Ibid. 7.
19 Wehbi S, and El-Lahib Y, "Sit (or stand) and be counted! campaigning for the voting rights of people with disabilities in Lebanon" (2008) *Disability Studies Quarterly* 28(2).
20 Anspach R, *From stigma to identity politics: Political activism among the physically disabled and former mental patients* (13A, Social Science and Medicine, 1979). Schur L. A, "Disability and the psychology of political participation" (1998) *Journal of Disability.*
21 Ibid.
22 Scotch R K, "Disability as the basis for a social movement: Advocacy and the politics of definition" (1988) *Journal of Social Issues* 44(1).

An Australian study found that activists with intellectual disabilities had backgrounds in self-advocacy and that a supportive collegial milieu was important for them to participate meaningfully in government disability advisory boards.[23]

Becoming a disability rights activist may occur in a number of ways. Some people experience a defining event or act of discrimination that motivates them to become politically active. For example, a U.S. woman in a wheelchair prior to the ADA found there were no accessible dressing rooms in a department store and was told to take the clothes home to try them on; she then began a successful campaign to require accessible dressing rooms in every clothing store.[24] Also, another U.S. woman had negative rehabilitation experiences that led her to embark on a personal campaign to force rehabilitation hospitals to design more individualized programs. In contrast, other people develop into disability activists more slowly over time as they participate in organizations where they are exposed to role models and information on disability issues, and are likely to be recruited for political activities.[25]

Gaps in voting and other political activities

Despite the large and growing number of disability activists over the past few decades, people with disabilities in general tend to be less likely than non-disabled people to engage in standard political activities such as voting. Voting is the most basic form of political participation in a democracy. Data from the United States and European countries clearly show lower voter turnout among people with disabilities compared to non-disabled citizens, although the magnitude of the gap varies by country. Across twenty-seven countries in the European Union, a 2007 survey found that disability was linked to 2 percentage points lower turnout in the most recent national elections, after controlling for income and demographic characteristics.[26] There was especially high turnout of people with disabilities relative to non-disabled citizens in Estonia, Slovenia, Luxemburg, and Lithuania, and especially low relative turnout in Finland, Italy, and Sweden.[27] The lower turnout of people with disabilities is backed up by other studies: in the 2005 national elections in the UK, people with disabilities were significantly less likely to vote than citizens without disabilities and only 34% of those with learning difficulties in the East of England were registered to vote compared to 51% for other potential voters.[28] An earlier study of the 1994 Swedish elections found that only 31% of citizens with intellectual disabilities voted, compared to 86% of the total Swedish population.[29]

---

23 Frawley P, and Bigby C, "Inclusion in political and public life: The experiences of people with intellectual disability on government disability advisory bodies in Australia" (2011) *Journal of Intellectual and Developmental Disability* 36(1).

24 Schur L A, "Disability and the psychology of political participation" (1998) *Journal of Disability Policy Studies* 9(2).

25 Ibid.

26 Grammenos S, *Indicators of disability equality in Europe, ANED 2010 task 4* (Academic Network of European Disability Experts, Centre for Disability Studies, University of Leeds, 2010).

27 Ibid.

28 Clarke P J, Ailshire J A, Nieuwenhuijsen E R, and de Kleijn–de Vrankrijker Marijke W, "Participation among adults with disability: The role of the urban environment" (2011) *Social Science & Medicine* 72(10). Keeley H, Redley M, Holland A, and Clare I, "Participation in the 2005 general election by adults with intellectual disabilities" (2008) *Journal of Intellectual Disability Research* 52(3).

29 Kjellberg A, and Hemmingsson H, "Citizenship and voting: Experiences of persons with intellectual disabilities in Sweden" (2013) *Journal of Policy and Practice in Intellectual Disabilities* 10(4).

The disability turnout gap appears to be generally larger in the United States than in Europe. Twelve U.S. surveys using varying samples and definitions of disability found turnout to be 4 to 21 percentage points lower among people with disabilities over the 1992–2012 period.[30] More recent U.S. surveys using larger samples and a consistent disability definition found disability turnout gaps of 7% in 2008, 3% in 2010, and 6% in 2012.[31] The smaller gap in 2010 reflects especially low turnout in midterm elections by young voters, who are generally less likely to have disabilities. Broken down by major type of disability, the turnout was lower in 2012 among people with visual, mobility, and cognitive impairments, but people with hearing impairments were as likely as people without disabilities to vote. Turnout was also low among those who reported difficulty going outside alone, or difficulty with daily activities inside the home. When demographic characteristics (age, gender, race/ethnicity, and marital status) are held constant, the adjusted disability gap is close to 12 points in each year, which is larger than the 2-point disability gap found in Europe.

There appears to be a smaller disability gap in other forms of political activity based on data from the United States and UK. People with disabilities in the UK in the 2005–2010 period were about as likely as those without disabilities to engage in civic participation (contacting officials, taking part in public meetings or protests, or signing petitions), civic consultation (completing a questionnaire or attending a public meeting or discussing local services), and civic activism (holding some type of local government position or being part of a group making decisions about local services).[32] In the United States, people with disabilities in 2008 were just as likely as non-disabled citizens to have contacted a public official, and just slightly less likely to have attended a political meeting or rally, worked on or contributed to a political campaign, or taken part in a political meeting, rally, march, protest, or demonstration.[33]

These overall patterns of political participation are strongly influenced by age, since people with disabilities tend to be older on average than those without disabilities, and older people tend to have higher political participation in general. When comparing people with and without disabilities who have the same age and other demographic characteristics, an interesting pattern emerges: younger people with disabilities have similar participation levels as their non-disabled peers, while older people with disabilities have lower participation than their non-disabled peers. In a 2008 U.S. survey, for example, people with disabilities age 18–34 were slightly more likely than those without disabilities to have taken part in a political activity apart from voting in the past year (20% compared to 18%), while people with disabilities age 65 or older were significantly less likely than those without disabilities to have done so (21% compared to 28%).[34] As suggested earlier, this pattern may indicate generational differences, with greater perceptions of stigma and exclusion among older people with disabilities and greater willingness to be involved in community affairs among young people with disabilities.

---

30 Schur L, and Adya M, "Sidelined or mainstreamed? Political participation and attitudes of people with disabilities in the united states" (2013) *Social Science Quarterly* 94(3).

31 Schur L, Adya M, and Kruse D, *Disability, voter turnout, and voting difficulties in the 2012 elections* (U.S. Election Assistance Commission, 2013).

32 http://webarchive.nationalarchives.gov.uk/20111030141353/http://odi.dwp.gov.uk/roadmap-to-disability-equality/indicators.php, accessed December 2015.

33 Ibid. 9.

34 Ibid. 9. The activities were: contacted a public official; attended a political meeting or rally; worked on or contributed to political campaign; and took part in march, rally, protest, or demonstration. See Schur et al. (2005) for similar results using earlier surveys.

Explaining the political participation gap

Why are people with disabilities less likely to vote and to engage in other political activities? The factors that shape political participation can be viewed under the general framework of resources, recruitment, and psychological factors.[35] People with disabilities tend to have fewer resources for political participation, including lower average education and income levels, and often must spend extra money, time, and energy on disability-related matters, which further decreases their ability to participate in politics. The recruitment of people with disabilities for political activity is often limited by their relative social isolation, which provides fewer opportunities for friends, neighbors, co-workers and others to encourage them to vote or become involved in other activities.

Several studies indicate that lower levels of resources, especially income and education, help account for their lower participation.[36] They are also less likely to be recruited for voting by friends, family members, co-workers, and political organizations, which reflects their greater isolation. Consistent with this, people with disabilities in the United States were less likely to report that they frequently discuss politics with family members or friends.[37]

Psychological factors can also limit the participation of people with disabilities, particularly low feelings of efficacy or a sense that one's participation matters, reflected in the extreme by a sense of fatalism that discourages all action (as noted earlier in discussing disability activism). People with disabilities express lower levels of political efficacy in general, which plays a role in their lower levels of political participation.[38] Psychological factors may account for the finding that recent onset of disability appears to discourage political participation, consistent with studies of the effects of other major life transitions on participation.[39] Learning to live with a disability can be difficult and many people with new disabilities may feel overwhelmed and have less time, energy, and interest available for political activities. Also, Jennings argues that pain and loss have a de-politicizing effect, which may wear off as people learn to manage their new situations.[40] This is consistent with findings that disability activists tend to have lived with their disabilities for longer periods of time than people with disabilities who are not politically active.[41]

Resources, recruitment, and psychological factors help explain the positive role that employment plays in the political participation of people with disabilities; voter turnout is very similar between employed people with and without disabilities, but is depressed among non-employed

35 Verba S, Schlozman K L, and Brady H. E, *Voice and Equality: Civic Voluntarism in American Politics* (Harvard University Press, 1995).
36 Shields T G, Schriner K, and Ochs, L.D "Disenfranchised: People with disabilities in American electoral politics" in Altman B, and Barnartt S, (eds.) *Expanding the scope of social science research on disability* (Emerald Group Publishing, 2000). Schur L, Shields T, Kruse D, and Schriner K "Enabling democracy: Disability and voter turnout"(2002) *Political Research Quarterly* 55(1). Schur L, Shields T, and Schrine K, "Generational cohorts, group membership, and political participation by people with disabilities" (2005) *Political Research Quarterly* 58(3).
37 Schur L, Adya M, and Kruse D, *Disability, voter turnout, and voting difficulties in the 2012 elections* (U.S. Election Assistance Commission, Washington, DC, 2013).
38 Ibid. 36 Shur et al. 2002, 2005. See also Schur L, "Employment and the creation of an active citizenry" (2003) *British Journal of Industrial Relations* 41(4).
39 Stoker L, Jennings M K, "Life-cycle transitions and political participation: The case of marriage" (1995) *American Political Science Review* 89(2), 421.
40 Jennings M K, "Political responses to pain and loss presidential address, American Political Science Association 1998" (1999) *American Political Science Review* 93(1).
41 Schur L A, "Disability and the psychology of political participation" (1998) *Journal of Disability Policy Studies* 9(2).

people with disabilities relative to those without disabilities.[42] This may reflect an especially strong effect of employment on the resources and recruitment opportunities of people with disabilities (through increased income, skills, and social contacts at work), or on their feelings of efficacy, self-esteem, and interest in public issues.

The standard predictors of political participation do not, however, fully explain the gap in turnout.[43] External barriers such as laws, public policies, and the organization of public space may also prevent or limit participation. It has often been assumed that people with disabilities cannot or should not participate in civic life, which has frequently been expressed in public policies that isolate people with disabilities and exclude them from citizenship.[44] For example, many countries have laws disqualifying people with mental and other disabilities from voting and serving on juries.[45] In earlier periods this was even more common, as noted by Schriner et al and Carey in regard to state laws in the United States.[46] The view that people with mental illness or intellectual disabilities do not deserve the basic rights of citizenship was strongly articulated in a 1927 Supreme Court case, *Buck v. Bell*, which upheld a state statute permitting the compulsory sterilization of "unfit" people, especially those with intellectual disabilities.[47] While substantial progress has been made over the past century, people with disabilities still receive "mixed messages" in laws and policies about the extent of their rights of citizenship.[48]

When people with disabilities are not explicitly excluded, the arrangement of public space has nonetheless often reflected the assumption that they will not participate in public life (Hastings and Thomas, 2005; Hahn, 1988). One of the clearest examples is the inaccessibility of many polling places in the United States, despite the legal requirements for accessibility (GAO, 2009).

Voting can be discouraged by barriers getting to or using polling places, which make voting more time-consuming and difficult. There is evidence that living in an area with streets in poor condition is linked to substantially lower voter turnout among people with mobility limitations, and that difficulty finding and getting to the polling place lowers voter turnout among people in general.[49] Such difficulties may also decrease feelings of efficacy by sending the message that people with disabilities are not fully welcome in the political sphere.[50] Furthermore, informal "gatekeeping" decisions, such as family or caregivers' pressure to vote for particular candidates or

---

42 Schur L A, and Kruse D L, "What determines voter turnout? Lessons from citizens with disabilities" (2000) *Social Science Quarterly* 81(2). Schur L, Shields T, and Schriner K, Can I make a difference? Efficacy, employment, and disability (2003) *Political Psychology* 24(1).

43 Ibid. 36 Shur et al. 2002.

44 U.S. Commission on Civil Rights, *Accommodating the spectrum of individual abilities* (Clearinghouse Publications, 1983).

45 Prince M J, *The electoral participation of persons with special needs* (Ontario: Elections Canada, 2007). Fiala-Butora J, Stein M A, and Lord J E, "The democratic life of the union: Toward equal voting participation for Europeans with disabilities" (2014) 55 *Harvard International Law Journal* 71.

46 Schriner K, Ochs L. A, and Shields T G, "The last suffrage movement: Voting rights for persons with cognitive and emotional disabilities" (1997) *The Journal of Federalism* 27(3). Carey A C, *On the margins of citizenship: Intellectual disability and civil rights in twentieth-century America* (Temple University Press, 2009).

47 *Buck v. Bell* 274 U.S. 200 (1927).

48 Ibid. 46 Carey.

49 Clarke P J, Ailshire J A, Nieuwenhuijsen E R, and de Kleijn–de Vrankrijker Marijke W, "Participation among adults with disability: The role of the urban environment" (2011) *Social Science & Medicine* 72(10). Brady H E, and McNulty J E, "Turning out to vote: The costs of finding and getting to the polling place" (2011) *American Political Science Review* 105(1).

50 Schneider A, and Ingram H, Social construction of target populations: Implications for politics and policy (1993) *American Political Science Review* 87(2).

their decision not to assist an individual with a disability who needs help registering or casting a ballot, can discourage citizens with disabilities from voting.[51]

Despite the existence of laws requiring polling place accessibility, the U.S. Government Accountability Office found that only 27% of polling places in 2008 had no potential impediments to access by people with disabilities, a modest improvement from 16% in 2000.[52] The majority of impediments occurred outside of or at the building entrance, such as lack of accessible parking spaces, steep ramps or curb cuts, unpaved surfaces in the path leading from the parking lot or route to the building entrance, and door thresholds exceeding 0.5 inch in height. The GAO found that 46% of polling places had an accessible voting system that could pose a challenge to certain voters with disabilities. While the proportion of polling places with four or more potential impediments dropped from 29% in 2000 to 16% in 2008, the percentage with one to three potential impediments stayed about the same.[53]

The GAO findings are reinforced by a U.S. voter survey following the 2012 elections, which found that almost one-third (30%) of voters with disabilities reported difficulty in voting at a polling place in 2012, compared to 8% of voters without disabilities.[54] The most common problems reported by voters with disabilities were reading or seeing the ballot, understanding how to vote or use the voting equipment, waiting in line, and finding or getting to the polling place. A positive finding is that 84% of people with disabilities felt that election officials treated them very respectfully, and 87% of those who needed help reported that the election officials were very helpful. Some contrary evidence comes from a British study that found that one in five people with a "learning impairment" reported that staff at polling stations were unhelpful.[55]

People with disabilities may especially benefit from flexible opportunities to vote, including being able to vote before election day at a more convenient time or location (e.g., when accessible transportation is more easily available) or to vote by mail, which may be of particular value for those who have difficulty getting to a polling place. Several U.S. studies have found that people with disabilities, particularly those with mobility impairments, are more likely to vote by mail than are people without disabilities, although they are not more likely to vote before election day when that option is available.[56]

While voting by mail has advantages for many people with disabilities, it also can pose challenges. For example, the prevalent model requires voters to take the first step, by initiating contact with election officials to request and return the ballot, which may be difficult for some people with disabilities.[57] People with visual or cognitive impairments may have trouble following complicated written instructions, and those with limited fine motor skills may find it hard to record their vote. As with in-person voting, people who need assistance may be reliant on family members or caregivers who can provide or withhold assistance, or can apply pressure to vote for particular candidates. In the 2012 U.S. survey, close to one-tenth of people with disabilities who

51 Tokaji D P, and Colker R, "Absentee voting by people with disabilities: Promoting access and integrity" (2007) *McGeorge Law Review* 38. See also ibid. 19.
52 Government Accountability Office, *Voters with disabilities: More polling places had no potential impediments than in 2000, but challenges remain* (No. 09-685, 2009).
53 Ibid.
54 Ibid. 37.
55 Scott R, and Crooks A, *Polls apart 4: Campaigning for accessible democracy* (Scope, 2005). Shields T G, Schriner K, and Ochs, L D "Disenfranchised: People with disabilities in American electoral politics" in Altman B, and Barnartt S, (eds.) *Expanding the scope of social science research on disability* (Emerald Group Publishing, 2000).
56 Ibid. 30, 37.
57 Ibid. 46.

voted by mail reported having difficulties in doing so, and the need for assistance in filling out or sending the ballot.[58]

An additional obstacle to mail voting in twenty-one states in the U.S. is the requirement of an excuse when applying for a mail ballot, which can discourage mail voting due to the stigma of recording a disability on an official government document. In contrast, twenty states allow a mail ballot without an excuse but the request has to be renewed each election, while seven states and the District of Columbia have a permanent no-excuse mail ballot available, and two states have mail-only voting.[59] These provisions appear to affect turnout: the requirement of an excuse correlates with lower turnout among eligible citizens with disabilities in 2010, and among registered voters both with and without disabilities in 2008 and 2010.[60] In addition, in states with no-excuse and all-vote-by-mail systems, non-voters were less likely to report illness or disability as a reason for not voting in 2008 and 2010.

Despite the advantages of mail voting, most people both with and without disabilities express a preference for voting at a polling place. A 2012 U.S. survey found that 58% of people with disabilities, and 68% of people without disabilities, said they would prefer to vote at a polling place, while one-fourth (25%) of people with disabilities said they would prefer to vote by mail, compared to about one-seventh (14%) of people without disabilities. People with disabilities were relatively more likely to prefer voting by telephone (5% compared to 2%), and less likely to prefer voting on the Internet (10% compared to 16%).

The lower likelihood of preferring Internet voting among people with disabilities is probably due to their low rate of Internet access: a 2011 U.S. Department of Commerce report found that more than half (54%) of U.S. households headed by someone with a disability had no Internet access from home, compared with 25% of households headed by someone without a disability.[61] This also probably explains why people with disabilities in the United States are less likely than people without disabilities to say that the Internet has affected their own political activity.[62] The European Union has also identified a disability gap in computer access in its member nations.[63] The fact that relatively few people with disabilities have access to computers is due both to economic factors, such as lower income levels, and to technological barriers.[64]

Despite the disability gap in computer access, new technologies have the potential to make it easier for people with disabilities to vote, and help increase their overall political participation through increased access to information, networking, and recruitment. For example, increased availability and knowledge about short messaging services provided by the Election Commission in Pakistan enabled more people with disabilities to find their polling stations and vote.[65] The

---

58 Ibid. 37.
59 National Conference of State Legislatures, "Absentee and Early Voting," at http://www.ncsl.org/legislatures-elections/elections/absentee-and-early-voting.aspx
60 Schur L A, and Kruse D L, "Disability and election policies and practices" in Burden B.C, and Stewart C, (eds.) *The measure of American elections* (Cambridge University Press, 2014).
61 U.S. Department of Commerce, *Exploring the digital nation: Computer and internet use at home* (U.S. Department of Commerce, 2011).
62 Ibid. 30.
63 Vicente M R, and López A J, "A multidimensional analysis of the disability digital divide: Some evidence for internet use" (2010) *Information Society* 26(1).
64 Jaeger P T, "Telecommunications policy and individuals with disabilities: Issues of accessibility and social inclusion in the policy and research agenda" (2006) *Telecommunications Policy* 30(2).
65 Mahmood Q K, Ali H, and Raza H, "The effect of SMS service on the political participation of person with disabilities (PWDs) in Khyber Pakhtunkhwa (Pakistan)" (2013) *World Applied Sciences Journal* 25(5).

Internet has become a vital tool for mobilizing political activities among people with disabilities, as noted earlier.

To address disability-related voting problems, the UN Convention's Article 29 commits nations to "Ensuring that voting procedures, facilities and materials are appropriate, accessible and easy to understand and use" and "Protecting the right of persons with disabilities to vote by secret ballot in elections and public referendums without intimidation."[66] While the Article spells out the general requirements, it remains up to the individual countries to implement the provisions. This Article has been used by both international and local organizations to monitor and improve election procedures, such as in Mexico, Bosnia-Herzegovina, and the Philippines.[67] Efforts to implement this Article often involve diverse groups of stakeholders – "non-governmental organizations, democracy activists, election management professionals, political party represent-atives, disabled advocates, media specialists, and others" – who work to interpret and implement Article 29 in "locally relevant ways."[68] In the United States, the 2002 Help America Vote Act (HAVA) encouraged adoption of computer technologies and required electronic voter registra-tion at disability agencies, at least one fully accessible voting system at each polling place, the provision of all voting-related materials in alternative formats, and disability etiquette training for poll workers.[69] Disability rights advocates have criticized HAVA, however, for not being strong enough to fully protect the voting rights of people with disabilities, and the U.S. GAO found that limited oversight of HAVA requirements as of 2009 left gaps in ensuring voting accessibility for people with disabilities.[70]

Social participation

Just as there are gaps in political participation, people with disabilities also face gaps in social participation. People with disabilities have less social contact in general; they are more likely to live alone, less likely to be married, and less likely to socialize than people without disabilities.[71] A study in Ireland found that the likelihood of having "an evening out" in the previous 2 weeks declined by 17 percentage points after the onset of disability, although there was no substantial decline in other social activities (including membership in a club, and meeting or talking to people).[72] In the UK, people with disabilities were more likely than those without disabilities to report barriers to participating in a range of social activities, including going on holiday, visiting friends, spending time with family, engaging in sports, going to a museum or place of historic interest, going to the theatre, cinema, or other arts activity, and going to the library or archive.[73]

66 http://www.un.org/disabilities/default.asp?id=289, accessed December 2015.
67 See www.article29.org, accessed December 2015.
68 Tucker F K, (2009). Achieving progress towards reasonable accommodation on Article 29 of the United Nations Convention on the Rights of Persons with Disabilities, accessed December 2015.
69 The earlier National Voter Registration Act (NVRA) in 1993 required states to offer voter registration in conjunction with any business at public service or assistance agencies, but full implementation was delayed and a 2000 survey showed that many agencies were not aware of their NVRA responsibilities.
70 Barbara Bovbjerg, *Voters with Disabilities: Challenges to Voting Accessibility*, U.S. GAO, Statement before the National Council on Disability, April 23, 2013, available at http://www.ncd.gov/events/OtherEvents/04232013/.
71 Ibid. 30, 31.
72 Gannon B, and Nolan B, "The impact of disability transitions on social inclusion" (2007) *Social Science & Medicine* 64(7).
73 https://www.gov.uk/government/uploads/system/uploads/attachment_data/file/180903/leisure_community_civic_life.pdf, accessed December 2015.

The barriers included the expense, lack of public transport, concern over discrimination and attitudes of others, and being too busy. Adults with disabilities in the United States were less likely than those without disabilities to report socializing with friends, neighbors, or relatives at least twice a month (79% compared to 90%), or going to a restaurant at least twice a month (48% compared to 75%).[74] They were less likely to have attended a group or organization meeting in the past 12 months (18% compared to 24%), or to be officers or committee members in groups or organizations (8% compared to 12%). They were also less likely to go out to the movies, theater, live music performances, sports events, or events related to hobbies such as dancing, art shows, or events for collectors.[75] The gaps in socializing in the United States do not appear to have changed in the past two decades.[76]

An important form of social contact for many people is attendance at religious services. While people with disabilities in the United States are equally likely as those without disabilities to say that religious faith is very important to them,[77] they are less likely to attend religious services at least once a month (50% compared to 57% in 2010).[78]

One encouraging sign is that there tend to be smaller disability gaps in social participation among young people, and in fact young adults with disabilities appear just as likely as their non-disabled peers to socialize with friends, neighbors, or relatives, and to have attended a group or organization meeting in the past 12 months.[79]

The types and extent of participation depend on context. For example, an Australian study found that people with disabilities who lived outside of cities had lower employment levels and incomes than those in urban areas, and were less likely to socialize frequently with family members and friends, but they were more likely to do volunteer work and attend community events, and had stronger feelings of being part of the community.[80] The two groups reported similar overall levels of life satisfaction.

Transportation difficulties contribute to the generally lower levels of social participation among people with disabilities. In a 2010 U.S. survey, one-third of people with disabilities reported that inadequate transportation was a problem for them, compared to one-sixth of people without disabilities,[81] while in a 2010 UK survey, 23% of people with disabilities reported transportation difficulties. People with disabilities in the United States are less likely than non-disabled people to have or be able to drive a private vehicle,[82] and vehicle modifications for people with disabilities are often expensive.[83] Public transportation systems are often inaccessible, which has led to protests by disability activists (e.g., the ADAPT protest against inaccessible buses in Denver, Colorado; Lamp, 2006: 1321).

74 Kessler, NOD, Harris, *The ADA, 20 years later* (Harris Interactive, 2010). NOD/Harris, 2000 *national organization on Disability/Harris survey of Americans with disabilities* (Harris Interactive, 2000).

75 Ibid. NOD/Harris (2000).

76 Ibid. 69 Kessler, NOD, Harris 2010.

77 NOD/Harris, *2004 national organization on Disability/Harris survey of Americans with disabilities* (Harris Interactive, 2004).

78 Ibid. 69 Kessler, NOD, Harris 2010.

79 Ibid. 30, 31. 69 Kessler, NOD, Harris 2010.

80 McPhedran S, "Disability and community life: Does regional living enhance social participation" *Journal of Disability Policy Studies* 22(1).

81 Ibid. 69 Kessler, NOD, Harris 2010.

82 Ibid. 36 Schur, Shields, Schrine (2005).

83 Berkowitz M, O'Leary P K, Kruse D L, and Harvey C, *Spinal cord injury: An analysis of medical and social costs* (Demos Medical, 1998).

Accessible transportation is specified as a key right in Article 9 of the Convention. Many governments have taken steps to increase the accessibility of transportation systems, as described in WHO/World Bank.[84] In India, for example, design teams found inexpensive ways to make small vans accessible and developed a type of pedicab that is easier for people with restricted mobility to use. Cities such as New Delhi and Beijing have introduced major policies to upgrade their public rail systems and make them more accessible. Wheelchair-accessible, low-floor buses have been installed in various cities in India, Colombia, Ecuador, the United Republic of Tanzania, and Brazil. Other examples include Helsinki, Finland, which made its tram system accessible by buying new vehicles and renovating stops and stations, and the United Kingdom, which adopted a special initiative to make all taxis in the country wheelchair accessible.

Social stigma is another factor that can lead to lower participation among people with disabilities. Multiple studies have documented the stigma associated with disability in many countries.[85] For example, a 2010 U.S. survey found that 27% of people with disabilities said that others generally treated them differently after learning of their disability, with 14% saying that people generally avoid further contact once they learn of their disability.[86]

Low employment levels also contribute to decreased participation, as both quantitative and qualitative research suggests that employment is linked to greater social inclusion for people with disabilities.[87] Not only are many workplaces important sources of social contact, but non-employed people may reduce their social activities due to embarrassment over their status as well as their limited financial resources.[88]

While people with disabilities overall are less likely to participate in social activities than their non-disabled peers, many have active social lives based on networks built through family, friends, neighbors, employment, political activities, Centers for Independent Living, and other groups. For those with computer skills and access, social media such as Facebook and LinkedIn can play an important role in fostering social participation and a sense of community.[89]

Conclusion

Articles 29 and 30 of the UN Convention affirm the principles of full equality and inclusion for people with disabilities in all areas of life. While there has been tremendous progress in the status of people with disabilities around the world over the past few decades, they continue to experience lower levels of political and social participation than people without disabilities.

This chapter has discussed political and social participation separately, but they are clearly linked to each other as well as to broader inclusion in society. Political participation can lead to greater social participation, and vice versa. For example, the achievements of the disability rights movement have enabled millions of people with disabilities to participate more fully in social activities, and have helped changed attitudes toward disability. In turn, participation in social activities and

---

84 WHO/World Bank, *World report on disability* (World Health Organization and World Bank, 2011).
85 Ibid. 30, 31, 37.
86 Ibid. 69 Kessler, NOD, Harris 2010.
87 Morris A, and Abelló D, *Disability support pension new customer focus groups* (Social Policy Research Centre, 2005).
88 Morrison R L, and Nolan T, "I get by with a little help from my friends . . . at work" (2009) *New Zealand Journal of Social Sciences Online* 4(1).
89 Baker P, Bricout J C, Moon N W, Coughlan B, and Pater J, "Communities of participation: A comparison of disability and aging identified groups on Facebook and LinkedIn" (2013) *Telematics and Informatics* 30(1).

networks often exposes people with disabilities to political information, issues, and recruitment opportunities that can lead them to become more politically involved. Political and social participation can be seen as a virtuous circle, in which each can lead to and reinforce the other.

While this chapter focuses on political and social participation, it must be recognized that they are strongly shaped by economic participation. The low employment levels and the high poverty rates of people with disabilities around the globe constrain the financial resources available to many people with disabilities.[90] Such constraints can greatly limit the opportunities for people with disabilities to take part in many political and social activities, although these constraints can also serve as the basis for disability activism to improve opportunities and resources for people with disabilities. In addition, employment can play an important social and psychological function, providing social networks and a sense of efficacy that increases the likelihood of participating in political and social activities.

Bibliography

Books

Anspach R, From stigma to identity politics: Political activism among the physically disabled and former mental patients (13A, Social Science and Medicine, 1979).

Barnes C, and Mercer C, *Exploring disability* (2nd ed., Polity Press, 2010).

Berkowitz M, O'Leary P. K, Kruse D. L, and Harvey C, *Spinal cord injury: An analysis of medical and social costs* (Demos Medical, 1998).

Carey A. C, *On the margins of citizenship: Intellectual disability and civil rights in twentieth-century America* (Temple University Press, 2009).

Flynn E, *From rhetoric to action: Implementing the UN convention on the rights of persons with disabilities* (Cambridge University Press, 2011).

Kessler, NOD, and Harris, *The ADA, 20 years later* (Harris Interactive, 2010).

Lamp S, "Public transportation" in Albrecht G, Bickenbach J, Mitchell D, Schalick W, and Snyder S, (eds.), *Encyclopedia of disability* (Sage Publications, 2006).

Morris A, and Abelló D, *Disability support pension new customer focus groups* (Social Policy Research Centre, 2005).

NOD/Harris, *2004 national organization on disability/Harris survey of Americans with disabilities* (Harris Interactive, 2004).

Oliver M, *The politics of disablement* (MacMillan, 1990).

Power D, and Power M, "The internet and government disability policy development in the united kingdom" (Internet, Politics, Policy 2010: An Impact Assessment, 2010). http://epublications.bond.edu.au/cgi/viewcontent.cgi?article=1491&context=hss_pubs

Prince M. J, *The electoral participation of persons with special needs* (Elections Canada, 2007).

Rimmerman A, *Social inclusion of people with disabilities: National and international perspectives* (Cambridge University Press, 2013).

Schur L, Adya M, and Kruse D, *Disability, voter turnout, and voting difficulties in the 2012 elections* (U.S. Election Assistance Commission, 2013).

Schur L, and Kruse D. L, "Disability and election policies and practices" in Burden B.C, and Stewart C, (eds.), *The measure of American elections* (Cambridge University Press, 2014).

Scott R, and Crooks A, *Polls apart 4: Campaigning for accessible democracy* (Scope, 2005).

Shields T. G, Schriner K, and Ochs, L. D, "Disenfranchised: People with disabilities in American electoral politics" in Altman B, and Barnartt S, (eds.), *Expanding the scope of social science research on disability* (Emerald Group Publishing, 2000).

NOD/Harris, *2000 national organization on Disability/Harris survey of Americans with disabilities* (Harris Interactive, 2000).

90 Ibid. 79, 31, 30.

Journals

Baker P, Bricout J. C, Moon N. W, Coughlan B, and Pater J, "Communities of participation: A comparison of disability and aging identified groups on facebook and LinkedIn" (2013) *Telematics and Informatics* 30(1).

Barnartt S, "The globalization of disability protests, 1970–2005: Pushing the limits of cross cultural research?" (2010) *Comparative Sociology* 9(2).

Bates P, and Davis F. A, "Social capital, social inclusion and services for people with learning disabilities" (2004) *Disability & Society* 19(3).

Brady H. E, and McNulty J. E, "Turning out to vote: The costs of finding and getting to the polling place" (2011) *American Political Science Review* 105.

Clarke H, Sanders D, Stewart M, and Whiteley P, "Taking the bloom off new labour's rose: Party choice and voter turnout in Britain 2005" (2006) *Journal of Elections Public Opinions and Parties* 16(1).

Clarke P. J, Ailshire J. A, Nieuwenhuijsen E. R, and de Kleijn–de Vrankrijker Marijke W, "Participation among adults with disability: The role of the urban environment" (2011) *Social Science & Medicine* 72(10).

Fiala-Butora J, Stein M. A, and Lord J. E, "The democratic life of the union: Toward equal voting participation for Europeans with disabilities" (2014) 55 *Harvard International Law Journal* 71.

Frawley P, and Bigby C, "Inclusion in political and public life: The experiences of people with intellectual disability on government disability advisory bodies in Australia" (2011) *Journal of Intellectual and Developmental Disability* 36(1).

Gannon B, and Nolan B, "The impact of disability transitions on social inclusion" (2007) *Social Science & Medicine* 64(7).

Gayle A, and Palmer D, "The activism of persons with disabilities in Jamaica: An evaluation of the impact" *Social and Economic Studies* 54(4).

Hahn H, "The politics of physical differences: Disability and discrimination" (1988) *Journal of Social Issues* 44(1).

Hastings J, and Thomas H "Accessing the nation: Disability, political inclusion and built form" (2005) *Urban Studies* 42(3).

Hayashi R, and Okuhira M, "The disability rights movement in Japan: Past, present and future" (2001) *Disability & Society* 16(6).

Holland D, "The current status of disability activism and non-governmental organizations in post-communist Europe: Preliminary findings based on reports from the field" (2008) *Disability & Society* 23(6).

Jaeger P. T, "Telecommunications policy and individuals with disabilities: Issues of accessibility and social inclusion in the policy and research agenda" (2006) *Telecommunications Policy* 30(2).

Jennings M. K, "Political responses to pain and loss presidential address, American political science association 1998" (1999) *American Political Science Review.*

Keeley H, Redley M, Holland A, and Clare I, "Participation in the 2005 general election by adults with intellectual disabilities" (2008) *Journal of Intellectual Disability Research* 52(3).

Kelly C, "Towards renewed descriptions of Canadian disability movements: Disability activism outside of the non-profit sector" (2013) *Canadian Journal of Disability Studies* 2(1).

Kjellberg A, and Hemmingsson H, "Citizenship and voting: Experiences of persons with intellectual disabilities in Sweden" (2013) *Journal of Policy and Practice in Intellectual Disabilities* 10(4).

Mahmood Q. K, Ali H, and Raza H, "The effect of SMS service on the political participation of person with disabilities (PWDs) in Khyber Pakhtunkhwa (Pakistan)" (2013) *World Applied Sciences Journal* 25(5).

McPhedran S, "Disability and community life: Does regional living enhance social participation" *Journal of Disability Policy Studies* 22(1).

Mekosha H, "Virtual activists? women and the making of identities of disability" (2002) *Hypatia* 17(3).

Moriarity L, and Dew K, "The united nations convention on the rights of persons with disabilities and participation in aotearoa New Zealand" (2011) *Disability & Society* 26(6).

Morrison R. L, and Nolan T, "I get by with a little help from my friends . . . at work" (2009) *New Zealand Journal of Social Sciences Online* 4(1).

Rimmerman A, and Herr S. S, "The power of the powerless: A study on the Israeli disability strike of 1999" (2004) *Journal of Disability Policy Studies* 15(1).

Schneider A, and Ingram H, "Social construction of target populations: Implications for politics and policy" (1993) *American Political Science Review* 87(2).

Schriner K, Ochs L. A, and Shields T. G, "The last suffrage movement: Voting rights for persons with cognitive and emotional disabilities" (1997) *The Journal of Federalism* 27(3).

Schur L, "Disability and the psychology of political participation" (1998) *Journal of Disability Policy Studies* 9(2).

Schur L, "Contending with the "double handicap": Political activism among women with disabilities" (2003a) *Women and Politics* 25(1/2).

Schur L, "Employment and the creation of an active citizenry" (2003b) *British Journal of Industrial Relations* 41(4).

Schur L, and Adya M, "Sidelined or mainstreamed? Political participation and attitudes of people with disabilities in the united states" (2013) *Social Science Quarterly* 94(3).

Schur L, and Kruse D. L, "What determines voter turnout? Lessons from citizens with disabilities" (2000) *Social Science Quarterly* 81(2).

Schur L, Shields T, Kruse D, and Schriner K, "Enabling democracy: Disability and voter turnout" (2002) *Political Research Quarterly* 55(1).

Schur L, Shields T, and Schriner K, "Can I make a difference? Efficacy, employment, and disability" (2003) *Political Psychology* 24(1).

Schur L, Shields T, and Schrine K, "Generational cohorts, group membership, and political participation by people with disabilities" (2005) *Political Research Quarterly* 58(3).

Scotch R. K, "Disability as the basis for a social movement: Advocacy and the politics of definition" (1988) *Journal of Social Issues* 44(1).

Stoker L, and Jennings M. K, "Life-cycle transitions and political participation: The case of marriage" (1995) *American Political Science Review* 421.

Tokaji D. P, and Colker R, "Absentee voting by people with disabilities: Promoting access and integrity" (2007) *McGeorge Law Review* 38.

Verba S, Schlozman K. L, and Brady H. E, "Voice and equality: Civic voluntarism in American politics" (1995) Harvard University Press.

Vicente M R, and López A J, "A multidimensional analysis of the disability digital divide: Some evidence for internet use" (2010) *Information Society* 26(1).

Wehbi S, and El-Lahib Y, "Sit (or stand) and be counted! campaigning for the voting rights of people with disabilities in Lebanon" (2008) *Disability Studies Quarterly* 28(2).

Weis C. J, "Why the help America vote act fails to help disabled Americans vote" (2005) *Legislation & Public Policy* 421.

Official publications

Government Accountability Office, *Voters with disabilities: More polling places had no potential impediments than in 2000, but challenges remain* (No. 09-685, 2009).

Grammenos S, *Indicators of disability equality in Europe, ANED 2010 task 4* (Academic Network of European Disability experts, Centre for Disability Studies, University of Leeds, 2010).

U.S. Commission on Civil Rights, *Accommodating the spectrum of individual abilities* (Clearinghouse Publications, 1983).

U.S. Department of Commerce, *Exploring the digital nation: Computer and internet use at home* (U.S. Department of Commerce, 2011).

WHO/World Bank, *World report on disability* (World Health Organization and World Bank, 2011).

PART III

Emerging fields in disability law

Introduction

The contributors to this final section examine leading edge developments in disability law and policy. From multiple disciplinary viewpoints, the authors reflect on the past, and they foretell the possibilities for future advancements to ensure the rights of individuals with disabilities.

There are more than one billion individuals with disabilities around the globe with expectations for self-determination, and for full and equal involvement in their communities. These individuals are living longer, yet most still live in poverty. The majority of people with disabilities live in developing nations (Mary Keogh). These individuals presently experience low levels of literacy, education and employment, and disparities in access to basic resources in social services, healthcare, rehabilitation and technology. Despite recognition of and exponential increases in age-related disabilities (Eilionóir Flynn), women and men with disabilities across the globe continue to experience dire conditions for economic and social advancement.

In light of these developments, the contributors to this section further articulate the modern recognition of the right of people with disabilities to be included in their communities (Ciara Brennan). Equally as significant, they consider the sea of change towards active citizenship by people with disabilities. In this regard, the chapters foreshadow a 'next wave' of activism as envisioned by the CRPD and focused on ensuring that people with disabilities have access to decision-making supports to help them to live and work in integrated, community settings (Anna Arstein-Kerslake and Elizabeth Kamundia).

Within 20 years, the number of persons over age 65 also will have increased exponentially. These individuals, many with disabilities, along with their family members, will require access to supports and services to support independence in all aspects of their daily lives (Arie Rimmerman). They must be afforded equal access to emerging healthcare services, including genetic testing and intervention strategies, in ways that do not result in stigma and discrimination (Aisling de Paor). Additionally, as citizens of the world, individuals with disabilities must be assured the right to full and equal access to the ubiquitous online society (Peter Blanck, Abigail Rekas).

Taken together, the chapters in this section foreshadow how disability law and policy, at the domestic and supranational levels, must continue to promote the liberties of citizenship, independence and human dignity, not only for persons with disabilities but for us all.

9

LEGAL CAPACITY

A global analysis of reform trends

Lucy Series, Anna Arstein-Kerslake
and Elizabeth Kamundia

Introduction

The right to legal capacity in Article 12 of the Convention on the Rights of Persons with Disabilities (CRPD) has prompted controversy that began with the negotiation of the Convention[1] and continues. The heart of the controversy lies in in the call for equality inherent in the right. Article 12 enumerates a right to legal capacity for people with disabilities on an *equal basis* with others. This means that any denials of legal capacity must be on the same basis for people with and without disabilities. This requires respecting the decision-making skills of people with disabilities – including intellectual and psychosocial disabilities – to the same degree as decision-making is respected for people without disabilities. Many people are fully ready to embrace equal rights for people with disabilities, until they are confronted with the challenge of respecting legal capacity on an equal basis. It asks for a true move away from the charity model of disability. It demands that society not only provide people with disabilities services and supports, but also that people with disabilities are recognized as full persons before the law with equal respect for their rights, wills and preferences.

This chapter aims to give a snapshot of the current state-of-play of the right to equal recognition before the law for people with disabilities. It will discuss the interpretation of Article 12 CRPD given by the CRPD Committee – the UN monitoring body for the CRPD – in their recent General Comment on Article 12. It will also provide examples of reform efforts from Africa, the United Kingdom (UK) and other jurisdictions to give a context for how the implementation of Article 12 is progressing on the ground. The purpose of this chapter is to both provide information about how the CRPD Committee has envisioned compliance with Article 12 as well as a look at the successes and challenges of recent reform efforts.

---

1 For a discussion of the negotiation of the right to legal capacity in Article 12 of the CRPD, see Amita Dhanda, (2006–2007) "Legal Capacity in the Disability Rights Convention: Stranglehold of the Past or Lodestar for the Future?," *Syracuse Journal of International Law and Commerce*, 34(2), 429–462.

Interpreting Article 12: The general comment and its discontents

Until April 2014, there was relatively little information available regarding the CRPD Committee's interpretation of Article 12. The most significant statement that the Committee had made up to that point was that supported decision-making regimes must replace substituted decision-making regime.[2] This statement was very important in shaping the interpretation of Article 12 because it strongly suggested that existing regimes such as guardianship, interdiction and wardship are contrary to Article 12. This garnered support from Disabled People's Organizations (DPOs) and disability human rights scholars. However, there was no detail available from the Committee on what exactly State Parties were required to do in order to achieve the replacement of substituted decision-making regimes with supported decision-making regimes. There was also no official definition of either type of regime. Based on this gap, and on the fact that it became increasingly apparent that State Parties did not clearly understand the state obligations and individual rights held in Article 12, in early 2014 the Committee came forward with its first general comment, which focused on illuminating the text of Article 12.

The General Comment on Article 12 contains many concepts that were discussed throughout the drafting process of the Convention itself.[3] It is also a reflection of scholarly work[4] and the advocacy work of DPOs[5] since the adoption of the Convention by the United Nations (UN) in 2006. It is a statement of the Committee's interpretation of Article 12 and it is the yardstick by which the Committee will review State Parties for compliance with Article 12.[6]

The General Comment attempts to cover a significant amount of ground. It includes background information on the importance and relevance of the right to equal recognition before the law for people with disabilities, a description of the normative content of Article 12, the State Party obligations connected to the rights in Article 12, and an explanation of the relationship that Article 12 has to the other articles in the Convention. Three of the key innovations of the General

---

2 See for example the Committee's concluding observations on the state report of Australia, *Concluding observations on the initial report of Australia*, paragraph 25, UN Doc No. CRPD/C/AUS/CO/1, adopted by the Committee at its tenth session (2–13 September 2013).

3 *Supra* note.

4 For example, Eilionóir Flynn & Anna Arstein-Kerslake, (2014) "Legislating Personhood: Realizing the Right to Support in Exercising Legal Capacity," *International Journal of Law in Context*, 10(1), 81; Tina Minkowitz, (2006–2007) "The United Nations Convention on the Rights of Persons with Disabilities and the Right to Be Free from Nonconsensual Psychiatric Interventions," *Syracuse Journal of International Law and Commerce*, 34, 405; Gerard Quinn and Anna Arstein-Kerslake, "Restoring the 'Human' in 'Human Rights': Personhood and Doctrinal Innovation in the UN Disability Convention," in C. Gearty and C. Douzinas (eds.), *The Cambridge Companion to Human Rights Law* (Cambridge University Press, 2012); and Amita Dhanda, "Universal Legal Capacity as a Universal Human Right," in Michael Dudley, Derrick Silove and Fran Gale (eds.), Mental Health and Human Rights: Vision, Praxis, and Courage, 177 (Oxford University Press, 2012). Quinn, Dhanda, etc.

5 For example, "Legal Capacity as Right, Principle and Paradigm: Submission to the Committee on the Rights of Persons with Disabilities in response to its Call for Papers on theoretical and practical implementation of Article 1," World Network of Users and Survivors of Psychiatry (WNUSP) (17 June 2011); and "Independent but Not Alone: A Global Report on the Right to Decide," Inclusion International (12 June 2014).

6 For example in the State Reports that are due 2 years after ratification and then every 4 years proceeding that date. Article 35, Convention on the Rights of Persons with Disabilities (CRPD), 2515 U.N.T.S. 3 (13 December 2006). The General Comment will also be used it interpreting Article 12 for the purposes of individuals complaints and other inquiries under the Optional Protocol. Optional Protocol to the Convention on the Rights of Persons with Disabilities (CRPD), UN Doc. No. A/RES/61/106 (13 December 2006).

Comment are: 1) the definition of 'substituted decision-making' regimes that are contrary to Article 12; 2) the move from 'best interests' decision-making to 'will and preference' support; and 3) the clear delineation of 'legal capacity' as a separate concept from 'mental capacity'.

The General Comment is the first major piece of work that defines impermissible 'substituted decision-making'. It defines substituted decision-making as systems where: 1) legal capacity is denied, 2) an outside decision-maker is imposed, and 3) decisions are made in the 'best interest' of the individual as opposed to based on the will and preference of the individual.[7] This has serious implications for most jurisdictions. There may be some jurisdictions that can reform existing decision-making systems to ensure that they are not substituted decision-making regimes. However, many systems will require a reconstruction from the ground up. It is important to note that this definition does not include circumstances in which an individual nominates someone to make decisions on his or her behalf. This type of nominated decision-maker is permitted under the General Comment because it does not deny the legal capacity of the individual – in fact, it is an exercise of the individual's legal capacity when he or she nominates a decision-maker. It is also permissible because it is not imposed against the person's will. Further research and scholarship is needed to examine national systems to discover whether they are impermissible substituted decision-making according to the General Comment.

The move from 'best interest' to 'will and preference' is not novel in the General Comment. It has been discussed in advocacy documents[8] and academic work[9] from various jurisdictions. There is an emerging literature on the meaning of 'will and preference' and how to arrive at an individual's will and preference through a process of support.[10] The General Comment highlights that where a person is using assistance in decision-making, that assistance is operating based on what they believe, in good faith, is the will and preference of that individual. If the will and preference is not precisely knowable, then the assistant must operate based on his or her best interpretation of what that individual's will and preference is.[11]

The final significant innovation in the General Comment is the establishment of mental capacity and legal capacity as separate and distinct concepts. This is important because of the long history of conflating these concepts. The distinction is a critical one. Legal capacity is a legal construct that, when recognized, acknowledges the individual as a person before the law – as a subject of the state with rights and responsibilities. Mental capacity, on the other hand, is simply an individuals cognitive skills and decision-making abilities. Mental capacity varies between individuals based on personality, environment, education, disability, and other factors. The General Comment firmly establishes that all people, regardless of level of 'mental capacity' are due 'legal capacity' on an equal basis – that is, all people of all different levels of cognitive ability have a right to be persons before the law.

---

7 Committee on the Rights of Persons with Disabilities, General Comment No. 1, Article 12: Equal Recognition Before the Law, paragraph 27, UN Doc. No. CRPD/C/GC/1 (April 2014).
8 For example, Inclusion International *supra* note 5 at pages 19, 55, 115, and 118; and Position on Legal Capacity, Canadian Association for Community Living (June 2010).
9 For example, Flynn and Arstein-Kerslake *supra* note; and Michael Bach and Lana Kerzner, "A New Paradigm for Protecting Autonomy and the Right to Legal Capacity," prepared for the Law Commission of Ontario (October 2010).
10 For example, Michelle Browning, Christine Bigby and Jacinta Douglas, (2014) "Supported Decision Making: Understanding How its Conceptual Link to Legal Capacity is Influencing the Development of Practice," *Research and Practice in Intellectual and Developmental Disabilities*, 1(1), 34–45; and Piers Gooding, (2013) "Supported Decision-Making: A Rights-Based Disability Concept and Its Implications for Mental Health Law," *Psychiatry, Psychology and Law*, 20(3), 431–451.
11 Committee on the Rights of Persons with Disabilities, General Comment No. 1, Article 12: Equal Recognition Before the Law, paragraph 21, UN Doc. No. CRPD/C/GC/1 (April 2014).

The General Comment clarifies the rights in Article 12. It also presents the challenges that Article 12 makes to existing legal capacity law. It has sparked controversy – particularly in fields that are reliant on denials of legal capacity tied to mental capacity, such as psychiatry. There is potential for further conflict to arise based on the understanding that the General Comment gives of Article 12 – however, instead of seeing barriers and a battleground, the General Comment should be seen as an opportunity to re-examine existing laws and policies in light of the principles within the General Comment and to challenge the effectiveness of those laws and policies in securing the rights of people with disabilities.

Reform in Africa: The rays of hope and the stumbling blocks

Introduction

In June 2014, a workshop on 'Latest developments on legal capacity in Africa' was held in Nairobi, Kenya, with participants drawn from a diverse range of African countries including Zambia, Uganda, Tanzania, Malawi, Nigeria, South Africa, Zimbabwe, Rwanda and Kenya.[12] The workshop discussed various topics including laws that limit legal capacity in the represented countries, the role of customary law in upholding and denying legal capacity, the right to own and manage property and finances by persons with disabilities, and implementing the supported decision-making model in the African context. Most of the participants are part of an online list serve community called 'Legal Capacity Network-Africa' formed in January 2014. The online community keeps members up to date on legal capacity developments in the respective countries within Africa, and provides a space for members to discuss issues related to legal capacity.

The countries represented in the workshop are at various stages in the legal capacity law reform process. Kenya and Zambia are leading the continent on legal capacity-related initiatives and as such will feature prominently in this section. In both countries, legal capacity law reform is mainly being pushed by civil society, Disabled People's Organizations (DPOs) and, in the case of Kenya, the National Human Rights Institution. Open Society Foundations funds DPOs that are implementing projects on legal capacity in several African countries including Kenya, Zambia and Tanzania.

This section outlines development in legal capacity law in Africa. It explores potential openings for change, showcases organizations that are focused on change in select countries, identifies barriers that may prevent change from occurring and highlights pathways towards the realization of the right to legal capacity in Africa.

Legal capacity law reform: Progress made

Regional level

At the African regional level, the African Commission on Human and Peoples' Rights has developed a draft protocol on the rights of persons with disabilities in Africa. Article 7 of the draft protocol is on equal recognition before the law.[13] While the article largely echoes the provisions of Article 12 of the CRPD, it also addresses issues that are specific to the exercise of the right to

---

12 The workshop, which was held at Sarova – Panafric Hotel, Nairobi, Kenya on 11th and 12th June 2014 was funded by Open Society Foundations.

13 African Commission on Human and Peoples' Rights, 'Comments Invited on Draft Protocol on the Rights of Persons with Disabilities in Africa', available at http://www.achpr.org/news/2014/04/d121 accessed 4 December 2015.

legal capacity within the African continent. In addition to the provisions of the CRPD, Article 7 of the draft protocol requires States Parties to ensure that non-State actors and other individuals do not violate the right of persons with disabilities to realize their right to legal capacity and that persons with disabilities have the equal right to hold documents of identity and other documents that may enable them to exercise their right to legal capacity.

Despite being part of the law in many African countries, formal guardianship is not an often-employed mechanism in the African context;[14] the more prevalent situation is that of informal substituted decision-making within families and communities.[15] Article 7(a) of the draft protocol responds to this reality by expressly prohibiting non-State actors and other individuals from violating the right of persons with disabilities to realize their right to legal capacity.

Studies on the right to legal capacity in Kenya identify that persons with disabilities often do not have national identification cards and other documents of identity:

> Many people with intellectual disabilities with whom MDAC researchers spoke did not have a national identification card because no one had supported them to get one.[16]
>
> Persons with intellectual disabilities in Kenya tend not to have identity documents as 'many families do not register their child with an intellectual disability at birth'.[17]

In responding to this reality, Article 7(d) of the draft protocol recognizes the right of persons with disabilities to hold documents of identity.

The African Commission on Human and Peoples' Rights is still addressing itself to comments received upon the release of the draft protocol.

National level

There has been limited progress on legal capacity law reform at the national level in most African countries.[18] In the countries where there has been progress, the form this progress has taken is legislation as well as reports laying the foundation for reform by identifying for amendment laws that run counter to Article 12 of the CRPD. With regard to legislation, Section 8(1) of Zambia's Persons with Disabilities Act 2012 states that 'A person with disability shall enjoy legal capacity on an equal basis with others in all aspects of life'. It is the only country in Africa whose domestic law explicitly recognizes the right to legal capacity, despite the fact that most African countries have ratified the CRPD.[19] There have been two key reports on legal capacity in Kenya; the first by the Kenya National Commission on Human Rights and the second by the Mental Disability Advocacy Centre.

---

14 Workshop on 'Latest Developments on Legal Capacity in Africa' (Nairobi, Kenya, 11–12 June 2014).
15 Mental Disability Advocacy Centre, 'The Right to Legal Capacity in Kenya', available at: http://mdac. info/sites/mdac.info/files/mdac_kenya_legal_capacity_2apr2014.pdf accessed 4 December 2015.
16 *Id.*
17 Kenya National Commission on Human Rights, 'How to Implement Article 12 of the Convention on the Rights of Persons with Disabilities Regarding Legal Capacity in Kenya: A Briefing Paper', available at http://www.knchr.org/ReportsPublications/ThematicReports/GroupRights.aspx accessed 4 December 2015.
18 Workshop *supra* note.
19 UN Enable, 'Convention and Optional Protocol Signatures and Ratifications', available at http://www. un.org/disabilities/countries.asp?id=166 accessed 4 December 2015.

In 2013, the Kenya National Commission on Human Rights (KNCHR) together with the Open Society Initiative for Eastern Africa commissioned a briefing paper on how to implement Article 12 of the Convention on the Rights of Persons with Disabilities regarding legal capacity in Kenya.[20] Through interviews, the study revealed the situation of persons with disabilities in Kenya with regard to Article 12 of the CRPD, highlighting local good practice models on implementing the right to legal capacity. The study also highlighted the dilemmas in implementing Article 12 in the Kenyan context; and finally made recommendations on the process as well as the content which should be included in policy, law and procedures to effect Article 12 of the CRPD in Kenya.

The Mental Disability Advocacy Centre also published a paper on the right to legal capacity in Kenya.[21] The report highlights the voices of people with mental disabilities themselves, outlining the need for substantial legal and social reform. The report provides comprehensive recommendations to bring Kenya in line with international law, and specifically the right to legal capacity guaranteed by Article 12 of the CRPD.[22]

Potential openings for change

The laws of many countries in Africa run contrary to Article 12 of the CRPD as they allow substituted decision-making and fail to make provision for access to support in the exercise of legal capacity by persons with disabilities. To illustrate:

> Section 7 of Uganda's Mental Health Treatment Act, 1964 allows for the involuntary detention of 'a person alleged to be of unsound mind'.[23]
> Section 101(e) of Tanzania's Law of Marriage Act allows a person to petition for divorce on the grounds that the spouse is 'suffering from an incurable mental illness'.[24]
> Sections 80(7)a and 94(3)b (*inter alia*) of Malawi electoral laws run counter to the right of persons with disabilities to stand for elections and/or to effectively hold office.[25]

Potential openings for change vary widely, depending on the context of the country. In countries that are reforming their Persons with Disabilities Acts (such as Kenya and Mozambique), or their Mental Health laws (such as Kenya, Uganda and Zambia) the law reform process presents a huge potential for change. Because Africa lacks huge guardianship infrastructure, it should be easier, theoretically, to advocate for law reform to abolish guardianship. However, the extent to which law reform can be used to yield laws that provide for equal legal capacity remains to be seen.[26]

---

20 Kenya National Commission on Human Rights *supra* note.
21 Mental Disability Advocacy Centre *supra* note.
22 *Id.*
23 World Health Organisation, 'WHO Mind Bank: More Inclusiveness Needed in Disability and Development', available at http://www.mindbank.info/item/881 accessed 4 December 2015.
24 The Law of Marriage Act, available at http://polis.parliament.go.tz/PAMS/docs/5–1971.pdf accessed 30 August 2014.
25 Malawi Electoral Commission, 'Malawi Electoral Laws', available at http://www.mec.org.mw/LinkClick.aspx?fileticket=EYRmv9D7DYk%3D&tabid=178 accessed 30 August 2014.
26 See section 'Limited expertise on the right to legal capacity', which uses Kenya's Mental Health Bill to illustrate the shortcomings of law reform in circumstances of limited understanding of the concept of legal capacity.

The second opening for change has to do with addressing the issues that give rise to informal substituted decision-making within the community. The key finding from the KNCHR briefing paper is that formal guardianship is not widespread in Kenya and the exercise of the right to legal capacity in Kenya is hindered by factors such as societal attitudes that continue to hold persons with disabilities as objects of care as opposed to rights holders, lack of alternatives to psychiatric solutions within the mental healthcare sphere, inaccessibility of the environment, limited state support to persons with disabilities and their families, and poverty and high unemployment rates among persons with disabilities.

The third opening for change is presented by DPOs of persons with psychosocial disabilities and DPOs of persons with intellectual disabilities which are leading the way towards supported decision-making, mainly through projects on awareness-raising within families and communities, peer support groups and self-advocacy.

Organizations that are focused on change

Zambia

The two organizations in Zambia that are leading the work on Article 12 of the CRPD are the Zambian Federation of the Disabled (ZAFOD) and the Mental Health Users Network of Zambia (MHUNZA).[27] The two DPOs are engaged in mental health law reform (advocating for the recognition of the right to legal capacity in Zambia's Mental Health Bill), community advocacy on legal capacity, peer networks and individual and family supports projects.[28]

In responding to the Zambian context, one of the objectives of pilot projects is to develop and implement practical strategies for social and *economic* inclusion. The objectives of the pilot projects also highlight the need to empower and engage not just people with disabilities but their families as well.[29] Further, the need to develop and implement community-based mental health supports is highlighted. It is planned to develop information tools for training self-advocates and mental health users on the right to legal capacity.[30]

Kenya

In Kenya, there are ongoing initiatives on actualizing Article 12 of the CRPD for Persons with Intellectual Disabilities as well as for persons with psychosocial disabilities. The Kenya Association of the Intellectually Handicapped (KAIH)[31] works on actualizing Article 12 for persons with intellectual disabilities in six regions within Kenya while USP-Kenya[32] works

27 Institute for Research and Development on Inclusion and Society, 'Iris International Work on Legal Capacity – Zambia', available at http://irisinstitute.ca/2013/12/21/iris-international-work-on-legal-capacity-zambia/ accessed 4 December 2015.

28 The Institute for Research and Development on Inclusion and Society is supporting ZAFOD and MHUNZA in pilot projects on Article 12 — Michael Bach, 'How can we create change in the legal framework, in the community and in our social systems?' Paper Given at a Workshop on 'Latest Developments on Legal Capacity in Africa' (Nairobi, Kenya, 11–12 June 2014).

29 *Id.*

30 *Id.*

31 Kenya Association for the Intellectually Handicapped, available at http://kaihid.org/ accessed 4 December 2015.

32 Users and Survivors of Psychiatry-Kenya, available at http://www.uspkenya.com/ accessed 1 September 2014.

on realizing Article 12 for persons with psychosocial disabilities in four counties in Kenya.[33] The two organizations focus on legislative reform, peer support groups, self-advocacy and awareness-raising.

Barriers to change

Limited expertise on the right to legal capacity

While the CRPD Committee has issued its General Comment on Article 12, the issue as to exactly what Article 12 of the CRPD means with regard to law reform and practice on the ground remains contentious.[34] Using the General Comment on Article 12 as the guiding framework, it is clear that there are huge contradictions in some of the mental health laws that are being formulated post CRPD. For example, Kenya's draft Mental Health Bill, 2014, at Clause 17(1) states that 'Persons with disabilities shall enjoy legal capacity on an equal basis with others'. Immediately following this provision, Clause 17(4) states that 'the court shall make a determination as to whether a person has legal capacity'.[35] In addition, recent cases on guardianship did not mention the CRPD at all.[36]

Families

The majority of persons with disabilities in Kenya live with their families in a context of limited state support. This is compounded by the fact that most people with disabilities are unemployed and therefore economically dependent on their families.[37] Families are critical allies in the exercise of legal capacity by persons with disabilities in Kenya; yet while some families are very supportive of their family member with a disability, others are not. According to KAIH:[38]

> Initially, families are sceptical about allowing their family members with intellectual disabilities to make their own decisions. Families are worried about having to 'pick up the pieces' in case their family member with intellectual disability makes a 'bad' decision. When support persons are not family members, families are concerned, for instance, about their family member with an intellectual disability being exploited financially.

33 Kenya National Commission on Human Rights *supra.*
34 Examples are declarations to the Convention by Australia http://www.bayefsky.com//html/australia_t2_disability.php and Canada http://www.bayefsky.com//html/canada_t2_disability.php both accessed 4 December 2015.
35 See http://kenyalaw.org/kl/fileadmin/pdfdownloads/bills/2014/MentalHealthBill2014.pdf accessed 1 September 2014.
36 In the matter of Leah Wachu Waiganjo, available at http://kenyalaw.org/caselaw/cases/view/80879 accessed 4 December 2015 and generally Section 3.2.1 of Kenya National Commission on Human Rights *supra.*
37 Office of the High Commissioner for Human Rights 'CRPD Future Sessions', available at http://tbinternet.ohchr.org/_layouts/treatybodyexternal/SessionDetails1.aspx?SessionID=800&Lang=en accessed 4 December 2015.
38 Kenya National Commission on Human Rights *supra.*

Limited financial resources

Currently, there is no state-funded system of support for decision-making for people with disabilities in Kenya. Some persons with disabilities do not have family to fall back on for support; in such circumstances, such persons end up homeless on the streets.[39] In the absence of a state-funded system of support (even for basic livelihood issues such as food and housing) a question arises as to whether it is reasonably foreseeable that the Kenyan state will fund a system of support for decision-making for people with disabilities in the future.[40]

Limited financial resources also limit the extent to which DPOs can act as change agents. For example, USP-K's peer support groups are only running in four out of forty-seven counties; while KAIH's runs in six regions only. This is largely out of insufficient funds to replicate the same throughout the country.

Limited alternatives in mental healthcare

Recognizing the right to refuse psychiatric services requires that the State provide alternative services outside of the medical paradigm.[41] In Kenya, there are no state-funded alternatives to medication in the context of psychosocial disability.

Conclusion

Overall, the change process on legal capacity in Africa is slow-going. However, even at this early stage, certain lessons regarding how to make Article 12 of the CRPD real in law and practice can be drawn. First, it is important to contextualize the right to legal capacity in the specific context, without of course derogating from the core of the right. In the African context, bringing families and entire communities on board with universal legal capacity is especially pertinent, given the limited nature of state support to people. Second, it is critical that the process is led by DPOs, civil society and self-advocates. Given the relative 'newness' of the right, the need for practical models on the ground formulated by persons with disabilities cannot be gainsaid. Third, there is dire need of expertise on legal capacity, and need for the expertise to seep into the various arms of government.

Reform in the United Kingdom: Palpable resistance and positive practices

Introduction

In contrast with other common law jurisdictions such as Ireland, Australia and Canada, the separate jurisdictions that make up the United Kingdom (UK) – England and Wales, Scotland and Northern Ireland – have been slow to engage with the requirements of Article 12 CRPD.

---

39 *Id.*

40 This is not said to diminish the importance of the right to legal capacity (which is of the nature of a civil and political right) only to show the reality of the situation, i.e. how useful is the guarantee of the right to choose when there is nothing to choose between, as in the mental health context?

41 Office of the High Commissioner for Human Rights, Committee on the Rights of Persons with Disabilities Day of General Discussion on Article 12 of the CRPD – The Right to Equal Recognition Before the Law (21 October 2009) Ubuntu Centre of South Africa, 'Supported Decision-Making', available at http://www.ohchr.org/EN/HRBodies/CRPD/Pages/DayGeneralDiscussion21102009. aspx accessed 30 May 2014.

Until relatively recently, awareness that domestic legal capacity legislation might diverge from the requirements of Article 12 CRPD was confined to a small circle of legal academics.[42] As engagement with the normative content of Article 12 CRPD has increased, there are signs that it has prompted serious reflection on existing practices in some places, whilst encountering palpable resistance in others. This section briefly summarizes existing capacity legislation in the UK, explores what limited engagement there has been with Article 12 CRPD, and suggests some areas of existing good practice which the CRPD could be used to strengthen and develop.

Capacity legislation in England and Wales, Scotland and Northern Ireland

Each UK jurisdiction has undergone, or is undergoing, relatively recent reforms to capacity legislation. Proposals for legal capacity law reform were drawn up by law reform commissions in England and Wales[43] and Scotland[44] during the 1990s, and were enacted in the Mental Capacity Act 2005 (MCA) of England and Wales and the Adults with Incapacity (Scotland) Act 2000 (AWIA). Meanwhile, Northern Ireland has embarked upon an attempt at 'fusion law', whereby a single statute based on the concept of 'incapacity' provides for both traditional 'guardianship' mechanisms, as well as measures such as detention and involuntary treatment that are the traditional preserve of mental health law.[45]

Part of the reason for reluctance to engage with the CRPD's different approach to legal capacity in the UK may therefore simply be the recentness of these reforms (or proposed reforms) and a desire to avoid revisiting old debates or opening new areas of controversy. Policymakers and campaigners may also mistakenly assume that the normative content of the CRPD is identical to older human rights instruments which more closely resemble these reforms.[46] In the UK, there is also a growing backlash against international human rights instruments,[47] perhaps coupled with a view in some places that the UK is already world leading in human rights, which may lead to a degree of parochialism and resistance to international human rights instruments.

42 Bartlett, P. (2009) "The United Nations Convention on the Rights of Persons with Disabilities and the future of mental health law," *Psychiatry*, 8(12), 496–498; Bartlett, P. (2012) "The United Nations Convention on the Rights of Persons with Disabilities and Mental Health Law," *Modern Law Review*, 75(5), 752–778; Richardson, G. (2012) "Mental Disabilities and the Law: From Substitute to Supported Decision-Making?," *Current Legal Problems*, 65(1), 333–354; Richardson, G. (2013) "Mental capacity in the shadow of suicide: What can the law do?," *International Journal of Law in Context*, 9 (Special Issue 01), 87–105; Fennell, P. and Khaliq, U. (2011) "Conflicting or complementary obligations? The UN Disability Rights Convention on Human Rights and English law," *European Human Rights Law Review*, (6), 662–674. See also: Donnelly, M. (2010) *Healthcare Decision-Making and the Law: Autonomy, Capacity and the Limit of Liberalism*, Cambridge University Press; Dimopoulos, A. (2010) *Issues in Human Rights Protection of Intellectually Disabled Persons*, Ashgate Publishing Ltd.
43 Law Commission (1995) *Mentally Incapacitated Adults*, London: HMSO.
44 Scottish Law Commission (1995) *Report on Incapable Adults*, Edinburgh.
45 Department of Health, Social Services and Public Safety, (2014) *Draft Mental Capacity Bill (NI) Consultation Document*, Belfast.
46 Council of Europe (1999) *Recommendation (99) 4 on Principles Concerning the Legal Protection of Incapable Adults*, (Adopted by the Committee of Ministers on 23 February 1999); United Nations (1991) *The Protection of Persons with Mental Illness and the Improvement of Mental Health Care*, (the "MI Principles").
47 Commission on a Bill of Rights (2012) *A UK Bill of Rights? The Choice Before Us (Volume 1)*, Ministry of Justice; Commission on a Bill of Rights (2012) *A UK Bill of Rights? The Choice Before Us (Volume 2)*, Ministry of Justice.

The Draft Mental Capacity Bill in Northern Ireland (MCB NI), the AWIA and the MCA all contain elements that are problematic from the perspective of the CRPD. They all include functional tests of mental capacity.[48] All contain the potential for 'substitute decisions': the MCA[49] and the MCB NI[50] explicitly permit 'best interests' decisions whilst the AWIA[51] permits 'interventions' for the 'benefit of' people who are considered 'incapable' of making decisions for themselves.

The UK approach to support for decision-making is also somewhat embryonic and atomized, focusing on support for isolated decisions rather than taking a coordinated, holistic and longitudinal approach. The AWIA's support provision simply specifies that a person should not be considered 'incapable' 'by reason only of a lack or deficiency in a faculty of communication if that lack or deficiency can be made good by human or mechanical aid (whether of an interpretative nature or otherwise)'.[52] The MCA specifies that 'A person is not to be treated as unable to make a decision unless all practicable steps to help him to do so have been taken without success'[53] and that 'A person is not to be regarded as unable to understand the information relevant to a decision if he is able to understand an explanation of it given to him in a way that is appropriate to his circumstances (using simple language, visual aids or any other means).'[54] The MCB NI contains slightly more detailed provisions on supporting a person to make a decision by providing appropriate information, selecting an optimal time and place to discuss decisions, and involving others who could assist with understanding and communication.[55] However, neither the MCA, the AWIA nor the MCB NI contains a framework enabling a person to formally nominate a supporter, as required by the GC (§25), and such as those provided for Canada, and proposals in Ireland and Australia.[56] Whilst the MCA and the MCB NI do include provisions for independent advocacy,[57] these advocates' roles are primarily conceived of in terms of representing a person who has already been assessed as lacking mental capacity and better informing best interests decisions. They are not explicitly required to support a person in making decisions for themselves.

The AWIA and the MCA were passed before the United Nations General Assembly adopted the CRPD, meanwhile the fusion bill in Northern Ireland is based on proposals that 'mental incapacity' is a less problematic and less discriminatory basis for non-consensual interventions than risk and mental disorder.[58] These laws have proven to be remarkably popular amongst lawyers,

---

48 S2–3 MCA; s1(6) AWIA; s3 MCB NI.
49 s4 MCA.
50 s6 MCB NI.
51 s1 AWIA.
52 s1(6) AWIA.
53 s1(3) MCA.
54 s3(2) MCA.
55 s4 MCB NI.
56 On Canada, see: James, K. and Watts, L. (2014) *Understanding the Lived Experience of Supported Decision-Making in Canada*, Law Commission of Ontario. For proposals in Ireland see the Assisted Decision-Making (Capacity) Bill 2013 (Ireland). For proposals in Australia see: Victorian Law Reform Commission (2012) *Guardianship Final Report 24*, Melbourne, Australia.
57 s33–41 MCA, see also The Mental Capacity Act 2005 (Independent Mental Capacity Advocates) (General) Regulations 2006; MCB NI s35–36.
58 Campbell, T. and Heginbotham, C. (1991) "Chapter 4: Paternalism and Civil Commitment" in *Mental Illness: Prejudice, Discrimination and the Law*, Dartmouth Publishing Company Ltd; Richardson, G. (1999) *Report of the Expert Committee: Review of the Mental Health Act 1983*, Saks, E. (2002) *Refusing Care: Forced Treatment and the Rights of the Mentally Ill*, University of Chicago Press; Dawson, J. and Szmukler, G. (2006) "Fusion of mental health and incapacity legislation," *The British Journal of Psychiatry*, 188(6), 504–509.

academics, policymakers, health and social care professionals and many disability organizations. For example, a recently established House of Lords Committee on the MCA heard evidence from a wide range of sources that although its application could be unduly paternalistic and even oppressive, its core principles were sound.[59] It seems that few in the UK countenance the idea that there might be an inherent problem with mental capacity laws themselves, and prefer to blame troubling outcomes upon misapplication on the ground.

Engagement with Article 12 CRPD in the UK

If the UK government was aware, when it signed and ratified the UN CRPD, that the MCA and AWIA might not satisfy the requirements of Article 12 CRPD, it gave no sign of it.[60] Despite a burgeoning industry of academic research and comment on the MCA, until very recently there has been very limited engagement among UK academics with the 'support paradigm' literature that was emerging in connection with the CRPD. Some interpreted the CRPD to permit substitute decisions where people lacked mental capacity.[61]

Although disability organizations and human rights bodies have campaigned using Article 19 CRPD – the right to independent living[62] – there are few signs of any campaigns around rights connected with Article 12 CRPD.[63] Perhaps surprisingly given the influence of bodies such as the World Network of Users and Survivors of Psychiatry on the development of Article 12 CRPD, there are no prominent campaigns by UK-based user and survivor organizations basing their advocacy on the CRPD.[64] Although denial of opportunities to make decisions, and support

59 House of Lords Select Committee on the Mental Capacity Act 2005 (2013) *Oral and Written Evidence – Volume 1 (A–K)*, House of Lords, UK Parliament; The Select Committee on the Mental Capacity Act 2005 (2013) *Oral and Written Evidence – Volume 2 (L–W)*, House of Lords, UK Parliament; House of Lords Select Committee on the Mental Capacity Act 2005 (2014) *Mental Capacity Act 2005: Post-legislative Scrutiny*, TSO.
60 Unlike Australia and Canada, for example, it did not enter any interpretive reservation to the effect that Article 12 permitted substitute decisions. See also: Office for Disability Issues (2011) *UK Initial Report On the UN Convention on the Rights of Persons with Disabilities*, London. pp. 32–36.
61 Donnelly, M. (2010) *Healthcare Decision-Making and the Law: Autonomy, Capacity and the Limits of Liberalism*, Cambridge University Press; Dimopoulos, A. (2010) *Issues in Human Rights Protection of Intellectually Disabled Persons*, Ashgate Publishing Ltd.
62 For example, Disability Rights UK, Mencap and Scope have all campaigned against cuts to benefits and services by citing Article 19 CRPD. See also: Joint Committee on Human Rights (2012) *Implementation of the Right of Disabled People to Independent Living*, 1, (HL Paper 257, HC 1074). London.
63 Although, a recent event organised by Mencap and the Northern Ireland Association for Mental Health (NIAMH) in Northern Ireland, entitled 'Our lives, our decisions: Event focuses on controlling your destiny' did discuss Article 12 CRPD, available at www.mencap.org.uk/news/article/our-lives-our-decisions-event-focuses-controlling-your-destiny, accessed 4 December 2015.
64 See, for example, the websites of the National Survivor User Network (www.nsun.org.uk/), and the Scottish organisation *Voices of Experience* (www.voxscotland.org.uk/). Neither are prominent mental health organizations that are not user led, such as Mind (www.mind.org.uk/), Rethink (www.rethink.org/) or the Mental Health Foundation (www.mentalhealth.org.uk/). However, NSUN has in its newsletters been promoting a petition to 'Repeal illegal mental health laws – which do not comply with the CRPD'. It is unclear from its wording whether this petition opposes all forced treatment, or only forced treatment of those regarded as having mental capacity (available at https://secure.avaaz.org/en/petition/Rt_Hon_Jeremy_Hunt_MP_Secretary_of_State_for_Health_United_Kingdom_Repeal_illegal_mental_health_laws_which_do_not_comply/?neHOFdb) all websites accessed on 4 December 2015.

to make decisions, is a key concern of disabled people and self-advocates,[65] it seems that – in the UK at least – their representative organizations have yet to harness the potential for advocacy based on Article 12 CRPD.

As awareness of the 'support paradigm' has grown, some in the UK have voiced confusion or concern about its content. In Scotland, Adrian Ward – an influential mental health solicitor – has described the CRPD as a product of 'inept drafting', which itself discriminates against people with disabilities,[66] and his criticisms appear to have been adopted by the Law Society of Scotland.[67] A comparatively large number of UK academics responded to the CRPD Committee's call for comments on a draft General Comment on Article 12 (DGC); many of these defended 'mental capacity' based approaches.[68] No UK disabled people's user-led organizations submitted comments on the DGC, but Colin Harper – a Belfast-based researcher and activist who is playing a key role in coordinating a UK shadow report on the CRPD – highlighted a number of concerns and expressed doubts about the 'universal legal capacity' formulation. Meanwhile, the UK's national equality and human rights commissions[69] submitted a joint comment on the DGC arguing, *inter alia*, for a qualified approach to legal capacity that still permitted substitute decision-making.

Many of the concerns expressed in the UK related to a lack of clarity as to how the support paradigm could accommodate situations where it was difficult to ascertain a person's 'will and preferences', as well as concerns about situations of risk and emergency. To win support in the UK, advocates of the CRPD will need to address these concerns, but that does not negate a need at the domestic level for academics and activists to engage in a respectful way with the existing literature on the CRPD and even take responsibility for constructively developing our understanding of how Article 12 could be implemented.

An opportunity to reconsider the MCA in light of the CRPD arose when the House of Lords established a Select Committee to conduct post-legislative scrutiny of the Act, following concerns that it might be implicated in human rights violations.[70] The Committee called for evidence on twenty-six questions relating to the MCA, with the final question relating to its compliance with the CRPD. In the event, the Committee declined to review the compatibility of the MCA with the CRPD, on the basis that the purpose of post-legislative scrutiny is to consider compliance with the intentions of legislators.[71] However, it was gratifying to see several responses to the Committee from bodies such as the Law Society calling for examination of how the MCA could be adapted to better comply with the CRPD, although some bodies such as

65 Inclusion International (2014) *Independent But Not Alone: A Global Report on the Right to Decide*, London.
66 Ward, A. (2011) "Adults with incapacity: freedom and liberty, rights and status: Part 1," *Scots Law Times*, (5), 21–25.
67 See overlap between: Ward, A. (2014) "Abolition of all guardianship and mental health laws?," *Elder Law Journal*, 4(1), 71 and Law Society of Scotland (2014) *Comments on Draft General Comment on Article 12 of the Convention*, Submitted to the United Nations Committee on the Rights of Persons with Disabilities.
68 See responses from: Essex Autonomy Project, University of Essex; University of Cambridge Intellectual & Developmental Disabilities Research Group; George Szmukler, Kings College London; Jill Stavert, Edinburgh Napier University. To view responses, available at http://www.ohchr.org/EN/HRBodies/CRPD/Pages/DGCArticles12And9.aspx, accessed 4 December 2015.
69 Equality and Human Rights Commission, Equality Commission for Northern Ireland, Northern Ireland Human Rights Commission and Scottish Human Rights Commission.
70 *Supra* note.
71 Bartlett, P. (2014) "Good Act, Poor Implementation: The Report of the House of Lords Post-Legislative Scrutiny Committee on the Mental Capacity Act 2005," *Elder Law Journal*, June, 157.

the British Medical Association raised concerns about the Convention.[72] Many responses to the Committee, however, suggested a lack of awareness of Article 12 CRPD from professionals and organizations on the ground.

In oral evidence to the Committee, the government announced that following concerns raised by the senior judiciary, they were conducting a review on its compatibility with the CRPD.[73] These concerns may have been raised by Senior Judge Lush of the Court of Protection, who has recently written that the MCA is unlikely to be compatible with Article 12 as it does not contain 'a detailed and viable framework for supported decision-making in the exercise of legal capacity'.[74] The Essex Autonomy Project at the University of Essex[75] arranged a series of policy roundtables to assist the Ministry of Justice in its review. Attendance was by invitation only, and delegates included philosophers, judges, mental health law academics, psychiatrists, civil servants and public officials, barristers and representatives from civil society organizations; two of the authors of this chapter[76] attended. As a published record of the meetings reports, they 'were characterised by vigorous debate and some significant disagreements', however by the end a consensus had emerged that the MCA was not compliant with the CRPD.[77] Specifically, there was consensus that the MCA's 'diagnostic threshold'[78] constituted a form of disability discrimination, that the 'best interests' approach of the MCA did not sufficiently respect 'will and preferences' and that the MCA did not go far enough in providing support for decision-making.[79] There was not agreement, however, as to the extent or nature of reforms that would be necessary to bring the UK into compliance with the CRPD. The final report giving the government's view of these matters has not yet been published.

The CRPD has frequently been deployed in litigation in the UK.[80] However, Article 12 itself has only been explicitly considered in one case concerning the MCA, when Senior Judge Lush declined to appoint a 'deputy' to make decisions on behalf of a person against their wishes.[81] The CRPD as a whole has been cited in several judgments about the MCA, but sometimes in rulings explicitly endorsing measures that conflict with a person's expressed will and preferences.[82]

---

72 *Supra* note.
73 Oral evidence of John Hall on 18 June 2013, Q5.
74 Lush, D. (2013) "The 2nd World Congress on Adult Guardianship," *Elder Law Journal*, 3(1).
75 'MCA Compliance with the UNCRPD' (2014), available at http://autonomy.essex.ac.uk/mca-compliance-with-the-uncrpd, accessed 4 December 2015.
76 Anna Arstein-Kerslake and Lucy Series.
77 Martin, W. (2014) "Mental Capacity Law Discussion Paper: Consensus Emerges in Consultation Roundtables: The MCA is Not Compliant with the CRPD," *39 Essex St Mental Capacity Law Newsletter*, August (Issue 49).
78 s2(1) MCA; similar provisions are contained within the definition of incapacity in s1(6) AWIA and s2(1) MCB NI.
79 *Supra* note.
80 For England, see: *R(NM) v. Secretary of State for Justice* [2011] EWHC 1816 (Admin); *AH v. West London MH NHS Trust* [2011] UKUT 74 (AAC); *R (NM) v. London Borough of Islington & Ors* [2012] EWHC 414 (Admin); *Burnip v. Birmingham City Council & Anor (Rev 1)* [2012] EWCA Civ 629; *R (Bracking & Ors) v. Secretary of State for Work and Pensions* [2013] EWHC 897 (Admin); *R (MA & Ors) v. The Secretary of State for Work and Pensions & Ors* [2013] EWHC 2213 (Admin); *R (D) v. Worcestershire County Council* [2013] EWHC 2490 (Admin); *Bracking v. Secretary of State for Work and Pensions* [2013] EWCA Civ 1345. For Northern Ireland, see: *PF & Anor, Re Application for Judicial Review* [2011] NIQB 20; *Re SB Judicial Review* [2012] NIQB 71.
81 *London Borough of Haringey v. CM* [2014] EWCOP B23.
82 On sterilization, see *A NHS Trust v. DE* [2013] EWHC 2562 (Fam); on deprivation of liberty see *P v. Cheshire West and Chester Council and another; P and Q v. Surrey County Council* [2014] UKSC 19.

Although under the MCA the Court of Protection has on several occasions made decisions requiring particular measures to be adopted to support a person in making decisions[83] the support principle has sometimes been used to justify intrusive or highly coercive interventions.[84] A Scottish court held that a 3-year renewal period for a guardianship order better complied with Article 12(4) than an indefinite order.[85] These cases highlight a lack of engagement on the part of the UK courts with underlying normative differences between the 'support paradigm' and UK law.

Positive developments

Despite a widespread lack of awareness of the CRPD, and resistance in places, there are developments in the UK that suggest there is real room for progress. Many of these initiatives and developments do not cite the CRPD as an inspiration, or use it as an advocacy tool, although there is often a harmony between their approach and that of Article 12.

A number of UK initiatives – especially around people with learning disabilities – have emphasized the importance of rights for people to make decisions for themselves, and to receive support in doing so. Fostering the rights, independence and choices of people with learning disabilities was adopted as an official policy in England and Wales in *Valuing People*.[86] There are also a number of user-led organizations,[87] provider networks,[88] training and development agencies[89] – and in particular organizations involved in developing person-centred planning[90] – whose approaches enjoy considerable overlap with the ethos of Article 12 CRPD. Many techniques developed in these areas, such as circles of support, could be developed as supports for the exercise of legal capacity in accordance with Article 12. Meanwhile in Scotland, there are tentative steps towards advance planning instruments in psychiatric care that could be built upon in connection with the CRPD.[91]

One of the most interesting legal developments in England and Wales are proposals connected with new legislation governing public provision of care and support.[92] Draft guidance on support planning states that 'The modern care and support system will routinely provide supported decision-making'.[93] When assessing a person or planning support local authorities will be under a duty to involve the person,[94] no matter how complex their needs.[95] Where a person might have

---

83 For decisions about residence, see *CC v. KK and STCC* [2012] EWHC 2136 (COP); for decisions about sex, see *D Borough Council v. AB* [2011] EWHC 101 (COP).

84 *A Local Authority v. TZ (No. 2)* [2014] EWHC 973 (COP); *The Mental Health Trust & Ors v. DD & Anor* [2014] EWCOP 13.

85 *Re JM* [2011] ScotSC 107, paragraphs 72–73.

86 *Valuing People: A New Strategy for Learning Disability for the 21st Century* (2001) Valuing People: A New Strategy for Learning Disability for the 21st Century.

87 For example, CHANGE – a human rights NGO led by people with learning disabilities, available at http://www.changepeople.org/.

88 For example, Keyring (www.keyring.org/). the Housing and Support Alliance (www.housingandsupport. org.uk), and Choice Support (www.choicesupport.org.uk).

89 For example, Paradigm (www.paradigm-uk.org/).

90 For example, Helen Sanderson Associates (www.helensandersonassociates.co.uk/).

91 Stavert, J. (2013) "Added value: Using human rights to support psychiatric advance statements," *Edinburgh Law Review*, 17(2), 210–223.

92 Care Act 2014.

93 Department of Health (2014) *Draft guidance on care and support plans*, London. Paragraph 10.4.

94 s67 Care Act 2014.

95 Department of Health (2014) *Draft guidance on independent advocacy*, London. Paragraph 7.5.

difficulty understanding, retaining, evaluating or communicating information about assessment and support planning, local authorities must consider whether there is an 'appropriate person' to represent and support the person, and if not, they must make a referral to an independent advocate.[96] The draft regulations explicitly specify that the advocates' role is to assist the person in understanding the information, communicating their 'views, wishes or feelings', making decisions, understanding their rights and the local authority's obligations, and challenging its decisions if they so wish.[97] It is unclear whether these proposals were explicitly inspired by Article 12 CRPD, but it certainly suggests a change in approach to advocacy and support than models of advocacy that were developed under the MCA.[98]

Conclusion

Overall, the UK has lagged behind other commonwealth jurisdictions in engaging with Article 12 CRPD and the support paradigm. The response in the UK has sometimes been less 'how can we fulfil the requirements of Article 12 CRPD?' than 'how can we defend the status quo *against* the CRPD?' Instead of viewing uncertainties around the implementation of the support paradigm as opportunities for critical reflection and learning from other countries, not to mention tapping into existing UK practical knowledge on supporting people in making choices, the support paradigm has often been engaged with somewhat reluctantly, where there is engagement at all. This is a shame, as the UK has a wealth of knowledge – legal, practical and academic – that could be productively brought to bear on questions connected to the support paradigm. UK-based organizations and individuals with concerns about paternalistic use of capacity legislation could make good use of the CRPD in their advocacy. The forthcoming examination of the UK by the CRPD Committee in 2015, and the production of shadow reports by disability organizations, may well prompt a broader conversation about the compatibility of the CRPD and UK capacity laws. There are some encouraging signs of interest and progress, but there is much work yet to be done.

Dual track reform required: Law reform alongside support practices

Every jurisdiction is going to need to develop culturally and economically appropriate laws, policies, and practices to implement Article 12. However, there are key principles, outlined in the General Comment, which must be consistent across jurisdictions. Additionally, the effective implementation of Article 12 requires a two-track approach to reform. It requires both the reform of laws and policies that are denying legal capacity to people with disabilities on an unequal basis and the development and fostering of positive practices that support individuals to exercise their legal capacity.

This dual track approach is noted in the General Comment[99] along with frameworks for reform of the law and principles for the development of supported decision-making and other

---

96 S67 Care Act 2014; see also s68 Care Act 2014 for similar provisions regarding adult safeguarding.

97 Department of Health (2014) *The Care and Support (Independent Advocacy Support) Regulations 2014.* London. See, in particular, Regulation 5.

98 Known as Independent Mental Capacity Advocates (IMCAs), see ss35–41 MCA. See also: The Mental Capacity Act 2005 (Independent Mental Capacity Advocates) (General) Regulations 2006 SI 2006/1832.

99 Committee on the Rights of Persons with Disabilities, General Comment No. 1, Article 12: Equal Recognition Before the Law, paragraph 28, UN Doc. No. CRPD/C/GC/1 (April 2014).

methods for support for the exercise of legal capacity.[100] The General Comment is the best guide for State Parties and others to use in developing law, policy, and practice in line with Article 12.

The importance of the dual-track approach lies in the interaction between law and practice. Law itself plays a major force in daily life. However, there are many pockets of the world and of daily experience which law does not touch. Conversely, the existence of the law itself – even aside from enforcement practices – can be a very powerful societal force. For example, the existence of a law in Ireland criminalizing sexual contact with a person with intellectual disability outside of marriage has had a chilling effect on relationships for people with intellectual disabilities for many years. This is occurring despite the fact that the law itself is sparsely enforced, and rarely used in prosecutions.[101]

The law often does not have a significant grasp in areas involved with daily decision-making and familial or personal relationships. Therefore, it may be easy for some activity to go undetected. This has developed as a largely intentional aspect of the relationship between the individual and the state. The state has been quite carefully excluded from the private lives of individuals in certain domains.[102] Overall, most would agree, that this arms-length distance between the state and the individual is a positive thing. The context of disability – created both by the nature of impairment itself and by the social construction of segregation and dependence that has emerged – has resulted in both an overly intrusive role of the state and outside decision-makers in the private lives of people with disabilities as well as often relatively unchecked power for family members, supporters, and others to substitute their decision-making for that of the individual with a disability. For this reason, in order to achieve Article 12 compliance and implementation, there is a need to both ensure that the laws are in line with Article 12 and to ensure that people with disabilities, and their families, friends and supporters have all the tools on both an informal and formal level to enable support for the exercise of legal capacity.

Two exemplars of jurisdictions that are attempting this two-track approach to reform are Australia and Ireland. Neither jurisdiction has necessarily coordinated and planned this two-track approach to the implementation of Article 12. Instead, both movements for change have developed organically from advocacy within the disability rights movement as well as political will within the government and legislature.

In Ireland, the government committed to reforming its antiquated wardship law before ratification of the Convention, in order to bring Irish laws into compliance with the Convention before the point of ratification. This has spurred a drive from disability rights groups, the law reform commission, government and the legislature to create law that is in compliance with Article 12. The precise interpretation of Article 12 and the content of Article 12 compliant law has not always been consistent among these groups, however all would express a desire for Article 12 compliance. The result has been a series of reports and events coming from many different places that have fostered and explored Article 12 compliant legal capacity legislation. The government has published an Assisted Decision-Making (Capacity) Bill in 2013,[103] which takes a stab at

---

100 Committee on the Rights of Persons with Disabilities, General Comment No. 1, Article 12: Equal Recognition Before the Law, paragraphs 24–30, UN Doc. No. CRPD/C/GC/1 (April 2014). For further discussion, see earlier section Interpreting Article 12.

101 See [Irish] Criminal Law (Sexual Offences) (Amendment) Bill 2014 [Seanad] [Private Members Bill] Explanatory Memorandum, sponsored by Senator Katherine Zappone (Bill 41 of 2014).

102 See for example, Article 8 of the European Convention on Human Rights.

103 [Irish] Assisted Decision-Making (Capacity) Bill 2013, available at http://www.oireachtas.ie/documents/bills28/bills/2013/8313/b8313d.pdf.

Article 12 compliance. The Bill has been criticized by academics and disability groups as not going far enough towards compliance with the principles of Article 12.[104] However, the Bill is still a good example of law reform attempts toward Article 12 compliance.

Simultaneously in Ireland, there are many people developing positive supported decision-making practices on the ground and often quite separately from the law reform efforts.[105] These two-tracks will soon meet at the point of the entry into force of any new legal capacity legislation. There may be some conflicts in the way the law formulates the principles of Article 12 and in the way that they have been developed on the ground. However, the two will hopefully help to inform each other and will result in more comprehensive compliance with Article 12 than would have occurred if either movement were taking place in isolation.

In Australia, there has been a strong move toward supported decision-making practices. Pilot projects in supported decision-making have sprung up in several different Australian states, including South Australia, Victoria and New South Wales.[106] Simultaneously, there is an effort underway in several offices of public advocates and in the law reform commission and the human rights commission to explore what law reform is required for the implementation of Article 12.[107] Similar to Ireland, the hope is that these dual-tracks of reform will meet and will, at that point, secure the right to equal recognition before the law enumerated in Article 12 on both the legal front and on the more informal level of interpersonal relationships and service provision.

Conclusion

The aim of this chapter was provide to a brief exploration of the interpretation of Article 12 of the Convention and a snapshot of reform efforts in a few corners of the globe. On the whole, there has been significant progress towards law reform and a conceptual shift towards the concepts of Article 12. However, some are still struggling with how to implement Article 12. Particularly, fields that are dependent upon legal capacity denials are finding the concept of a right to legal capacity difficult to comprehend and implement. For example: psychiatry, where some practitioners are dependent upon forced treatment and detention; institutional settings, where choice is largely removed from residents and placed in staff and the institutional administration; social work, in certain jurisdictions, where they are empowered to make best interests determinations if they deem someone to 'lack capacity,' among others. Article 12 poses a specific challenge to these fields. However, it is not an insurmountable challenge. It is one that is already beginning

104 See, for example, "Equality, Dignity and Human Rights: Does the Assisted Decision-Making (Capacity) Bill 2013 fulfil Ireland's human rights obligations under the Convention on the Rights of Persons with Disabilities?," authored by the coalition for the reform of capacity law in Ireland: Centre for Disability Law and Policy at the National University of Ireland, Galway; Age Action; Amnesty Ireland; the Alzheimer's Society; et al., available at http://www.nuigalway.ie/cdlp/documents/amendments_to_bill.pdf.

105 For example, the new StepIn Supported Living Networks. For more information, see stepin.ie.

106 See Margaret Wallace, Evaluation of the Supported Decision Making Project, South Australia Office of the Public Advocate (November 2012); Support Decision-Making Pilot Project Description, Victoria Office of the Public Guardian (Ongoing 2014), available at http://www.publicadvocate.vic.gov.au/file/file/Research/Current%20projects/SDM%20project%20flyer%20FINAL.pdf; and "Supported Decision-Making Pilot," Fact Sheet, Issue No. 1, joint project by Ageing, Disability and Home Care, New South Wales Trustee and Guardian and the Public Guardian (October 2013), available at http://www.adhc.nsw.gov.au/__data/assets/file/0003/279039/SDMP_fact_sheet_Oct2013.pdf.

107 See, for example, "Equality, Capacity and Disability in Commonwealth Laws," (Discussion Paper 81) Australian Law Reform Commission (22 May 2014).

to be met through shifts towards the recognition of the will and preference of the individual and practices supporting individuals, even in crisis situations and other situations where communication is very difficult.[108]

Article 12 presents an opportunity to achieve real equality for people with disabilities. Not only formal equality before the law, but also an equal recognition of people with disabilities as decision-makers on the same basis as people without disabilities. This has the potential to revolutionize the manner in which disability is treated in modern society. Many examples of reform have already begun, and this appears to be the beginning of a larger movement towards achieving equal recognition before the law of people with disabilities.

---

108 For example: the personal ombudsman system in Skane, Sweden, see "Swedish user-run service with Personal Ombud (PO)," available at http://www.po-skane.org/ombudsman-for-psychiatric-patients-30. php; and peer support networks such as Intentional Peer Support in Vermont, see www.intentional peersupport.org.

10

ARTICLE 19 AND THE NORDIC EXPERIENCE OF INDEPENDENT LIVING AND PERSONAL ASSISTANCE

Ciara Brennan

Article 19 of the United Nations Convention on the Rights of Persons with Disabilities (CRPD) outlines the right to live independently in the community. The choice of where to live, access to a range of services including personal assistance, and access to mainstream social services are outlined as steps toward Article 19. In theory, the Convention represents an important milestone for the international independent living movement, which has campaigned for choice, control and participation in society on an equal basis with other citizens. The core principles of Article 19 require a paradigm shift in countries where institutions, segregated services or unpaid care is the norm. Rather than exploring progressive realisation of Article 19, the objective of this chapter is to reflect on developments in three Nordic countries that have relatively lengthy experiences of deinstitutionalisation, community living and personal assistance. Drawing on policy reviews and the findings of in-depth qualitative research in Sweden, Norway and Iceland, it will address the following three questions that cut deep into the heart of the relationship between the provisions of the CRPD and the implementation of policy in practice. (1) What were the key steps towards establishing policies to support independent living in Nordic countries prior to the CRPD? (2) How have policies to support independent living and personal assistance developed in the three Nordic countries under consideration? (3) Can lessons learned in Nordic countries offer insights into the implications for other countries seeking to develop independent living and personal assistance?

This study was undertaken as part of a larger investigation which charted progress toward independent living and user-led personal assistance across Europe. The findings have been presented at numerous international conferences and have generated considerable interest among persons from countries that have not implemented policies that support independent living in the community. Hence, these questions were designed to respond to frequently asked questions by persons wishing to advance Article 19 in other countries that want to or are attempting to promote independent living and personal assistance. This chapter outlines pragmatic steps, common success factors, as well as challenges for the CRPD in countries that have implemented policies to support independent living in the community. The intention is to reflect on lessons learned in the hope that it will advance knowledge for persons who are interested or invested in these issues.

Terms and definitions

Article 19 does not contain a specific definition of independent living or community living. However, the wording of Article 19 encompasses the key demands of the independent living movement, which predates the Convention by five decades. Ed Roberts is known as the father of independent living. He described the movement as 'the wave of protest against segregation and discrimination and an affirmation of the right and ability of disabled persons to share fully in the responsibilities and joys of our society'.[1] Independent living advocates have pointed out that independence does not refer to doing everything by oneself or in isolation from others. Rather, it means having choice and control over services to enable full participation in society.[2] The independent living movement called for an end to institutionalisation and segregation preventing participation in society. An institution is defined by the European Coalition for Community Living as:

> any place in which people who have been labelled as having a disability are isolated, segregated and/or compelled to live together. An institution is also any place in which people do not have, or are not allowed to exercise control over their lives and their day-to-day decisions. An institution is not defined merely by its size.[3]

Personal assistance emerged from the independent living movement. It has become one of the cornerstones of independent living (IL) in Nordic countries for persons who require extensive support on a daily basis. The Convention does not contain a specific definition of personal assistance. Therefore, it is appropriate to draw on the definition made by the largest independent living organisation in Europe. Personal assistance (PA) is defined by the European Network for Independent Living (ENIL) as follows:

> PA is a tool which allows for IL. PA is purchased through earmarked cash allocations for disabled people, the purpose of which is to pay for any assistance needed. PA should be provided on the basis of an individual needs assessment and depending on the life situation of each individual. The rates allocated for personal assistance to disabled people need to be in line with the current salary rates in each country. As disabled people, we must have the right to recruit, train and manage our assistants with adequate support if we choose, and we should be the ones that choose the employment model which is most suitable for our needs. PA allocations must cover the salaries of personal assistants and other performance costs, such as all contributions due by the employer, administration costs and peer support for the person who needs assistance.[4]

---

1 Roberts, E. (1977). Forword. In S. Pflueger (Ed.), *Independent Living: Emerging Issues in Rehabilitation*. Washington: Institute for Research Utilization. p. ii.
2 Glasby, J., and Littlechild, R. (2010). *Social Work and Direct Payments*. Bristol: The Policy Press. Morris, J. (1993). *Independent Lives: Community Care and Disabled People*. Basingstoke: Macmillan Press. Ratzka, A. (2003). *What is Independent Living? A personal definition*. http://www.independentliving.org/def.html
3 European Coalition for Community Living (2015). *What is the European Coalition for Community Living?* http://community-living.info/about-eccl/
4 ENIL. (2014). *ENIL's Key Definitions on Independent Living*. Retrieved 25 September 2014, from ENIL's key definitions on Independent Living.

It is important to note that, where it has been implemented, personal assistance has primarily applied to a minority of disabled persons who are deemed to have the largest support requirements resulting from impairments.[5] For instance, the Swedish law, which translates as 'Act concerning support and service provision for persons with certain functional impairments' LSS (1993:387), contains ten rights including the right to personal assistance. The law outlines the basic needs which must be measured to evaluate the number of personal assistance hours of personal assistance an individual is entitled to. These basic needs include dressing and undressing, hygiene and eating (LSS: 1993:387). Therefore, personal assistance primarily relates to persons described as 'those who require more intensive support' in the CRPD.

The Nordic context

Cross-country analyses of policies to support independent living in the community reveal vast differences and variations across Europe.[6] Therefore, it is important not to generalise, but to understand policies within a specific context. Nordic countries may offer valuable insight into the implications and challenges of policies aimed at living independently in the community. Some Nordic countries have been among those making the most progress towards the rights outlined in Article 19 the CRPD. Sweden, Norway and Iceland implemented policies and legislation on deinstitutionalisation and personal assistance in the absence of an overt supranational obligation to do so. This is not to say that policies developed at the same time or to the same scale. The Nordic countries have been categorized as belonging to a particular kind of welfare state, and have been identified as 'social democratic welfare states'.[7] Despite this, there are significant variations between and within each of these three Nordic countries.[8] This chapter highlights both the similarities and differences between these three Nordic countries and explores some of the issues that have arisen at different stages in their implementations of policies to support independent living.

Over the past five decades, Nordic countries have already addressed similar challenges to those that many European countries face today. Institutions and unpaid family care was the rule in the Nordic region in the 1950s, 1960s and 1970s.[9] In the early 1990s, Sweden and Norway implemented policies to close all institutions. This resulted in the closing or downsizing of institutions, most of which were replaced by group homes, apartment clusters and similar residential services. Nordic disability policy has been closely linked to the welfare state.[10] However, many

---

5 Berg, S. (2005). Personal Assistance Reforms in Sweden: Breaking the Assumption of Dependency? In C. Barnes and G. Mercer (Eds.), *The Social Model of Disability: Europe and Majority World*. Leeds: The Disability Press. pp. 32–48.
6 Townsley, R., Abbott, D., and Williams, V. (2009). The Implementation of Policies Supporting Independent Living for Disabled People in Europe: Synthesis Report. In ANED (Ed.), *Academic Network of European Disability Experts*. Leeds: ANED.
7 Esping-Andersen, G. (1990). *The Three Worlds of Welfare Capitalism*. Princeton: Princeton University Press.
8 Askheim, O. (2008). Personal Assistance in Sweden and Norway: From Difference to Convergence? *Scandinavian Journal of Disability Research*, 10(3), 179–190.
9 Tøssebro, J., Bonfils, I. S., Teittinen, A., Tideman, M., Traustadóttir, R., and Vesala, T. (2012). Normalization Fifty Years Beyond – Current Trends in the Nordic Countries. *Journal of Policy and Practice in Intellectual Disabilities*, 9(2), 134–146.
10 Gustavsson, A., Tøssebro, J., and Traustadóttir, R. (2005). Introduction: Approaches and Perspectives in Nordic Disability Research. *Resistance, Reflection and Change. Nordic Disability Research*. Lund: Studentiltterature.

arguments for policies to support independent living have been constructed outside a welfare state context. Some critics of Nordic disability policies have argued that demands for user-led and individually tailored services, including personal assistance, were a response to the poor standards and inflexibility of services following the closing of institutions.[11] Personal assistance is either offered as a cash payment or is provided as a service through a local government.[12] Those in receipt of a cash payment have several options of service providers if they choose not to be the sole employer of personal assistants. For instance, in Sweden there are many private for-profit companies offering to employ personal assistants on the user's behalf. Another option is to employ personal assistants through centres for independent living (CILs). The first CIL was established in Sweden in the early 1980s, in Norway in 1993 and in Iceland in 2010. CILs comprised primarily of disabled individuals offering services such as peer counselling, independent living skills training, information and training in the independent living ideology.[13] In addition, many CILs developed a personal assistance user co-operative which employs personal assistants on behalf of members. In turn, members are responsible for recruitment, supervising and scheduling personal assistants.[14]

One of the major points of interest, from a human rights perspective, is the relatively extensive and diverse group of users entitled to personal assistance in Nordic countries. For instance, in Sweden personal assistance is available to adults and children with intellectual impairments and autism, brain injuries and physical impairments not resulting from ageing (LSS: 1993:387). A number of mechanisms are in place to enable persons with intellectual disabilities to access personal assistance with the support of others. A Swedish independent living organisation, JAG, developed a model in which an individual or several individuals are responsible for ensuring quality, continuity and safety for a person who requires somebody else to manage personal assistance on his or her behalf.

Three steps towards legislation

What were the key steps towards establishing policies to support independent living in Nordic countries prior to the CRPD? In the absence of a supranational expectation to implement policies to support independent living, individuals and grassroots organisations were instrumental in persuading governments to enact policies and legislation to support independent living and personal assistance. A comprehensive review of the lead up to the development of policy and legislation in Sweden, Norway and Iceland reveals several explanations for the shift in thinking and in policy. Despite time differences, there were three common steps evident in all three countries: transfer of knowledge from other countries, the establishment of centres for independent living, and finally, convincing governments to initiate pilot projects to prove the viability and desirability of personal assistance provisions.

11 Berg, S. (2005). Personal Assistance Reforms in Sweden: Breaking the Assumption of Dependency? In C. Barnes and G. Mercer (Eds.), *The Social Model of Disability: Europe and Majority World*. Leeds: The Disability Press. pp. 32–48.
12 Askheim, O. P. (2005). Personal Assistance – Direct Payments or Alternative Public Service. Does It Matter for the Promotion of User-Control? *Disability and Society, 20*(3), 247–260.
13 White, G. W., Simpson, J., L., Gonda, C., Ravesloot, and Coble, C. J. (2010). Moving From Independence to Interdependence: A Conceptual Model for Better Understanding Community Participation of Centres for Independent Living Consumers. *Journal of Disability Policy Studies, 20*(4), 233–240.
14 Ratzka, A. (1996). *STIL, the Stockholm Co-operative for Independent Living*. Retrieved 13 March 2012, from http://www.independentliving.org/docs3/stileng.html

The first step was the transfer of knowledge from other countries. The independent living ideology originated in Berkeley, California in the late 1960s. Inspired by the civil rights movement, a small group of disabled university students demanded the right to personal assistance and accommodations to enable them to study and live alongside their peers on campus.[15] These demands spread outside the campus, and inspired similar movements throughout the United States. The independent living movement in the Nordic countries can be traced back to Adolf Ratzka, who is considered the most influential figure in the European independent living movement. As a student in California, he witnessed the rise of the independent living movement. In the following extract, he explains the contrast between his experience in the United States and in Sweden:

> As a student at the University of California at Los Angeles in the 1960's and early 1970's I had contact with the incipient Independent Living movement in California. Also, I had a scholarship which included an allowance for personal assistance. With these funds I recruited, hired, trained and scheduled my own personal assistants which were for the most part fellow college students. When I moved to Sweden in 1973 to do field work for my dissertation and became entitled to the Swedish public home helper service, I experienced an enormous difference in my quality of life.[16]

The second step was the establishment of Centres for Independent Living (CILs). Ratzka returned to Sweden and organised a seminar on Independent living in 1983.[17] He was among the founding members of the Stockholm centre for Independent Living (STIL), which was formally established in 1984. In 1989, Ratzka was one of the founding members of the European Network on Independent Living (ENIL), which has campaigned for independent living in Europe ever since. Inspired somewhat by STIL, a Norwegian CIL, ULOBA was established in 1993. In 2009 an organisation for independent living was established to develop the independent living ideology in Iceland. The decision to establish a centre for independent living was made following a visit to Sweden to meet with and learn from leaders of Swedish and Norwegian centres for independent living. In 2010 a personal assistance co-operative was established in Iceland.[17] To date, it is the only independent living co-operative in Iceland.

Two distinct kinds of CILs emerged in Norway and Sweden. The first comprises a wide spectrum of personal assistance users, but with a majority of persons with physical impairments. The second kind of user co-operative has exclusive membership of persons who require another person to manage and arrange personal assistance on their behalf. Around the same time STIL was established, a group of Swedish mothers of disabled children and adults began discussing alternatives to unpaid care for their son or daughters. Inspired by the independent living movement they established a non-profit organisation, JAG, in 1992. The founders of JAG were innovators of a system that would enable persons with multiple impairments including intellectual disabilities, autism and acquired brain injuries to access personal assistance with the support of a legal representative and an individual who takes on the responsibility for ensuring the quality, safety

---

15 De Jong, G. (1983). Defining and Implementing the Independent Living Concept: Developing, Implementing, and Evaluating Self-Help Rehabilitation Programs. In N. Crewe and I. Zola (Eds.), *Independent Living for Physically Disabled People*. San Francisco: Jossey-Bass.

16 Ratzka, A. (1993). *The User Cooperative Model in Personal Assistance: The Example of STIL, the Stockholm Cooperative for Independent Living*. http://www.independentliving.org/docs5/ratzka199301.html

17 NPA miðstöðin (the NPA Centre). (NPA stands for Notendastýrð Persónulega Aðstoð – User-led Personal Assistance).

and continuity of personal assistance.[18] In December 2009, a Norwegian JAG association was established. Like its Swedish counterpart, JAG Norway provides personal assistance for persons who require another person to support them with arranging and managing personal assistance.

The third step was to demonstrate that personal assistance was not merely viable but also desirable as a service option. At political level, centres for independent living aimed to convince local governments to pay the costs of providing services directly to the individuals so that they could hire their own personal assistants.[19] Pilot projects in Sweden and Norway were precursors to implementing legislation at national level. Pilot projects were the first formal steps towards legislating for personal assistance. The first pilot project took place in Stockholm in 1987. Six local governments participated. The pilot project lasted for 2 years and was considered a success, receiving widespread political and public support.[20] Pilot projects began in Norwegian local governments in 1994. ULOBA petitioned the government for a pilot project. A personal assistance pilot project took place between 1994 and 1997.[20] The pilot was considered a success and municipalities were positive about the outcome.[21] Pilot projects placed personal assistance on the national political agenda. For instance, it was outlined as a priority in the Norwegian government's plan of action for the disabled 1994–1997.[22] In 2012, the Icelandic Ministry of Welfare released guidelines for a personal assistance. Municipalities could choose whether or not to partake in the pilot. Eleven of the seventy-four Icelandic municipalities offered personal assistance contracts during the pilot. A review of the pilot is due to be published in 2016.

How have policies to support independent living developed?

Independent living advocates were successful at placing independent living on the national agenda in all three countries, but how has this developed? The influence of the independent living movement in the lead up to legislation generated high expectations from legislation and policy.[23] The extent to which the aims of these laws and policies have been realised varies in practice. Discrepancies between aims and realities have led to tensions between those who wish to maintain and advance the legislation and those responsible for controlling and monitoring policy and legislation.

A 'menu' of services to support independent living in the community is available in Nordic countries. For example, the Swedish Act concerning support and service provision for persons with certain functional impairments outlines ten rights (LSS: 1993:387). The key goals of this legislation are arguably, the most comprehensive articulation of independent living in national legislation. The key goals are 'equality in living conditions', 'full participation in the life of the community', 'to live as others do' and 'self-determination and privacy'. However,

18 JAG. (2005). *Ten Years with Personal Assistance: The Knowledge Project.* Stockholm: JAG.
19 Ratzka, A. (1993). *STIL, the Stockholm Co-operative for Independent Living.* Retrieved 13 March 2012, from http://www.independentliving.org/docs3/stileng.html
20 Christensen, K. (2012). Towards a Mixed Economy of Welfare of Long Term Care in Norway? *Critical Social Policy, 32*(4), 576–596.
21 Guldvik, I. (1998). Kommunenes erfaringer med brukerstyrt personlig assistanse [*The Muncipalities Experiences of Personal Assistance*]. Lillehammer: Eastren Norway Research Institute.
   Omsorgstjenester, R. f. (1997). Brukerstyrt Personlig Assistanse. En begrenset evaluering av virkningen av stimuleringstilskudd til kommunene [*User-Controlled Personal Assistance: a Restricted Evaluation of the Consequences of the Financial Contribution from the State to the Municipalities*]. Report April 1997.
22 Askheim, O. (2008). *Personal Assistance Service in Norway.* Riga. Available online: http://www.apeirons.lv/down/PA/1_PA_service_in_Norway_OlePetterAskheim.pdf (accessed 20 May 2013).
23 Andersen, J. (2003). Personal Assistance as a Strategic Game between State and Municipalities in Norway. *Scandinavian Journal of Disability Research, 5*(2), 140–159.

the legislation contains ten rights, some of which appear entirely contradictory to its goals. For instance, the rights include residential arrangements for children who cannot live with their family, residential arrangements for adults and daily activities for unemployed people.

The right which has received the most attention and acclaim from the independent living movement is personal assistance. Personal assistance has received the most attention of all the ten rights in LSS. Sweden is often considered the 'golden standard' of personal assistance in Europe.[24] In 2013, 15,970 people were entitled to personal assistance at the Swedish Social Insurance Agency, with an average of 122 hours per week.[25] Norwegian legislation was more restrictive when it was first implemented. Personal assistance is outlined in the Social Services in 2000 and is described as 'practical assistance and training including user-controlled personal assistance for those who are in special need of assistance owing to illness, disability or other reasons' (Social Services Act, 2000). Local governments are responsible for administering personal assistance in Norway. Although it is outlined in the legislation, to date, local governments have had discretionary powers to decide whether an applicant can have personal assistance or avail of the more traditional municipal services. In 2014, the Norwegian government revealed plans for an individual right to personal assistance, which should, in theory, weaken the discretion of local governments. Another interesting development in Norway has been the diversification of personal assistance users since the legislation was introduced.[27] In the beginning, access was limited to persons who could arrange and manage their own personal assistance. The legislation was amended in 2006, which opened up the possibility for people with intellectual disabilities to have personal assistance with the support of a legal representative. A survey carried out in 2010[26] reported that 19% of personal assistance users had an acquired brain injury, 12% had intellectual impairments and 5% had psycho-social disabilities, furthermore, 8% of users were under 18 years old. Iceland is the most recent Nordic country to introduce a personal assistance pilot project. Fifty-five people, including nine children, received temporary contracts during the pilot project. However, local governments are not obliged to offer personal assistance until legislation is enacted.

While Nordic policies and legislation are relatively extensive compared to other European countries, they have proven to be contentious and vulnerable to financial, political and attitudinal changes. For example, the thresholds for accessing personal assistance have changed in scale and nature throughout the years, sometimes encompassing more persons, and at other times, restricting them. For example, in Sweden, applicants must be assessed as needing more than 20 hours of personal assistance per week in order to receive personal assistance from the national Social Insurance Agency. There has been an increase in the numbers of refusals for personal assistance at the Social Insurance Agency since 2009, in which case applicants have had to reapply for personal assistance at their local government.[26] This has resulted in an unstable situation for some recipients, particularly those who are close to the 20 hour threshold for personal assistance. Administrative and financial challenges have arisen as barriers to the full realisation of the aims of legislation.

24 Anderberg, P. (2009). *ANED Country Report on the Implementation of Policies Supporting Independent Living for Disabled People*. Sweden: ANED. Retrieved 05 April, 2012, from http://www.disability-europe. net/content/aned/media/SE-6-Request-07%20ANED%20Task%205%20Independent%20Living%20 Report%20Sweden_to%20publish_to%20EC.pdf

25 Assistanskoll. (2014). Statistik om Personlig Assistans Och Sssistansanordnare [*Statistics on Personal Assistance and Assistance Providers*]. Retrieved 20 February 2014 from http://assistanskoll.se/assistans-statistik. php

26 Askheim, O., Andersen, J., Guldvik, I., and Johansen, V. (2013). Personal Assistance: What Happens to the Arrangement When the Number of Users Increases and New User Groups are Included? *Disability and Society, 28*(3), 353–366.

Financial concerns are a primary challenge among administrators and policymakers. The past 20 years has seen an unprecedented rise in the cost of personal assistance in Sweden. In 1994, personal assistance cost €207.5 million whereas in 2010 it cost €2.65 billion.[27] The early stages of policy development in Iceland administrators at local government have expressed concerns about their financial capacity to meet the demands for personal assistance arising from persons who did not avail of social services in the past by relying on informal care. Personal assistance in Sweden was characterised by a relatively unregulated market of for profit companies offering services for a portion of the direct payment.[28] New mechanisms for monitoring payments have been implemented in recent years following reports of misuse of payments. Norwegian local governments, on the other hand, have exercised more control and paternalism over the legislation.[29] Local governments in Norway can choose which providers can offer personal assistance at their municipality. For instance, in 2011 fourteen municipalities terminated their relationship with the largest Norwegian co-operative, so they could not offer assistance provision in these municipalities.

Can lessons learned in Nordic countries offer insights into the implications for other countries seeking to develop independent living and personal assistance?

Nordic countries offer paradoxical insights to the implications of policies and legislation. On one hand, they are considered leaders in policy for independent living in the community. However, they have ratified the Convention at a time of turmoil and uncertainty about the future of independent living and personal assistance and are struggling to uphold and sustain the current system. Yet, independent living movements outside the Nordic region are looking to them for inspiration. Although Nordic countries display some of the most promising practices, this could prove problematic if they are considered a litmus test for policymakers elsewhere. For example, the CRPD comes into force at a time of turmoil and uncertainty for the future cutbacks of personal assistance in Sweden. Twenty years after the enactment of LSS, personal assistance is under review and scrutiny. Discourses in the mainstream media highlight the negativity towards personal assistance in the public domain. For instance, an article which appeared in the Ledare newspaper argued that 'good institutions must become a worthy alternative' to personal assistance.[30] Unfortunately, these discourses are not limited to the media. Recent reports illustrate regressive measures in Norway and Sweden. There are reports of a counterrevolution in Norway, with an increase in 'small community institutions', some with more than twenty-five residents.[31] In 2012 a Swedish report

27 Social Insurance Agency. (2013). *Attendance Allowance*. Retrieved 16 April 2013, from http://www.forsakringskassan.se/wps/wcm/connect/f2331695-f616–4730–9ff3-f715f51cc572/assistansersattning_eng.pdf?MOD=AJPERES&CACHEID=f2331695-f616–4730–9ff3-f715f51cc572&useDefaultText=0&useDefaultDesc=0
28 Askheim, O. (2008.) Personal Assistance in Sweden and Norway: From Difference to Convergence? *Scandinavian Journal of Disability Research, 10*, 179–190.
29 Askheim. (2005). Personal Assistance – Direct Payments or Alternative Public Service. Does It Matter for the Promotion of User-Control? *Disability and Society, 20*(3), 247–260.
30 Wetterberg, G. (2012). Passing Round the Clock Becomes Too Expensive. *Ledare*. Retrieved January 14, 2013, from http://www.expressen.se/ledare/gunnar-wetterberg/passning-dygnet-runt-blir-for-dyrt/
31 Tøssebro, J., Bonfils, I. S., Teittinen, A., Tideman, M., Traustadóttir, R., and Vesala, T. (2012). Normalization Fifty Years Beyond – Current Trends in the Nordic Countries. *Journal of Policy and Practice in Intellectual Disabilities, 9*(2), 134–146.

entitled *Measures to Combat Fraud and Misconduct with Assistance Allowance* was published by an Inquiry on State Assistance (2012). The report attributed some of the cost of assistance to the lack of controls, application problems, processing errors and financial incentives to cheat.[32] The report estimated that between 9% and 15% of the total amount of assistance benefit paid in 2010 was fraudulent or misguided. It recommended that the social insurance agency have more opportunities to investigate and control assistance benefits. Other reports from Sweden show an increase in the numbers of rejections and refusals for personal assistance.[33] This has been recognised by the United Nations Committee on the Rights of Persons with Disabilities. In its concluding observations of Sweden, the Committee criticised cuts to personal assistance and stricter needs assessments.

> The Committee is concerned that State-funded personal assistance has been withdrawn for a number of people since 2010 due to a revised interpretation of "basic needs" and "other personal needs", and that persons who still receive assistance have experienced sharp cutbacks, the reasons for which are unknown or only seemingly justified. It is further concerned at the reported number of positive decisions under the Swedish Act concerning Support and Service for Persons with Certain Functional Impairments that are not executed.[34]

The cost of personal assistance in Sweden could be a deterrent for extending rights in other countries. This has been the case, even in the Nordic countries, where the high cost of personal assistance in Sweden has influenced a more cautious approach among Norwegian policy makers.[35]

Therefore, the CRPD has been ratified at a problematic period for Nordic disability policy and places considerable uncertainty over the progress that can be made in countries that have made relative progress in the past. There is some scepticism towards the implications that the CRPD will have in practice. For instance, in Sweden, critics have pointed to the mistranslation of the Swedish version of Article 19 of the CRPD. Personal assistance is translated as personal support. At the same time, there is good news from Iceland regarding personal assistance. Although Iceland has not ratified the CRPD, independent living has been successfully articulated by grass roots independent living advocates who, interestingly, succeeded in convincing the government to enact a personal assistance pilot project despite the country's significant financial crisis in 2008. Although the outcome of the pilot project remains to be seen, the Ministry of Welfare has explicitly committed to establishing personal assistance as one of the 'main pillars of services to disabled people in the future'.[36]

32 Inquiry on assistance compensation costs. (2012). Measures to Combat Fraud and Misconduct with Assistance Allowance. Retrieved 14 January 2013, from http://regeringen.se/content/1/c6/18/63/04/7bc4f4f9.pdf
33 Assistanskoll. (2014). Statistik om Personlig Assistans Och Sssistansanordnare [*Statistics on Personal Assistance and Assistance Providers*]. Retrieved 20 February 2014 from http://assistanskoll.se/assistans-statistik.php
34 Committee on the Rights of Persons with Disabilities. (2014). *Concluding Observations on the Initial Report of Sweden CRPD/C/SWE/CO/1*. Retrieved 12 September 2014, from http://tbinternet.ohchr.org/_layouts/treatybodyexternal/Download.aspx?symbolno=CRPD%2fC%2fSWE%2fCO%2f1&Lang=en
35 Askheim, O. (2008). Personal Assistance in Sweden and Norway: From Difference to Convergence? *Scandinavian Journal of Disability Research, 10*(3), 179–190.
36 Ministry of Welfare. (2012). Handbók um NPA (Handbook on UPA). Retrieved 12 March 2012, from http://www.velferdarraduneyti.is/media/npa/NPA_Handbok_10022012.pdf

Conclusion

There are many lessons to be learned from the Nordic experience of independent living and personal assistance. While there are many positive examples to be derived from each country, it is also useful to reflect on some of the challenges. Nordic countries are a good example of how a grass roots social movement can impact national level policy and legislation. Furthermore, the findings illustrate the transfer of knowledge and of principles of independent living between countries. The development of legislation and policy over time reveals a complex and contentious process. No doubt, some of the challenges encountered demystify independent living in Nordic countries. Financial and administrative challenges could be a deterrent for other countries considering policies that support independent living in the community. However, this is not to say that policies in Sweden, Norway or Iceland have failed. Quite the contrary. Those who have benefited from the progress made are defending their right to live independently. Ed Roberts, who is considered the father of independent living, once argued that 'when there's maximum danger, and when our programs are in the most jeopardy, there's also maximum opportunity. To make changes . . . to fight for what we know we need, to make them more responsible for the needs of our people to and let's take advantage of that'.[37] Roberts, however, was speaking at a time when independent living was evolving. On the other hand, independent living in Nordic countries has evolved to a point where there is a lot to lose. There is so much at stake in the future.

37 Roberts, E. (1989). *Speech at Research and Training Centre on Independent Living at the University of Kansas.* For full transcript of speech see: http://ollibean.com/2013/08/22/you-ed-roberts/

11

eQUALITY

The right to the web

Peter Blanck

Introduction

This chapter and the book it is based upon, *eQuality: The Struggle for Web Accessibility by Persons with Cognitive Disabilities* (2014, Cambridge University Press), was spurred several years ago by Dr. David Braddock, Executive Director of the Coleman Institute for Cognitive Disabilities. Dr. Braddock asked me to examine the right under the Americans with Disabilities Act (ADA) to web access for people with cognitive and other disabilities.

Given the ubiquity of online activity in the United States and most of the world, as well as the shifting of nearly all daily interactions and activities to the Internet, the right under the ADA and other laws to web equality may seem obvious. However, establishing the rights of individuals with disabilities, and in particular of individuals with cognitive disabilities – intellectual and developmental disabilities, autism, traumatic brain injury, and other conditions – has seldom come without legal and political struggle, which also is necessary to achieve a broader shift in attitudes and practice.[1]

This chapter continues a line of study examining the full and equal enjoyment (accessibility and usability) of web content with particular reference to people with cognitive disabilities. It explores how web content equality grounded in law and policy is necessary for people with cognitive and other disabilities, such as adults aging with the onset of cognitive and physical disabilities, to fully partake and flourish in the information age.[2] To that end, this chapter gives an overview of the struggle for web equality for people with cognitive disabilities. It presents definitions, legal challenges and rights that are developed more fully in *eQuality*, and it reflects on new developments associated with the Semantic Web and the "Internet of Things," and in disability law and policy in the United States (e.g., Section 508 refresh and web equality case law) and globally (e.g., developments in CRPD Articles 9 and 12, and European standardization efforts) since *eQuality* was published.

---

1 *See, e.g.*, Peter Blanck and Mollie W. Marti, Attitudes, Behavior, and the Employment Provisions of the Americans with Disabilities Act, *Villanova Law Review*, 42(2), 345–408 (1997).

2 *See, e.g.*, Peter Blanck and Jonathan J. Martinis, "The Right to Make Choices": National Resource Center for Supported Decision-Making, *Inclusion*, 3(1), 24–33 (2015); Michelle, Putnam, Bridging network divides: Building capacity to support aging with disability populations through research, *Disability and Health Journal*, 7(1), S51–S59 (2014).

Defining web eQuality

Full and equal access to the Internet's World Wide Web (web) is an enabler of other basic human and civil rights.[3] The web supports the freedoms of speech, association, and civic engagement.[4] Yet, while it is fundamental to exercising one's rights of citizenship,[5] access to the technology tools of the Internet alone is not sufficient to guarantee web equality. Overly complex interfaces, lack of information alternatives (e.g., symbols along with text, captions instead of audio), and the inability to transform content presentation all prevent effective use of the tool that is the Internet's web. *Access alone is not web content equality.*

I have described web *eQuality* as the opportunity for *full and equal enjoyment* of web content across all its technologies and interfaces:

> Full and equal enjoyment of the web is to have the meaningful and reasonably comparable opportunity to enjoy – access and use – web content, and to not be excluded from that prospect on the basis of cognitive and other disabilities, either by individuals, organizations, or through the design of web technology.[6]

This proposition, including the opportunity for active citizenship, is "the right to share in the full social heritage," as embodied in civic, educational, economic, and social information available to autonomous citizens.[7] The elements of citizenship include the opportunity to participate in the democratic endeavor and to be meaningfully heard as a part of that community. In this sense, web content equality is a fundamental right and an enabler of other human and economic liberties. It is a means for fulfillment through human cognition. Web technology has the unique potential to reduce the attitudinal, behavioral, and structural barriers encountered by individuals with a range of cognitive, physical, and sensory capabilities.

I take a civil and human rights approach to disability and frame web equality within the norms and legal obligations of the ADA and the U.N. Convention of the Rights of Persons with Disabilities (CRPD).[8] These and other legal instruments, and their associated regulations and commentaries, articulate this right as the opportunity for comparable use of web content by

---

3 Stephen B. Wicker and Stephanie M. Santoso, Access to the Internet Is a Human Right, *Communications of the ACM*, 56(6), 45–46 (June 2013).

4 *See also* Ivan Illich, *Tools for Conviviality*; *available at*: http://www.preservenet.com/theory/Illich/IllichTools.html (last visited Jan. 13, 2015).

5 *See* G. Anthony Giannoumis and Jennifer Kline, Active Citizenship through the Use of New Technologies–The Experiences of Three Generations of Persons with Disabilities, *DISCII*, 7.2 (2015); Delia Ferri, Analytical Framework for a Comparative Analysis of Accessible Technology Law and Policy, *DISCII*, 7.1 (2014); Rune Halvorsen and Bjørn Hvinden, Active Citizenship for Persons with Disabilities-CURRENT Knowledge and Analytical Framework, *DISCII*, 2.1 (2013).

6 Peter Blanck, *eQuality: The Struggle for Web Accessibility by Persons with Cognitive Disabilities*, at 245 (Cambridge, UK: Cambridge University Press 2014) [hereinafter "*eQuality*"].

7 T.H. Marshall, *Citizenship and Social Class: And Other Essays*, at 150, 154, (Cambridge, UK: Cambridge University Press 1950).

8 The Committee on the Rights of Persons with Disabilities, Eleventh session, 31 March–11 April 2014, in its General comment No. 2 (May 22, 2014) on Article 9: Accessibility writes: "Accessibility is a precondition for persons with disabilities to live independently and participate fully and equally in society. Without access to . . . information and communications technologies and systems, . . . persons with disabilities would not have equal opportunities for participation in their respective societies. It is no coincidence that accessibility is one of the principles on which the Convention on the Rights of Persons with Disabilities is based."

persons with disabilities in ways reasonable under the circumstances. They direct that freedom from discrimination in the digital online experience is achieved when persons with disabilities have the meaningful opportunity, with or without accommodation, to equivalent web usage as those without disabilities, and not only by access to separate or alternative knowledge and services. The power of the web is in its potential to mitigate barriers to knowledge that drive and inform human cognition, speech and ideas. The web increases the opportunity for individuals and collectives to share knowledge, although structural barriers such as poverty and a lack of access to technology continue to stand in the way of full access to the information society.

Presently, to approach web equality, people with a range of disabilities require modifications and accommodations in service design when reasonable and feasible to do so. These accommodations alone do not, and cannot, guarantee that in all circumstances people with disabilities will have the same outcomes from their activities on the web. In this sense, *web equality does not necessarily equate with content impartiality*, because there may be judgment at some point prior to the end user to determine what information will be offered and how. While it is expected that content transformations and substitution of equivalent information would be directed by the end user, there is still a filtering process that may raise concerns about how web content is selected. Would certain alternate content be favored over another and, if so, why?

With such caveats, I use the term *eQuality* to emphasize two ideals: the first is the conception of equality and justice under law. Thus, in the ADA there may be found a justiciable right to web equality for persons with cognitive and other disabilities. The second is the conception of "electronic *quality*," which is to signify that the meaningful and objective opportunity for the comparable use of web content by persons across the spectrum of disability is possible, with particular reference to individuals with cognitive disabilities. The right to enjoy digital knowledge and social interaction is encompassed by the freedom from discrimination solely as a consequence of disability, and is established by the ADA and recognized in the CRPD.

Rights of persons with cognitive disabilities

Although in the United States the ADA has been in effect for 25 years and there has been a concordant growth in the strength of the disability rights movement worldwide,[9] web equality for people with cognitive disabilities has received limited attention, and when examined has faced resistance and pushback.[10] Under the ADA, the right to web equality, as for other rights assuring nondiscriminatory access to society, is considered on an individualized basis in circumstances involving human and computer interaction. Those individuals with cognitive and other disabilities who choose to engage with the web must have the prospect for reasonably equivalent and comparable use of its electronic content, as do others without disabilities in the same situation.

Nondiscrimination in the full and equal enjoyment of web content offered by commercial entities is addressed by the ADA's third chapter (title III), which covers services offered by "public accommodations," including those of online service providers. Freedom from discrimination because of disability in the use of the online activities of public accommodations (and of state and local governments under ADA title II), and the corresponding obligation to make modifications

---

9 *See* Peter Blanck, ADA at 25 and Persons with Cognitive Disabilities: From Voice to Action, *Inclusion*, 3(2), 46–54 (2015); Blanck, P. (2016). ADA at 25 and Persons with Cognitive Disabilities: From Action to Inclusion, *Inclusion*, 4(1): 1–5.

10 *See infra* (U.S. Access Board Section 508 "refresh" excludes functional criteria for individuals with cognitive disabilities). *See also* Eli Pariser, *The Filter Bubble: What the Internet is Hiding from You*, (New York: Penguin), at 5 (2011).

within reason to ensure that services offered are equally enjoyable, are among the means by which people with disabilities meaningfully participate in the digital information society.

The ADA's preamble establishes its mandate as to ensure equal opportunity, inclusion, independent living, and opportunity for economic self-sufficiency.[11] The web is a major driver of these principles.[12] For this reason, the lack of equal opportunity to participate on the web, whereby separate access to web content becomes the default means for interaction, is *inherently not equal* for people with cognitive and other disabilities who aim to enjoy such services.[13] The full and equal enjoyment of web content requires at least the fair opportunity for substantive equality in online participation.

The World Wide Web Consortium (W3C) defines equivalent web content as that which is an "acceptable substitute," adaptation, and alternative that "fulfills essentially the same function or purpose as the original content upon presentation."[14] Alternative content removes reliance upon any one mode and cognitive mechanisms for comprehension: text can be heard instead of seen, audio can be read instead of heard, images are described instead of seen, symbols replace words, and so on. This seemingly complex suspension of modal reliance is actually and often achieved simply in web content as well as in other digital content. An illustration of a common adaptation is transformations in presentation, such as text enlargements and higher contrasts. Provision of equivalent content, or the capacity for web content to be transformed, is a central element of web equality.

Practically speaking, the enjoyment of web content must be considered in context. This is why laws like the ADA approach such fact-based determinations on a case-by-case basis, and not in terms of prescriptive compliance with web content technical standards and functional performance criteria. This also is the reason that American courts tend to view web equality in accord with notions of the fair and equivalent *opportunity* to participate regardless of disability.[15] The concept of web equality then embodies the comparable choice to participate online, with or without appropriate supports, and without discrimination on the basis of disability.

Given historical and present attitudinal discrimination, web equality is a means to ensure that disability is respected as an element of human diversity, when individuals and communities otherwise would directly or indirectly exclude disabled individuals. The ADA accords people with disabilities individual and collective rights to web equality, regardless of obvious or hidden characteristics that may subject them to artifactual, invidious, and paternalistic forms of prejudice and discrimination. The CRPD's Article 9, for instance, conceives of web accessibility as the opportunity to have equivalent access to and use of web content, and for individuals not to be excluded unreasonably from that prospect because of disability.[16]

---

11 *See, e.g.,* Fatima A. Boujarwah, Hwajung Hong, Gregory D. Abowd, and Rosa I. Arriaga, Towards a framework to situate assistive technology design in the context of culture, In *ACM, Proceedings of the 13th International ACM SIGACCESS Conference on Computers and Accessibility*, 19–26 (2011).

12 *See* Rob Imrie, Universalism, Universal Design and Equitable Access to the Built Environment, *Disability & Rehabilitation*, 34(10): 873–882 at 880 (2012). For empirical analyses of access issues facing persons with cognitive and other disabilities, *see* Lisa Schur, Douglas Kruse, D., and Peter Blanck, *People with Disabilities: Sidelined or Mainstreamed?* (Cambridge, UK: Cambridge University Press, 2013) (people with cognitive disabilities are among the most stigmatized and underemployed in society).

13 G. Anthony Giannoumis, Regulating Web Content: The Nexus of Legislation and Performance Standards in the United Kingdom and Norway, *Behavioral Sciences & the Law*, 32(1), 52–75 (2014).

14 *See* W3C, [DRAFT] Basic Glossary for WAI Documents (Aug. 9, 2005); *available at:* http://www.w3.org/WAI/lexicon/#equiv (last visited Jan. 13, 2015).

15 *See, e.g.,* K.M. v. Tustin Unified School District, and K.H. v. Poway Unified School District, 725 F.3d 1088, 1096–97, 1101 (9th Cir. 2013). *Compare* T.H. Marshall, *Citizenship and Social Class*, 148–54, at 148 (1950), in *Inequality and Society* (Eds. Jeff Manza and Michael Sauder, New York: Norton, 2009).

16 *See* Committee on the Rights of Persons with Disabilities, Eleventh session, *supra.*

Global context

The human rights of disabled people set out in the CRPD are recognized by more than 150 nations that have ratified the treaty.[17] The CRPD reflects a commitment by member states to value participation and citizenship by persons with disabilities in the global community. Article 1 of the CRPD states as its purpose "to promote, protect and ensure the *full and equal enjoyment* of all human rights and fundamental freedoms by all persons with disabilities, and to promote respect for their inherent dignity."[18] Persons with disabilities are those with long-term physical, sensory, mental, and cognitive impairments who face societal barriers that "hinder their *full and effective participation in society* on an equal basis with others" without such conditions.[19]

The CRPD's human rights lens is similar to, but different than, that of the ADA's civil rights approach. Its enumerated fundamental liberties are expressed as universal and interrelated conditions arising from the human experience. These liberties are not granted by governments or laws. Rather, they are fundamental to personal dignity and fulfillment, autonomy and capacity, regardless of disability.

Among its protections, the CRPD (Article 9, Accessibility) establishes obligations for States Parties to ensure comparable access to communications technology.[20] Johan Borg and colleagues argue that the CRPD declares for people with disabilities the right to technology equality "to ensure their *full and equal enjoyment* of all human rights and fundamental freedoms."[21] Although as of yet the U.S. Senate has declined to ratify the CRPD, the ADA directs that in a free society, people with disabilities have the equal right to use online materials to learn, work, play, communicate, shop, and participate fully in their communities.

Web ubiquity

Almost one-half (42%) of the world's 7 billion individuals use the web.[22] During the prior 15 years, web usage has increased globally at a tremendous rate. Web usage is expected to further

---

17 Convention on the Rights of Persons with Disabilities, GA Res 61/106, UN Doc. A/RES/61/106 (Dec. 13, 2006) (hereinafter, CRPD); *available at*: http://www2.ohchr.org/english/law/disabilities-convention.htm (last visited Jan. 13, 2015). *See also* David Sloan and Sarah Horton, Global Considerations in Creating an Organizational Web Accessibility Policy, In *Proceedings of the 11th Web for All Conference*, p. 16. *ACM* (2014).

18 CRPD, *supra* (emphasis added). *See also* Jerome E. Bickenbach, Disability, Culture and the U.N. Convention, *Disability and Rehabilitation*, 31, 1111–1124 (2009; Court of Justice of the European Union, Press Release No. 82/13, Luxembourg (July 4, 2013); re: Judgment in Case C-312/11: Commission v. Italy; *available at*: http://curia.europa.eu/juris/documents.jsf?num=C-312/11 (last visited Jan. 13, 2015).

19 CRPD, *supra* (Article 1) (emphasis added).

20 CRPD, *supra*.

21 Johan, Borg, Stig Larsson, and Per-Olof Östergren, The Right to Assistive Technology: For Whom, for What, and by Whom?, *Disability & Society*, 26(2), 151–167, at 165 (2011) (emphasis added). *See also* Johan Borg, Ann Lantz, and Jan Gulliksen, Accessibility to Electronic Communication for People with Cognitive Disabilities: A Systematic Search and Review of Empirical Evidence, *Universal Access in the Information Society*, 1–16 (2014); Gerard Goggin, Communication Rights and Disability Online: Policy and Technology After the World Summit on the Information Society, *Information, Communication & Society*, 1–15 (2014) (disability, Internet, and citizenship policy discussions at the World Summit on the Information Society (WSIS) in 2014 and 2015).

22 *See* Internet World Stats, http://www.internetworldstats.com/stats.htm (last visited Jan. 13, 2015) (based on web usage and world population statistics as of June 30, 2014). *See also* Wolfgang F.E. Preiser and Korydon H. Smith, Introduction, *Universal Design Handbook*, at xxvii–iii at xxviii (2nd ed. 2011) (Hereinafter "*UD Handbook*").

accelerate for those who previously have faced barriers to it, including those with cognitive disabilities and those who are aging (or who acquire cognitive disabilities with age), those living in poverty, and others who face economic and political restrictions to web access. More people use mobile and tablet devices to access the web than desktop personal computers.[23] In 2014, there were more than one billion smartphones and tablets bought worldwide, and this number is set to double by the end of 2015.[24] In the past 3 years, there have been billions of mobile subscriptions accessed across the globe and tens of billion mobile applications ("apps") downloaded.[25]

How many of these apps are accessible to and usable by persons with cognitive disabilities? At astounding rates, people are accessing web content on multiple devices, and often simultaneously, expecting real-time responsiveness and ubiquitous usage across contexts and environments. Do persons with cognitive disabilities have such equivalent opportunities?

Web content

Computer engineers and scientists, policymakers, and disability advocacy groups consider web content to be online digital information derived from human and machine operations and transferred to users by various means. Nonetheless, the definition of web content is far from clear for purposes of legal analysis.[26]

Social networking websites often distinguish among web content, online data, and metadata ("data that explains or describes other data").[27] However, each are forms of knowledge-based digital information that allow for online participation and the sharing of electronic text, images, and other modes of communication, and are expressed in computer code, data, and semantic information in machine readable formats.[28] The W3C's Web Content Accessibility Guidelines (WGAG, presently in version 2.0) conceives of web content as the "information and sensory

---

23 *See generally* Henry Blodget, *The Future of Digital, Business Insider* (2014) (smart phones and tablets out sell PCs); *available at*: http://www.businessinsider.com/the-future-of-digital-2014-slide-deck-2014-12#-70 (last visited Jan. 13, 2015).

24 *See, e.g.,* Natasha Lomas, Gartner: 1.2 Billion Smartphones, Tablets to be Bought Worldwide in 2013; 821 Million This Year: 70% of Total Device Sales, *AOL Tech* (Nov. 6, 2012); *available at*: http://techcrunch.com/2012/11/06/gartner-1–2-billion-smartphones-tablets-to-be-bought-worldwide-in-2013–821–million-this-year-70-of-total-device-sales/ (last visited Jan. 13, 2015); Jun Yang, Smartphones in Use Surpass 1 Billion, Will Double by 2015, *Bloomberg* (Oct 17, 2012); *available at*: http://www.bloomberg.com/news/2012–10–17/smartphones-in-use-surpass-1-billion-will-double-by-2015.html (last visited Jan. 13, 2015); Mobiforge, 36 Must-know Mobile Market Statistics for 2014 (Jan. 6, 2015); *available at*: http://mobithinking.com/mobile-marketing-tools/latest-mobile-stats & http://mobiforge.com/research-analysis/36-must-know-mobile-market-statistics-2014 (last visited Jan. 13, 2015) (number of smartphones worldwide expected to hit over 1.3 billion during 2014).

25 *See, e.g.,* Mobiforge, *supra.*

26 *See, e.g.,* European Commission, Proposal for a Directive of the European Parliament and of the Council on the Accessibility of Public Sector Bodies' websites, at 14 (Dec. 3, 2012) (web "content" is information communicated to user by user agent, including code or mark-up that defines content structure, presentation, and interactions); *available at*: http://ec.europa.eu/digital-agenda/en/news/proposal-directive-european-parliament-and-council-accessibility-public-sector-bodies-websites (last visited Jan. 15, 2015).

27 *See, e.g.,* Facebook, Statement of Rights and Responsibilities (Date of Last Revision: Nov. 15, 2013); *available at*: http://www.facebook.com/legal/terms (last visited Jan. 15, 2015). *See also* W3C, Web Services Glossary (Feb. 11, 2004); *available at*: http://www.w3.org/TR/ws-gloss/ (last visited Jan. 15, 2015).

28 Facebook, Data Use Policy: Information We Receive About You; *available at*: http://www.facebook.com/about/privacy/your-info (last visited Jan. 15, 2015).

experience to be communicated to the user by means of a user agent (e.g., a browser), including code or markup that defines the content's structure, presentation, and interactions."[29]

User-based content

The web's architecture enables online service providers, such as social media services, to organize and maintain digital information about users in computer code. One common form of such metadata collection is "cookies," which are tracking devices that create summaries of user data.[30] Other metadata content derive from the use of the web and its applications, such as information about electronic book (eBook) usage and purchases made using a browser service.[31]

Location-based web content and services may be offered using metadata, such as information retrieved from a device's global positioning system (GPS) and Internet Service Provider (ISP). This information may be used by the web service to provide a user with information such as advertisements tailored to user preferences and choices in situ. "Click data" from the user's interaction with an advertisement, for instance, is assessed by advertisers to determine an ad's effectiveness and resultant closure of e-sales.

Websites often create other data from user information, for instance, using GPS and other sensors that collect location information and provide contextual real-time information and content feedback to the user. Many ecommerce organizations sell this content to external third-party enterprises for marketing and other purposes. This web content is dynamic, in part because it is user-generated and collected via multiple sensors and offered in multiple formats from text, photos, movies, and audio. User-based content exemplifies the extraordinary capacity of online service providers to provide personalized and customized experiences to individual visitors and to respond to the needs and preferences of the individual.

Semantic content

The web's inventor, Tim Berners-Lee, along with his colleagues, conceived of the web as a responsive (experiential) and machine-assisted "Semantic Web." The Semantic Web is a term that refers to a common structure for understanding and processing web content with the assistance of computer algorithms (rules for computer processing).[32] The conception of a Semantic Web draws on advances in natural language processing (NLP: computers drawing meaning from human language) and the ability of machines to recognize human speech and convert it to electronic text.[33]

---

29 *See* W3C, Definition of a Web Content; *available at*: http://www.w3.org/TR/WCAG20/ (last visited Jan. 15, 2015).
30 *See, e.g.,* LinkedIn, Cookies on the LinkedIn Site (Sept. 26, 2012); *available at*: http://www.linkedin.com/legal/cookie_policy (last visited Jan. 15, 2015. *See also* Paul Baker, John C. Bricout, Nathan W. Moon, Barry Coughlan, and Jessica Pater, Communities of Participation: A Comparison of Disability and Aging Identified Groups on Facebook and LinkedIn, *Telematics and Informatics*, 30, 22–34 (2012).
31 Facebook, Data Use Policy: Information We Receive About You, *supra*.
32 *See* W3C, *W3C Semantic Web Activity*; *available at*: http://www.w3.org/2001/sw/ (last visited Jan. 15, 2015). *See also* Lee Feigenbaum, Ivan Herman, Tonya Hongsermeier, Eric Neumann, and Susie Stephens, The Semantic Web in Action, *Scientific American*, 297, at 90–97 (Dec. 2007).
33 *See* Ross Lazerowitz, What Is Natural Language Processing?, Information Space, School of Information Studies, Syracuse University (May 11, 2012); *available at*: http://infospace.ischool.syr.edu/2012/05/11/what-is-natural-language-processing/ (last visited Jan. 15, 2015).

The Semantic Web is a conceptual, machine-based framework that enhances access to and use of web content by diverse users. It does this by aiding in the understanding, organization, and interpretation of digital information. Intelligent web design conceived presently has not and may never replicate the intricate state of human knowledge processing and interaction; however, it has the promise to make web content accessible and usable (in its broadest form, universally usable) by persons with cognitive and other disabilities. The Semantic Web, along with other innovations, is poised to support the opportunity for web enjoyment to be individualized and contextualized in consideration of a user's preferences, skills, motivation, use of assistive technology (AT, such as screen reader software used by individuals with visual impairments), and myriad applications across desktop and mobile platforms, operating systems, and devices.

The capacity for semantic and user-based content to form *both* universal and individualized web content for persons with cognitive disabilities is further supported and increasingly delivered through Cloud Computing.[34] The Cloud, more precisely public and private Clouds of Clouds, allows web users ubiquitous access as they move through contexts and settings in their day and interact with web-enabled and interconnected devices. Through access to software stored in the Cloud, users are not inexorably tied to one access configuration, one location, one device, and one form of AT. Cloud computing enables a user to use AT and invoke preferences on any enabled device. No longer is the individual bound to the device that has AT or preferences installed; instead, they may enjoy the freedom of web content equality in an information technology ecosystem that undergoes continuous and dynamic change (e.g., updating of content), and which leverages the exponential power of computer data mining, search capacity, and semantic content generation and interpretation.[35]

Cognitive disabilities and the web

Besides attitudinal discrimination and technological barriers, there are structural reasons why people with cognitive disabilities face exclusion from the web. Poverty and lack of inclusive education, inadequate job training, and negative expectations limit the opportunity to access computer technology and services provided online. There are associated barriers facing those across the spectrum of disability in transportation, healthcare, social activities, and housing.

The particular examination of cognitive disability and web equality involves consideration of arguably the largest meta-group of people with disabilities.[36] Admittedly, it is artificial to consider cognitive disability as a discrete category or condition, as cognition itself is linked to intellectual,

---

34 *See generally* Amrish Chourasia, Dan Nordstrom, and Gregg Vanderheiden, State of the Science on the Cloud, Accessibility, and the Future, *Universal Access in the Information Society*, 13(4), 483–95 (2014).

35 *See also* Elizabeth Ellcessor, Captions On, Off, on TV, Online: Accessibility and Search Engine Optimization in Online Closed Captioning, *Television New Media*, 13: 329–52, at 329–30 (2012); Matt Huenerfauth and Pengfei Lu, Effect of Spatial Reference and Verb Inflection on the Usability of Sign Language Animations, *Universal Access in the Information Society*, 11: 169–184 (2012).

36 *See,* Frank La Rue, Report of the Special Rapporteur on the Promotion and Protection of the Right to Freedom of Opinion and Expression, United Nations, General Assembly, Human Rights Council, A/HRC/17/27 (May 16, 2011) at 6; Michael Schaten, Accessibility 2.0–New Approach to Web Accessibility for People with Cognitive and Intellectual Disabilities. In T. Amiel and B. Wilson (Eds.), *Proceedings of World Conference on Educational Multimedia, Hypermedia and Telecommunications*, at 2868–2877 (2012). *See also* Kate Ellis and Mike Kent, *Disability and New Media*, at 7 (2011).

sensory, emotional, and motivational characteristics and preferences.[37] Moreover, within cognitive disabilities there are individual disparities in access to and use of online services.[38] Nonetheless, there is a general lack of commitment to web equality for cognitive disability[39] despite the fact that technological advances for persons with cognitive disabilities complement and extend access strategies for those with visual, hearing, dexterity, and other conditions.[40] Many presupposed barriers to web equality not only are surmountable, but also are capable of resolution for individuals with diverse text- and print-related, intellectual, developmental, and neurological impairments.

Web content is produced by developers using HTML5 and Cascading Style Sheets 3 (CSS3) to present and format the information. Digital content is available on browsers used on desktop computers and mobile devices capable of multimedia presentation.[41] For web content to operate with a user agent (e.g., browsers, AT screen reader software), it must be machine-readable.[42] Computer code allows AT software to convert content to speech for screen reading functions and audio information to text for captioning.[43]

People with cognitive disabilities benefit from these same mechanical and verbatim translations. As for blind individuals who use screen readers and deaf individuals who use captioning to access web content, people with cognitive disabilities profit from conversions that format text to audio and the reverse, as well as from the opportunity to use content presented in multiple communication modalities and to alter the viewing format of the information presented. This is the case where text alternatives for audio information are presented as captions and include important non-dialogue audio information such as sound effects.[44] The use of text to explain audio information that is integral to the plot helps individuals understand and note significant nonverbal information.

Sometimes, however, people with cognitive disabilities face additional challenges in the use of web content as expressed purely in text alternatives. A user's reading level, which is not a monolithic characteristic, affects comprehension and understandability, and the processing of text. Individuals with cognitive impairments who may have hearing impairments often have lower levels

37 *See, e.g.,* Michael D. Melnick, Bryan R. Harrison, Sohee Park, Loisa Bennetto, and Duje Tadin, A Strong Interactive Link between Sensory Discriminations and Intelligence, *Current Biology* 23, 1013–1017, at 1015 (2013).

38 *See* Singanapalli Balaram, *UD Handbook, supra,* at 3.8.

39 Elizabeth Ellcessor, Access Ability: Policies, Practices, and Representations of Disability Online, A dissertation submitted in partial fulfillment of the requirements for the degree of Doctor of Philosophy (Communication Arts), University of Wisconsin-Madison, at 342 (2012).

40 Ellcessor, *supra* (2012, dissertation) 342–343.

41 For review, *see* Kevin Cullen, Lutz Kubitschke, David McDaid, Peter Blanck, William Myhill, Gerard Quinn, Patrick O'Donoghue, and Rune Halverson, Accessibility of ICT Products and Services to Disabled and Older People: Evidence-Based Analysis for a Possible Coordinated European Approach to Web Accessibility, *European Commission Information Society & Media Directorate,* at 16 (2008); *available at:* http://ec.europa.eu/information_society/activities/einclusion/docs/access/comm_2008/coordinated_approach.doc (last visited Jan. 15, 2015). *See also* Jaka Sodnik, Matija Jekovec, Grega Jakus, and Sašo Tomažič, The Future of the Web, *E-Society Journal: Research & Applications,* 2(1), 27–38 (July 2011).

42 *See* W3C, Understanding Conformance (*available at:* http://www.w3.org/TR/UNDERSTANDING-WCAG20/conformance.html (last visited Jan. 15, 2015).

43 *See* W3C, Understanding Conformance, *supra.*

44 *See* Captions (Live): Understanding SC 1.2.4, W3C; *available at:* http://www.w3.org/TR/UNDERSTANDING-WCAG20/media-equiv-real-time-captions.html (last visited Jan. 15, 2015). For an excellent discussion, *see* Ellcessor, *supra* at 342 (2012 article) ("visual cues, movements, expressions, and sounds that add to the tone or plot may be left out of online captioning, leaving deaf and hard-of-hearing users with a somewhat impoverished version of the original.").

of linguistic capabilities especially if a gestural language such as American Sign Language (ASL) is their first language. Some individuals may require ASL, or other sign languages not based in English grammar to aid in web content usability and comprehensibility.[45] Consequently, within the domain of content transformation and modification, there is a need to consider an array of cross and coexisting characteristics.

Cognitive disabilities

David Braddock and colleagues describe cognitive disabilities as "a substantial limitation in one's capacity to think, including conceptualizing, planning, and sequencing thoughts and actions, remembering, interpreting subtle social cues, and understanding numbers and symbols."[46] Cognitive disability covers conditions that may be based on the interaction of biology and environment over the life course – autism, intellectual and developmental disabilities, cerebral palsy, traumatic brain injury, brain injury acquired from aging, physiological and environmental conditions, post-traumatic stress disorder, dyslexia and learning disorders, and other conditions called print-related disabilities.[47] Often, these conditions coexist with sensory and physical impairments, with mental health conditions (e.g., depression and bipolar disorder), and have a diversity of causes, severity, and episodic presentation. Cognitive disability is affected separately and in combination by individual characteristics, environmental demands, and social supports.

The International Classification of Functioning, Disability and Health (ICF) is the World Health Organization's (WHO) framework for measuring health domains by use of functional capacity in a social context. Although not without its limitations, the ICF attempts to "'mainstream'[] the experience of disability and recognises it as a universal human experience."[48] The ICF approach reduces reliance on the medical model to adopt the social model of disability as applied in the ADA, the CRPD, and other disability rights laws. It recognizes the importance of individual characteristics and the environment in defining disability.[49]

Although in instances cognitive disability may be associated with lower levels of intelligence as defined by standard tests and measures of daily functioning, this is not necessarily the case. Many individuals with cognitive disabilities have average and high levels of daily life functioning and intellectual skills. These individuals, whether with dyslexia or autism, may experience limitations in social and communication abilities due to a range of factors.[50] Moreover, contrary to popular belief, the majority of individuals with cognitive disabilities have conditions that are relatively

---

45 *See* Web Content Accessibility Guidelines (WCAG) 2.0, W3C Recommendation (Dec. 11, 2008), *supra*.

46 David Braddock, Mary Rizzolo, Micah Thompson, and Rodney Bell, Emerging Technologies and Cognitive Disability, *Journal of Special Education Technology*, 19(4), 49–56, at 49 (2004). *Id.* at 50 (citations omitted).

47 *See, e.g.,* Autistic Self Advocacy Network (ASAN), *About Autism; available at*: http://autisticadvocacy. org/about-autism/ (last visited Jan. 15, 2015).

48 *See* WHO, *International Classification of Functioning, Disability and Health (ICF), available at*: http://www. who.int/classifications/icf/en/ (last visited Jan. 15, 2015).

49 *See, e.g.,* K-R. Foley, P. Dyke, S. Girdler, J. Bourke, and H. Leonard, Young Adults with Intellectual Disability Transitioning from School to Post-School: A Literature Review Framed within the ICF, *Disability & Rehabilitation*, 34(20), 1747–1764 (2012); Borg et al., *supra* at 153.

50 Referring to Autism Spectrum Disorder, which includes autistic disorder, Asperger Syndrome, and some pervasive developmental disorders. *See* E. Michael Foster and Erin Pearson, Is Inclusivity an Indicator of Quality of Care for Children with Autism in Special Education?, *Pediatrics*, 130, S179–85 (2012) at S180.

mild and moderate.[51] Having said this, the experience of severe cognitive disability over the life course is not a presumption against the same opportunity for individual preference and choice in daily life, often with human and technological supports in certain circumstances. For people with some cognitive disabilities, autonomous choice takes on new meaning when "supported decision-making"[52] is bolstered by on-demand technological and web-based supports across the life cycle to maximize independence and fulfillment.[53]

Cognitive disabilities, therefore, represent an array of conditions and behaviors, which may be present at birth such as Down syndrome, acquired by a life event, or result from the aging process. These conditions coexist with others. Individuals with Down syndrome, for instance, often have vision, hearing, and dexterity impairments.[54] For these reasons, generalizations across individuals are made with caution.

Cognitive load

The process and rate involved with the delivery and transformation of electronic text generally determines the "cognitive load" that the information presents to an individual and that person's capacity to meaningfully acquire the information. Cognitive load is affected by how online tasks (websites) are designed and presented, as well as by individual characteristics.[55]

Generally, for all individuals, with and without disabilities, the proliferation of online devices, services, and multitasking has made cognitive load a crucial functional and performance issue of the information age.[56] In interacting with a web service, there is an expected distribution of cognitive load to be generated across the population of users. Unfortunately, web services typically are designed to be accessible and usable only to a limited range of the distribution of web users and often to an idealized "normal user" without consideration of cognitive disability, and the effects of other factors: environment, task, individual or collective interaction.

Disability anti-discrimination laws set out parameters to define when that "range of usage" is unfairly limited due to disability and hence discriminatory, which to date have been used in ADA actions primarily by the blind and deaf communities, and to a lesser extent by persons with cognitive disabilities. The requirement for reasonable modifications is meant to mitigate such unfair restrictions, as long as they do not fundamentally alter the essence of the task or present

---

51 Richard Hemp reviewed disability prevalence rates as reported in the World Report on Disability (2011); *available at*: http://whqlibdoc.who.int/publications/2011/9789240685215_eng.pdf (last visited Jan. 15, 2015). *See also* David Braddock, Richard Hemp, Mary C. Rizzolo, Emily Shea Tanis, Laura Haffer, Amie Lulinski, and Jiang Wu, *State of the States in Developmental Disabilities*, at 72 (2013) (hereinafter "States of the States").
52 Peter Blanck and Jonathan Martinis, "The Right to Make Choices": National Resource Center for Supported Decision-Making, *Inclusion*, 3(1), 24–33 (2015).
53 *See, e.g.,* Terry Carney, Participation and Service Access Rights for People with Intellectual Disability: A Role for Law? *Journal of Intellectual & Developmental Disability*, 38(1): 59–69 (2013); Nina A. Kohn, Jeremy A. Blumenthal, and Amy T. Campbell, Supported Decision-Making: A Viable Alternative to Guardianship? *Penn State Law Review*, 117, 1111–57 (2012).
54 Ruimin Hu, Jinjuan Feng, Jonathan Lazar, and Libby Kumin, Investigating Input Technologies for Children and Young Adults with Down Syndrome, *Universal Access in the Information Society*, at 2; online 10.1007/s10209–011–0267–3 (2011). *See generally* Feng, Lazar, Kumin, and Ozok, *supra*.
55 John Sweller, Paul Chandler, Paul Tierney, and Martin Cooper, Cognitive Load as a Factor in the Structuring of Technical Material, *Journal of Experimental Psychology: General*, 119(2), 176–192, at 176 (1990).
56 *See* Tony Schwartz, Faced with Overload, a Need to Find Focus, Life@Work, *NY Times* (May 17, 2013) *available at*: http://dealbook.nytimes.com/2013/05/17/faced-with-overload-a-need-to-find-focus/ (last visited Jan. 15, 2015).

an undue burden to the content producer. This general conception applies across disability types and functional severity, although cognitive disabilities by description directly implicate issues of cognitive load.

Although screen reader software and augmentative technologies may transform electronic content to aural presentation, for instance, the structure of the website, its navigability, and the complexity of its organization may independently affect comprehensibility and hence cognitive load.[57] Cognitive load or capacity is tested further when considering multimedia and dynamic (constantly updated) web content and interactions across platforms and interfaces. For example, cognitive disabilities may result in memory processing limitations that affect attention capabilities, which reduce the ability to perform certain sequenced web-based tasks.[58] Without the opportunity for alternatives, augmentations, sequenced feedbacks and supports, web use is effectively limited.[59]

Susan Feinberg and Margaret Murphy distinguish extraneous from intrinsic cognitive load in the development of online web educational materials.[60] Intrinsic cognitive load is implicated in the processing of the substantive task at issue, while extraneous cognitive load is tapped when processing the presentation and format of web content.[61] Often, without the opportunity for effective modifications, online services make cascading demands on cognitive resources, creating an overload that makes extrinsic and intrinsic cognitive processing unnecessarily difficult. A website's presentational (navigational) format itself, as John Sweller and colleagues comment, may require considerable cognitive capacity.[62]

In principle, accessible and usable web design offers the opportunity to reduce *unnecessary* cognitive load, especially those substantive and presentational formats that are cumbersome or nonessential to the meaning of web content.[63] Of course, "unnecessary" cognitive load is a relative term and often depends on the perspectives of the content owner and producer, and the individual user.

---

57 *See, e.g.,* Yury Puzis, Yevgen Borodin, Faisal Ahmed, and I. V. Ramakrishnan, An intuitive Accessible Web Automation User Interface, *ACM, Proceedings of the International Cross-Disciplinary Conference on Web Accessibility*, 41–44 (2012).

58 *Compare* Peter G. Fairweather, How Older and Younger Adults Differ in their Approach to Problem Solving on a Complex Website, *ACM ASSETS'08*, 67–72, at 67 (Oct. 13–15, 2008). *See also* Harper and Yesilada, *supra* at 16. *Id.* at 17; Iosif Klironomos and Julio Abascal, An Introduction to the Key Issues Relating to Accessible User Interfaces, *Cardiac-EU, available at*: http://www.cardiac-eu.org/user_interfaces/key.htm (last visited Jan. 15, 2015); John Gill & Julio Abascal, Accessible User Interfaces: Priorities for Research, *Cardiac-EU*; *available at*: http://www.cardiac-eu.org/deliverables/accessible_user_interfaces.htm (last visited Jan. 15, 2015); Julio Abascal, Coordination Action in R&D in Accessible and Assistive ICT, CARDIAC—Coordination Action in R&D in Accessible and Assistive ICT, Deliverable D3.2: Trends on Inclusive User Interface Design, ADVANCE DRAFT REPORT (2012); *available at*: http://www.cardiac-eu.org/deliverables/d3–2.pdf (last visited Jan. 15, 2015).

59 Fairweather, *supra* at 71.

60 Susan Feinberg and Margaret Murphy, Applying Cognitive Load Theory to the Design of Web-Based Instruction, In *IPCC/SIGDOC '00 Proceedings of IEEE Professional Communication Society International Professional Communication Conference and Proceedings of the 18th Annual ACM International Conference on Computer Documentation: Technology & Teamwork*, 353–60, at 354 (2000).

61 Feinberg and Murphy, *supra* at 354. *See also* Puzis et al., *supra*, at 41.

62 Sweller, *supra* at 176. *See also* Peter G. Fairweather, How Older and Younger Adults Differ in their Approach to Problem Solving on a Complex Website, *ACM ASSETS'08*, 67–72, at 67 (2008).

63 *See, e.g.,* Shawn Lawton Henry, Shadi Abou-Zahra, and Judy Brewer, The Role of Accessibility in a Universal Web, In *Proceedings of the 11th Web for All Conference*, at 17, *ACM* (2014) ("'Universal design' is the process of creating products (devices, environments, systems, and processes) which are usable by people with the widest possible range of abilities, operating within the widest possible range of situations (environments, conditions, and circumstances). It is related to approaches called inclusive design, design for all, digital inclusion, and universal usability.") (citation omitted).

Universal design

When the opportunity for web content accessibility and usability is possible in the broadest sense, it trends towards "universal design" (UD), which enables participation by diverse users to the maximum degree possible.[64] UD is well beyond a minimum standard of accessibility.[65] As formulated by Ron Mace, it is "the design of products and environments to be usable by all people, to the greatest extent possible, without the need for adaptation or specialized design."[66]

Rob Imrie has described UD as "making products *easier to use by reducing their complexity* and minimizing individuals' reliance on their physical and cognitive capabilities in interacting with them."[67] Reductions in task complexity, and conveyance of information via alternative channels of communication, reduce cognitive demands because capacity is effectively deployed and not expended on extraneous and multiple tasks and decision-making processes. Individual cognitive capacity may be increased with the use of universal adaptation and customization strategies (which may be thought of as individualized accommodations) that allow for tasks to be broken down into accessible and alternative components that are presented in different and multiple modalities.

In theory, UD exists when there is an equivalent opportunity for diverse individuals to use web content easily and comprehensibly, and within reasonable bounds. To paraphrase Imrie, it is an "avoidance of discriminatory design" in the technological world, with similar although less ubiquitous consequence in physical world design.[68] In practice, UD represents an aspiration to achieve equal and individualized participation regardless of disability and other human characteristics, as mediated by the unique characteristics of design, deployment, and integration with other related products and services.

Universal design and web *eQuality*

Without web equality, people with cognitive and other disabilities often "end up on the side of the [digital] divide with others who do not have access to or use technology."[69] This divide means a lack of access to comparable web content within and across multiple devices, platforms, and browsers (e.g., cross-platform compatibility).[70] The lack of functional and equivalent access to

---

64 *See, e.g.,* Judy Brewer, Accessibility of the World Wide Web: Technical and Policy Perspectives, *UD Handbook, supra,* at 33.2. For review, *see* Edward Steinfeld and Jordana Maisel, *Universal Design: Creating Inclusive Environments* (2012).

65 *See* Jack L. Nasser, Are Retrofitted Wheelchair Entries Separate and Unequal?, *UD Handbook, supra,* at 41.2.

66 *See* Rob Imrie, Universalism, Universal Design and Equitable Access to the Built Environment, *Disability & Rehabilitation,* 34(10): 873–882, at 873 (2012) (*citing* Ronald Mace, *Universal Design: Housing for the Lifespan of All People,* at 1 (1988)).

67 Imrie, *supra* at 873. Jim Tobias, Universal Design: Is it Really about Design? *Information Technology & Disabilities,* 9(1): 2–10 (2003).

68 Imrie, *supra* at 875–876.

69 Emily Shea Tanis, Susan Palmer, Michael Wehmeyer, Daniel K. Davies, Steven E. Stock, Kathy Lobb, and Barbara Bishop, Self-Report Computer-Based Survey of Technology Use by People with Intellectual and Developmental Disabilities, *Intellectual and Developmental Disabilities,* 50(1), 53–68, at 53 (2012).

70 *See, e.g.,* La Rue, Report of the Special Rapporteur, *supra* at 4, 17. *See also* Tania Sebastian, 'Copyright World' and Access to Information: Conjoined *via* the Internet, *Journal of Intellectual Property Rights,* 17, 235–42, at 235 (2012); International Telecommunication Union (ITU) (hereinafter "ITU 2013") at 4 (May 2013); *available at:* http://www.itu.int/dms_pub/itu-d/opb/reg/D-REG-TTR.14-2013-SUM-PDF-E.pdf (last visited Jan. 15, 2015); Anthony Giannoumis, *supra* (2014); Anthony Giannoumis, The Web as a Site of Intractable Governance, in H.A. Caltenco, P-O. Hedvall, and Andreas Larsson (Eds.), *Universal Design 2014: Three Days of Creativity and Diversity: Proceedings of the International Conference on Universal Design,* UD 2014 Lund, Sweden, Vol. 35, at 384 (June 16–18, 2014).

web content affects individuals across the spectrum of disability, as well as other "non-standard" web users. However, persons with cognitive disabilities are among those most profoundly affected by web content inequality. This is because, as a general proposition, *web equality for people with cognitive disabilities necessitates consideration of the meaning of web content.*

For instance, a web user with memory processing limitations likely will benefit (e.g., in terms of web accessibility and usability) from the opportunity to choose clearer and more concise language, which requires developers to consider the meaning of text-based web content they employ.[71] It is essential, therefore, to examine the intended purpose of web content and the design of the online service itself. Analysis requires an examination of the "equivalent enjoyment of web content" from the perspective of the content owners and designers, and the content users and their contextual environments.

Given the web's inclusive UD possibilities, it is fitting to aim for the development of a principled basis in law to web equality for persons with cognitive disabilities. This endeavor is not to divert attention for web equality from those with other disabilities; rather, it is to focus attention on a stigmatized and ostracized segment of individuals on the disability spectrum.[72] Moreover, the potential UD benefits of web content equality for those with cognitive disability transcend cognitive disability and apply to many other coexisting conditions, such as to sensory and mobility related impairments.

In *eQuality*, I proposed that for people with cognitive disabilities there may be at least two recognized meta-functional dimensions of web content equality: (1) *ease of use of web content*, for instance, in navigational and multimedia access and operability; and (2) *comprehensibility of web content*, for instance, in its understandability and substantive usability.[73] These dimensions of web content equality are not zero-sum choices nor independent of one another. Rather, they reflect a continuum of user experience that must be considered in context, with or without the use of AT and other supports.[74] They further are multidimensional concepts that are influenced by, and which affect individual preferences and differences, interaction with Semantic content on the web. Individuals with similar backgrounds and characteristics may prefer different ways to interact with web content in different situations and under varying conditions.[75]

Nevertheless, preference in web use does not necessarily equate with simplification (and is relative to context), and greater comprehensibility (or simplicity) is not necessarily synonymous

---

71 I thank Anthony Giannoumis for this example.

72 *See, e.g.,* Mark C. Weber, Disability Harassment, at 23–24 (2007). *See also* Elizabeth F. Emens, Disabling Attitudes: U.S. Disability Law and the ADA Amendments Act, *American Journal of Comparative Law*, 60, 220–33 (2012); Brigida Hernandez, Christopher Keys, and Fabricio Balcazar, Employer Attitudes toward Workers with Disabilities and their ADA Employment Rights: A Literature Review, *Journal of Rehabilitation*, 66(4), 4–16 (2000); Nicole Ditchman, Shirli Werner, Kristin Kosyluk, Nev Jones, Brianna Elg, and Patrick W. Corrigan, Stigma and Intellectual Disability: Potential Application of Mental Illness Research, *Rehabilitation Psychology*, 58(2), 206–16, 208 (2013); Shira Yalon-Chamovitz, Invisible Access Needs of People with Intellectual Disabilities: A Conceptual Model of Practice, *Intellectual & Developmental Disabilities*, 47, 395–400 (2009).

73 *See, e.g.,* Kasper Hornbaek, Current Practice in Measuring Usability: Challenges to Studies and Research, *International Journal of Human-Computer Studies* 64(2), 79–102, at 91 (2006).

74 *See, e.g.,* Diana Ruth-Janneck, An Integrative Accessibility Engineering Approach Using Multidimensional Classifications of Barriers in the Web, In *Proceedings of the International Cross-Disciplinary Conference on Web Accessibility*, ACM, at 10–13 (2011). *See also* Katie Ellis and Mike Kent, *Disability and New Media*, at 26–27 (2011).

75 *See* Fairweather, *supra* at 71.

with intellectual challenge and cognitive demands.[76] Although individuals with autism may experience differences in sensory and speech processing, and in sensitivities to the human voice itself, these characteristics in social communications are not necessarily tied to individual intelligence and capabilities.[77]

For many people with cognitive disabilities ease of use and simplicity directly tie to the nature of web content accessibility and usability.[78] Melissa Dawe Schmidt conducted an ethnographic study with young adults with cognitive disabilities.[79] The study, entitled "Desperately Seeking Simplicity," found overwhelmingly that these participants desired developers to "keep it small and simple, please!", and among the most desirable features were ease of use, functionality, and portability. The opportunity for ease of use and comprehensibility was among the central means for sustaining interest.[80]

For web developer Jamie Knight, "cognitive accessibility" (and usability) means that individuals with cognitive and other disabilities have the same opportunity to receive, process, and act on online information, as do others without such conditions.[81] Cognitive accessibility, according to Knight, is related to functional dimensions affecting reading comprehension, visual and content load capacity, and web layout.[82]

Towards web eQuality

By the year 2040, at the fiftieth anniversary of the ADA and the thirty-second anniversary of the CRPD, will a generation of individuals with cognitive disabilities be engaged fully and equally with the web? More and more students with cognitive disabilities will have attended post-secondary education and be seeking to enter the competitive workforce.[83] By that time, the number

76 Micah Mazurek, Paul Shattuck, Mary Wagner, and Benjamin P. Cooper, Prevalence and Correlates of Screen-Based Media Use Among Youths with Autism Spectrum Disorders, *Journal of Autism & Developmental Disorders* (published online Dec. 2011). *See also* Cecilia Li-Tsang, Susanna Yeung, Chetwyn Chan, and Christina Hui-Chan, Factors Affecting People with Intellectual Disabilities in Learning to Use Computer Technology, *International Journal of Rehabilitation Research*, 28(2), 127–133, at 132 (2005); Daniel Davies, Steven Stock, and Michael Wehmeyer, Enhancing Independent Internet Access for Individuals with Mental Retardation through Use of a Specialized Web Browser: A Pilot Study, *Education and Training in Mental Retardation and Developmental Disabilities*, 36(1), 107–113 (2001); Alex Wong, Chetwyn Chan, Cecilia Li-Tsang, and Chow Lam, Competence of People with Intellectual Disabilities on using Human–Computer Interface, *Research in Developmental Disabilities*, 30; 107–123 (2009).
77 *See, e.g.,* Daniel A. Abramsa, Charles J. Lynch, Katherine M. Cheng, Jennifer Phillips, Kaustubh Supekar, Srikanth Ryali, Lucina Q. Uddin, and Vinod Menon, Underconnectivity between Voice-Selective Cortex and Reward Circuitry in Children with Autism, *Proceedings of the National Academy of Sciences*, at 4 (2013) (citations omitted).
78 *See* Gregg Vanderheiden, Fundamental Principles and Priority Setting for Universal Usability, *CUU '00 Proceedings on the 2000 Conference on Universal Usability*, ACM, 32–38, at 36 (2000).
79 Melissa Dawe, Desperately Seeking Simplicity: How Young Adults with Cognitive Disabilities and their Families Adopt Assistive Technologies, *ACM, CHI 2006*, 1143–1152, at 1143, 1147–49 (Apr. 22–27, 2006).
80 Dawe, *supra* at 1148.
81 Jamie Knight, Cognitive Accessibility 101 – Part 1: What is Cognitive Accessibility (2015); *available at*: http://jkg3.com/Journal/cognitive-accessibility-101-part-1-what-is-cognitive-accessibility (last visited Mar. 13, 2015).
82 Jamie Knight, Cognitive Accessibility 101 – Part 2: How it Effects Me & the Tools I Use; (2015); *available at*: http://jkg3.com/Journal/cognitive-accessibility-101-part-2-how-it-effects-me-the-tools-i-use (last visited Mar. 13, 2015).
83 *See* Association of Research Libraries, Report of the ARL Joint Task Force on Services to Patrons with Print Disabilities, at 6, 14 (Nov. 2, 2012).

of persons over age 65 in the United States will have doubled, and many people will use the web to support independence in all aspects of their daily lives.[84]

Fortunately, there is a growing body of expertise in accessibility to meet the increasing demand to make web technologies accessible. There is now an International Association of Accessibility Professionals (IAAP): "a global community for people and organizations working in accessibility to share expertise and resources, support one another's work, and follow developments in this fast-changing field."[85] This sharing of resources and standards of practice is an important part of building universal web equality.

Optimistically, before too long, binary views of web accessibility and usability will be relics of the past. Instead of "one size fits all" web content for standard users, there will be opportunities for auto-personalization "one size fits one"[86] web content, reflecting a globalized alignment of the web as an enabler of human rights as envisioned by the CRPD.[87] Still, even with such technological optimism, there will be complexities to the mass customization of web content, such as the need for developers to maintain design simplicity and ease of use with the proliferation of niche technologies, which is where open source ecosystems that promote universal access and use also will come into play.[88]

Hardware and software architectures will coexist with smart environments – homes, schools, libraries, workplaces, and health care centers. Embedded ambient intelligence will converge in Cloud infrastructures, and web content will be semantically responsive and intuitive, and less design and code dependent.[89] Content will be available in real-time on-demand services on and in the person (through wearables and nanorobotics),[90] in homes (through automation and

---

84 *See* Braddock, et al., *supra* (2012), at 82 (citing U.S. Census Bureau, 2012). *See also* Blanck, P. (2016). The First "A" in the ADA: And 25 More "A"s Toward Equality for Americans with Disabilities, *Inclusion*, 4(1): 46–51.

85 Rob Sinclair, Microsoft Will Help Launch a New Association for Accessibility Professionals (December, 17, 2013); *available at*: http://blogs.msdn.com/b/accessibility/archive/2013/12/17/microsoft-will-help-launch-a-new-association-for-accessibility-professionals.aspx (last visited Jan. 15, 2015).

86 *See* Jutta Treviranus, You Say Tomato, I Say Tomato, Let's Not Call the Whole Thing Off: The Challenge of User Experience Design in Distributed Learning Environments, *eLiterate* (July 1, 2008); *available at*: http://mfeldstein.com/you-say-tomato-i-say-tomato-let%E2%80%99s-not-call-the-whole-thing-off-the-challenge-of-user-experience-design-in-distributed-learning-environments/ (last visited Jan. 15, 2015).

87 *See* Gary Heil, Tom Parker, and Deborah C. Stephens, *One Size Fits One: Building Relationships One Customer and One Employee at a Time* (New York: Van Nostrand Reinhold, 1999); Jordan Novet, The Web Isn't One-Size-Fits-All Anymore, So the as-a-Service World Just Keeps on Growing, *Gigaom* (May 31, 2013); *available at*: http://gigaom.com/2013/05/31/the-web-isnt-one-size-fits-all-anymore-so-the-as-a-service-world-just-keeps-on-growing/ (last visited Jan. 15, 2015); WebAim, Design Considerations. One Size Fits All? (2013) *available at*: http://webaim.org/articles/design/ (last visited Feb. 16, 2015).

88 *Compare* One Size Fits One: Tailoring Technology to Consumer Needs, Knowledge@Wharton (Apr. 20, 2005); *available at*: http://knowledge.wharton.upenn.edu/article.cfm?articleid=1178 (last visited Jan. 15, 2015).

89 *See* Tim Berners-Lee, Weaving the Web, at 159, 168 (1999); G. Liotta, E. DiGiacomo, R. Magni, and F. Corradi, Web Solutions for Rehabilitation and Daily Life, in *Assistive Technology Assessment Handbook*, Stefano Federici and Marcia Scherer (Eds.), at 366 (Boca Raton: CRC Press, 2012); Rich Picking, Alexia Robinet, John McGinn, Vic Grout, Roberto Casas, and Ruben Blasco, The Easyline+ Project: Evaluation of a User Interface Developed to Enhance Independent Living of Elderly and Disabled People, *Universal Access in the Information Society*, 11, 99–112 (2012).

90 In addition, 3-D printers will have new benefits for consumers, for example, to aid in development of products and services that enhance participation by persons with disabilities in daily life. *See, e.g.,* Jacqueline Mroz, Hand of a Superhero: 3-D Printing Prosthetic Hands that Are Anything but Ordinary, *NY Times* (Feb. 16, 2015); *available at*: http://www.nytimes.com/2015/02/17/science/hand-of-a-superhero.html?hp&action=click&pgtype=Homepage&module=photo-spot-region&region=top-news&WT.nav=top-news&_r=0 (last visited Feb. 17, 2015).

appliances),[91] schools (with online teaching materials) and workplaces (with job training and advancement programs). The web will provide options for collaborative crowd-sourced feedback and services for individuals, groups, and communities from the management of health care and financial transactions, to emergency preparedness for natural and manmade disasters. Digital cooperatives not only will enhance the sharing and development of knowledge, but also will be central to the management and growth of a free and open information society.[92]

Functional eQuality

Although aspects of online solutions increasingly will be tailored for all persons, the WCAG 2.0 and other standards also will have preferably trended towards functional use criteria for universal applicability.[93] Discussion will not be one of whether online services must be universally usable versus disability-specific. Consider Elizabeth Ellcessor's view that "[e]quality does not require uniformity,"[94] nor need it result in mediocrity. Rather, *personalization as an option will be offered across a range of digital inclusive environments.*

Ideally, corresponding concepts of accessibility and usability will fade, replaced by a paradigm shift towards innovation in web content regardless of disability. The inventor of the web, Tim Berners-Lee, understood this centrality of choice and cohesiveness to web content equality when he said that its "flexibility and openness" make it possible "to build services and applications that are truly accessible for people with disabilities, as well as [for] people who need to transform content for purposes other than that for which it was originally intended."[95]

To "transform content for purposes other than that for which it was originally intended" is to provide meaningful and autonomous choice in the web ecosystem. It is to reach diverse audiences, without stifling innovation and creativity, without trampling on individual privacy, and by spurring market growth and consumer loyalty, and importantly, participation in one's community.

Before there was established law on the right to the web, Berners-Lee said:

> we have to be careful that [the web] allows for a just and fair society. The Web must allow equal access to those in different economic and political situations; to those who

91 *See* Evan Brown, Best Practices for Providers of Goods and Services on the Internet of Things; *available at:* http://blog.internetcases.com/2015/01/27/best-practices-for-providers-of-goods-and-services-on-the-internet-of-things/ (2015) (last visited Feb. 15, 2015) (company practice need not impede device usability).

92 *See* Gregg C. Vanderheiden, Jutta Treviranus, Maria Gemou, Evangelos Bekiaris, Kasper Markus, The Evolving Global Public Inclusive Infrastructure (GPII), In *Universal Access in Human-Computer Interaction. Design Methods, Tools, and Interaction Techniques for eInclusion, Lecture Notes in Computer Science*, Vol. 8009, 2013, pp. 107–116. For the Prosperity4All project, I serve as legal advisor on international copyright issues and on the connection to Prosperity4All services and software services and guidelines for their use.

93 Simon Harper and Yeliz Yesilada, (2011). Chapter 11—Web Accessibility: Current Trends, 172–90, at 175, In Javier Pereira (Ed.), *Handbook of Research on Personal Autonomy Technologies and Disability Informatics* (Hershey, PA: Medical Information Science Reference, 2011).

94 Ellcessor, *supra* at 346 (2012 article). *Id.* at 347. *See also* Stein et al., *supra* (2014).

95 *See* Timothy Berners-Lee, Testimony Before the United States House of Representatives Committee on Energy and Commerce Subcommittee on Telecommunications and the Internet Hearing on the "Digital Future of the United States: Part I—The Future of the World Wide Web", at 1, 4 (Mar. 1, 2007).

have *physical or cognitive disabilities*; those of different cultures; and those who use different languages with different characters that read in different directions across a page.[96]

A number of coming technologies will further support an inclusive web. Semantic web content will provide a basis for establishing a Cloud-driven Semantic Web, a "social-semantic" web[97] that will provide the opportunity for contextually-aware multichannel communications, using facial expressions and tone of voice, eye blinks and movements, gestures, and sign languages.[98]

Such breakthroughs will facilitate mass interoperability and personalization among the components of the entire online ecosystem.[99] Legal and policy regimes domestically and transnationally will need to keep pace with these advances to support harmonization and innovation in web content ownership, licensing and open source agreements, and security and privacy of user agents built into the systems and accessed externally by web interfaces and the Cloud.[100] These systems will experience constant updating, given dynamic operating schemes and websites, and the means to aggregate and summarize web content.

These imaginings follow on existing automation capabilities to simplify user interfaces. Yury Puzis and his colleagues comment that screen reader software presently allows users to develop their own macros for automation of certain tasks, such as to look up unknown words in a dictionary.[101] These researchers, and others, are examining the means to automate web content to reduce unnecessary cognitive load and to maximize cognitive flourishing. The release of Microsoft's Windows 8, and its built-in AT, hinted at some of the future opportunities for personalization of web content.[102] For people with cognitive and other disabilities, consider its "Ease of Access Center," with customizable commands.[103]

Human–computer interaction (HCI) researchers are developing on-demand analytics for web content that incorporate individual learning, and reading histories and styles. IBM researcher Eser

---

96 Berners-Lee, *supra* at 165 (emphasis added).

97 Mark Greaves and Peter Mika, Editorial, Semantic Web and Web 2.0, *Web Semantics: Science, Services and Agents on the World Wide Web*, 6, 1–3, at 1 (2008).

98 *See, e.g.,* Aleksandra Krolak and Paweł Strumiłło, Eye-Blink Detection System for Human–Computer Interaction, *Universal Access in the Information Society*, 11, 409–419, at 418 (2012). *See, e.g.,* Whistle (2013) (web-based monitor for dogs); *available at*: http://www.whistle.com/company/ (last visited Jan. 15, 2015); Mike Hendricks and Roxie Hammill, New Devices Mind Pets While Owners Are Away, *NY Times* (Sept. 11, 2013) (listing products similar to Whistle); *available at*: http://www.nytimes.com/2013/09/12/technology/personaltech/new-devices-mind-pets-while-owners-are-away.html?src=dayp&_r=1& (last visited Jan. 15, 2015).

99 Denis Anson, Email to Author and Attached Memorandum (Mar. 20, 2013) (available from author).

100 In 2013, NIDRR issued the proposed research priority "Inclusive Cloud and Web Computing", *Federal Register*, 78(10), at 2919–23 (Jan. 15, 2013). *See also* Anson Memo, *supra*.

101 Puzis et al., *supra* at 42.

102 Accessibility in Windows 8 (2013); available at: http://www.microsoft.com/enable/products/windows8/ (last visited Jan. 15, 2015). *Compare*, Anirban Lahiri, Is Windows 8 a Step Back in Accessibility?, *SSB Bart Group* (Oct. 31, 2012) *available at*: https://www.ssbbartgroup.com/blog/2012/10/31/is-windows-8-a-step-back-in-accessibility/ (last visited Jan. 15, 2015); Mardon Erbland, How Good Are Windows 8 Accessibility Features for the Blind?, *betanews* (2012); *available at*: http://betanews.com/2012/03/02/how-good-are-windows-8-accessibility-features-for-the-blind/ (last visited Jan. 15, 2015).

103 *See, e.g.,* Jessica Hullman, Nicholas Diakopoulos, and Eytan Adar, Contextifier: Automatic Generation of Annotated Stock Visualizations, *ACM CHI 2013* (Apr. 27–May 2, 2013); David McNaughton and Janice Light, The iPad and Mobile Technology Revolution: Benefits and Challenges for Individuals who require Augmentative and Alternative Communication, *Augmentative and Alternative Communication*, 29(2), 107–16, at 109 (2013) at 110.

Kandogan is developing "just-in-time descriptive analytics" using means in real-time "to help users easily understand the structure of data as seen in visualizations."[104] Kandogan's image-to-text analytics identify informational trends automatically and are able to "*decrease the cognitive load on users by automatically explaining structure in real-time as they interact.*"[105] The annotation model is user-driven at the time of interaction to enhance understanding. With a similar outcome in mind, Bill Gates and his co-inventors have submitted a patent filing for a technology application to autogenerate video from electronic text.[106] These advances will enhance web content equality through the integration of automated annotation and summarization techniques with semantic, perceptual, cognitive, communication, lingual and features based on personal preferences and capabilities, all in real-time.

The W3C and other groups are developing complementary tools to support the inclusive web, such as the Web Ontology Language (OWL V.2), for web applications to process content.[107] Ontologies are vocabularies of web content – terms, words, microformats, and metadata – organized by rules and their relationships to other terms.[108] These capabilities, when combined with collective and machine-based knowledge from cataloguing and search capabilities, offer personalized opportunities for people to interact with the web. The late disability leader and historian Paul Longmore pointed out that critics of disability rights laws complain that people with disabilities "want it both ways," that is, to have equality and full integration along with the opportunity for "special treatment" such as accommodations.[109] In the advancing world of the web, both are possible, not only for the disabled, but for all. The full and equal enjoyment of the web means the opportunity for equivalent and comparable engagement, but not necessarily identical usage.

Raising the Floor (RtF) for people with cognitve and other disabilities

Cloud-based educational, rehabilitation, job training, financial, and leisure programs and services increasingly act as daily life supports for individuals with an array of cognitive disabilities.[110] The Cloud has the potential to seamlessly augment communication, memory and concentration skills in real-time by aiding in customization and operability across digital devices, browsers, and systems.[111]

---

104 *See* Eser Kandogan, Just-in-Time Annotation of Clusters, Outliers, and Trends in Point-Based Data Visualizations, *IEEE TVCG*, 73–82, at 73 (2012).
105 Kandogan, *supra* at 73–74.
106 *See* Victoria Slind-Flor, Bill Gates, HP, Warner Music, Deere: Intellectual Property, *Bloomberg News* (Aug. 20, 2013); *available at*: http://www.businessweek.com/news/2013–08–20/bill-gates-hp-warner-music-deere-intellectual-property (last visited Jan. 15, 2015).
107 *See* W3C, OWL Working Group; *available at*: http://www.w3.org/2007/OWL/wiki/OWL_Working_Group (last visited Jan. 15, 2015).
108 *See* W3C, OWL 2 Web Ontology Language Document Overview, W3C Recommendation 27 October 2009; *available at*: http://www.w3.org/TR/owl2-overview/ (last visited Jan. 15, 2015). *See also* Anupriya Ankolekar, Markus Krotzsch, Thanh Tran, and Denny Vrandecic, The Two Cultures: Mashing up Web 2.0 and the Semantic Web, *Web Semantics: Science, Services and Agents on the World Wide Web*, 6, 70–75, at 71 (2008).
109 Paul K. Longmore, Disability Policy and Politics: Considering Consumer Influences, *Journal of Disability Policy Studies*, 11: 36–44, at 43 (2000).
110 *generally* Blanck, *eQuality*, *supra*.
111 *See, e.g.,* National Council on Disability. *The Power of Digital Inclusion: Technology's Impact on Employment and Opportunities for People with Disabilities* (NCD, 2011). The U.S. Department of Defense also uses online services for veterans and their families to address disability stigma and post-deployment work adjustment. *See, e.g.,* After Deployment, http://www.afterdeployment.org/ (last visited Jan. 15, 2015) (programs for PTSD emphasize online ease of use and comprehensibility).

The Raising the Floor (RtF) Consortium, and its partners engaged with the Global Public Inclusive Infrastructure (GPII) initiative and projects such as Cloud4All and Prosperity4All,[112] are developing a real-time Cloud-based ecosystem to provide customized user profiles to enhance online access for people with cognitive and other disabilities.[113] The goal is to provide auto-personalized options for users to simplify operations and interfaces, and for individuals with disabilities who use assistive technologies (AT: e.g., screen reader software) to make web operations adaptable and compatible across devices. The overarching aim of these projects is to create the means for individuals to effectively use any digital device and system encountered in their daily activities. This objective is furthered by use of open source and commercially viable Cloud-based technologies that support web equality.[114]

To approach these goals, Rtf is developing a MasterList (database) of strategies designed to support universal solutions for web content equality.[115] The majority of the MasterList entries are directly applicable to individuals with cognitive disabilities; for example, the MasterList includes Cloud-based solutions designed for:

- Reading text aloud and highlighting functions for those who use screen readers to enhance content comprehension for persons with cognitive disabilities.
- Reorganizing and simplifying text with the use of customized style aids to help in interoperability with AT used by those with print disabilities.
- Reorganizing text in navigation menus and to develop consistent and contextual navigation controls, page layout, labels and icons, notices within and across pages to aid persons with memory impairments.
- Audio enhancements to reduce background noise and adjust pace and volume of audio to aid in comprehension by persons with Autism.
- Accessible authentication (security) methods for online use to help those with learning disabilities.
- Functions for pronunciation and help support on demand, and the ability to correct speech-synthesis pronunciations to help those with Traumatic Brain Injury (TBI).
- Customization by ability to reorganize and translate content, and choice to modify background color, contrast, magnification, and font adjustments to facilitate reading for those with dyslexia.

112 *See* Raising the Floor, *Mission and Beliefs* (RtF); *available at*: http://raisingthefloor.org/about/mission (last visited Jan. 15, 2015). Launched in 2010, RtF was conceived by Gregg Vanderheiden during his term as co-chair and editor of WCAG 2.0. RtF members are individuals and organizations who believe the right to the web is "no longer optional" and access and usability solutions must be made universalized for persons with cognitive disabilities. I am founding member and President of RtF USA, which is a not-for-profit organization based in Washington, D.C.

113 *See* Global Public Inclusive *Infra*structure (GPII); *available at*: http://gpii.net/index.html (last visited Jan. 15, 2015). *See also* Gregg Vanderheiden & Jutta Treviranus, Creating a Global Public Inclusive Infrastructure, In *Proceedings of the 6th International Conference on Universal Access in Human-Computer Interaction: Design for All and Einclusion – Volume Part I*, Orlando, FL, 2022652, 517–26 (2011).

114 The W3C is examining other ways users may maintain personal security, with authentication systems embedded in online services. *See* W3C, *User Identity on the Web Community Group*, W3C.org; *available at*: http://www.w3.org/community/w3Id/ (last visited Jan. 15, 2015).

115 *See, e.g., Who We Are: The People and Organizations that Make Up the RtF Initiative*, Raising the Floor (listing members); *available at*: http://raisingthefloor.org/about/who (last visited Jan. 15, 2015). *Solutions MasterList*, Raising the Floor; *available at*: http://raisingthefloor.org/projects/masterlist/currentmaster-list (last visited Jan. 15, 2015).

- Simplification and customization of pages and browsers in different modes of presentation, and to translate and retrieve content in simplified language and symbols.
- Adjustable time limits and functions that may be paused for reading, listening, and required actions for those with intellectual and developmental disabilities.

There are other solutions to supplement web content with automated tools and AT. These include development of customized dictionaries and glossaries in multiple languages, and usage profiles to share with others, as well as customized cues for prompting use and function, and real-time assistance. Solutions allow for customize keyboard, mouse, and voice controls for text and input entry, along with use of specialized "hotkeys," shortcuts to simplify actions. Error prevention, correction, and recovery solutions are provided. Privacy and safety functions allow for automatic and pre-set assessments of website credibility and authenticity for trusted websites. Security functions are presented to support ease of use and comprehensibility for a range of users in ecommerce, social media, and gaming, and multichannel support functions are suggested to organize and adjust the amount of information presented. The use of GPS navigation provides for wayfinding, communication, and use of mobile devices in real time as well as to aid in information processing and comprehensibility of content.

The RtF MasterList furthers the design of new web tools and infrastructure to enhance customized, affordable and cost-effective ways to present web content.[116] The RtF, along with the GPII, with activities operating within the larger digital ecosystem, aims to enable individuals with diverse backgrounds and cognitive skills to learn about and select strategies to create and access their personalized profiles stored in the Cloud.[117] The preferences are to be available on-demand, across platforms and devices, and aimed at spurring innovation in proprietary and open source web products and services. Leading web researcher Gregg Vanderheiden believes that such a paradigm shift is essential because "access to the Internet and its information, resources and services is no longer optional."[118]

The RtF and other projects are helping to make online technologies universally available to those with cognitive and other disabilities, which also will benefit those with lower reading skills and digital literacy, print-related, lingual, and aging-related barriers. These efforts build on the principles set out in the ADA and the CRPD to promote web equality as a principal enabler for full and equal participation, and active citizenship, across life circumstances.[119]

Semantic Web and the "Internet of Things"

According to Anthony Giannoumis, *eQuality's* "idea that semantic web content provides a means for achieving universal design in practice *is the missing link* between what we know and understand

---

116 *See* Raising the Floor Projects, http://raisingthefloor.org/projects (last visited Jan. 15, 2015).

117 *See generally* Blanck, *eQuality*, *supra*. The GPII proposes Cloud-based user profiles (Personal Needs and Preferences (PNP) files) to enhance web use for people disabilities. *See* Global Public Inclusive Infrastructure; *available at*: http://gpii.net/index.html (last visited Jan. 15, 2015).

118 *See* Vanderheiden and Treviranus, *supra*, at 517.

119 *See also* G3ICT, ITU. e-Accessibility Policy Toolkit for Persons with Disabilities: A Joint ITU/G3ict Toolkit for Policy Makers Implementing the Convention on the Rights of Persons with Disabilities. [cited 2014 Mar. 22]; *available at*: http://www.e-accessibilitytoolkit.org/toolkit/annexes/Text%20of%20the%20Convention#expression (last visited Jan. 15, 2015).

about accessibility and what we want to achieve with universal design."[120] In this chapter, I have tried to clarify this view and extend its centrality as the Semantic Web and the Internet of Things (IoT; e.g., web-activated household appliances) continue to evolve. As Giannoumis has suggested, one main consideration regarding the principles of accessibility, usability, and universal design going forward in relation to the IoT is that new and non-traditional platforms and web interfaces will become even more ubiquitous, yet increasingly personalized.

At the present time, we are experiencing an inflection point at which web developer and service provider norms and standards are shifting from primarily user-driven interfaces to the IoT's hybrid of user-intelligent machine interfaces. For example, rather than programming a website to interact with particular assistive technology, a developer will program everyday household appliances to interact with Cloud-based auto-personalization services.[121] The objective is to allow users with diverse backgrounds and skills, and under varying environmental conditions, to access the IoT through the platforms and input devices the *user* chooses, anyplace and anytime.

The shift towards the ubiquitous IoT, in user practice and from a developer organizational perspective, should reduce the need for prescribed web content design standards. Rather, the pendulum of "responsibility" may swing from user-interaction designers and developers to international collaboratives aimed at maximizing innovative machine-to-machine interfaces, which the IoT envisions. However, despite attempts at harmonization, there are no globally accepted norms and values to spur such efforts, which is why the web and the IoT risk fragmentation.[122]

Section 508 refresh: Missed opportunity in the United States?

In 2015, the U.S. Architectural and Transportation Barriers Compliance Board ("Access Board") proposed an update or "refresh" of the accessibility guidelines and standards for electronic and information technologies, including web services, under Section 508 of the Rehabilitation Act of 1973 and Section 255 of the Communications Act of 1934.[123] According to the Access Board, this effort is in response to "a technological revolution" in web design and usage driven technologies, services, and products.[124] For instance, in the 15 years since adoption of the prior

---

120 Anthony Giannoumis email correspondence to author (Feb. 15, 2015). *See also* G. Anthony Giannoumis, Articulating a right to the Web for persons with cognitive disabilities, Universal Access to the Information Society; DOI 10.1007/s10209-015-0432-1 (2015).

121 Again, I thank Anthony Giannoumis for this example.

122 *See, e.g.,* Colin Gibbs, Challenges and Opportunities Abound in the Fragmented IoT, *Gigaom Research* (Oct. 8, 2014); *available at*: http://research.gigaom.com/2014/10/challenges-and-opportunities-abound-in-the-fragmented-iot/ (last visited Feb. 15, 2015) (fragmented operating systems in the IoT).

123 *See* U.S. Access Board, Proposed Information and Communication Technology (ICT) Standards and Guidelines, to be published in the *Federal Register* at 36 CFR Parts 1193 and 1194 [Docket No. ATBCB-2015-0002] RIN 3014-AA37 (Feb. 18, 2015); *available at*: http://www.access-board.gov/guidelines-and-standards/communications-and-it/about-the-ict-refresh/news-release (last visited Feb. 20, 2015).

124 *See* U.S. Access Board, Proposed Information and Communication Technology (ICT) Standards and Guidelines, *supra* at Executive Summary.

Section 508 standards, "smart" mobile phones and tablets have overtaken desktop computers as the primary means for information technology communications.[125]

The proposed rules replace the current "product-based approach with requirements based on functionality" to ensure accessibility and usability for people with disabilities in "hardware, software, *electronic content*, and support documentation and services."[126] They incorporate the WCAG 2.0 and make them applicable to web content and to web electronic documents and software.[127] The Access Board identifies as among the potential beneficiaries of its proposal people who are deaf and hard of hearing, for instance, to have faster and enhanced natural language communications. It also acknowledges that the proposal is intended to help improve online services and supports for individuals with visual impairments.

The Board does not take the opportunity to address those particular web accessibility and usability issues facing individuals with cognitive disabilities. It does acknowledge, however, that aspects of the proposed functional performance criteria relate to cognitive functioning – for example, in regard to improved functionality for web application timing adjustments, and for blinking, scrolling, and auto-updating information to aid in comprehension.[128] The earlier referenced RtF MasterList identifies many of these same considerations.[129]

It is curious why the Access Board chose not to include specific guidelines for functional performance criteria relating to cognitive disabilities.[130] The Board's stated reason is that its

125 *Id.*
126 *Id.*
127 *Id.* ("electronic content would have to be accessible, with "content" encompassing all forms of electronic information and data. . . . [with] real-time text (RTT) functionality. . . . The guidelines define "usable" as providing access to information about how to use a product, and direct that instructions, product information, documentation, and technical support for users with disabilities"). *Id.* at V. Major Issues (A. Electronic Content: proposed rule would delineate "scope of covered electronic content, as well as specifying concrete, testable, technical requirements to ensure the accessibility of such content. . . . all covered electronic content would be required to conform to WCAG 2.0 Level A and Level AA Success Criteria . . . . [including] public-facing content" – which encompasses electronic information and data made available by agencies to members of the general public).
128 *See, e.g.,* U.S. Access Board, Proposed Information and Communication Technology (ICT) Standards and Guidelines, *supra* at V. Major Issues, B. WCAG 2.0 Incorporation by Reference ("proposed standards would provide a single set of requirements for websites, documents, and software. . . . New requirements in WCAG 2.0 also address gaps in the existing 508 Standards. Examples include: a requirement for a logical reading order, the ability to resize text, and the ability to turn off background audio that might interfere with comprehension and screen reading software."). *Id.* at VI. Section-by-Section Analysis, Functional Performance Criteria ("Timed Response . . . where a timed response is required, ICT would have to alert the user visually, as well as by touch or sound. . . . The intent of this section is to afford people with certain disabilities – namely, those relating to manual dexterity, *cognitive disabilities, or otherwise affecting response time* – additional time to complete a task, if needed.") (emphasis added). *Id.* at VI. Section-by-Section Analysis, D. Functional Performance Criteria ("Captioning is critical for persons with hearing impairments *to use and understand information presented* in a video format.") (emphasis added); *Id.* Functional Performance Criteria ("[S]pecifications for ICT documentation in terms of accessibility and compatibility features that assist users with disabilities. Such documentation includes installation guides, user guides, online support, and manuals that describe features of a product and how it is used. . . . [B]ecause some users with disabilities have complained about a lack of information available *to help them understand the accessibility and compatibility features of some ICT*.") (emphasis added).
129 *See eQuality, supra* at 167–74.
130 *Id.* ("The existing 255 Guidelines provide a criterion for at least one mode of operation that minimizes cognitive skills required of the user [], while the existing 508 Standards have no parallel provision. Such a criterion has not been included in the proposed rule on the advice of the Advisory Committee, which recommended deletion of this criteria pending future research.").

Advisory Committee was not able to reach consensus on requirements for web accessibility for individuals with cognitive disabilities, and that there was a lack of adequate research on related metrics to verify functional conformance.[131] Yet, there are recognized metrics useful for assessing functional performance, in the WGAG 2.0 and elsewhere, for individuals with cognitive disabilities and older adults. Many such criteria may be derived from extant research and are relevant to individuals with visual, hearing, and dexterity conditions, as referenced by the Board.[132]

An additional objective of the Access Board's 508 refresh is to harmonize the existing Section 508 and 255 standards with corresponding guidelines in the global communications and technology markets to spur international advancement and innovation.[133] The Access Board references that in 2013, the European Commission published its draft Mandate 376 standards for "Accessibility requirements for public procurement of ICT products and services in Europe,"[134] which was completed in 2014 and subsequently adopted by the major European standards organizations.[135] Mandate 376, like the 508 guidelines, provides technical specifications for the public procurement of web and communications technology products to harmonize these products and services within Europe.[136]

Mandate 376 tracks functional performance criteria similar to that identified in the Access Board's proposed guidelines.[137] However, Mandate 376 includes functional criteria for web usage

---

131 *Id.* at VI C. 255 ("In the 2010 ANPRM, the Board followed this recommendation and proposed removal of the existing functional performance criterion specifically directed to cognitive disabilities. The Board did, however, seek public input on whether other proposed functional performance criteria adequately addressed cognitive impairments . . . Some commenters believed that cognitive disabilities were already sufficiently addressed through other criteria and requirements, while others preferred inclusion of a functional performance criterion for cognitive disabilities but offered no substantive proposals. Still other commenters – particularly those representing the IT community – thought more research was needed before meaningful requirements could be crafted. Given the variety of commenters' views and the inherent difficulty in creating a single functional performance criterion that adequately covers the wide spectrum of cognitive and intellectual disabilities, the Board elected not to reinstate this functional performance criterion.").

132 Existing 255 Guidelines have functional criteria such that under "1193.41 (i) Operable with limited cognitive skills. Provide at least one mode that minimizes the cognitive, memory, language, and learning skills required of the user."). *See id.* at V. Major Issues. C. Functional Performance Criteria; VII. Regulatory Process Matters. A. 4. Benefits of the Proposed Rule, Table 5 ("Time savings by people with hearing, cognitive, speech, and manual dexterity or motor impairments from improved federal websites.").

133 *Id.* at IV. Rulemaking History, F. Harmonization with European Activities.

134 *Available at*: http://www.etsi.org/deliver/etsi_en/301500_301599/301549/01.00.00_20/en_301549v010000c.pdf (last visited Feb. 24, 2015).

135 *Id.* at IV. Rulemaking History, F. Harmonization with European Activities (Mandate 376 "required the three European standards organizations – European Committee for Standardization (CEN), European Committee for Electrotechnical Standardization (CENELEC) and European Telecommunications Standards Institute (ETSI) – to: inventory European and international accessibility requirements; provide an assessment of suitable testing and conformity schemes; and, develop a European accessibility standard for ICT products and services along with guidance and support material for public procurements including an online toolkit.").

136 *See* http://www.mandate376.eu/ (last visited Feb. 24, 2015). *See also* Loïc Martínez and Michael Pluke, Mandate M 376: New Software Accessibility Requirements, *Procedia Computer Science*, 27, 271–80 (2014) (Mandate 376 functional performance clause for persons with physical, cognitive and sensory disabilities to access full functionality and documentation of web services and ICT, with and without use of assistive technology).

137 *See, e.g.,* European Commission, Standard-EN 301 549, Accessibility requirements suitable for public procurement of ICT products and services in Europe, Accessible ICT Procurement Toolkit, Functional Performance Statements (2014) (for Usage without vision, with limited vision, without perception of

(and for ICT) by individuals with limited cognition: "Some users will need [web services] to provide features that enable them to make better use of their limited cognitive capabilities."[138] This clause addresses functional needs of persons with cognitive, language, and learning impairments. It includes specifications for adjustable timings, error indications and suggestions, and logical focus ordering as examples of design features that satisfy this requirement. Building on the European approach elaborating functional performance criteria for individuals with cognitive, language and learning disabilities, and for older adults,[139] comments likely will be offered to the Access Board during the proposal notice period urging it to reconsider inclusion of functional performance criteria applicable to young and older individuals with cognitive disabilities, and to spur additional research in the area.

Closing

Vast numbers of individuals with disabilities with divergent interests increasingly are using the web. In the past, many of these individuals were among those least able to participate online and to exert pressure for web content equality. This is the reason why a new generation of disability advocates are vigorously defending their right to the web.[140] Three recent legal cases illustrate the ongoing struggle for web equality across platforms, apps, and services offered such as in Massive Open Online Courses (MOOCs), IoT devices, and crowd-sourced apps (e.g., Uber-type

---

colour, without hearing, with limited hearing, without vocal capability, with limited manipulation or strength, with limited reach, to Minimize photosensitive seizure triggers, with limited cognition); *available at*: http://mandate376.standards.eu/standard/functional-statements (last visited Apr. 23, 2015).

138 *See* Draft EN 301 549 V1.0.0 (2013–02), European Standard, Accessibility requirements for public procurement of ICT products and services in Europe, at 17 (2013) (4.2.10: Usage with limited cognition); *available at*: http://www.etsi.org/deliver/etsi_en/301500_301599/301549/01.00.00_20/en_301549v010000c.pdf (last visited Feb. 24, 2015). *Id.* at 12.1.2 ("Accessible documentation: . . . providing alternate formats that meet the needs of some specific type of users (e.g. Braille documents for blind people *or easy-to-read information for persons with cognitive impairments*") (emphasis added). *Id.* at 13.1.5 ("Any speech to speech relay service shall enable speech *or cognitively impaired telephone users and any other user to communicate by providing assistance between them."*) (emphasis added). *See also* Anthony Giannoumis, Transatlantic Learning: From Washington to Brussels and beyond (*Inclusion*, this volume) (British Standards Institution [BSI] standards on web accessibility (BS 8878:2010) recognize complex web navigation, content, and layout accessibility and usability for people with cognitive disabilities [*citing* BSI, Draft BS 8878:2009 Web accessibility – Building accessible experiences for disabled people – Code of practice: BSI.2009]).

139 *See, e.g.,* Terms of Reference—Specialist Task Force STF ZV (TC HF) Recommendations to allow people with cognitive disabilities to exploit the potential of mobile technologies, ToR STT 488 (TC HF), ETSI (Jan, 28, 2015) (proposed action for research to support standards that enable older people and people with cognitive, language, and learning disabilities to use mobile devices with simplicity and predictability to access e-information and services, such as e-learning, e-communicating, and e-interacting with public services, necessary for independent living and quality of life); *available at*: http://portal.etsi.org/STFs/STF_HomePages/STF488/STF488.asp (last visited Mar. 29, 2015); European Telecommunications Standards Institute (ETSI) (produces globally applicable standards for ICT) and recognized by European Union as a European Standards Organization; *available at*: http://www.etsi.org/about (last visited Mar. 29, 2015).

140 *See* Peter Blanck, Justice for All? Stories About Americans with Disabilities and their Civil Rights, *Journal of Gender, Race & Justice*, 8(1), 1–32 (2004); Peter Blanck, Americans with Disabilities and their Civil Rights: Past, Present, Future, *University of Pittsburgh Law Review*, 66, 687–719 (2005); Blanck, P. (2016). The First "A" in the ADA: And 25 More "A"s Toward Equality for Americans with Disabilities, *Inclusion*, 4(1): 46–51.

transportation services).[141] In this environment, *web content is king*, and full and equal access to it is crucial in all aspects of daily life.

In the first case, in 2015, a group of U.S. disability advocates – individuals who are deaf and with hearing impairments, along with the National Association of the Deaf (NAD) – sued Harvard University and the Massachusetts Institute of Technology (MIT) under the ADA.[142] They alleged that these universities' online web-based content (for example, in MOOCs) was not captioned and often was unintelligibly captioned, making the information not accessible and incomprehensible.[143] These individuals stated: "[j]ust as buildings without ramps bar people who use wheelchairs, online content without captions excludes individuals who are deaf or hard of hearing."[144]

While the Harvard and MIT cases were awaiting determination, later in 2015, the U.S. Department of Justice (DOJ) reached a settlement with edX, Inc. edX is a not-for-profit provider of MOOCs that was created by Harvard and MIT in 2012. It serves as an online platform for a consortium of approximately sixty other partnering universities providing hundreds of courses to over 3 million individuals worldwide.[145] The DOJ had alleged violations of ADA title III because

141 *See eQuality, supra* at 188–90 (discussion of MOOCs). *See also* National Federation of the Blind et al., v. Uber technologies, Inc., et al., Order Denying Motion to Dismiss (Case No. 14-cv-04086, NCDC ND CA 2015) (UberX is a transportation service that uses mobile software applications to arrange rides between passengers and Uber's fleet of drivers; plaintiffs allege UberX drivers violated ADA title III by denying access to blind individuals and their guide dogs; court denied Uber's motion to dismiss and found that Uber's potential liability as a public accommodation under ADA title III, and under California state law Unruh Act and Disabled Persons Act (DPA), required further factual development).

142 Harvard and MIT are places of public accommodation under the ADA. *See* Peter Blanck, Eve Hill, Charles D. Siegal, Michael Waterstone, *Disability Civil Rights Law and Policy: Case and Materials* (St. Paul, MN: West Publishers, 3rd ed., 2014) at 26.

143 *See* NAD, NAD Sues Harvard and MIT for Discrimination in Public Online Content (Feb. 12, 2015); *available at*: http://nad.org/news/2015/2/nad-sues-harvard-and-mit-discrimination-public-online-content (last visited Feb. 17, 2015). *See also* National Association of the Deaf et al., v. Harvard University, Class Action Complaint for Declaratory and Injunctive Relief (West. Div. D. Mass., Feb. 12, 2015); National Association of the Deaf et al., v. Massachusetts Institute of technology, Class Action Complaint for Declaratory and Injunctive Relief (West. Div. D. Mass., Feb. 12, 2015) (hereinafter "NAD Complaints").

144 NAD Complaints, *supra* at 2. *See also* Casey Fabris, Technology: As High-Tech Teaching Catches On, Students with Disabilities Can Be Left Behind, *Chronicle of Higher Education* (Feb. 25, 2015) ("Peter Blanck, chairman of the Burton Blatt Institute at Syracuse University and author of *eQuality: The Struggle for Web Accessibility by Persons with Cognitive Disabilities* (Cambridge, UK: Cambridge University Press, 2014), said blind and deaf students need to be considered when shifting core parts of teaching to the Internet. 'So far, it's been kind of an incremental struggle by persons with disabilities to have full and equal access to the web,' he said."); *available at*: http://m.chronicle.com/article/As-High-Tech-Teaching-Catches/190341/?key=SWN2cl9hMndFYXthYjZDZ2oAanJqYx0hMnNIPnwnbl5XFw== (last visited Feb. 26, 2015). *See also* Patrick Henry Wilson, The Next 50 Years: A Personal View, *Biologically Inspired Cognitive Architectures*, 1, 92–99, at 95 (2012). *See also* ADA Story Teller Project, Southwest ADA Center (2013); *available at*: http://www.southwestada.org/html/adastoryteller/about.html (last visited Jan. 15, 2015).

145 *See* Justice Department Reaches Settlement with edX Inc., Provider of Massive Open Online Courses, to Make its Website, Online Platform and Mobile Applications Accessible Under the Americans with Disabilities Act, DOJ Website (Apr. 2, 2015) (edX courses offered largely for free in areas such as business, computer sciences, hard sciences, food and nutrition and social sciences); *available at*: http://www.justice.gov/opa/pr/justice-department-reaches-settlement-edx-inc-provider-massive-open-online-courses-make-its (last visited Apr. 2, 2015); Settlement Agreement between the United States of

edX's website and platform for providing MOOCs were not fully accessible to individuals who are blind or with low vision, who are deaf or hard of hearing, and who have physical disabilities affecting manual dexterity (e.g., from videos without captions, and information not usable and lacking compatibility with screen-reader software applications). The allegations did not include that edX's online platform and apps, and related activities and services, were not fully accessible to individuals with cognitive and learning impairments. Nonetheless, the remedies adopted likely will benefit individuals across the spectrum of physical, sensory, and cognitive disability (e.g., compare the RtF Masterlist entries listed earlier).

The settlement agreement specifically requires edX to modify it website platform and mobile applications to conform with the WCAG 2.0 AA and to provide guidance and authoring tools to entities that create and post edX courses to ensure that the course content offered is accessible.[146] The 4-year agreement also requires edX to make its mobile applications and learning and content management systems fully accessible, to offer university course creators best practices for making online courses fully accessible, and to adopt web accessibility trainings and policies overseen by the company's Web Accessibility Coordinator.

The edX agreement does not necessarily resolve all the accessibility issues alleged in the Harvard and MIT litigation mentioned earlier. Universities and other online providers still must provide their information and course materials to edX and to other content management service providers in formats that are capable of accessible digital transmission. However, the edX agreement puts universities and other online information providers on notice that they must offer information in accessible formats when using the tools and means made available by edX and other like entities.[147]

In yet a third landmark legal development in 2015, the National Federation of the Blind (NFB) and its members brought suit against Scribd, Inc., which is a California-based digital library that operates reading subscription services on its website and on applications for mobile

---

America and edX Inc., Under the Americans With Disabilities Act, DJ No. 202-36-255 (Apr. 2, 2015); *available at*: http://www.justice.gov/sites/default/files/opa/press-releases/attachments/2015/04/02/ edx_settlement_agreement.pdf (last visited Apr. 2, 2015). *See also* Casey Fabris, edX to Improve Access to MOOCs for People With Disabilities, *Chronicle of Higher Education* (Apr. 3, 2015) ("Peter Blanck, . . . author of eQuality: The Struggle for Web Accessibility by Persons With Cognitive Disabilities . . . said edX was part of a new generation of services that are essentially content-management services rather than content providers. The settlement acknowledges that, he said. 'It's reflective of a recognition of the responsibility of these new content-provider management systems to enable a platform that is accessible with content,' . . . The settlement also acknowledges 'the responsibility of all parties to work together,' he added, in that it holds edX and its member colleges accountable.").

146 edX Settlement Agreement, *supra* at 8 ("incorporate accessibility in www.edx.org, its mobile applications, and its Platform to meet a wide variety of requirements of Participants with disabilities to enable Content Providers to develop accessible course content"). *See id.* Definitions ("'Content Management System' or 'CMS' means the components of the edX software platform with which Course Creators interact, including, without limitation, the HTML editor, video upload screens, assessment authoring, and studio.edx.org, and excluding, for purposes of clarity, Course Content. EdX calls its CMS 'Studio.' 'Content Provider' means any non-edX organization or institution that creates and/or provides content on www.edx.org, the Platform, or edX's mobile applications. 'Course Content' means any information published to www.edx.org, edX's mobile applications, or the Platform by a Content Provider, including, but not limited to, courses or specific plug-ins or tools related to any course.").

147 *See also* Casey Fabris, edX to Improve Access to MOOCs for People with Disabilities, *supra* (Eve Hill, DOJ Deputy Assistant Attorney General for Civil Rights noted that the edX agreement "is different because it concerns both platform technology, created by edX, and the content itself, which is largely created by the consortium's member colleges.").

phones and tablets.[148] The Plaintiffs contended that Scribd's website and apps were not accessible to individuals with visual impairments and who are blind in violation of the ADA because the company uses "an exclusively visual interface" and lacks non-visual means of operation, such as use with screen reader software to convert graphical information into audio and Braille formats.

In a decision of first impression for its jurisdiction,[149] the Vermont federal district court concluded that a defendant such as Scribd, which offers commercial services solely via the web, provides services to the public within the purview of the ADA. Thus, Scribd may not discriminate against individuals with disabilities in their full and equal opportunity to enjoy the website and the apps offered to the public. The court wrote that "the site of the sale is irrelevant. All that matters is whether the good or service is offered to the public."[150] It reasoned:

> Now that the Internet plays such a critical role in the personal and professional lives of Americans, excluding disabled persons from access to covered entities that use it as their principal means of reaching the public would defeat the purpose of this important civil rights legislation.[151]

The recent legal developments that I have highlighted are part of a progressive effort to eliminate disability discrimination in education, employment, health care, housing, and access to the built and digital environments.[152] Change is being achieved incrementally through advocacy, where

---

148 National Federation of the Blind et al., v. Scribd, WL 1263336 (D.Ct. D. Vermont, Mar. 19, 2015) ("Scribd's customers pay a monthly fee to gain access to its collection of over 40 million titles, including e-books, academic papers, legal filings, and other user-uploaded digital documents. Scribd's digital software program is accessed over the Internet.").

149 The jurisdiction of United States Court of Appeals for the Second Circuit. Although the U.S. Court of Appeals for the First Circuit takes a similar approach, other Circuits require a "nexus" between the physical and digital worlds for the ADA to apply. *See eQuality, supra* at 81 and *passim* (discussion of "place" nexus requirement). *See also* Cullen, et al. v. Netflix, No. 13-15092: D.C. No. 5:11-cv-01199-EJD (9th Cir. Apr. 1, 2015) ("We have previously interpreted the statutory term "place of public accommodation" to require "some connection between the good or service complained of and an actual physical place." *See Weyer v. Twentieth Century Fox Film Corp.*, 198 F.3d 1104, 1114 (9th Cir. 2000). Because Netflix's services are not connected to any "actual, physical place[]," Netflix is not subject to the ADA."); Earll v. eBay, No. 13-15134: D.C. No. 5:11-cv-00262-EJD (9th Cir. Apr. 1, 2015) (same). In a separate action in the First Circuit, Netflix was deemed a place of accommodation for purposes of ADA title III. *See eQuality, supra* at 171 and *passim*.

150 NFB v. Scribd, *supra* at 10 ("It would be "absurd" to conclude people who enter an office to purchase a service are protected by the ADA but people who purchase the same service over the telephone or by mail are not."). *Id.* at 12 ("Otherwise, a company could freely refuse to sell its goods or services to a disabled person as long as it did so online rather than within the confines of a physical office or store."). *Id.* at 16 ("it would make little sense if a customer who bought insurance from someone selling policies door to door was not covered but someone buying the same policy in the parent company's office was covered."). *Compare* Eric Goldman, Scribd Must Comply with the Americans with Disabilities Act, *Forbes* (Mar. 26, 2015) ("ADA doesn't expressly apply to Internet retailers, and stretching the statutory language to include online-only activities requires awkward interpretive contortions. . . . As a result [of the *Scribd* decision], many thousands of websites may have to incur substantial remediation expenses to comply with the ADA. In the interim, this opinion could produce a litigation tsunami against sites that aren't in compliance."); *available at:* http://www.forbes.com/sites/ericgoldman/2015/03/26/scribd-must-comply-with-the-americans-with-disabilities-act/ (last visited March 28, 2015). Many disability advocates await the coming "litigation tsunami."

151 NFB v. Scribd, *supra* at 23–24.

152 *See generally* Robert Silverstein, The Emerging Disability Policy Framework: A Guide for Developing Public Policy for Persons with Disabilities, *Iowa Law Review*, 85, 1691 (2000).

discrimination is challenged and brought to the fore. The ADA and the CRPD serve as principled bases in law to end segregation on the basis of disability.[153]

It would be unfair, however, to suggest that disability advocates are alone in pursuit of web equality. Many technology, educational, and business leaders support this endeavor.[154] Nonetheless, the community of individuals with cognitive and other disabilities, and their families, have experienced, and continue to experience, discrimination.[155] Inaccessible and unusable online content is one aspect of that negative experience because it sends the message to "keep off the web." Inclusion and active participation have always been the remedy to segregation and discrimination, and they are the principles set forth in disability right laws for equal opportunity, independent living, and economic self-sufficiency.[156]

The ADA has yet to be applied in a principled manner to achieve web content equality for people with cognitive disabilities.[157] However, this chapter has argued that full and equal access to the web for all individuals increasingly is recognized. In 2015, U.S. Supreme Court Justice Anthony Kennedy wrote: "The Internet has caused far-reaching systemic and structural changes in the economy, and, indeed, in many other societal dimensions."[158]

In the coming years, it may be that in the United States amending the ADA, revising its implementing regulations, and seizing the opportunity to modify the Access Board's Section 508 refresh are among actions required to ensure that web content equality is a right available to all persons with disabilities, including those with cognitive conditions.[159] Nonetheless, the possibility for *eQuality* – the full and equal enjoyment of the web – for persons with cognitive and other disabilities in the United States and globally is on the horizon.

153 In 2015, the European Disability Forum called for "An inclusive digital continent" for its 80 million citizens with disabilities, with passage of a legal framework that offers a right to digital inclusion. *See* European Disability Forum, 80 Million Persons with Disabilities Call for Accessible Information & Communication Technologies (Feb. 21, 2015); *available at*: http://www.edf-feph.org/Page_Generale. asp?DocID=13855&thebloc=34202 (last visited Feb. 21, 2015).

154 *See* James Sullivan, Clayton Lewis, and Jeffery Hoehl, (2011). Implications of Cloud Computing for People with Cognitive Disabilities, in C. Stephanidis (Ed.), *Universal Access in HCI, Part II* (New York: Springer), pp. 372–381.

155 *See, e.g.,* Harold Pollack, Do Liberals Disdain the Disabled?, *NY Times* (Feb. 27, 2012); *available at*: http://www.nytimes.com/2012/02/27/opinion/do-liberals-disdain-the-disabled.html?_r=2 (last visited Jan. 15, 2015).

156 *See, e.g.,* Michael Morris, Christopher Rodriguez, and Peter Blanck, (2016). ABLE Accounts: A Down Payment on Freedom, *Inclusion*, 4(1): 21–29.

157 *See, e.g.,* Eve Hill, Legal and Policy Implications of Cloud Computing, *Lecture Notes in Computer Science*, 6765, 478, 481 (2011). Encouragingly, *see* Coleman Institute for Cognitive Disabilities, Declaration of the Rights of People with Cognitive Disabilities to Technology and Information Access, In *Thirteenth Annual Coleman Institute National Conference on Cognitive Disability and Technology*, Broomfield, Colorado (Oct. 2, 2013).

158 Direct Marketing Association v. Brohl, Executive Director, Colorado Department of Revenue, 135 S.Ct. 1124, at 1135 (U.S. 2015) (Kennedy, J., concurring decision).

159 *See generally* Steven E. Stock, Daniel K. Davies Michael L. Wehmeyer, and Yves Lachapelle, Emerging New Practices in Technology to Support Independent Community Access for People with Intellectual and Cognitive Disabilities, *NeuroRehabilitation*, 1; 28(3): 261–269 (Jan. 2011). *See also* Catherine Easton, The Web Content Accessibility Guidelines 2.0: An Analysis of Industry Self-regulation, *International J.L. & Information Technology*, 19(1), 74–93, at 89–92 (2010); Elizabeth Ellcessor, <ALT="Textbooks">: Web Accessibility Myths as Negotiated Industrial Lore, *Critical Studies in Media Communication*, 1–16 (2014) (debunking "web accessibility myths" such as that accessibility compromises good web design, cost-effectiveness, and aesthetics).

12

DISABILITY AND AGEING

Bridging the divide?
Social constructions and human rights

Eilionóir Flynn

Introduction

In the past decade, significant discourse has developed on the relationship between disability and ageing. One factor which prompts this discussion is the truism that many people with disabilities are living longer, and conversely that many people without disabilities will acquire disabilities as they age.[1] However, the growing global awareness of a demographic trend towards an ageing population is not the only reason to investigate the connections between disability and ageing. In the field of international human rights law, the UN Convention on the Rights of Persons with Disabilities is the most recent UN human rights treaty to be adopted, and a process is ongoing at the UN level to consider whether a new treaty on the rights of older people might be developed.[2] Given that the experience of people with disabilities in advocating, and securing, a UN treaty is comparatively recent, there is much to share and learn from that experience with advocates for a Convention on the Rights of Older Persons.

There are also synergies in the kinds of stereotypes that may be applied to both older people and people with disabilities in contemporary society – that is that they are economically unproductive, a burden on the welfare state, and objects of pity and care, rather than subjects or citizens with equal rights.[3] In the parallel literatures of disability studies and social gerontology, there are similarities in how social and political responses to people with disabilities and older people are understood. For example, both literatures have separately developed an understanding of both

---

1 See World Health Organization and World Bank, *World Report on Disability* (Geneva: WHO), pp. 24–31; 34–36.
2 This process is ongoing within the UN Open-Ended Working Group on Ageing. For more detail on the process and advocacy strategies employed, see Sciubba, J.D., "Explaining campaign timing and support for a UN Convention on the Rights of Older People" (2014) 18(4–5) *International Journal of Human Rights* 462.
3 See for example, Davidson, K., "Sociological Perspectives on Ageing" in Stuart-Hamilton, I. (ed), *An Introduction to Gerontology* (Cambridge; New York: Cambridge University Press, 2011) 226–251 at 228; and Barnes, C., Mercer, G. and Shakespeare, T. (eds), *Exploring Disability: A Sociological Introduction* (Cambridge; New York: Cambridge University Press, 1999).

chronological age[4] and disability as social constructions,[5] connected to, but distinct from, the biological impact of impairment and the ageing process. While there are many differences in the lived experiences of people with disabilities and older people, and indeed, neither community can be described as a homogenous group, there are some interesting similarities in some of the core human rights violations that affect both communities.

Two human rights concerns common to both communities are the exercise of legal capacity and the concepts of independent living and community inclusion.[6] These issues will be discussed in further detail throughout this chapter, as themes which demonstrate the interconnectedness of disability and ageing discourse, and indeed, demonstrate how both communities might learn from each other in how these core human rights are constructed and applied. Before examining these concrete rights, this chapter will provide an overview of the conceptualisations of disability and ageing which might influence human rights discourse, and then consider how these two human rights, as illustrative examples, can be framed and applied to both communities. Finally, a brief comparative analysis will be undertaken of the negotiation which led to the elaboration of a UN Convention on the Rights of Persons with Disabilities (CRPD) and the discussions underway in the UN Open-Ended Working Group on Ageing, provide some tentative recommendations on how advocacy for a Convention on the Rights of Older Persons might be advanced at the UN level.

Social constructions of disability

Many phrases have been used in law and policy to describe people with disabilities since laws and policies were first specifically applied to this group of people. Retarded, handicapped, mentally disordered, chronically ill, infirm, and disabled are a selection of the initial terms used.[7] However, in recent times, many of these phrases have been regarded as offensive or inappropriate for a myriad of reasons, but primarily because they were overly reliant on a medical or individualist conception of 'disability', one which labelled people according to their impairment and viewed all the problems experienced by people with disabilities as a direct result of their impairment, rather than problems arising from a society which was structured according to the needs of the majority, who did not experience disability.

This critique led to the development of a social model of disability, which viewed 'disability' as separate from 'impairment'. 'Impairment' is the term used to describe the medical condition affecting a particular individual, whereas 'disability' is the term given by sociologists to the societal barriers experienced by people with physical or mental impairments. Although many people suffer societal disadvantage due to gender, race, sexuality or poverty, the term 'disability' applies solely to the type of disadvantage suffered specifically by people with impairments. Of course,

---

4 For a discussion of the critical gerontology approach to a social construction of chronological age, see Phillipson, C., *Reconstructing Old Age: New Agendas in Social Theory and Practice* (Thousand Oaks; London; New Delhi: SAGE Publications, 1998), Chapter 3 "Constructing Old Age" pp. 29–43.
5 See for example, Oliver, M., *The Politics of Disablement* (London: Macmillan, 1990).
6 These concepts are among the issues identified by Kanter of relevance for both people with disabilities and older people. See Kanter, A. "The United Nations Convention on the Rights of Persons with Disabilities and its implications for the rights of elderly people under international law" (2009) 25 *Georgia State University Law Review* 527.
7 See further, Dajani, K., "Other research – What's in a name? Terms used to refer to people with disabilities" (2001) 21(3) *Disability Studies Quarterly* 196.

this is not to state that people with disabilities cannot suffer multiple types of societal disadvantage due to other factors such as those outlined earlier; it is merely to clarify that a particular type of societal disadvantage affects individuals who have impairments and to recognise that specific redress for this disadvantage must be sought through reform of law and policy. In addition, the use of the term 'people with disabilities' does not deny that impairment can have a significant impact on individuals' daily lives; rather, it seeks redress for this situation on a societal, as well as an individual, level.

This term also reflects the language chosen in the UN CRPD, which contains the term 'persons with disabilities' in its title.[8] An underlying factor in the choice of this term can also be found in one of the major shifts in terminology in recent years – the move from 'disabled persons' to 'persons with disabilities'.[9] This shift was spearheaded by a self-advocacy group of people with intellectual disabilities, known as People First, whose claim that people with disabilities are people first, and that disability is secondary to their human citizenship,[10] is particularly important given the nature of advocacy for people with disabilities, which is to ensure that the voices of people with disabilities are heard in decision-making processes which affect them.

In terms of the use of the social model of disability as the basis for understanding the position of people with disabilities in society and justifying law reform in the manner suggested by this thesis, it is important to understand that this model is not intended to ignore or deny the suffering caused to individuals by impairment. As Oliver has more recently stated:

> I want to make three general points about the social model. Firstly, it is an attempt to switch the focus away from the functional limitations of individuals with an impairment on to the problems caused by disabling environments, barriers and cultures. Secondly, it refuses to see specific problems in isolation from the totality of disabling environments: hence the problem of unemployment does not just entail intervention in the social organisation of work and the operation of the labour market but also in areas such as transport, education and culture. Thirdly, endorsement of the social model does not mean that individually based interventions in the lives of disabled people, whether they be medically, rehabilitative, educational or employment based, are of no use or always counterproductive.[11]

Kayess and French highlight the dual purposes of the social model of disability[12] – as a theory of disability and as a disability rights manifesto, in their analysis of the drafting process of the UN CRPD. This concept will be discussed in further detail below in the context of the Ad Hoc Committee negotiations which led to the drafting of a Convention.

---

8 UN Convention on the Rights of Persons with Disabilities (2006).

9 It should be noted that many disability advocates, especially those in the UK, prefer the term 'disabled persons/people' which they see as a signifier of solidarity and more closely aligned with the social model. For more, see Barnes, C., Oliver, M. and Barton, L. (eds), *Disability Studies Today* (London: Wiley Publishers, 2002).

10 People First of Spokane Washington, *People First History* (Washington: People First, 2002) available at http://www.peoplefirstsv.com/people_first_history.htm (last accessed 29 March 2009).

11 Oliver, M., "The social model in action: If i had a hammer" in Barnes, C. and Mercer, G. (eds), *Implementing the Social Model of Disability: Theory and Research* (Leeds: The Disability Press, 2004), pp. 18–20.

12 Kayess, R. and French, P., "Out of darkness into light? Introducing the convention on the rights of persons with disabilities" (2008) 8(1) *Human Rights Law Review* 1, 7.

Social constructions of ageing and synergies with disability/impairment

Recent developments in social gerontology, particularly the political economy of ageing and critical gerontology, emphasise how chronological age is socially constructed.[13] Research on the political economy of ageing uncovers how old age is constructed by the state in its laws and policies to ensure that the interests of the most powerful members of society are prioritised in an effort to maintain economic, political and social capital. This theory was emerging around the same time that the social model of disability, discussed earlier, was being developed in Britain, and many of the theorists in both strands of literature identified the structural barriers facing both communities as part of a class struggle, in which older people and people with disabilities were marginalised.[14] Further developments in critical gerontology explore the combined impact of biological, psychological, social and environmental factors on the ageing process, and attempt to consider the diverse experiences of older people from different genders, ethnicities and social classes. These approaches also have a resonance within critical disability studies, where the inter-sectionality of identities held by disabled people are also explored.[15]

As a whole, the most recent social gerontology literature demonstrates that societal expectations of people of a certain age, for example, people over 65, include a number of assumptions – that they will become frail, have greater care needs and increased dependency on others, retire or withdraw from active participation in the open labour market, etc. The chronological age at which these expectations are imposed can vary widely depending on geographic location and cultural context – so that there are great variations across the globe in the chronological age at which a person is considered to be 'old'. Gorman writes that:

> In many parts of the developing world, chronological time has little or no importance in the meaning of old age. Other socially constructed meanings of age are more significant such as the roles assigned to older people; in some cases it is the loss of roles accompanying physical decline which is significant in defining old age. Thus, in contrast to the chronological milestones which mark life stages in the developed world, old age in many developing countries is seen to begin at the point when active contribution is no longer possible.[16]

The potential of older people to make an active contribution to society is clearly not biologically determined by a particular chronological age. Nevertheless, some experiences associated with old age, such as retirement[17] and frailty,[18] are fraught with societal expectations and contribute to

---

13 Heckhausen, J. and Lang, F. "Social construction and old age: Normative conceptions and interpersonal processes" in Semin, G. and Fiedler, K. (eds), *Applied Social Psychology* (London: SAGE Publications Ltd., 1996), pp. 374–399.
14 See for example, Oliver, M., *The Politics of Disablement* (London: Macmillan, 1990).
15 Goodley, D. "Dis/entangling critical disability studies" (2013) 28(5) *Disability & Society* 631–644.
16 Gorman, M., "Development and the Rights of Older People" in Randel J., German T., Ewing D., Help-Age International, (eds), *The Ageing and Development Report: Poverty, Independence and the World's Older People* (London: Earthscan Publications Ltd., 1999), pp. 3–21.
17 Phillipson, C., "The Social Construction of Retirement" in *Reconstructing Old Age: New Agendas in Social Theory and Practice* (Thousand Oaks; London; New Delhi: SAGE Publications, 1998), Chapter 3 "Constructing Old Age", pp. 55–64.
18 Kaufman, Sharon R. "The social construction of frailty: An anthropological perspective" (1994) 8(1) *Journal of Aging Studies* 45–58.

the social construction of old age. In the context of retirement, for example, the imposition of a mandatory retirement age, a political decision, sends a clear message to older people about their expected social role.[19] Many social policies also delineate eligibility for social benefits to people with disabilities – placing an upper age limit (often equivalent to the retirement age) after which a person is no longer recognised as a person with a disability, but is simply an older person, who may be entitled to a different kind of social benefit, one which is often less likely to meet his or her disability-related needs.[20]

These examples demonstrate the intersectionality of discrimination faced by older people, many of whom acquire disabilities as they age, and people with disabilities, who are increasingly living longer, with differing needs as they age.[21] The communities of older people and people with disabilities clearly share many of the same human rights concerns, including, but not limited to, the right to lifelong learning, work and employment, and the right to health and accessibility. In the following section, I will focus on two specific human rights issues which resonate deeply in both communities, namely, the right to live independently and be included in the community, and the right to equal recognition before the law, which includes the enjoyment of legal capacity on an equal basis with others.

Legal capacity and community living in the context of ageing and disability

The rights to legal capacity and community living have been specifically chosen for further exploration in the context of older people and people with disabilities for a number of reasons. First, these two rights are intimately connected and dependent upon each other. For example, an individual's skills in self-determination are often dependent on that person's contact with and participation in the broader community and opportunities to exercise choices – and the recognition of an individual's legal capacity is often essential in enforcing and acting upon that person's decisions about where and with whom to live (including entering legally binding tenancy agreements, accessing credit for mortgages, or claiming housing benefits).

Secondly, these issues have been identified by international organisations, and organisations of older people and people with disabilities, as core human rights concerns, long before they were recognised in legally binding international human rights instruments, such as the UN Convention on the Rights of Persons with Disabilities. For example, the issue of 'ageing in place', and maintaining the right of older persons to live in their own homes as long as possible, has been recognised in international literature since at least the 1980s,[22] and the independent living movement in the disability community developed in the 1960s and 1970s,[23] even though legal recognition of these rights was not widespread until the entry into force of the CRPD in 2007.

---

19 For more, see Sargeant, M. "Mandatory retirement age and age discrimination" (2004) 26(2) *Employee Relations* 151–166.
20 See for example, Office of the Ombudsman, *Too Old to be Equal? An Ombudsman Investigation Into the Illegal refusal of Mobility Allowance to People Over 66 Years of Age* (Dublin: Stationery Office, 2012).
21 See World Health Organization and World Bank, *World Report on Disability* (Geneva: WHO), pp. 24–31; 34–36.
22 See for example, World Assembly on Ageing, Vienna International Plan of Action on Ageing 1982, adopted by the UN General Assembly on 3 December 1982, A/RES/37/51, Recommendation 19.
23 DeJong, Gerben. "Independent living: From social movement to analytic paradigm" 60(10) (1979) *Archives of Physical Medicine and Rehabilitation* 435–446.

Finally, the reason for focusing on these core rights is that they have been particularly controversial in their negotiation in the UN Convention on the Rights of Persons with Disabilities, their subsequent interpretation and implementation in practice – and they present interesting tensions between and among the disability and ageing communities in terms of how they can be realised in practice. Since these two rights, and all human rights, are intended to be universal in nature, then any tensions or conflicts in their application to different groups are worth exploring and clarifying. It is particularly timely to undertake such an analysis now, before any new norm-setting process begins at the international level in clarifying the application of existing human rights to the lived experience of older people. In the following sections I will set out the existing rights to equal recognition before the law and living independently as they are framed in the CRPD, and their interpretation and implementation in the context of disability, before considering how such rights might be framed in the context of older people and the similarities and differences which may emerge.

Equal recognition before the law and legal capacity

The right to legal capacity is recognised in Article 12 CRPD on equal recognition before the law. Article 12 represents a paradigm shift in understanding the right to legal capacity. Prior to the entry into force of the Convention, there was no international human rights standard that guaranteed to persons with disabilities the enjoyment of legal capacity on an equal basis with non-disabled people. As a result, in many countries around the world, people with disabilities were deprived of their legal capacity – meaning that they were denied the right to make many legally binding decisions – including entering contracts, voting, retaining legal representation and consenting to (or refusing) medical treatment. In many liberal democracies today, it is still considered acceptable to deny people with disabilities the right to exercise their legal capacity, based on the person's 'mental capacity' or decision-making ability. This particularly affects those with intellectual disabilities, psycho-social disabilities, dementia, autism and other neurological or cognitive disabilities – whose choices are more likely to be challenged on the basis that they lack the necessary 'mental capacity' to make a binding legal decision, and are often asked to pass a 'functional test' of mental capacity to demonstrate that they understand the reasonably foreseeable consequences of their decision. Older people too, often find the legality of their decision-making to be challenged by others, including family members and professionals who deem them to lack the requisite understanding to make a binding decision. While it is clear from the text that Article 12 applies to older people with disabilities including people with dementia, a new human rights instrument could usefully extend this recognition to all older persons, regardless of whether or not an older person also identifies as a person with a disability.

Article 12(1) reaffirms the status of persons with disabilities as persons before the law, that is as individuals possessing legal personality, with legal status and agency. This is confirmed by Article 12(2), which extends the right to enjoy legal capacity on an equal basis with others to all aspects of life. Article 12(3) CRPD contains a novel addition to international human rights norms – a state obligation to provide the supports required to exercise legal capacity. This support can take many forms, including, but not limited to, formal agreements with supporters who assist in certain areas of decision-making.[24]

Article 12(4) then addresses the safeguards required for all measures regarding the exercise of legal capacity. Some argue that this provision allows for some limited forms of guardianship

---

24 Committee on the Rights of Persons with Disabilities, *General Comment on Article 12* (CRPD/C/GC/1) at para 15.

to remain if the appropriate safeguards are in place;[25] however, the Committee on the Rights of Persons with Disabilities has not accepted this argument from any of the countries it has examined to date – even those countries which have interpretative declarations or reservations on Article 12 which state that Article 12 permits some limited forms of substituted decision-making.[26]

The key phrase in Article 12(4), and one which has been used repeatedly by the Committee on the Rights of Persons with Disabilities in its concluding observations on the countries examined to date, is that safeguards should be designed to respect the 'rights, will and preferences' of the person. The term 'best interests' does not appear in paragraph four, or in Article 12 at all. Therefore, it is clear that safeguards which are paternalistic in nature, or which envisage the use of substitute decision-making, are not permitted under Article 12. Finally, Article 12(5) refers specifically to the need to respect legal capacity with regard to financial affairs and property – an issue which was subject to extensive debates during the negotiation of the CRPD.

The Committee on the Rights of Persons with Disabilities, which monitors the CRPD, has repeatedly called for the abolition of regimes of substitute decision-making and their replacement with systems of supported decision-making in each of the ten concluding observations it has issued to date.[27] In each of its Concluding Observations on these countries, the Committee expressed concern 'that no measures have been undertaken to replace substitute decision-making by supported decision-making in the exercise of legal capacity'.[28] With respect to all countries, the Committee has recommended that the states 'review the laws allowing for guardianship and trusteeship, and take action to develop laws and policies to replace regimes of substitute decision-making by supported decision-making, which respects the person's autonomy, will and preferences'.[29]

---

25 *See* Canada's Reservation to the CRPD, Article 12 (11 March 2010). However, the United Nations Committee on the Rights of Persons with Disabilities (CRPD) has recently noted in several of its concluding observations that steps should be taken to replace substituted decision-making with supported decision-making. *Consideration of reports submitted by States parties under article 35 of the Convention: concluding observations, Tunisia,* Committee on the Rights of Persons with Disabilities (CRPD), 5th Sess., at 4, UN Doc CRPD/C/TUN/CO/1 (April 11–15, 2011); *Consideration of reports submitted by States parties under article 35 of the Convention: concluding observations, Spain,* Committee on the Rights of Persons with Disabilities (CRPD), 6th Sess, at 5, UN Doc CRPD/C/ESP/CO/1 (September 19–23, 2011).

26 See for example *Consideration of reports submitted by States parties under article 35 of the Convention: concluding observations, Australia,* Committee on the Rights of Persons with Disabilities (CRPD), 10th Sess., UN Doc CRPD/C/AUS/CO/1 (September 2–13, 2013).

27 See for example *Consideration of reports submitted by States parties under article 35 of the Convention: concluding observations, Tunisia,* Committee on the Rights of Persons with Disabilities (CRPD), 5th Sess., at 4, UN Doc CRPD/C/TUN/CO/1 (April 11–15, 2011); *Consideration of reports submitted by States parties under article 35 of the Convention: concluding observations, Spain,* Committee on the Rights of Persons with Disabilities (CRPD), 6th Sess, at 5, UN Doc CRPD/C/ESP/CO/1 (September 19–23, 2011).

28 *Consideration of reports submitted by States parties under article 35 of the Convention: Concluding observations of the Committee on the Rights of Persons with Disabilities,* Committee on the Rights of Persons with Disabilities: Fifth session, 4 (April 11–15, 2011), http://www.ohchr.org/EN/HRBodies/CRPD/Pages/Session5.aspx (last accessed 26 April 2013).

29 *Consideration of reports submitted by States parties under article 35 of the Convention: Concluding observations of the Committee on the Rights of Persons with Disabilities,* Committee on the Rights of Persons with Disabilities: Sixth session, 5 (September 19–23, 2011), http://www.ohchr.org/EN/HRBodies/CRPD/Pages/Session6.aspx (last accessed 17 May 2013).

The General Comment on Article 12 developed by the Committee clearly states, for the first time in international human rights law, that an individual's mental capacity cannot be used as a reason to deprive that person of legal capacity, even if the deprivation of legal capacity relates to a single decision.

> Legal capacity and mental capacity are distinct concepts. Legal capacity is the ability to hold rights and duties (legal standing) and to exercise these rights and duties (legal agency). It is the key to accessing meaningful participation in society. Mental capacity refers to the decision-making skills of an individual, which naturally vary among individuals and may be different for a given individual depending on many factors, including environmental and social factors. . . . Under article 12 of the Convention, perceived or actual deficits in mental capacity must not be used as justification for denying legal capacity.[30]

More guidance has also been provided by the Committee in its General Comment on the definitions of 'substitute decision-making regimes' and 'supported decision-making' respectively. Substitute decision-making is defined as follows:

> where 1) legal capacity is removed from the individual, even if this is just in respect of a single decision; 2) a substituted decision-maker can be appointed by someone other than the individual, and this can be done against his or her will and 3) any decision made is bound by what is believed to be in the objective 'best interests' of the individual – as opposed to being based on the individual's own will and preferences.[31]

By contrast, the Committee provides a broad interpretation of 'supported decision-making', as 'a cluster of various support options which give primacy to a person's will and preferences and respect human rights norms'.[32] A non-exhaustive list of support options is provided in the General Comment, from relatively minor accommodations, such as accessible information, to more formal measures such as supported decision-making agreements nominating one or more supporters to assist the individual in making and communicating certain decisions to others.[33]

These developments in the interpretation of the right to legal capacity in Article 12 CRPD have significant implications for the recognition of the legal capacity of older persons in any new international human rights treaty. The CRPD and treaty body, the Committee, have set clear standards in terms of the expectations on States to protect the right of persons with disabilities to enjoy and exercise legal capacity (with support, if desired) on an equal basis with others. The following section will address the extent to which these new interpretations of the CRPD are filtering through to discussions in the UN Open Ended Working Group on Ageing (OEWGA) on the legal capacity of older persons.

---

30 Committee on the Rights of Persons with Disabilities, *General Comment on Article 12* (CRPD/C/GC/1) at para 12.
31 Committee on the Rights of Persons with Disabilities, *General Comment on Article 12* (CRPD/C/GC/1), at para 23.
32 Committee on the Rights of Persons with Disabilities, *General Comment on Article 12* (CRPD/C/GC/1), at para 25.
33 Committee on the Rights of Persons with Disabilities, *General Comment on Article 12* (CRPD/C/GC/1), at para 15.

Legal capacity of older persons – on an equal basis with others?

At the time of writing, no formal negotiation has commenced of a draft Convention on the rights of older persons. Nevertheless, the issue of legal capacity has been subject to some discussion in the five sessions to date of the Open Ended Working Group on Ageing. While many civil society organisations and speakers in the sessions have highlighted the importance of self-determination and autonomy for older persons, there seemed to be less resistance, at least in the early sessions, to the idea that the exercise of legal capacity will be limited for older people as they acquire disabilities such as dementia, when compared with the discussions on legal capacity that took place in the Ad Hoc Committee. Evidence of this is found in the discussions of regional developments such as draft Conventions, protocols and recommendations on the human rights of older persons at the OEWGA from Africa, the Americas and Europe, have tended to contain weaker protections of the right to legal capacity for older people when compared with the right as framed in Article 12 CRPD, discussed earlier. For example, an early draft of the Organization of American States Convention on the Rights of Older Persons in 2012 stated that 'any and all restrictions on legal capacity must be properly substantiated, limited in time, subject to periodic review and applied solely to specific decisions in which a lack of capacity and the need for proxy consent has been determined'.[34] That draft also used the terms 'legal representative' or 'legal proxy' to describe 'a person who under the law has the duty to represent the interests of an older person who is incapable of taking decisions in a particular area, or to exercise specific rights on behalf of the person'.[35] However, the most recent draft of the OAS Convention from 2014 shows alterations to the text, which now reflect exactly the provisions of Article 12 CRPD.[36] This new draft also requires 'respect for the autonomy of older persons in making their decisions, and their independence in the actions they undertake'[37] and recognises that 'older persons have the inalienable right to express their [prior and] informed consent' on healthcare treatment.[38]

Similarly, the Council of Europe Committee on Human Rights of Older Persons published a recommendation in 2014. While the language of the final recommendation broadly reflects the principles of Article 12 CRPD, it also refers to 'possible restrictions' on the legal capacity of older persons 'which may be required for protection purposes'.[39] This seems to be an implicit

---

34 Permanent Council of the Organization of American States, Committee on Juridical and Political Affairs, Working Group on protecting the Human Rights of Older Persons, *Preliminary Draft Inter-American Convention on Protection of the Human Rights of Older Persons*, OEA/Ser.G CAJP/GT/DHPM-37/12 30 April 2012, Article 31(b).
35 Permanent Council of the Organization of American States, Committee on Juridical and Political Affairs, Working Group on protecting the Human Rights of Older Persons, *Preliminary Draft Inter-American Convention on Protection of the Human Rights of Older Persons*, OEA/Ser.G CAJP/GT/DHPM-37/12 30 April 2012, Article 2.
36 Permanent Council of the Organization of American States, Committee on Juridical and Political Affairs, Working Group on protecting the Human Rights of Older Persons, *Preliminary Draft Inter-American Convention on Protection of the Human Rights of Older Persons*, OEA/Ser.G CAJP/GT/DHPM/INF.34/14 17 November 2014, Article 30.
37 Ibid., Article 7(a).
38 Ibid., Article 11.
39 Council of Europe, Steering Committee For Human Rights (CCDH), Recommendation CM/Rec(2014)2 of the Committee of Ministers to Member States on the promotion of the human rights of older persons CM/Rec(2014)2, available at http://www.coe.int/t/dghl/standardsetting/hrpolicy/other_committees/cddh-age/Document_CDDH_AGE/CMRec(2014)2_en.pdf (accessed 9 February 2015).

endorsement of adult guardianship systems which restrict the legal capacity of older persons and persons with disabilities in the name of 'protection'. Speaking about the development of this recommendation at the UN OEWGA, Nicola-Daniele Cangemi, Head of the Human Rights Law and Policy Division from the Council of Europe, stated that 'I think it is important not to be afraid to speak about protection, and to be felt as taking a "paternalistic" approach.'[40] While Cangemi acknowledged that the recommendation drew on the text of Article 12 CRPD for inspiration, he also suggested that 'our member states took the view that the recommendation could not simply endorse the CRPD provisions, but should adapt them to the specificities of the older persons'.[41]

The African Commission's Working Group on the Rights of Older Persons and People with Disabilities also developed a Draft Protocol to the African Convention on Human and People's Rights on the Rights of Older Persons, which was discussed at the fourth session of UN OEWGA. However, this protocol contains a very problematic statement on the right to legal capacity in its Article 7, which requires States to '[e]nsure that, in the event of incapacity, Older Persons shall be provided with such support as legal aid and accompaniment by social and legal personnel in order to make decisions that are in their best interest and wellbeing'.[42] The references to 'incapacity' and the appointment of personnel to make decisions in the 'best interest' of older persons, stand in stark contrast to the strong right to legal capacity available to persons with disabilities under Article 12 CRPD.

Although the UN OEWGA is not currently negotiating a draft text of a Convention, civil society organisations have begun to formulate the elements they believe should be present in a legally binding human rights instrument. Following a global consultation with older people, the Global Alliance for the Rights of Older People has developed a draft of these elements which contains strong statements about the right to legal capacity. This draft states that older people should have 'legal capacity on an equal basis with others in all aspects of life' and the 'support required to exercise legal capacity and to be complete citizens and to be an equal member of the family and of society'.[43] Similarly, it states that older people have a right to 'autonomy, self-determination and choice in all aspects of older people's lives including in making decisions about their support and care and leisure time, property, income, finances, place of residence, health and medical treatment or care, and funeral arrangements'.[44] In the context of the right to health, this draft states that older persons should have 'autonomy in terms of informed consent for, and choice of, treatment' and the 'opportunity to make advance instructions about health care, including palliative and end of life care'.[45]

---

40 UN Open-ended Working Group on Ageing, Fourth working session, International frameworks and instruments on the human rights of older persons and identification of existing gaps at the international level Panel 2: Update on multilateral processes, Nicola-Daniele Cangemi, Head of the Human Rights Law and Policy Division Directorate General of Human Rights and Rule of Law, Council of Europe (New York: UN, 13 August 2013) available at: http://social.un.org/ageing-working-group/documents/fourth/presentation/NicolaDanieleCangemi.pdf (accessed 10 February 2015).

41 Ibid. at p. 5.

42 African Union, Draft Protocol to the African Charter on Human and Peoples' Rights on the Rights of Older Persons in Africa, 26–30 May 2014, CAMSD/EXP/4(IV) available at: http://sa.au.int/en/sites/default/files/Protocol%20Older%20Person%20-%20English%20-%20Final.pdf (last accessed 11 February 2015), Article 7(2).

43 GAROP, A New Convention on the Rights of Older Persons – A Proposal by the Global Alliance for the Rights of Older People (New York: December 2014), draft on file with author, p. 2.

44 Ibid.

45 Ibid., p. 4.

These examples demonstrate the opportunities and challenges facing the drafting of a new Convention in terms of the framing of a right to legal capacity for older persons. On the one hand, there is a risk that this right will be framed more restrictively for older persons than it currently is for persons with disabilities – as evidenced by the regional developments discussed earlier. However, on the other hand, there is a real opportunity to expand the existing right to legal capacity for persons with disabilities to all older persons, and also to reconceptualise how this right can be framed positively in the context of making advance decisions – something which was not fully addressed in the CRPD. New interpretations of this right for older persons could in turn influence the development of new ideas in the disability movement on the recognition and protection of legal capacity for all.

Article 19 of the CRPD: The right to live independently and be included in the community

The twin concepts contained in Article 19 of the CRPD[46] are particularly important for people with disabilities and indeed for older people without disabilities, although there are a number of perceived tensions between the right to 'independent living' and the right to be included in the community. Many people with disabilities had traditionally been – and continue to be – institutionalised and forced to live in congregated settings, and therefore, the right to 'independent living', and the subsequent obligation on states to provide financial support (including personal assistance) to facilitate this is a rallying cry of the disability rights movement.[47]

However, throughout the drafting process of the CRPD,[48] it was argued that this right to independent living should not become a justification for the isolation or victimisation of people with disabilities who live in the community with their non-disabled peers, or the removal of State support to facilitate participation and inclusion in community life. Concerns were also raised about ensuring that people with disabilities could continue to live within the community with their families if they so wished, and the need for state support to families to achieve this. Given these challenges, the inclusion of Article 19 in the CRPD is a major achievement. Some of the key commitments in Article 19 which are relevant to people with disabilities and older people alike include the right to live in the community with choices equal to others; the right to choose where and with whom to live (Article 19(a)); the right to targeted services, including 'access to a range of in-home, residential and other community support services, including personal assistance necessary to support living and inclusion in the community, and to prevent isolation or segregation from the community' (Article 19(b)); and the right to access mainstream community services (Article 19(c)). This includes the availability on an equal basis to people with disabilities of '[c]ommunity services and facilities for the general population', which should be 'responsive to their needs'.

The success of Article 19 is also due in large part to sustained advocacy by disabled people's organisations (DPOs) throughout the drafting process. These organisations and advocates insisted

---

46 The full text of Article 19 is available at: http://www.un.org/disabilities/default.asp?id=279 (last accessed 23 January 2015).
47 For information on the origin of the independent living movement see the UC Berkeley archive, available at http://bancroft.berkeley.edu/collections/drilm/ (last accessed 2 February 2015). See also the websites of the European Network of Independent Living (ENIL) http://enil.eu/ and Inclusion International http://www.inclusion-international.org/priorities/living-in-community/ (last accessed 2 February 2015).
48 The archive of the negotiations on the Convention on the Rights of Persons with Disabilities is available at: http://www.un.org/disabilities/default.asp?id=1423 (last accessed 3 February 2015).

that the inclusion of Article 19 was key to the entire Convention, that it fulfilled the promise of 'nothing about us without us' on the basis of which DPOs had participated in the drafting process, and provided the essential tools to combat the kinds of invidious discrimination which people with disabilities had been subject to at state level (e.g. with respect to access to housing and in-home supports).[49]

The CRPD protects Article 19 rights and freedoms for all people with disabilities, including older people with disabilities, and through the work of the UN OEWGA, it may be possible to extend this recognition to all older people so as to prevent the institutionalisation and segregation of older people, simply on the basis of their age, a growing phenomena in many parts of the world. A key argument in progressing these rights, and one which was repeated throughout the work of the Ad Hoc Committee which drafted the CRPD, is that the CRPD contains no new rights, but draws on existing international human rights norms and applies them to the particular circumstances of people with disabilities. However, it is clear that while the particular circumstances of people with disabilities led to the framing of Article 19 CRPD, the right to live independently and to be included in the community for older people may have a different framing or context, as discussed further in the following section.

Ageing in place and long-term support for independent living

The global experience of older persons in respect of living in the community differs in some important respects from that of persons with disabilities. Given the historical trajectories of both communities, much of the efforts of the disability rights movement have been to reverse the process of institutionalisation by getting people with disabilities out of institutions and back into the community[50] – whereas for older persons, advocacy is more targeted at keeping people in their own homes for as long as possible.[51] There is perhaps greater acceptance among the civil society organisations that represent the concerns of older persons that institutionalisation, or residential care, is inevitable at a certain point. This stands in contrast with the strident advocacy of many disability rights activists, who increasingly argue that there is no justification for institutionalisation, regardless of the severity of the individual's disability. While civil society organisations have repeatedly highlighted the abuses and rights violations which older people experience in segregated residential settings such as social care institutions and nursing homes, there has not to date been any consensus in the deliberations of the UN OEWGA that the mere placement of older people in segregated residential facilities could constitute a human rights violation. Indeed, when Eric Rosenthal from Disability Rights International suggested at a side event during the second session of the UN OEWGA that all segregated residential settings from orphanages to nursing homes are institutions which violate human rights, he encountered serious resistance to this idea from civil society organisations representing older people.[52]

49 Lord, J. and Kayess, R., "Living Your Own Life" (Galway: Summer School From Paper Rules to Action, Centre for Disability Law and Policy, NUI Galway & Harvard Project on Disability, 8 June 2011).
50 See for example, ENIL, "Free Our People Now" (European Network on Independent Living, 2014), available at: http://www.enil.eu/campaigns/free-our-people-now/ (last accessed 20 February 2015).
51 See Wiles, J. L., Leibing, A., Guberman, N., Reeve J., and Allen, R. E. S., "The meaning of 'aging in place' to older people" (2011) 52(3) *The Gerontologist* 357–336.
52 See Flynn, E., Lewis, O., Laurin-Bowie, C., and Rosenthal, E., 'The rights of older persons: Lessons from the process and text of the UN convention on the rights of persons with disabilities' discussion paper presented at the UN Open-Ended Working Group on Ageing side event, second session, New York, 1 August 2011.

Nevertheless, in more recent sessions of the UN OEWGA, the concept of living independently and being included in the community has emerged as an important issue for older people. Civil society organisations representing older persons tend to use slightly different language to describe the concepts of retaining independence and remaining in the community – such as 'ageing in place'[53] or 'long-term support', reflecting the unique experiences of older people; however, the basic concepts resonate deeply with the underlying principles in Article 19 CRPD. In the third session of UN OEWGA, one of the panel discussions was dedicated to 'autonomy, independent living and healthcare'.[54] Within this discussion, Nena Georgantzi from AGE Platform Europe, argued that 'we need to guarantee that older persons are not forced against their will to enter in any type of care setting, whether residential or home care'.[55] She highlighted that '[i]n care delivery, older people often don't have a say on what to eat, what to wear, what time to go to bed or even whether to use the bathroom. Caregivers sometimes carry out even the most intimate tasks, without discussing the older person's preferences. Older persons may have no control of the visits they receive and can even be forced to stay in bed for long periods of time.' Georgantzi's presentation made explicit the potential for human rights violations which are present in segregated residential care facilities, and those which can be experienced by older people being cared for at home.

At the fourth session of UN OEWGA, where States and civil society organisations for the first time had an opportunity to discuss the possible elements of a new human rights instrument for older persons, many delegations raised the issue of maintaining autonomy and independence in care, and some focused explicitly on independent living. Age UK argued that any new human rights instrument should include the 'right to support and services, including long term care, for people who need support to live independent lives' and the 'right to live independently, in your own home and to participate in the community'.[56] The draft proposal for a Convention developed by the Global Alliance for the Rights of Older People also addresses this issue, and suggests the inclusion of a 'right to long term support for independent living', encompassing 'choice of, and access to, a range of options for where and with whom to live, who provides support and when; which support the ability to live independently'.[57] This draft also recommends a separate right to 'age in place' whereby older people are not 'obliged to live in any particular living arrangement', can 'choose living arrangements, where and with whom they live and have the 'right to remain in the community, regardless of physical or mental status'.[58]

These examples demonstrate the unique framing of the right to live in, and be part of, the community, for older people. The inclusion of such a right in any new human rights instrument would provide an important opportunity to build on the foundation of the CRPD and acknowledge that segregation and institutionalisation of older people without their consent constitutes a

---

53 See Wiles, J. L., Leibing, A., Guberman, N., Reeve J., and Allen, R. E. S., 'The meaning of "aging in place" to older people' (2011) 52(3) *The Gerontologist* 357–336.

54 UN Open-Ended Working Group on Ageing, Third Session, Proposed Programme of Work (21–24 August 2012), available at: http://social.un.org/ageing-working-group/documents/third/programme ofwork.pdf (last accessed 10 February 2014).

55 Georgantzi, N., "The right to autonomy, health and independent living" paper presented at UN Open-Ended Working Group on Ageing, Third Session (UN: New York) 22 August 2012.

56 Bluestone, K. *Consultation Response: Main Elements for Inclusion in an International Human Rights Instrument for Older People* (London: Age UK, 2013).

57 GAROP, *A New Convention on the Rights of Older Persons – A Proposal by the Global Alliance for the Rights of Older People* (New York: December 2014), draft on file with author, p. 3.

58 Ibid., p. 2.

human rights violation. However, the experiences of older people demonstrate that the violation of the rights to privacy and autonomy experienced in residential care are also at risk in the informal care or home setting, and that equal protection against both kinds of violations are necessary. This would expand upon the existing statement of the right contained in Article 19 CRPD and indeed has the potential to broaden our understanding of the human rights to autonomy and participation beyond the context of disability and ageing.

Comparative processes of treaty negotiation – some brief reflections

At first glance, there are many similarities between the processes undertaken by the Ad Hoc Committee which drafted the CRPD and the UN OEWGA. For example, both processes were initiated by Latin American countries in favour of drafting new legal instruments.[59] In both processes, many of the same countries were initially opposed to the development of a new human rights instrument – including the United States, EU and China.[60] The same arguments for and against a treaty have been made in both processes – with those in favour arguing that a treaty is needed due to an invisibility of the target group in existing international human rights law, and those opposed arguing that the group is already protected by existing human rights norms, and that the introduction of a new treaty with an associated monitoring body would overburden an already stretched UN treaty body system.[61]

However, there are also some stark differences between these processes – primarily in the pace of negotiation and in the advocacy strategies employed. The CRPD is often referred to as the fastest negotiated human rights treaty in UN history[62] – the process took just over 5 years from the formation of the Ad Hoc Committee to the adoption of the final Convention text. The UN OEWGA has at the time of writing held five annual sessions, yet there is still no consensus on the need to begin drafting a treaty as part of this process. It should be noted however that the CRPD was unusual in the speed of its negotiation, and that most human rights treaty processes take much longer – therefore it is still eminently possible that a treaty will emerge from the UN OEWGA process in the future.

The other key difference worth mentioning here is the level of direct involvement of rights holders; namely, people with disabilities and older people, in both processes. The participation of people with disabilities in the Ad Hoc Committee was significant at all levels. The majority of civil society organisations in the Committee's deliberations were DPOs – organisations run and controlled by disabled people themselves. People with disabilities were also well-represented among the National Human Rights Institutions that participated in the discussions, and towards the end of the negotiation process, many of the State delegations included people with disabilities as representatives.[63] By contrast, the majority of civil society organisations in UN OEWGA are not representative organisations *of* older people, but rather groups that work *for*

59 Kayess, R. and French, P., "Out of darkness into light? Introducing the convention on the rights of persons with disabilities" (2008) 8(1) *Human Rights Law Review* 1, 7.
60 See Flynn, E., "International discourse on ageing – The journey towards a convention" in Ruebner, R., Do, T. and Taylor, A. (eds), *International Elder Law and Policy* (Chicago: Vandeplas Publishers, 2015) forthcoming.
61 Sciubba, J.D., "Explaining campaign timing and support for a UN convention on the rights of older people" (2014) 18(4–5) *International Journal of Human Rights* 462.
62 Kayess, R. and French, P., "Out of darkness into light? Introducing the convention on the rights of persons with disabilities" (2008) 8(1) *Human Rights Law Review* 1, 4.
63 Ibid.

older people – such as the International Federation on Ageing, HelpAge International, Global Action on Ageing, the International Network on the Prevention of Elder Abuse, etc. There are some notable exceptions to this rule, such as AGE Platform Europe and Gray Panthers – but these are in the minority.

The reasons for this difference in the involvement of rights holders in UN OEWGA are complex, and a detailed discussion of possible factors is outside the scope of this chapter.[64] However, one possible reason which should be mentioned here is the absence of a global social movement of older people themselves. If the UN OEWGA commences negotiations on a human rights treaty, there will certainly be a greater need for the involvement of rights holders, and perhaps such a development in the work of UN OEWGA might encourage older people to come together to form a global social movement in order to influence this process.

Conclusion

Since the CRPD is the most recent international human rights treaty and a Convention on the Rights of Older Persons may be the next new human rights treaty, the two instruments and processes will inevitably be compared and contrasted. Such comparisons may tend to focus on the substantive rights these instruments contain as well as the advocacy strategies employed to achieve these ends. The exploration of the interlinked rights to legal capacity and independent living undertaken earlier provides an interesting example of what advocates for older people can learn from the framing of these rights in the CRPD, and indeed, how the reframing of similar rights in a new instrument on older people can contribute substantively to deepen our understanding of these fundamental rights. It seems that in the UN OEWGA process, there is an understandable unwillingness to simply restate CRPD rights without further adaptation to the unique lived experience of older persons.[65] The articulation of the rights of older persons from first principles is an important part of any treaty negotiation process which may emerge from UN OEWGA. As Gerard Quinn has noted:

> You can do that based on your theory of age, your understandings of why age is discounted in existing human rights doctrine and therefore the new space needed to valorize the rights of older people. This is unlikely to overlap substantially with any other ground including disability. Don't cut and paste from another treaty – including the disability treaty – work it out for yourselves freed from the dead hand of another treaty.[66]

64 For a more extensive discussion of this phenomenon, see Sciubba, J.D., "Explaining campaign timing and support for a UN convention on the rights of older people" (2014) 18(4–5) *International Journal of Human Rights* 462 and Flynn, E., "International discourse on ageing – The journey towards a convention" in Ruebner, R., Do, T. and Taylor, A. (eds), *International Elder Law and Policy* (Chicago: Vandeplas Publishers, 2015) forthcoming.

65 See for example, the Council of Europe contribution to the third session of UN OEWGA, UN Open-ended Working Group on Ageing, Fourth working session, International frameworks and instruments on the human rights of older persons and identification of existing gaps at the international level Panel 2: Update on multilateral processes, Nicola-Daniele Cangemi, Head of the Human Rights Law and Policy Division Directorate General of Human Rights and Rule of Law, Council of Europe (New York: UN, 13 August 2013) available at: http://social.un.org/ageing-working-group/documents/fourth/presentation/NicolaDanieleCangemi.pdf (accessed 10 February 2015).

66 Quinn, G., "The anatomy of the treaty drafting process: Lessons for the age treaty from the drafting of the UN Disability Treaty" in Ruebner, R., Do, T. and Taylor, A. (eds), *International Elder Law and Policy* (Chicago: Vandeplas Publishers, 2015) forthcoming.

The articulation of these rights and the demonstration of the added value which they would bring to international human rights law is a crucial next step for the advocates of a Convention on the Rights of Older Persons. Finally, drawing from the experiences of those who negotiated the CRPD as well as other activists who secured UN Conventions, it is clear that sustained advocacy from civil society, National Human Rights Institutions and States in favour of a Convention is needed to break down the resistance from those opposed to this development. In doing so, it is vital to strengthen the participation of older people themselves to articulate their human rights concerns. Such an approach could ensure that the mantra of 'Nothing About Us Without Us', which permeated the CRPD negotiations, becomes the clarion call of all future UN human rights treaties.

13

DISABILITY AND GENETICS

New forms of discrimination?

Aisling de Paor

Introduction

Rapid advances in genetic science and technology have presented a pandora's box of exciting insights, information and opportunities about the genetic make up of human beings. The discoveries made in the field genetic science throughout the twentieth and twenty-first centuries have contributed towards a more refined understanding of the connection between disease, genes and other external factors. These discoveries are continuing and will inevitably further progress in the future. In addition to general characteristics that determine an individual's physical appearance, such as height, eye colour and hair colour, individuals may also inherit diseases and disorders, such as heart disease, diabetes and different types of cancers, as well as disabilities. Genetic science is quickly advancing and genetic technologies are becoming increasingly available and accessible, offering the potential to revolutionise health care and the change the way disease and disability is detected, treated and even eradicated. Genetic testing can detect predisposition to a range of genetically based conditions and diseases. It may also offer the potential to detect the onset and possible severity of future disabilities. These genetic developments encourage greater awareness of the cause and effect of disease and disability and may potentially create a new paradigm of genetically oriented healthcare and medicine.

In conjunction with this promise of a genomic revolution, such scientific and technological advances create a minefield of ethical and legal dilemmas in relation to access to and use (including misuse) of genetic information. These concerns reflect an increasing interest in genetic technologies for non-medical purposes, particularly by interested third parties, such as employers and insurance companies, who often have a financial interest in accessing and using such information. These interested third parties may use this information to categorise and differentiate between individuals, potentially leading to discrimination, breach of privacy and the violation of a myriad of fundamental human rights.

This chapter proposes that misuse of genetic information in these circumstances (and indeed in a variety of social and economic contexts, as well as in society in general) exacerbates or heightens the susceptibilities of persons with disabilities (particularly putative disabilities), who are already in a vulnerable position in society and who already may be experiencing exclusion, isolation and discrimination. In addition, certain attitudes towards disability may operate to disable the individual, by imputing a disability to that individual on the basis of a positive genetic test result or on the basis of an undesirable family history of illness. Further, with an ageing population, it is inevitable that more and more individuals will be exposed as having putative disabilities, resulting in a greater proportion of the population who may be deemed 'at risk' of mistreatment and discrimination. Not only do advances in genetic technologies create the potential for discrimination on the basis of potential future disabilities and expose persons with putative disabilities, but such advances may also potentially operate to devalue the lives of persons with disabilities. This may further perpetuate further negative attitudes towards persons with disabilities, as well as adverse treatment, including discrimination.[1]

In light of the evident connection between disability and genetics, which will be explored in this chapter, and on account of the serious individual and societal implications of abusing genetic technologies, this chapter will highlight the current best thinking on the social construct of disability, and how it can shape the discussion in this area. This chapter acknowledges the discourse and theory surrounding the medical and transhumanist models of disability,[2] however, it focuses on the application of the social model of disability, as is most appropriate in this context. With an acknowledgement of historical abuses of genetic science, this chapter advocates a need to address and control the use of genetic information and genetic testing, with a view to anticipating the development of new forms of discrimination against persons with disabilities and indeed all individuals with putative disabilities (who encompass an increasing proportion of the population).[3]

Genetic science and technology

A scientific introduction

Before examining the connection between genetics and disability, it is important to provide a scientific and technological primer to this discussion. The past century has witnessed significant progress in genetics, from the discovery of the DNA double helix[4] to the successful completion of the Human Genome Project, which mapped the entire human genome.[5] As a result of the success of the Human Genome Project and related technological advances, genetics is playing an increasingly important role in the diagnosis, prevention and treatment of diseases. The Human Genome Project laid the foundations for a twenty-first century revolution in genetic research that offers longer, healthier and more informed futures for all individuals.

More recently, the Human Brain Project, another major scientific endeavour, aims to delve deeper into the human brain and discover new ways to understand and treat neurological conditions such as Parkinson's disease.[6] These and subsequent scientific developments have provoked

1 Janet Lord, 'Screened Out of Existence: The Convention on the Rights of Persons with Disabilities and Selective Screening Policies' (2012) 12 International Journal of Disability, Rehabilitation and Community 2.
2 Gregor Wolbring, 'A Disability Rights Approach to Genetic Discrimination' in Judit Sandor (ed) *Society and Genetic Information. Codes and Laws in the Genetic Era* (Central European University Press 2004) 161.
3 In comparison with the United States, which introduced federal level legislation in this area (the Genetic Information Non-Discrimination Act 2008), it is noted that there is currently no concrete regulatory framework in this area in the European Union, but rather a diverging patchwork of national level protections.
4 James D. Watson and Francis H.C. Crick, 'Molecular Structure of Nucleic Acids: A Structure for Deoxyribose Nucleic Acid' (1953) Nature 737 (announcing the discovery of the DNA double helix); Francis Crick, 'The Double Helix: A Personal View' (1974) 248 Nature 766.
5 Francis S. Collins, Michael Morgan and Aristides Patrinos, 'The Human Genome Project: Lessons from Large Scale Biology' (2003) 300 Science, 286.
6 Yves Fregnac and Gilles Laurent, 'Neuroscience: Where Is the Brain in the Human Brain Project' (2014) 513 Nature 7516.

a growing interest in genetics and have resulted in increasing endeavours to discover more about the genetic profile of human beings, as well as the causes of disease and disability. Technological innovation in this field offers the prospect of personalised medicine, which may potentially revolutionise health care in the future – with earlier diagnosis, more effective prevention and treatment of disease, and avoidance of drug side effects.[7] These new technologies are becoming more prevalent and are being used increasingly in mainstream health care practice, for example in the context of breast cancer diagnosis and treatment.[8]

Specifically, the use and availability of genetic testing has become more prevalent. The technique of genetic testing '*involves examining a person's DNA for some anomaly that flags a disease or disorder*'.[9] Genetic testing involves cells from the individual being tested, and generally, the cells used come from blood, saliva, the inside of the cheek, or any other human tissue. Suspected mutations and predisposition to disease can be confirmed by genetic testing in advance of the onset of symptoms.[10] The objective is that suspected genetic abnormalities and predisposition to disease can be confirmed or ruled out by genetic testing, before the expression of symptoms.

The speed at which science is advancing is becoming evident, as is the speed at which genetic technologies are becoming more sophisticated and more refined.[11] This results in a greater availability of and accessibility to genetic testing and genetic information. For example, in recent years, there has been a distinct increase in the profile and availability of direct-to-consumer (DTC) genetic testing.[12] DTC genetic testing, which is becoming cheaper, facilitates the direct provision of such tests to consumers, for example via the internet or through mail, usually without the need for a medical professional. Relying on the power of the Internet and recent genetic advances, '*an increasing number of companies are starting to offer health- related genetic testing services directly to the public*'.[13] Although raising significant legal and ethical concerns,[14] it is observed that the growing market for DTC genetic testing may promote awareness of genetic diseases, allowing consumers

---

7 Aisling de Paor and Noel Lowndes, 'Tracing the History, Evolution and Future Orientation of Genetic Science and Technology' in Gerard Quinn, Aisling de Paor and Peter Blanck (eds) *Genetic Discrimination – Transatlantic Perspectives on the Case for a European Level Legal Response* (Routledge 2014) 29.

8 Ibid. See also Yadak Sapkota *et al.*, 'Germline DNA Copy Number Aberrations Identified as Potential Prognostic Factors for Breast Cancer Recurrence' (2013) 8 Public Library of Science ONE 1: e53850.

9 Paul Steven Miller, 'Is there a Pink Slip in Your Genes? Genetic Discrimination in the Workplace' (2000) 3 Journal of Health Care Law and Policy 2 225, 229. See also Denise K. Casey, 'What Can the New Gene Tests Tell Us?' (1997) 36 The Judges Journal 14, 16.

10 Peter S. Harper, 'What do We Mean by Genetic Testing?' (1997) 34 Journal of Medical Genetics 749.

11 Jon Cohen, 'The Human Genome, A Decade Later', Technology Review (January/ February 2011) Available at: http://www.technologyreview.com/featured-story/422140/the-human-genome-a-decade-later/ (accessed 15 January 2015).

12 The increase in interest and availability of DTC genetic testing is partly the result of the emergence of several companies, such as: 23 and Me https://www.23andme.com/ (accessed 14 January 2015). See also Stuart Hogarth *et al.*, 'The Current Landscape for Direct-to-Consumer Genetic Testing: Legal, Ethical and Policy Issues' (2008) 9 Annual Review of Human Genomics and Human Genetics 161, 162. See generally John Lynch *et al*, 'Media Coverage of Direct-to-Consumer Genetic Testing' (2011) 20 Journal of Genetic Counselling 5 486.

13 Stuart Hogarth *et al.*, 'The Current Landscape for Direct-to-Consumer Genetic Testing: Legal, Ethical and Policy Issues' (2008) 9 Annual Review of Human Genomics and Human Genetics 161, 162. See generally John Lynch *et al.*, 'Media Coverage of Direct-to-Consumer Genetic Testing' (2011) 20 Journal of Genetic Counselling 5 486.

14 Stuart Hogarth *et al.*, 'The Current Landscape for Direct- to-Consumer Genetic Testing: Legal, Ethical and Policy Issues' (2008) 9 Annual Review of Human Genomics and Human Genetics 161, 162.

to take control of their genetic health and take a more proactive role in their health care. It also highlights the speed of technological progression.

There has also been particular technological advancement in the field of reproductive medicine. Genetic advances have propelled the development of innovative technologies in the area of reproduction and assisted reproduction, with the objective of identifying genetic abnormalities and future disabilities, at the prenatal stage, the antenatal stage and increasingly at the preimplantation stage. Prenatal diagnostic testing involves testing the foetus before birth to determine whether the foetus has certain abnormalities, including inherited or random genetic mutations (such as cystic fibrosis and sickle cell anaemia). Newborn screening, a technique used on newborn babies, can test for a range of genetic disorders, such as the *heel prick test*.[15] These technologies generally identify treatable genetic disorders, usually prior to the manifestation of conditions, with a view to earlier diagnosis, intervention and treatment.[16] Preimplantation genetic diagnosis is a more radical type of genetic technology, which involves screening embryos. It is a technique used to identify genetic abnormalities in embryos created through in vitro fertilisation.[17] This particular practice, although offering significant benefits to reproductive medicine and enhancing reproductive autonomy, produces many concerns in deciding in what circumstances to pursue pregnancy and arguably provokes ethical issues such as the value and dignity of all individuals, particularly persons with disabilities.[18]

The emerging technologies available in the reproductive and other contexts highlight the fast progression in the genetics field and the growing accessibility to such technologies.

What can genetic testing reveal?

By taking a genetic test, whether through traditional means via a medical practitioner or whether by availing of emerging technologies such as DTC genetic testing, an individual can discover what genes he/she may have that may potentially indicate predisposition to a range of conditions and diseases.[19] Genetic technology may offer the prospect of being able to detect the onset of future disabilities, thereby highlighting genetic predispositions to disability. In addition to identifying genetic markers for disease and disability, genetic testing may also identify potential behavioural and personality traits, thereby revealing further personal insights about individuals.[20]

Rapid evolution in the field of genetic science envisages a future in which a vast amount of information about genes and disease will be readily available and accessible. It is also inevitably that genetic technologies will become a more routine element of healthcare, creating exciting new horizons in the scientific and medical fields. However, in conjunction with acknowledging the enormity of scientific and technological advances in this field, it is important to be *mindful*

---

15 Stefan Timmermans and Mara Buchbinder, *Saving Babies – The Consequences of Newborn Genetic Screening* (University of Chicago Press 2013) 7.

16 Ibid.

17 Karen Sermon *et al.*, 'Preimplantation Genetic Diagnosis' (2004) 363 The Lancet 1633. See also Peter Braude *et al.*, 'Preimplantation genetic diagnosis' (2002) 3 Nature Reviews 941.

18 Erik Parens and Adrienne Asch, 'Disability Rights Critique of Prenatal Genetic Testing: Reflections and Recommendations' (2003) 9 Mental Retardation and Developmental Disabilities Research Reviews 40.

19 Denise K. Casey, 'What Can the New Gene Tests Tell Us?' (1997) 36 The Judges Journal 14.

20 Cynthia T. Garcia Coll *et al.*, *Nature and Nurture: The Complex Interplay of Genetic and Environmental Influences on Human Behaviour and Development* (Lawrence Erlbaum 2004); Mary Jeanne Kreek *et al.*, 'Genetic Influences on Impulsivity, Risk-taking, Stress, Responsibility and Vulnerability to Drug Abuse and Addiction' (2005) 8 Nature Neuroscience 11 1450.

of potential misuses, misunderstandings and pitfalls so that the promise of the genetic revolution in progress can be realised without undue costs and risks.[21] The genetic revolution taking place has generated a myriad of ethical and legal concerns, particularly regarding the misuse of genetic information and genetic testing.

A disability perspective

Connecting genetics and disability

In view of the fact that genetic testing offers the possibility of detecting the onset and the potential severity of future disability and disease, genetic technologies provide a new lens through which to view disability. The predictive power of these technologies draws attention to the concepts of future disability, perceived disability, and imputed or putative disability. It is also observed that perceptions of genetic testing and genetic test results may impact upon individuals' and third parties' view of disability and what it means to have a disability, as well as what it means to have a genetic predisposition to disability.

It is well established that the extent to which genetic technologies predict the onset of disease or disability is generally dependent upon a myriad of factors including environmental factors, as well as *'variances in gene expression, accuracy of the test, and the stability of linkage between genetic markers and suspect genes'.*[22] The technology, although advancing quickly, is still at a relatively early stage. It is also established that, to a certain extent, gene expression depends on whether a condition is a monogenic or a multifactorial disease.[23] Certain hereditary diseases can be explained by a single gene, or monogenic defect. However, the majority of hereditary diseases are multifactorial and are caused by the interaction of environmental factors and numerous abnormal genes.[24] Although there is still uncertainty in relation to the degree of probability with which a genetic test predicts the onset of disease or disability, some commentators have pointed out that *'despite these known uncertainties and imprecisions, our aversion to disability is so great that people who receive a positive result for a disabling genetic condition may be stigmatized'.*[25] Accordingly, such uncertainty and limited accuracy of genetic testing may impact upon and potentially skew perceptions of disability. It may also exacerbate existing stigmas surrounding disability, and perpetuate further stigma and negative attitudes.

On examining the connection between disability and genetics, it has further been suggested by some commentators that with rapid advances in genetic technology and the mapping of the human genome, these developments are changing the way we perceive who is *'normal'* and who is *'disabled'.*[26] Miller posed the question, *'if everyone has genetic conditions that are just waiting to express*

---

21 Rebecca Wolf *et al.*, 'Genes, Identity and Clinical Ethics Under Conditions of Uncertainty' in Gerard Quinn, Aisling de Paor and Peter Blanck (eds) *Genetic Discrimination – Transatlantic Perspectives on the Case for a European Level Legal Response* (Routledge 2014) 52.

22 James P. Evans *et al.*, 'The Complexities of Predictive Genetic Testing' (2001) 322 British Medical Journal 1052.

23 Neil Holtzman *et al.*, 'Predictive Genetic Testing: From Basic Research to Clinical Practice' (1997) 278 Science 602, 604.

24 Ibid.

25 Ani Satz and Anita Silvers, 'Disability and Biotechnology' in Thomas Murray and Maxwell Mehlman (eds) *Encyclopedia of Biotechnology: Ethical, Legal and Policy Issues* (Published online 15 October 2000) 173.

26 Paul Steven Miller, 'Genetic Testing and the Future of Disability Insurance: Thinking about Discrimination in the Genetic Age' (2007) 35 Journal of Law, Medicine and Ethics 47, 50.

themselves in the future, isn't everyone truly disabled'.[27] Considering that nobody has perfect genes, he further observed that '*as we will all have knowledge of the potential genetic disorder that we each harbor, disabled people may no longer remain stigmatized as "the other" in society'.*[28] It is pointed out that not only does this impact upon theories of disability, but it also can have a profound effect on the notion of personhood and core concepts of humanity.[29] Societal stigmas may shift and the notion of disability is likely to further transform and develop to encompass a larger portion of the population including those with genetic predisposition to disease or disability. The existence of an ageing population may further expand the proportion of individuals with genetic predispositions to a range of diseases and disabilities. In light of these additional theoretical considerations, and the impact of genetic technologies on the concept of disability, the next section will further explore the concerns arising as genetic science and technology advance.

Exploring genetic discrimination

This chapter aims to highlight a new layer of discrimination which is becoming apparent, as science and technology continue to advance. Discrimination may be described as '*the denial of equal treatment or the rejection of the equal worth of a person due to one or more characteristics he or she possesses or is thought to possess'.*[30] The concept therefore involves differentiating between individuals on the grounds of certain characteristics, such as age, race, disability or sex and using those distinctions as the basis for such differential treatment. Discrimination usually encompasses both direct and indirect discrimination.[31] The underlying concept of direct discrimination provides that individuals who are similarly or comparably situated should be treated as such and should not be treated less favourably or less fairly on the grounds of particular traits, characteristics or other grounds, such as disability or genetic information. Indirect discrimination occurs where a particular requirement, practice, provision or treatment, which appears to be neutrally applied, has a particular disadvantage or a disproportionately adverse effect on a particular group or population (e.g. race or ethnic group), and such requirement, practice, provision or treatment cannot be justified.[32]

The increasing use of genetic testing and the rise in the availability of genetic information have '*unveiled a new dimension or layer of human difference, that of genetic makeup'*,[33] which offers a new manner in which to differentiate between individuals. It effectively creates the potential for a new level of discrimination to arise, in which all individuals are potential victims, as everyone carries genes that predispose to a variety of common and more complex illnesses. Accordingly, all individuals potentially have putative disabilities, and are therefore susceptible to discrimination.[34]

---

27 Ibid.

28 Ibid.

29 Hugh Miller, 'DNA Blueprints, Personhood and Genetic Privacy' (1998) 8 Health Matrix 179, 187.

30 Aart Hendriks, 'The UN Disability Convention and (Multiple) Discrimination: Should EU Non-Discrimination Law be Modelled Accordingly?' in Gerard Quinn and Lisa Waddington (eds) 2 *European Yearbook of Disability Law* (Intersentia 2010) 10.

31 Aisling de Paor, 'Regulating Genetic Information – Exploring the Options in Legal Theory' (2014) 21 European Journal of Health Law 425, 435–436.

32 Ibid.

33 Anne Mainsbridge, 'Employers and Genetic Information: A New Frontier in Discrimination' (2002) 2 Macquarie Law Journal 61, 67.

34 See comments by Dr Francis Collins, Former Director, National Human Genome Research Institute, Regarding the Passage of Genetic Information Nondiscrimination Act of 2005 (S. 306) (17 February 2005), http://www.genome.gov/13014311 (accessed 16 February 2015).

The particular term of genetic discrimination has been explored extensively in literature. Genetic discrimination can refer to the differential treatment of individuals or their family on the basis of an apparent, or assumed variation from '*normal*' human genes.[35] It may be explained as a form of differentiation based on genetic features or based on genetic information. It has also been described as '*discrimination against an individual or against members of that individual's family solely because of real or perceived differences from the "normal" genome in the genetic constitution of that individual*'.[36] Rothstein describes such discrimination as the differential treatment based on genetic status.[37] The common theme identified is differential or discriminatory treatment on the basis of genetic information. Such discrimination indicates that the individual is treated in a more disadvantageous way than another comparable individual, '*solely or primarily because of his or her genotype or because of a specific genetic defect, without there being a sufficient and reasonable justification for such disadvantageous treatment*'.[38] Genetic discrimination has the potential of creating '*a new group of disadvantaged people*'.[39]

In further clarifying the concept of genetic discrimination, it is noted that it generally describes discrimination against asymptomatic individuals, in other words, those who have not yet expressed symptoms of disease or disability. Natowicz et al. '*distinguish genetic discrimination from discrimination based on disabilities caused by altered genes*', and thereby clarify that genetic discrimination is based on information inferred from an individual's genotype, as opposed to on the basis the current symptoms of an individual.[40] Yesley makes a similar point and notes that '*the quintessential feature of genetic discrimination is the use of genetic information about an asymptomatic person*'. If a genetic condition expresses itself, it can be categorised as a different type of discrimination, namely discrimination on the basis of current disability or health.[41]

It is relevant to note that genetic information can be obtained, not only from genetic test results, but also from other sources, such as through examination of one's family history. For example, one may discover genetic information through insights obtained from their own medical history, as well as details of family medical history.[42] Family medical history has traditionally been a reliable source of genetic information and individuals can obtain considerable knowledge from analysis of the medical history of one's blood relatives. Therefore, when discussing the use of genetic information, it is necessary to refer to both the results of genetic tests as well as information gained from family medical history, both of which can potentially be used as a means to

35 Aisling de Paor, 'The Regulation of Genetic Information in Ireland – Does It Strike an Appropriate Balance of Rights?' (2013) 19 Medico- Legal Journal of Ireland 97, 98.

36 Marvin R. Natowicz *et al.*, 'Genetic Discrimination and the Law' (1992) 50 American Journal of Human Genetics 465, 466. A similar definition has been given by Paul R. Billings *et al*, 'Discrimination as a Consequence of Genetic Testing' (1992) 50 American Journal of Human Genetics 476, 476.

37 Mark A. Rothstein, 'Genetic Discrimination in Employment: Ethics, Policy and Comparative Law' in Swiss Institute of Comparative Law (ed) *Human Genetic Analysis and the Protection of Personality and Privacy* (Schulthess Polygraphisher Verlag 1994) 129.

38 Janneke Gerards, 'General Issues Concerning Genetic Information' in Janneke H. Gerards, Aalt W. Heringa and Heleen L. Janssen (eds) *Genetic Discrimination and Genetic Privacy in a Comparative Perspective* (Intersentia 2005) 24.

39 Marvin R. Natowicz *et al*, 'Genetic Discrimination and the Law' (1992) 50 American Journal of Human Genetics 465, 465.

40 Ibid.

41 Michael S. Yesley, 'Protecting Genetic Difference' (1999) 13 Berkeley Technology Law Review 653, 662.

42 Paul Steven Miller, 'Is there a Pink Slip in my Genes? Genetic Discrimination in the Workplace' (2000) 3 Journal of Health Care Law and Policy 2 225, 231.

discriminate.[43] Similarly, the discriminatory use of genetic information identified from family history (and from other potential sources, such as an obituary in a newspaper, or social media) comes within the scope of the concept of genetic discrimination.

From a disability perspective, genetic testing and insights from family medical history can potentially predict a propensity to or probability of future disability. Genetic discrimination can therefore be described as discrimination on the basis of potential future disability, or on the basis of genetic predisposition to disability.[44] Similarly, genetic discrimination can indicate negative attitudes towards disability and genetic conditions, and the concept may also encompass assumed, perceived or imputed disability. On the basis of a family history of illness or following a positive genetic test result, it might be assumed either that a person has that illness or disability, or will develop a particular genetic condition. Accordingly, if genetic information is too freely accessible, it potentially exposes putative persons with disabilities to obvious discrimination, as well as more subtle and indirect discrimination.

Therefore, in accordance with established theories of non-discrimination, discrimination on the grounds of one's genetic information or genetic features may be either direct or indirect.[45] Direct discrimination may arise in circumstances where, for example, an employer refuses to hire an individual on the basis that the individual tested positive for the breast cancer gene, even though the individual is otherwise a suitable candidate for the job. Such discrimination may also arise, for example, where an employer refuses to hire (or otherwise discriminates against) an individual who has a family history of breast cancer, heart disease, diabetes or any other (genetically based) condition. Indirect discrimination may arise where, for example, an apparently neutral employment practice, such as a health and safety screening process that applies to all individuals, but may have the effect of highlighting (and potentially eliminating, or otherwise adversely effecting) those with a particular genetic predisposition or ethnic background.[46]

Individual and societal implications of genetic discrimination

Genetic discrimination and the misuse of genetic information raises a number of challenging issues from an individual's perspective and also from a wider societal perspective.

Discrimination which centres around actual or perceived genetic characteristics denies an individual equal opportunity on the basis of a genetic profile which he/she has no control over. Discrimination based on genetic information is arguably as unjust as that on the basis of similar immutable characteristics such as gender or race. It is noted that *the right to be treated equally and according to one's abilities in all the diverse aspects of human endeavour is a core social value*.[47] Genetic

---

43 Margaret Otlowski, Mark Stranger, Sandra Taylor, Kristine Barlow-Stewart, and Susan Treloar 'Practices and Attitudes of Australian Employers in relation to the use of genetic information: Report on a National Study' (2009–2010) 31 Comparative Labor Law and Policy Journal 637, 638.

44 See generally, Paul S. Miller, 'Genetic Testing and the Future of Disability Insurance: Thinking about Discrimination in the Genetic Age' (2007) Journal of Law, Medicine and Ethics 47. See also Gregor Wolbring, 'A Disability Rights Approach to Genetic Discrimination' in Judit Sandor (ed) *Society and Genetic Information: Codes and Laws in the Genetic Era* (Central European University Press 2004) 161.

45 Aisling de Paor, 'Regulating Genetic Information – Exploring the Options in Legal Theory' (2014) 21 European Journal of Health Law 425, 437.

46 Ibid.

47 Lawrence O. Gostin, 'Genetic Discrimination: The Use of Genetically Based Diagnostic and Prognostic Tests by Employers and Insurers' (1991) 17 American Journal of Law and Medicine 109, 112.

discrimination, as described in the previous section, therefore violates basic tenets of justice, as well as core societal values and is potentially harmful to fundamental human rights.

On highlighting the implications of genetic discrimination from an individual's perspective, this chapter draws particular attention to the context of employment and the use of genetic information by employers.[48] It is observed that employers may be interested in accessing and using an employee's genetic information, primarily for financial reasons and as a tool for selecting what are perceived to be the most desirable, genetically attractive employees. Employers arguably have no right to request or require that an individual undergo genetic testing (or use the results of genetic tests previously taken) when that individual shows no indication of a disease or disability that would impact upon the current ability to do a job. Making an employment decision on the basis of the probability of an individual developing a certain disease or disability, as opposed to on the actual ability to perform the work, may be deemed to be unlawful discrimination. In the European Union, there is strong legislation promoting equality in the workplace,[49] as there is in the United States.[50]

Individuals who are refused employment, or otherwise discriminated against on the basis of genetic information may be left without a job. This may negatively impact upon a person's general well-being, health and sense of purpose in society. Unauthorised access to and use of genetic information may also violate an individual's privacy.[51] This concern is particularly heightened given the uniquely personal and private nature of genetic information. In addition, access to fruitful employment may well act as a gateway to and may affect access to other social and economic goods and services (including health care and insurance). It may impact upon fulfilling civic engagement, including access to political life and active involvement in the community. Access to employment may also potentially affect an individual's social life, friendships and interaction with peers, which has a significant impact on inclusion and active participation in society. Therefore, from a fundamental perspective, the existence of barriers to employment by way of misusing genetic information may have a significant impact on an individual's private and professional life, as well as overall social inclusion.[52]

By excluding otherwise suitable individuals from employment, society is drained of skills and innovation. This exclusion *'promotes physical and economic dependency, draining rather than enriching social institutions'*.[53] Consequently, misuse of genetic technology can create employment barriers by effectively classifying individuals by potential future health risk. Society may lose out on the contribution of these individuals, who are in a position to make a positive and productive addition to the community, and who may be denied this opportunity, notwithstanding their current ability. This may result in the further exclusion and isolation of vulnerable persons, such as persons with putative disabilities and the elderly.

---

48 Although the example of the employment is highlighted in this chapter, it is acknowledged that misuse of genetic information can take place in a range of third-party and social contexts, including insurance, commercial lending, education, adoption and sport.

49 Council Directive 2000/78/EC of 27 November 2000 establishing a general framework for equal treatment in employment and occupation [2000] OJ L 303/16.

50 Title VII of the Civil Rights Act of 1964 Pub. L. No. 88-352 (1964); Americans with Disabilities Act of 1990, Pub. L. No. 101-336 (1991).

51 Graeme Laurie, *Genetic Privacy: A Challenge to Medico-Legal Norms* (Cambridge University Press 2002).

52 For discussion of the concept of "social inclusion", see Lisa Schur, Douglas Kruse and Peter Blanck, *People with Disabilities – Sidelined or Mainstreamed?* (Cambridge University Press 2013) 117.

53 Lawrence O. Gostin, 'Genetic Discrimination: The Use of Genetically Based Diagnostic and Prognostic Tests by Employers and Insurers' (1991) 17 American Journal of Law and Medicine 109, 112–113.

Ultimately, from a wider societal and public policy perspective, there is also the risk of the creation of a genetic underclass and the relegation of individuals deemed to be genetically undesirable in society.[54] Society may eventually view individuals according to their genes, differentiating according to what are deemed to be good genes and bad genes, leading to discrimination and segregation. We could potentially encounter a 'genetically cleansed' society and economy whereby only those who are considered low- risk are admitted to the mainstream. This potential towards a 'genetically cleansed' society may particularly target persons with disabilities and persons with putative disabilities. Fresh eugenic concerns arise in this context, and we can look to the past history of eugenics as an indicator of such potential abuse in the future.

Genetics and the history of eugenics

On exploring the connection between genetics and disability, and with a view to highlighting the real propensity for abuse in this new genetic era, it is relevant to consider the concept of eugenics and the eugenics movement which swept the early twentieth century. The history of the eugenics movement provides a framework for discussion of these challenging ethical dilemmas which are becoming increasingly apparent as genetic science and technology continue to advance today. An examination of the abuses of the past also offers insights into potential future misuse of science and technology, and warns against the creation of a genetic underclass in today's society.

Eugenics has been described as the 'conscious selection of humans by encouraging the production of those with desired inherited characteristics and for restricting those with undesirable inheritable characteristics'.[55] It can also be defined as 'the use of science applied to the qualitative and quantitative improvement of the human genome'.[56] The concept was pioneered by Francis Galton, with reinvigoration of the theory from Charles Darwin in the nineteenth century.[57] Since the nineteenth century, there has been an acknowledgement of the potential of using science and principles of inheritance to shape eugenic policies, with the result of creating a genetically cleansed society.[58]

Eugenics presents an extreme case of how genetic knowledge and a misinterpretation of genetic science can correspond with repressive public policy to deprive individuals of fundamental rights, particularly individuals with disabilities. Indeed, history is a reminder of the negative impact of eugenics. The eugenics movements of the early twentieth century, such as those in Europe and the United States (US) provide an insight into the potential misuse of science, and offer a framework for consideration of modern day eugenics and misuse of genetics. It has been observed that '*by remembering and understanding the past injustices and inhumanity of negative eugenics, further misuse of scientific information can be avoided*'.[59] In both Europe and the US, the aim of the

---

54 David A. Kirby, 'Extrapolating Race in GATTACA: Genetic Passing, Identity, and the Science of Race' (2004) 23 Literature and Medicine 1, 184–185.

55 Willi Rothley and Carlo Casini, 'Ethical and Legal Problems of Genetic Engineering and Human Artificial Insemination', (EU Committee on Legal Affairs and Citizen's Rights, 1990).

56 David J. Galton and Claire J. Galton, 'Francis Galton: And Eugenics Today' (1998) 24 Journal of Medical Ethics 99, 99.

57 Ibid. See also Francis Galton, *Inquiries Into Human Faculty and Its Development* (Dent and Sons 1907).

58 Peter Blanck and Aisling de Paor, 'US legislative and policy response: Some historical context to GINA' in Gerard Quinn, Aisling de Paor and Peter Blanck (eds) *Genetic Discrimination – Transatlantic Perspectives on the Case for a European Level Legal Response* (Routledge 2014) 98–99.

59 Kenneth L. Garver and Bettylee Garver, 'The Human Genome project and Eugenic Concerns' (1994) 54 American Journal of Human Genetics 148.

eugenics movement was to promote and advance genetic superiority, and it endeavoured to achieve this primarily by sterilising persons with disabilities and those deemed genetically undesirable.[60] In particular, the German T4 Euthanasia regime, which was initiated in 1939 had the objective of eliminating those with physical or mental disabilities, and other vulnerable members of society.[61]

Similarly, in the US, the history of eugenics is also very much apparent and has prompted a sense of fear in respect of science and genetics.[62] Eugenic policies in the US were experienced in many facets of society, including the areas of immigration and family life. In the 1920s, state fairs sponsored 'Fitter Families' contests which awarded prizes for 'Grade A individuals' in the 'human stock' category.[63] At this time many US states also introduced sterilisation laws targeting what were perceived to be genetically defective groups, following early developments in genetic science. The policy argument promoting such sterilisation was that those individuals were costly for society.[64] Indeed, thirty-two American states introduced compulsory eugenic sterilisation laws from 1907 to 1937, primarily with the objective of controlling the reproductive capacities of these genetically undesirable individuals.[65] The US Supreme Court promoted sterilisation in support of eugenics in its landmark decision of *Buck v. Bell*, with Justice Oliver Wendell Holmes infamously stating '*three generations of imbeciles is enough*'.[66]

Highlighting the reprehensible history of eugenics sheds light on potential future misuse of genetic science, and further mistreatment of persons with disabilities and perceived disabilities. With genetic science rapidly advancing and the benefits of science being realised, eugenics considerations are once again rising to the surface. New genetic technologies offer new means of differentiating and potentially discriminating against persons with disabilities. With this age of 'new genetics', the ethical, legal and social implications of genetic technologies have become more intricate, however, the controversies and societal risks it raises are effectively the same.[67] These new genetic technologies have the potential to idealise the perfect person, designer babies and a population founded upon genetic desirability.[68] It also has the potential of devaluing the lives of persons with disabilities and persons with future or putative disabilities. This potential

60 Iulia V. Motoc, 'The International Law of Genetic Discrimination: The Power of Never Again' in Therese Murphy (ed) *New Technologies and Human Rights* (Oxford University Press 2009).

61 M. Michael Cohen, 'Overview of German, Nazi and Holocaust Medicine' (2010) 152A American Journal of Medical Genetics 3 687. See also Rael D. Strous, 'Hitler's Psychiatrists: Healers and Researchers Turned Executioners and Its Relevance Today' (2006) 14 Harvard Review of Psychiatry 1 30.

62 Peter Blanck and Aisling de Paor, 'US legislative and policy response: Some historical context to GINA' in Gerard Quinn, Aisling de Paor and Peter Blanck (eds) *Genetic Discrimination – Transatlantic Perspectives on the Case for a European Level Legal Response* (Routledge 2014).

63 Daniel J. Kevles, *In the Name of Eugenics: Genetics and the Uses of Human Heredity* (Harvard University Press 1985) 62.

64 Lori B. Andrews, 'Past as Prologue: Sobering Thoughts on Genetic Enthusiasm' (1997) 27 Seton Hall Law Review 893, 894.

65 Edward J. Larson, 'Confronting Scientific Authority with Religious Values: Eugenics in American History' in Timothy J. Demy and Gary P. Stewards (eds) *Genetic Engineering: A Christian Response – Crucial Considerations in Shaping Life* 105, 106 (Kregal Publications 1999). See also Morse Hyun-Myung Tan, 'Advancing Civil Rights, the Next Generation: The Genetic Information Non Discrimination Act of 2008 and Beyond' (2009) 19 Health Matrix 63.

66 *Buck v. Bell* 274 U.S. 200 (1927).

67 See generally Troy Duster, *Backdoor to Eugenics* (2nd ed, Routledge, Chapman and Hall 2003).

68 Glenn E. McGee, *The Perfect Baby: A Pragmatic Approach to Genetics* (Rowman and Littlefield Publishers 1997) 111.

genetic underclass raises serious ethical and public policy concerns.[69] The advent of this new age of genetics and a new form of subtle eugenics gives rise to serious public policy concerns, and signals a need to anticipate the creation of a genetic underclass in society and respond to these issues.[70] Accordingly, questions arise as to how to address and control the use and potential misuse of genetic information, and it is recognised that appropriate regulation of this area is key.

Genetic discrimination and the social model of disability

On consideration of the speed at which genetic science is advancing, as well as the fundamental human rights at stake, particularly for persons with disabilities and persons with putative disabilities, the need arises to control the use and potential misuse of genetic information. On exploring the question of regulation in this area, from a disability perspective, it is submitted that the social model of disability provides an appropriate theoretical framework from which to approach these concerns.

This section will address the social model of disability, which was developed as a reaction to the undesirable connotations of and implications of the medical model of disability, as well as in response to the growing awareness of persons with disabilities as rights holders in society. This chapter proposes that in addressing the issue of discrimination in this field, which is becoming increasingly apparent as science and technology advance, the social model of disability is the most appropriate model to consider, in terms of recognising the rights of persons with disabilities and persons with putative disabilities.

Pursuant to the medical model, disability is seen as a problem inherent in the person, caused by biological defect, disease or other health condition.[71] It is generally viewed as giving rise to the perception of the individual being below normal and having a low quality of life.[72] Conversely, the social model of disability views disability primarily as a socially devised problem and with the aim of achieving the full integration of individuals with different abilities into society. The social model of disability was first pioneered in the late 1960s and 1970s. The theory was advanced in the publications of Vic Finkelstein and Michael Oliver in the 1980s, and Colin Barnes in the 1990s,[73] introducing a paradigm shift in thinking towards disability from a human rights perspective. The key message advocated by the social model is that persons with disabilities are not disabled by inherent defects or other internal sources, but through a variety of different barriers in the social environment.[74] It is therefore acknowledged that there are different barriers that can be created to disable an individual. Physical barriers can be created in the built environment, for example, an inaccessible public building or an inaccessible workplace.

69 Colin S. Diver and Jane Maslow Cohen, 'Genophobia: What is Wrong with Genetic Discrimination?' (2000–2001) 149 University of Pennsylvania Law Review 1440, 1447.
70 Aisling de Paor, 'US and EU Perspectives on Genetic Discrimination in Employment and Insurance: Striking a Balance in a Battlefield of Competing Rights' in Gerard Quinn, Lisa Waddington and Eilionóir Flynn (eds) 4 *European Yearbook of Disability Law* (Intersentia 2013) 99, 119.
71 Lisa Shur, Douglas Kruse and Peter Blanck, *People with Disabilities – Sidelined or Mainstreamed?* (Cambridge University Press 2013) 9.
72 For further discussion, see Mark Priestley, 'Constructions and Creations: Idealism, Materialism and Disability Theory' (1998) 13 Disability and Society 75.
73 Michael Oliver, *Understanding Disability: From Theory to Practice* (Macmillan Press Ltd 1996); Vic Finkelstein, '"We" are not disabled, "you" are' in Susan Gregory and Gillian Hartley (eds) *Constructing Deafness* (Continuum 1990). Colin Barnes, 'The Social Model of Disability: A Sociological Phenomenon Ignored by Sociologists?' in Tom Shakespeare (ed) *Disability Reader: Social Science Perspectives* (Continuum 1998).
74 Bill Hughes and Kevin Paterson, 'The Social Model of Disability and the Disappearing Body: Towards a Sociology of Impairment' (1997) 12 Disability and Society 3 325, 328.

From a social model of disability perspective, it is further observed that negative third-party or societal attitudes can also operate to disable a person. For example, third parties such as employers may not acknowledge the abilities of disabled people but instead see only the barriers that they encounter on account of the disability. By focusing on the disability rather than an individual's ability to perform the job, employers may be of the view that persons with disabilities are unsuitable for the position. This is clearly unfair – barriers can often be removed through the provision of accommodations or adjustments to work practices and/or the work environment, in line with the ethos of the social model of disability. Central to the social model of disability is therefore the concept of reasonable accommodation, as a tool to secure and advance the rights of persons with disabilities.[75]

This concept therefore adopts a theory that rejects the outdated medical view of disability to seeing disability as a consequence of societal barriers.[76] The built environment (and indeed social structures including attitudes) is generally designed and built for non-disabled individuals, thereby excluding persons with disabilities from actively participating and integrating in society.[77]

The social model of disability provokes a connection with a rights-based approach. In considering a rights-based approach, the social model views persons with disabilities as valued members of our societies, with rights, who are disabled by the physical and attitudinal barriers within societies that individuals create to exclude and stigmatise them. It has been noted that the social model theory has changed the status of persons with disabilities from passive '*objects of rehabilitation and cure*'[78] to '*rights holders entitled to make demands on social institutions*'.[79] An emphasis on rights '*changes the social status and social understanding of persons with disabilities from powerless recipients of their peers' charity to right-holders capable of making demands on the world*'.[80]

Viewing disability as a human rights issue requires us to recognise the inherent equality of all individuals, regardless of their abilities or disabilities, and obliges society to remove the attitudinal and physical barriers to achieve equality and inclusion of individuals with disabilities.[81]

Stigma and attitudes towards disability and genetic predispositions

On acknowledging the rationale of the social model, it is submitted that there is merit to applying this model to address the use of genetic information and genetic discrimination. It is important to highlight the impact of negative attitudes towards persons with disabilities. As noted, such attitudes can result in stigma and ultimately lead to social exclusion and isolation.[82]

---

75 For further discussion, see Anna Lawson, *Disability and Equality Law in Britain: The Role of Reasaonable Adjustment* (Hart Publishing 2008).

76 Michael Oliver, *Understanding Disability: From Theory to Practice* (Macmillan Press Ltd 1996).

77 Bill Hughes and Kevin Paterson, 'The Social Model of Disability and the Disappearing Body: Towards a sociology of impairment' (1997) 12 Disability and Society 3 325, 328.

78 Chai R. Feldblum, 'Definition of Disability Under Federal Anti-Discrimination Law: What Happened? Why? And What Can We Do About It? (2000) 21 Berkeley Journal of Employment and Labor Law 91, 94.

79 Vlad Perju, 'Impairment, Discrimination, and the Legal Construction of Disability in the European Union and the United States' (2011) 44 Cornell International Law Journal 279, 284.

80 Richard K. Scotch, 'Models of Disability and the Americans with Disabilities Act' (2000) 21 Berkeley Journal of Employment and Labor Law 213, 216 (quoting Paul C. Higgins, *Making Disability: Exploring the Social Transformation of Human Values* (Charles C Thomas Pub Ltd 1992) 199–200.

81 Michael L. Perlin, '"A Change is Gonna Come": The Implications of the United Nations Convention on the Rights of Persons with Disabilities for the Domestic Practice of Constitutional Mental Disability Law' (2009) 29 Northern Illinois University Law Review 483, 483–484.

82 Lisa Shur, Douglas Kruse and Peter Blanck, *People with Disabilities – Sidelined or Mainstreamed?* (Cambridge University Press 2013) 118.

Pursuant to the medical model of disability, persons with disabilities are defined by their disability and disempowered by the perception that they are ill and in need of a cure. Attitudinal barriers therefore often exacerbate the ethos of the medical model of disability and are contrary to the core rationale of the social model. Society has generally found it challenging to address difference and diversity.[83] This is particularly apparent as regards persons with disabilities and those perceived to be disabled.[84] People with disabilities have historically been segregated, isolated and abused, as society has struggled with dealing with those who are perceived to be inferior individuals. This inevitably leads to a breach of fundamental human rights and a disregard for core societal values. The societal struggle with difference has left persons with disabilities outside the *'paradigm of humanity'*.[85] Wendell argues that the non-disabled portion of society segregate persons with disabilities because *'they represent a threat to the security of their own perceptions of self which are embedded in a culture of perfection and control'*.[86]

It is submitted that this new genetic era has the potential to exacerbate these negative societal attitudes towards persons with disabilities, particularly persons with putative disabilities and those who are perceived to have disabilities or indeed genetic predispositions to disability. In addressing the issue of stigma attached to disability in this context, Bickenbach warns that genetic information has the potential to become *'the most profound form of stigmatising labeling people with disability have as yet experienced.'*[87] He postulates that *'human difference, when labeled genetically, opens the door to the most profound forms of stigmatisation'*.[88] Such stigmatisation may further translate into discrimination against individuals on the basis of genetic information, as well as other adverse treatment and even breach of privacy.

As discussed in an earlier section, the increasing availability of genetic technologies and use of genetic information therefore present new and novel tools to discriminate in areas such as employment (as well as insurance and a variety of commercial and social settings). Such technologies may ultimately isolate and further segregate persons with disabilities.

Attitudes towards disability provoke consideration of notions such as imputed disability and perceived disability, as discussed earlier. In this regard, a disability might be imputed to a person, regardless of the current abilities of the person. In the context of discussing genetic discrimination (and other misuse of genetic information), a third party, for example, an employer, may take the view that an individual with a genetic predisposition to a certain condition has a disability, and may therefore perceive the individual as unable or unsuitable to do a particular job. Third parties may therefore impute a disability to an individual or regard an individual as having a disability, on the grounds that an individual merely carries the gene for a particular condition or has a particular family medical history. Consequently, genetic advances operate to shape perceptions and attitudes towards disability in society. The ethos of the social model endorses positive attitudes to disability, and proscribes such negative attitudinal barriers, which operate as barriers to the full integration of persons with disabilities.

The social model of disability arguably provides the most appropriate framework from which to approach the issues arising at the intersection of genetics and disability. This model

---

83 Susan Wendell, 'Toward a Feminist Theory of Disability' in Helen Bequaert Holmes and Laura M. Purdy (eds) *Feminist Perspectives in Medical Ethics* (Indiana University Press 1992) 63, 74.
84 Ibid.
85 Ibid.
86 Ibid.
87 Jerome Bickenbach, 'The Perils of Human Genetics' (1996) 1 Ethics and Intellectual Disability 2, 2.
88 Ibid.

represents current best thinking on disability theory and applies a holistic approach in recognising and achieving the rights of persons with disabilities. Further, the social construction of disability under this model is broad enough to encompass individuals with putative disabilities or those with genetic predispositions to disability. It also focuses on the actions, intentions and attitudes of third parties, thereby taking the focus away from the individual. The emphasis on a rights-based theory, with non-discrimination as a focal point, as well as the promotion of positive attitudes towards disability and persons with disabilities reinforces the relevance of the social model in this debate.

From a regulatory perspective, this model provides a core rights-based lens, with the objective of acknowledging societal barriers, and recognising the equal rights of persons with disabilities and those with putative disabilities. In consideration of the significant potential for abuse of genetic information, it is observed that such a framework is best suited to address these challenging issues.

The United Nations Convention on the Rights of Persons with Disabilities

On addressing the connection between genetics and disability and the application of the social model of disability, international human rights law provides guidance on the challenging ethical and legal dilemmas arising in this field. This section will briefly highlight the relevance of the United Nations Convention on the Rights of Persons with Disabilities (CRPD)[89] in this context. As explained in earlier chapters of this book, the CRPD is the first international human rights treaty of the twenty-first century and its provisions been described as providing '*a moral compass for change*',[90] which aims to facilitate the fundamental human rights and equal treatment of persons with disabilities. The CRPD emphasises the social model of disability, thereby focusing outward toward the environment and other external factors as creating barriers and disabling a person.[91] Indeed the CRPD has been described as '*the highest legal manifestation and confirmation of the social model of disability on the international stage*'.[92] In the context of this debate, it has been observed that the CRPD '*provides a fresh human rights read on the interrelationship of genetic technology and disability rights as reflected in international human rights law*'.[93] It can certainly offer guidance on best practice and act as an international forum for discussion of these challenging issues.

Genetic discrimination or the discriminatory use of genetic information is arguably contrary to the CRPD. In particular, it is noted that the principles of non-discrimination and equality

---

89 United Nations Convention on the Rights of Persons with Disabilities (2006) G.A. Res 61/106 ("CRPD").
90 Gerard Quinn, 'The United Nations Convention on the Rights of Persons with Disabilities: Toward a New International Politics of Disability' (2009–2010) 15 Texas Journal on Civil Liberties and Civil Rights 1 33.
91 Lisa Waddington, 'Breaking New Ground: The Implications of Ratification of the UN Convention on the Rights of Persons with Disabilities for the European Community' in Oddný Mjöll Arnardóttir and Gerard Quinn (eds) *UN Convention on the Rights of Persons with Disabilities* (Martinus Nijhoff Publishers 2009) 115.
92 Ibid.
93 Janet Lord, 'Accommodating Genes: Disability, Discrimination and International Human Rights Law' in Gerard Quinn, Aisling de Paor and Peter Blanck (eds) *Genetic Discrimination – Transatlantic Perspectives on the Case for a European Level Legal Response* (Routledge 2014) 226.

feature strongly. Indeed, one of the main tools used in the CRPD is that of non-discrimination.[94] Through this framework, and in line with the social model of disability, the CRPD facilitates higher standards of non-discrimination and equality with respect to persons with disabilities. The CRPD is drafted broadly with the objective of promoting inclusion of all individuals with disabilities, including those with putative disabilities and genetic predisposition to disability.[95] In addition, the definition of disability discrimination and the objective of the substantive provisions of the CRPD can be interpreted as applying to the concept of genetic discrimination, thereby protecting genetic information.[96] The CRPD could well act as a catalyst to develop a wave of reform around the regulation of genetic information and initiate a deeper thinking around the concept of disability and disability discrimination, to encompass putative disability and genetic predisposition to disability.

Conclusion

Scientific and technological developments are propelling genetics and genetic technologies further into the public sphere. As groundbreaking scientific discoveries are being made in the genetics field, technological innovation is becoming more refined and is resulting in an increase in the use and availability of genetic testing, not only for medical objectives but also for economic or other non-medical purposes. It may also be used as a tool to identify future disabilities and these developments provoke consideration of the connection between genetics and disability as an emerging concern. Ultimately, advances in genetic science and technologies have the potential to expose a new category of individuals with putative disabilities in society.

On examination of the connection between genetics and disability, it is evident that the ethical and legal concerns arising with the advent of advances in genetics and technology may have a particularly adverse impact on persons with putative disabilities and persons with genetic predispositions to disabilities. In particular, an increasing prevalence of genetic technologies may lead to a new layer of discrimination against persons with disabilities, and therefore create novel ways of segregating and isolating these individuals.

On highlighting the fundamental human rights at stake, together with an awareness of the history of the eugenics movement, which acts as a stark reminder of the abuse of genetic science, this chapter proposes that the social model of disability provides the most suitable framework from which to view and address the challenging issues that arise at the intersection of advancing genetic science and disability. With a focus on the societal, attitudinal and other external barriers that disable an individual, it concentrates on acknowledging and achieving the rights of persons with disabilities. On considering questions of regulation, the social model of disability offers a rights-oriented lens from which to approach the emerging issues in this area. In line with the rationale of the social model, the CRPD provides an international framework for discussion in this area and may provoke consideration of best practice around disability law and policy in this field, as well as act as a potential impetus for any legislative intervention.

---

94 CRPD, Article 5.
95 European Foundation Centre, Study on challenges and good practices in the implementation of the UN Convention on the Rights of Persons with Disabilities VC/ 2008/ 1214 Final Report, p 54; Aisling de Paor, 'US and EU Perspectives on Genetic Discrimination in Employment and Insurance: Striking a Balance in a Battlefield of Competing Rights' in Gerard Quinn, Lisa Waddington and Eilionóir Flynn (eds) 4 *European Yearbook of Disability Law* (Intersentia 2013) 99, 141.
96 Ibid.

This chapter recognises the potential for new types of insidious discrimination to permeate society as genetic science and technological innovation become more widespread, refined and accessible. In order to ensure appropriate protections for persons with disabilities against discrimination on the grounds of genetic information, as well as to ensure that science and technology continue to flourish without the threat of misuse, safeguards and regulation are necessary. In the absence of appropriate controls, it is anticipated that more and more individuals with putative disabilities will be excluded from a range of social goods and services, potentially leading to a genetically cleansed society and a subtle reinvigoration of eugenic-based policies.

14

INCLUSIVE DEVELOPMENT AID

Mary Keogh

Introduction

In September 2015, world governments agreed on a new global framework for development. The proposed Sustainable Development Goals (SDGs) will shape how development cooperation policy and programmes are delivered for the coming years. So far the SDGs appear, at least on paper, to respond to some of the criticisms of their predecessor – the Millennium Development Goals (MDGs), particularly with respect to the lack of inclusion of persons with disabilities.[1] When the MDGs were developed over 10 years ago, disability, while established by the UN and some donor agencies as an issue for development cooperation to consider, remained on the periphery of international development. Since then, a number of factors such as the adoption of the Convention on the Rights of Persons with Disabilities (CRPD), a strong international disability movement and a number of committed donor governments, have resulted in persons with disabilities now being considered central to poverty reduction and to achieving effective development aid. For example donor governments such as Australia now recognize that the inclusion of persons with disabilities in their development cooperation is important for aid effectiveness.[2]

The challenge for the international community and the implementation of the new SDG goals is to ensure that women, men, girls and boys with disabilities benefit from and are included in development cooperation on an equal basis with others. This is clearly the intention behind Article 32 of the CRPD, which has at its core the principles of accessibility and inclusion of persons with disabilities in international development programmes.[3] However, the legal basis for inclusion and accessibility can only go so far.[4] Donor governments are limited

---

1 United Nations (2011) 'Disability and the Millennium Development Goals; A Review of the MDG Process and Strategies for Inclusion of Disability Issues in Millennium Development Goal Efforts'.
2 AusAID (2012) 'An Effective Aid Program for Australia: Making a Real Difference – Delivering Real Results'.
3 CRPD (2006) 'Article 32'.
4 The implementation of the CRPD is the responsibility of the ratifying government, development cooperation can play a role in helping governments fulfill their responsibilities' under the CRPD but the main responsibility lies with the government.

in their actions of achieving change through their development cooperation efforts, not least because countries in receipt of aid have their own sovereign identity, that is they make their own laws and policies. However, donor governments and the different actors associated with development cooperation can play an instrumental role in advancing equality for persons with disabilities in developing countries by first developing effective analytical tools for identifying where blockages exist for persons with disabilities, and second by developing and implementing programmes that are successful in overcoming these blockages. This will create opportunities for all women, men, girls and boys with disabilities to participate in and benefit from development cooperation.

Aim of this chapter[5]

The overall aim of this chapter is to put forward the argument that to build on the success made in disability-inclusive development so far, it is important to look at how we currently conceptualize equality for persons with disabilities. The central proposal this chapter makes is that in order for development cooperation to be effective and inclusive of women, men, girls and boys with disabilities, it needs to move beyond attributing the totality of discrimination experienced by persons with disabilities to identity alone. However, it is important to point out at the outset that this chapter is not suggesting a replacement of the category of disability or a dismantlement of it as a thematic issue in development and human rights narratives. The campaigns over recent years for a disability-inclusive post-2015 development framework demonstrate that at present there is no natural reflex associating disability as a development issue. Therefore the need for its visibility as a thematic issue is required.[6] However, the issue that emerges from this requirement for visibility is how to ensure that it is done in such a way that it does not contribute to further siloing and specialization of disability, but instead recognizes the different identities that persons with disabilities may have and captures the incidences of discrimination encountered by persons with disabilities which can be caused by other grounds (such as membership of race, gender) and different contexts (social, economic, cultural and political).

To facilitate this discussion the chapter is divided into a number of sections. The first section highlights how disability is not a new topic in development; intergovernmental agencies such as the United Nations and various governments have actively pursued the inclusion of persons with disabilities in developing countries over the past decades (e.g. the World Programme of Action on Disability and the UN Standard Rules on the Equalization of Persons with Disabilities).[7] The CRPD adopted in 2006 placed this pursuit of equal opportunities into a rights-based framework, increasing the momentum for government's development cooperation efforts to be inclusive of persons with disabilities.

The second section highlights the current legal protections that women, men, girls and boys with disabilities have under international law; it also highlights the multifaceted discrimination they face. The third section discusses what equality for persons with disabilities actually means in a development context. It outlines the different models of equality and asks the question – is our current approach of fixing disability within a single category limited? The fourth section

5 This chapter uses gender-differentiated language e.g. women, men, girls and boys with disabilities and non-gender differentiated language interchangeably.
6 United Nations (2011) 'Disability and the Millennium Development Goals; A Review of the MDG Process and Strategies for Inclusion of Disability Issues in Millennium Development Goal Efforts'.
7 United Nations General Assembly (1993) 'Standard Rules on the Equalization of Opportunities for Persons with Disabilities', A/RES/48/96.

introduces intersectionality and its potential to move beyond fixed categories. It explores how intersectionality can contribute to a deeper analysis in identifying the barriers persons with disabilities face in participating on an equal basis with others. The fifth section discusses the number of ways intersectionality can help disability inclusive development. The sixth section offers some concluding remarks as to how actors in development can utilize the SDGs as a means to ensure that persons with disabilities are considered part of the whole development process rather than being limited to the tradition areas such as education, health and welfare.

The emergence of disability as an issue for development actors

As in stated in the introduction, governments are making progress in recognizing that persons with disabilities must be able to access benefits from development cooperation on an equal basis with others. This is happening at the national government level, regional level and also international level. First, at the national level, prior to the adoption of the CRPD a number of governments such as the United States, Finland and Germany had policy commitments to include persons with disabilities in their development cooperation efforts.[8] These policies were based on a mixture of approaches including non-discrimination, equality of opportunity and mainstreaming of disability.[9] Since the adoption of the CRPD there has been a momentum building for inclusive and accessible development cooperation particularly with regard to the implementation of Article 32, which requires governments to adopt a range of measures to support disability inclusive development. Box 14.1 summarizes some of these actions from both donor governments and also from countries that would traditionally be in receipt of development aid.

Box 14.1   Examples of progress made by countries on disability inclusive development[10]

1.   Austria has released a manual that provides clear guidelines for including persons with disabilities throughout the project management cycle.
2.   Italy has included disability as a priority issue in its development cooperation action plan for the period 2014–2016.
3.   Denmark has reported persons with disabilities as a target group in its humanitarian action framework.
4.   Sweden has included persons with disabilities as one of its five main target groups for aid.

---

8   USAID (1997) 'Disability Policy'; Ministry for Foreign Affairs (2007) 'Development Policy Programme – Towards a Sustainable and Just World Community'; (2009) 'Cross-cutting themes in the Development Policy Programme of the Government of Finland'; (2012) 'Finland's Development Policy Programme Government Decision-in-Principle'.
9   For example, USAID understanding of disability is grounded in the principle of non-discrimination with the objective to 'to avoid discrimination against people with disabilities in programs which USAID funds'; The Ministry for Foreign Affairs in Finland explains that its concern for the status of disabled people is in the context of poverty reduction and human rights.
10   UN (2014) 'Report of the Secretary-General Realization of the Millennium Development Goals and Other Internationally Agreed Development Goals for Persons with Disabilities: A Disability-Inclusive Development Agenda towards 2015 and Beyond'.

5.   Spain has incorporated a specific indicator for disability in its international development cooperation framework for monitoring future cooperation programmes.

6.   Finland increased funding for its international cooperation and development programme by €3 million for development projects that target disabilities.

7.   The Philippines has formulated a National Plan of Action 2013–2022 to implement the Incheon strategy, which is the Asian-Pacific regional framework for disability rights.

8.   Indonesia has improved accessibility for persons with disabilities in public buildings and facilities, including for its parliamentary elections.

At the regional level, a number of instruments such as the Incheon Strategy in Asia-Pacific, the European Disability strategy and the African Union and its work on disability inclusive development have all had an impact on regional development.[11] For example, the Incheon Strategy sets out a number of specific goals, indicators and targets to achieve disability-inclusive development.

Finally, at the international level, the CRPD and its principles of equality of opportunity and non-discrimination have been successful in creating awareness and promoting the message that international frameworks such as the SDGs must consider persons with disabilities as they set out a road map for equality.[12] For example, the 2013 High Level Meeting on Disability and Development reiterated the point that for development frameworks to be disability-inclusive they must support the full implementation of the CRPD.[13] Furthermore, recent concluding observations and a general comment on accessibility issued by the CRPD Committee of Experts has expanded what Article 32 means for future development cooperation efforts.[14] For example, it asks that all new investments made within the framework of international/development cooperation should be used to encourage the removal of existing barriers and prevent the creation of new barriers and that new objects, infrastructure, facilities, goods, products and services must be fully accessible for all persons with disabilities.[15]

Persons with disabilities right to equality of opportunity and protection from discrimination

Equality of opportunity and the right to protection from discrimination is underpinned for persons with disabilities at the national, regional and international level. Each of these levels is relevant to persons with disabilities in developing countries. At the international level, persons with disabilities are protected by a number of layers of international law. For example the

---

11 UNESCAP (2012) 'Incheon Strategy to "Make the Right Real" for Persons with Disabilities in Asia and the Pacific'; European Commission (2010),' European Disability Strategy 2010–2020'.

12 UN (2014) 'Report of the Open Working Group of the General Assembly on Sustainable Development Goals'.

13 UN (2013) 'Outcome document of the high-level meeting of the General Assembly on the realization of the Millennium Development Goals and Other Internationally Agreed Development Goals for Persons with Disabilities: The Way Forward, a Disability-Inclusive Development Agenda towards 2015 and Beyond'.

14 OHCHR (2013) 'General Comment by the Committee of Experts on the Rights of Persons with Disabilities on Accessibility'.

15 Ibid.

early generation of human rights treaties such as the Universal Declaration of Human Rights (UNHDR); the International Covenant on Economic, Social and Cultural Rights (ICESCR); and the International Covenant on Civil and Political Rights (ICCPR). While none of these treaties make specific reference to persons with disabilities, each of their purpose and intent is broadly defined as ensuring that all people have rights and freedoms, which are then elaborated on in more specific detail.[16] Later jurisprudence on these treaties clarified to some extent their specific application to persons with disability.[17]

In addition, the adoption of the United Nations of the thematic treaties focused on women (Convention on the Elimination of Discrimination against Women), children (Convention on the Rights of the Child) and racial discrimination (Convention on the Elimination of Racial Discrimination) provide protection for persons with disabilities. CEDAW, while not explicitly referencing women and girls with disabilities, through two later general comments has made reference to women with disabilities.[18] The CRC includes specific articles on children with disabilities (Article 23) and also references to non-discrimination with respect to children with disabilities (Article 2(1)). Finally, CERD while also not specifically referencing persons with disabilities has been argued to be relevant to and also inclusive of persons with disabilities.[19]

Lastly, the adoption of the Convention on the Rights of Persons with Disabilities (CRPD) clarifies existing human rights from the perspective of women, men, girls and boys with disabilities. The CRPD sets out the main principles of non-discrimination, respect for difference, equality of opportunity and equality between men and women with disabilities, as a means of removing barriers so that people with disability can enjoy their human rights.[20] The CRPD's principle of non-discrimination is an 'overarching theory of non-discrimination'[21] that covers all of the CRPD's articles, including Article 32 on International Cooperation. It also includes articles that are specific to the rights of women and girls with disabilities (Article 6) and also children with disabilities (Article 7); these are relevant to all of the CRPD's articles, including Article 32 on International Cooperation.

16 For example, Article 2 of the Universal Declaration of Human Rights states that 'Everyone is entitled to all rights and freedoms set forth in the Declaration. Article 1 of the International Covenant on Economic, Social and Cultural Rights (ICESCR) and the International Convention on Civil and Political Rights share the same article that 'All peoples have the right of self-determination. By virtue of that right they freely determine their political status and freely pursue their economic, social and cultural development.'

17 For example, Quinn et al. (2002) 'Human Rights and Disability; The Current Use and Future Potential of United Nations Human Rights Instruments in the Context of Disability' argue that disability is covered by the term 'other status' in Articles 2 and 26, which together constitute the non-discrimination clauses of the treaty. In addition, the most recent general comment adopted by the Human Rights Committee who monitor the ICCPR general comment no 35 on ICCPR's Article 9: Liberty and Security of the Person (2014) makes reference to people with disability. With respect to the ICESCR, general comment no 5, a number of references to people with disability are made. For example in paragraph 11 the general comments states that 'non-public entities, including private employers and private suppliers of goods and services' must 'be subject to both non-discrimination and equality norms in relation to persons with disabilities'.

18 General comment No 18 on disabled women and general comment No 24 on CEDAW's Article 12 contains a reference to women with disabilities.

19 Quinn et al. (2002).

20 CRPD (2006) 'Article 3'.

21 Quinn, G (2009) 'Disability and Human Rights: A New Field in the United Nations' In: Krause, C and Scheinin, M (eds.), International Protection of Human Rights: A Textbook. Turku: Åbo Akademi University Institute for Human Rights, pg. 247.

The multifaceted discrimination and exclusion faced by persons with disabilities

The World Report on Disability states that over one billion people, or approximately 15% of the world's population have some form of disability.[22] It presents compelling evidence that across the world women, men, girls and boys with disabilities have poorer health, lower educational achievements, less economic participation and higher rates of poverty and inequality than persons without disabilities.[23] For the estimated 80% of persons with disabilities living in developing countries, these barriers to accessing services and participation can be intensified due to lack of functioning governance systems and infrastructure, the absence of social protection and the prevalence negative attitudes towards people with disabilities.

Discrimination encountered by women, men, girls and boys with disabilities impacts negatively on their human rights, and as highlighted earlier can reduce their opportunities for education and employment. For example, children with disabilities are less likely to attend school, which in turns decreases their chances of developing skills for future employment opportunities. This pattern of non-attendance is more pronounced in poorer countries and also among women and girls with disabilities.[24] With respect to employment and livelihood opportunities persons with disabilities, particularly women with disabilities, are more likely to be unemployed and earn less even when they are employed. For example, The World Report cites a study of fifty-one countries which highlights employment rates of 52.8% for men with disability and 19.6% for women with disability, compared to 64.9% for non-disabled men, and 29.9% for non-disabled women. This can become more acute for women with disabilities living in rural areas of developing countries, where research has found that more than 80% of women with disabilities have no independent means of livelihood, and are totally dependent on others for their very existence.[25]

What is important to recognize from the outset is that the discrimination faced by women, men, boys and girls with disabilities is multifaceted and can vary depending on their social, economic, cultural and political circumstances, and also because of their individual attributes and different identity groups they belong to. Persons with disabilities can experience discrimination differently depending on what identity they may have, the type of impairment they have, their social status or where they live. For example, reports from the World Health Organisation (WHO) and Human Rights Watch highlight that people with psychosocial disabilities experience discrimination and stigmatization and yet they remain largely invisible in development cooperation efforts.[26] Other reports have highlighted how identifying characteristics such as gender and age can contribute to incidences of discrimination experienced by persons with disabilities that may not be solely attributable to having impairments. For example, studies have shown how women with disabilities are adversely affected due to discrimination based on having dual

---

22 World Health Organization and World Bank (2011) 'World Report on Disability'.
23 Ibid.
24 UNDP (2013) 'Towards an Inclusive and Accessible Future for All'.
25 UNESCAP (2003) 'Final Report of the UN ESCAP Workshop on Women and Disability: Promoting Full Participation of Women with Disabilities in the Process of Elaboration on an International Convention to Promote and Protect the Rights and Dignity of Persons with Disabilities. 18–22 August 2003: Bangkok.
26 World Health Organisation (2010) 'Mental Health and Development: Targeting People with Mental Health Conditions as a Vulnerable Group' pg. 7.

identities, both of which are vulnerable to discrimination in the development context.[27] Finally, recent reports from Tanzania on men and women with albinism highlights how the lives of these men and women can be at risk due factors external to themselves, for example local myth and superstition.[28]

Unpacking equality for persons with disabilities in a development context

Much of the post 2015 narrative focused on the widening inequalities both between countries and within countries and between different groups and sectors. For example, it is estimated that most of the world's poor have shifted from low-income countries to middle-income countries.[29] International processes which have led to the publication of the high-level panel report and the SDGs have had at their core the recognition that in the pursuit for a better life for everyone, no-one should be left behind.[30] In order to achieve this, a series of measures such as affordable access to quality education, social protection and health care, as well as productive and remunerative employment opportunities, are presented as ways to progress towards equality for all, including persons with disabilities.[31]

Unpacking what equality means for persons with disabilities is not an easy task. The term equality has a number of different interpretations, ranging from 'treating likes alike, and un-likes alike',[32] as in the case of formal equality; to equality of opportunity, which as a redistributive justice model focuses on measures to rectify past discrimination; and finally, equality of outcome, which focuses on certain moral principles such as social and economic redistribution. Some authors have argued that the concept of disability equality remains contested and unexplored within the disability community.[33] Within the mainstream development narrative, the debate also continues on whether equality is about levelling the playing field by ensuring equality of opportunity for all, or about equality of outcome, which ensures that systems have factored in the different aspects that can put particular groups at a disadvantage.[34]

The CRPD gives guidance on this and positions equality for persons with disabilities within a human rights framework, which is meant to reflect the universality, indivisibility and interrelatedness

27 See the 'Rights of Special Groups with Disabilities', International Norms and Standards relating to disability' http://www.un.org/esa/socdev/enable/comp001.html, the UN reports which states that 'the combination of male preference in many cultures and the universal devaluation of disability can be deadly for disabled females'; see also Human Rights Watch (2010) 'As if We Weren't Human – Discrimination and Violence Against Women with Disabilities in Northern Uganda'.
28 Albinos in Africa (2015) http://www.stiefel.com/content/dam/stiefel/globals/images/products/Hats OnSkinHealth/Hats_On_For_Skin_Health_Fact_Sheet.pdf
29 Sumner, A. and Tiwari, M. (2011) 'Global Poverty Reduction to 2015 and Beyond', Journal of Global Policy, Vol. 2 No. 2.
30 United Nations (2013) 'A New Global Partnership: Eradicate Poverty and Transform Economics through Sustainable Development' among its recommendations it included 'data must enable us to reach the neediest, and find out whether they are receiving essential services. This means that data gathered will need to be disaggregated by gender, geography, income, disability, and other categories, to make sure that no group is being left behind.'
31 UN (2014) 'Report of the Open Working Group of the General Assembly on Sustainable Development Goals'.
32 Aristotle, 3 Ethica Nicomachea, 112–117, 1131a–1131b, Ackrill, J. L. and Urmson J. O. (eds.), W. Ross translation, New York: Oxford University Press, 1980.
33 See Bill Albert and Carol Miller (2005) 'Mainstreaming Disability in Development; Lessons from Gender Mainstreaming', http://r4d.dfid.gov.uk/PDF/Outputs/Disability/RedPov_gender.pdf
34 Fineman (2010) 'The Vulnerable Subject and the Responsive State', Emory Law Journal, Vol. 60, No. 2.

of all human rights. Arnadottoir contends that the CRPD has recognized that different models of equality have had limited success for persons with disabilities.[35] She claims the CRPD positions disability within the substantive disadvantage model, which focuses on the contextual and social structures of power and disadvantage and aims more clearly at the equality of results and makes a more profound call for change. Within this approach then, mechanisms such as positive obligations and reasonable accommodation are not seen as exceptions but as necessary elements to eradicate discriminatory practices and unequal social structures that perpetuate the exclusion of persons with disabilities. In essence the CRPD's approach to equality accepts that to achieve equality for persons with disabilities, a series of measures may be needed which may treat persons with disabilities differently, and in doing so reflect the diversity of the disability. For example, the CRPD in its general principles recognizes the importance of measures that promote non-discrimination and equality of opportunity, but also has respect for difference as part of the human condition.[36] These principles are intended to crosscut all of the articles of the Convention and therefore are applicable to how they are implemented, including Article 32 on International Cooperation.

The key issue then is how do agencies and NGOs responsible for the implementation of international development programmes reflect the diversity that exists among persons with disabilities and effectively analyze the multiple levels of discrimination experienced by persons with disabilities so that development interventions can be effective in their aim to promote equality for persons with disabilities. A number of authors have suggested that the discrimination and disadvantage experienced by many groups is not solely attributable to being a member of a particular identity group and analysis and policy responses on this basis alone can be limiting.[37] Discrimination and disadvantage can also happen because the state and its actors, through policies they presumed neutral or intentional, create disadvantage for certain groups of the population. Therefore, analysis of what creates barriers and discrimination for persons with disabilities must consider this. The limitations of taking an identity approach without recognizing the potential for intersecting identities and external factors, such as the social and political context, has also been criticized in international law. Bond argues while the recognition exists in international law of multiple and intersecting discrimination, the structures such as the treaty bodies and the United Nations continue to compartmentalize treaties and frustrate efforts to take an intersectional approach to human rights violations.[38] Furthermore it is claimed by De Silva that there needs to be synergies between treaties so there is an 'interlocking web of the human rights framework' which can provide the necessary safeguards against multiple and crosscutting forms of discrimination against women and children with disabilities.'[39]

35 See Arnadottoir, Oddy, 'What does Equality Mean for Persons with Disabilities? Lessons from the New UN Treaty on the Rights of Persons with Disabilities', paper given at public lecture, NUI Galway, September 2009. See also, Chapter 4, The UN Convention on the Rights of Persons with Disabilities: European and Scandinavian perspectives, edited by Quinn and Arnadottoir, 2009.
36 See Article 3 of the CRPD, which outlines the principles of the Convention including equality of opportunity, equality between men and women, and respect for difference and acceptance of persons with disabilities as part of human diversity and humanity.
37 Minnow, M (1990) 'Making all the Difference: Inclusion Exclusion and American Law' Chapter 1, pg. 20; more general see Fineman, Martha, 'The Vulnerability Theory'; Satz (2008) 'Vulnerability, and the Limits of Antidiscrimination', Washington Law Review, Vol. 83, pg. 153.
38 Bond, J (2003) 'International Intersectionality: A Theoretical and Pragmatic Exploration of Women's International Human Rights Violations', Emory Law Journal, Vol. 52, No. 71, pp 70–179.
39 De Silva, R (2009) 'Mining the Intersections: Advancing the Rights of Women and Children with Disabilities within an Interrelated Web of Human Rights', Pacific Rim Law and Policy Journal Association, Vol. 18, No. 1, pg. 294.

The next section discusses how intersectionality and intersectional analysis could be one way to deepen the analysis of the barriers persons with disabilities face to participating on an equal basis with others.

Intersectionality

Intersectionality has been described a tool for analysis, advocacy and policy development that addresses multiple discriminations and helps us understand how different sets of identities impact on access to rights and opportunities.[40] Kimberle Crenshaw, one of its original theorists, developed the thinking in response to black women's experience in employment. She claimed that a single axis framework, which is dominant in anti-discrimination law in the United States, erases black women in the conceptualization, identification and mediation of race and sex discrimination.[41] What this meant in effect is that the issues faced by black women in the cases analyzed by Crenshaw were not directly attributable to having a particular identity trait (e.g. woman, or African American) but instead were a result of other factors which contributed to their discrimination that were not included as protected grounds.[42]

Over recent years, intersectionality has become prominent in a number of ways. First, it considers the interaction of disability, race and gender as organizing structures of society. Second, it can be used as a way to analyze the intertwining of social and cultural categories.[43] Third, intersectionality can be a mechanism for moving beyond a single category perspective to a more complex understanding of difference and power, which understands that one voice does not represent all, and that the voices of those who are marginalized must be recognized.[44] Finally, in terms of international law it encourages analysis of human rights as they affect the whole person or the complex self rather than providing only a snapshot of identity frozen behind the lens of, gender, race or sexual orientation.[45] Finally, it recognizes that the context in which we situate ourselves is vital, in particular taking into account

40 AWID (2004) 'Intersectionality; A Tool for Gender and Economic Justice', Women's Rights and Economic Change, No. 9.
41 Rita Kaur Dhamoon (2011) 'Considerations on Mainstreaming Intersectionality', Political Research Quarterly Political, March 2011 Vol. 64, No. 1, pg. 230–243.
42 Crenshaw (1989) 'Demarginalizing the Intersection of Race and Sex', University of Chicago Legal Forum, pg. 139. Crenshaw discusses the case where a US court using a single axis approach e.g. gender or race failed to capture the fact that black women were discriminated against in a lay off of workers during a recessionary period as a result of not being part of the seniority team – the company had only started to hire black women a few years previous and therefore no black woman had made it to a seniority level as a result of not being in the company long enough. Crenshaw argued that existing legal evidence was seen through the eyes of white women and black men and not black women.
43 Knudsen, Susanne, Intersectionality – A Theoretical Inspiration in the Analysis of Minority Cultures and Identities in Textbooks. Knudsen describes it is where the relationship between gender, race, ethnicity and disability are examined.
44 Grillo (cited in Dhamoon) See Rita Kaur Dhamoon Political Research Quarterly 2011 Vol. 64, pg. 230 originally published online 22 September 2010) describes an important element of intersectionality is the move away from a unidimensional viewpoint such as gender or race to a more complex understanding of difference and power. This move to a more complex understanding it could be argued resonates with the social model of disability.
45 Bond, J. (2003) 'International Intersectionality: A Theoretical and pragmatic exploration of women's international human rights violations', Emory Law Journal, Vol. 52, No. 71; See also De Silva (2009) 'Mining the Intersections: Advancing the Rights of Women and Children with Disabilities within an interrelated web of Human Rights,' Pacific Rim Law and Policy Journal Association, Vol. 18, No. 1, pg. 294.

the historical, social and political context and the experience of the individual.[46] In essence, intersectionality recognizes that all people live multiple layered identities that are derived from social relations, history and the operation of structures of power. Therefore applying an intersectional approach moves away from directly focusing on the individual, to a much broader focus on context (be that economic, political or social) and is useful in investigating how inequalities are produced on the institutional scale through structures, processes and techniques of governance.[47]

All of these points have some form of relevance to the experience of persons with disabilities in developing countries and are discussed further in the next section. In terms of its direct application to disability studies, intersectionality has been discussed in the context of human rights, non-discrimination law and mental health.[48]

How intersectionality differs from single, dual and multiple discrimination

Both the development and disability discourse discuss how multiple discrimination impacts on people from different identity groups, for example, women, persons with disabilities and children. As intersectionality has gained traction in the development narrative, it is important to point out that the intersectionality analysis/approach is not about adding differing combinations of identities that are susceptible to discrimination. For example, it is not about assuming that because a person has a single, dual or multiple identities she or he will be discriminated against. Instead intersectionality is about understanding how the impact of converging identifies and the context they are in impact on access to rights and opportunities. Box 14.2 highlights the different distinctions between situations of discrimination.[49]

Box 14.2   Different distinctions between situations of discrimination

- The first is single discrimination where a person can experience discrimination solely on the grounds of one identity (e.g. disability).
- The second is multiple discrimination where a person can experience discrimination on one ground in one situation and on another ground in another situation.
- The third is compound discrimination which differs from multiple discrimination in that it describes a situation where a person suffers discrimination on the basis of two or more grounds at the same time and where one ground adds to discrimination on another ground.
- The fourth is 'intersectional discrimination' which refers to a situation involving discrimination which is based on several grounds operating and interacting with each other at the same time, and which produces very specific types of discrimination'.

---

46 See Ontario Human Rights Commission (2001) 'An Intersectional Approach to Discrimination Addressing Multiple Grounds in Human Rights Claims'.
47 Grabham, E., Cooper, D., Krishnadas, J., and Herman, D. (eds.) (2011) 'Intersectionality and Beyond, Law, Power and the Politics of Location' Oxon: Routledge-Cavendish.
48 De Silva (2009) 'Mining the Intersections: Advancing the Rights of Women and Children with Disabilities within an interrelated web of Human Rights', Pacific Rim Law and Policy Journal Association; Scheik and Lawson (2011) 'European Union, Non-Discrimination Law and Intersectionality', Vol. 18, No. 1; Degener, T (2013) 'Intersections between Disability, Race and Gender in Discrimination Law' In: Schieka, D and Lawson, A (eds), European Non-Discrimination Law and Intersectionality. Farnham: Ashgate; Janneke van Mens-Verhulst and Lorraine Radtke (2008) 'Intersectionality and Mental Health: A case study' (Chichester, West Sussex, UK: Wiley).
49 See Timo Makkonen (2002) 'Multiple, Compound and Intersectional Discrimination: Bringing the Experiences of the Most Marginalized to the Fore', Institute for Human Rights, Åbo Akademi University, pg. 10.

Intersectionality and its potential in a development context for persons with disabilities

As discussed earlier, despite the fact persons with disabilities are legally protected from discrimination, they are recognized as being one of the groups that are at higher risk of discrimination and exclusion.[50] This can be further intensified for persons with disabilities living in developing countries or in resource poor settings. In these scenarios attributing discrimination solely on the grounds of disability may not provide a comprehensive picture of why discrimination and barriers to participation occur. The following points highlight the potential of intersectionality to think beyond a disability lens and illuminate other factors which cause barriers for persons with disabilities to equal participation in international development.

First, intersectionality does not fix persons with disabilities into a single category. A positive aspect of intersectionality is that it takes into account people's experiences and identities without placing them into fixed categories. Persons with disabilities are members of more than one community or 'category', or have more than one identity. Yet for the most part, responses to disability cluster around the fact persons with disabilities are classified in a fixed category, whether that is for legal protection or for policy development, and are deemed in need of special protections and services. In recent years this has been challenged by the adoption of the CRPD and its requirements on governments to ensure that persons with disabilities can access the social, economic, cultural and political marketplace on an equal basis with others. It has also been challenged by a number of academics that highlight the consequences that can arise as a result of attributing a person with a disability to a fixed category. For example, first on an individual level, Amartya Sen points out that assignment to a particular category or group 'would be a major denial of the freedom each person has on how to decide how exactly to see himself or herself' and that not only is it an 'imposition of an external and arbitrary priority', it is a 'denial of an important liberty of the person who can decide their respective localities to different groups'.[51] Second, Shakespeare highlights how the continued insistence that persons with disabilities be considered as a separate political and social constituency means that disability becomes the defining characteristic. This can lead to disability being the dominant identity or lens that policymakers work through. Third, Satz contends that if we continue to conceptualize the discrimination that persons with disabilities face as discrete and isolated then disability will be conceptualized as fragmented, rather than as constant and part of the human condition.[52] This fragmentation it could be argued then could lead to policy focused specifically on disability rather than encouraging mainstream development to include disability as a crosscutting theme in development. As Bickenbach et al. comment, what we need to do is to help demystify disability and the notion of 'specialness' by recognizing 'that all people have needs that vary in predictable ways over the course of their life span'.[53] The OHCHR and the UN in 2010 have already highlighted this dilemma of having a persistent disability-specific

---

50 UN (2013) 'Outcome Document of the High-Level Meeting of the General Assembly on the Realization of the Millennium Development Goals and Other Internationally Agreed Development Goals for Persons with Disabilities: The Way Forward, a Disability-Inclusive Development Agenda Towards 2015 and Beyond'.

51 Sen (2009) 'The Idea of Justice', pg. 253–259.

52 Satz, Annie (2008) 'Disability, Vulnerability, and the Limits of Antidiscrimination', Washington Law Review, Vol. 83, pg. 153.

53 Bickenbach, J., Chatterji, S., Badley, E.M., and Üstün, T.B. (1999) 'Models of Disablement, Universalism and the International Classification of Impairments, Disabilities and Handicaps', Social Science and Medicine, Vol. 48, pg. 1173–1187.

focus. They highlight that the main activity in international development has been to focus on disability-specific interventions and that in some instances this has meant development aid funding has being used to fund projects that are in contradiction to the CRPD and also could be argued contribute to the disempowerment of people with disabilities.[54]

Second, intersectionality recognizes that persons with disabilities are not a homogenous group. For many of us working in disability inclusive development sector, our use of the term 'persons or people with disabilities' is underpinned by the understanding that persons with disabilities are not the same. Persons with disabilities have different identities and impairments and come from a variety of backgrounds. Yet for most policymakers, persons with disabilities remain an undifferentiated group and this results in the diversity that exists within the disability community going unrecognized. It can also result in development interventions failing to take into account the different needs of different types of persons with disabilities, for example, disability specific programmes not taking into account the specific needs of women and girls with disabilities.[55]

Third, intersectionality can capture the incidences of discrimination that happen at unique intersections that are not solely based on the ground of disability. It also recognizes that factors external to individuals and their identities can perpetuate discrimination, for example, institutional and structural causes, policy and practices. Therefore, analysis and thinking of what causes the exclusion of persons with disabilities from participating in their community and society in a development context needs to be expanded to include the fact that it is to do with more than just discrimination based solely on disability, but rather on how governments, their institutional policies and development processes continue to cause disadvantage for persons with disabilities.

Fourth, intersectionality helps move beyond identity and community politics. The current approach to claiming rights/entitlements is identity led (as evidenced by identity specific treaties and their separate treaty body committees) and as highlighted earlier, some have argued that this leads to a silo effect and separation of human rights. It is also recognized that it can and has led to competition among groups and also the perception by policymakers of an endless list of groups all claiming separate and individual rights and all vying for resources.[56] This has been explained by Martinez as 'the oppression Olympics' which is described as the scenario where groups compete for the mantle of the 'most oppressed' to gain attention and political support of dominant groups. Persons with disabilities usually come at the end of this list and their voices are less likely to be heard due to the fact that oftentimes they are more concerned for their mere survival.[57] Therefore intersectionality has the potential to overcome traditional policy responses

---

54 OHCHR (2010) 'Thematic study by the Office of the United Nations High Commissioner for Human Rights on the role of international cooperation in support of national efforts for the realization of the rights of persons with disabilities', A/HRC/16/38.

55 Research by Driedger and Groce (1991) cited in 'Women with Disabilities in the Developing World, Arenas for Policy Revision and Programmatic Change', Journal of Disability Policy, 1997, Vol. 8, pg. 177.

56 Bond, J. (2003) 'International Intersectionality: A Theoretical and Pragmatic Exploration of Women's International Human Rights Violations', Emory Law Journal, Vol. 52, No. 71; See also De Silva (2009) 'Mining the Intersections: Advancing the Rights of Women and Children with Disabilities within an interrelated web of Human Rights,' Pacific Rim Law and Policy Journal Association, Vol. 18, No. 1, pg. 294.

57 Arnadotttir and Quinn (2009) 'Resisting the Temptation of Elegance: Can the Convention on the Rights of Persons with Disabilities Socialise States to Right Behaviour?' Chapter 10.

of focusing on a singular aspect of a person's identity, and instead recognize a wider number of factors can be at play. It also helps build claims for rights that are not from any one-identity group's perspective but instead from the perspective of human rights for all. Claims for fairness and equality supported by a number of identity groups are harder to ignore. This is not to dismiss the fact the groups such as persons with disabilities, women and children have the right to make individual claims to realize their rights, but rather the fact that many of issues faced by different groups are common, for example, facing lack of access to justice as a result of being poor and a woman with a disability.

Finally, intersectionality recognizes that one voice does not represent all. Persons with disabilities and their representative organizations were successful in ensuring that the voices of persons with disabilities were heard during the CRPD negotiations and most recently with the post 2015 negotiations. In the recent inquiry by the UK government into international development aid and the inclusion of persons with disabilities, the voices of persons with disabilities were also present.[58] In many ways this is the aspect of intersectionality where some governments, intergovernmental organizations and civil society have demonstrated leadership. For example, Australia and the inclusive consultation it undertook to create its Development for All Strategy has been recognized as a good model of practice for including the voices of persons with disabilities.[59] The emphasis on including the voices of those who are most marginalized and absent from decision-making processes has the potential to go to the very core principles of the CRPD, which is 'Nothing about us, without us'. This slogan has been adopted by many different actors in development and it brings awareness to all organizations working in disability inclusive development that the voice of those who are the hardest to reach must be included if development is to be effective for all.

Equally, this is a challenge to organizations that are representative of persons with disabilities as it is to mainstream development organizations. Miles cites that 'at least 70% of global disability is experienced in countries and contexts upon which western ethics and philosophies impinge on peripherally'.[60] Yet the voice of persons with disabilities at 'the decision-making table' remains largely unrepresentative of persons with disabilities from the global south. There is also action needed to ensure that the voice of persons with disabilities include the diversity that exists both in identities and impairments. This is not a criticism unique to the disability community but to the development community in general when it comes to ensuring the voices of those most marginalized are heard.

Concluding remarks

As the world's governments have agreed on a new development framework and a set of goals to underpin this framework, this chapter explored the progress that has been made in disability-inclusive development and the challenges that remain. Persons with disabilities are included in the SDG's targets and indicators, which is a marked improvement on the MDGs where they were completely absent.

58 ADD International (2015) 'The Inquiry into Disability and Development'.
59 For example, the World Health Organisation and the World Bank (2011) *'World Report on Disability'* recognizes AusAID's Development for All Strategy as a best practice model for inclusive development.
60 Miles, M. (1993) 'Disability in an Eastern Religious Context: Historical Perspective' Disability and Society, Vol. 10, No. 1.

The key challenge now for the different actors involved in promoting the inclusion of women, men, girls and boys with disabilities in development is how to devise a set of analytical tools that capture the complexities faced by persons with disabilities in a development context. Having a focus on identifying the barriers that are specific to persons with disabilities is important, but using only a disability lens to dismantle barriers to participation and create pathways of inclusion has its limitations. This chapter has presented intersectionality as a potential approach to overcoming these limitations. Its potential to move beyond fixed categories of identity, shine a light on power structures that disadvantage persons with disabilities, highlight how discrimination is not always attributable to possessing a particular identity and the importance of giving recognition to the voices that are traditionally absent form the basis of a good starting point as to where future analysis can come from. This is helpful for disability-inclusive development and for development overall.

15

DISABILITY FAMILY POLICY AND THE UNITED NATIONS CONVENTION ON THE RIGHTS OF PERSONS WITH DISABILITIES (CRPD)

The case of Israel

Arie Rimmerman and Michal Soffer

Introduction

The family has undergone dramatic changes in its structure and functions, attributed to social, economic, technological, and cultural processes.[1] Nevertheless, in spite of these changes, the family remains "a central social institution and a key trope in the cultural imaginary."[2] Regardless of their ideology or political affiliation, families have strong political assets that are often being used in their engagement with local and national authorities.[3]

Although family matters are increasingly acknowledged by policymakers and national and local leaders, there is a lack of consensus about the definition and essence of "family policy."[4] Kamerman and Kahn tried to provide a general definition: "everything that government does to and for the family."[5] However, it appears that this definition is too loose and may include any policy or legislation that touches upon the family, intentionally and unintentionally. Ooms provided boundaries to family policy, arguing that it primarily geared to families of children who are younger than 18 years of age or those whose offspring are enrolled in full-time education, have

---

1 Furstenberg, F. F., "On a new schedule: Transitions to adulthood and family change" (2010) The Future of Children 20(1) 67–87.
2 Budgeon, S., and Roseneil, S., "Editors' introduction: Beyond the conventional family" (2004) Current Sociology 52(2) 127–134.
3 Bogenschneider, K., *Family policy matters: How policymaking affects families and what professionals can do* (Routledge, 2014).
4 Ibid. See also Kamerman, S. B., and Kahn, A. J., "Families and the idea of family policy" in Kamerman S.B., and Kahn, A.J., (eds.), *Government and families in fourteen countries* (Columbia University Press, 1978).
5 Aldous, J., and Dumon, W., "Family policy in the 1980s: Controversy and Consensus" (1990).

not left the parental household or are not married or in a relationship.[6] Bogenschneider defined family policy according to core family functions: (a) family creation policy, which is policy that facilitates development of human capital and not necessarily consumption.[7] This includes policy concerning marriage, divorce, adoption and foster care; (b) policy that deals with the economic supports and infrastructure that assist families to care for their members; (c) policy that fosters and secures attachment relationships between family members. Such policy is pivotal to raising caring and committed citizens; (d) policy that is geared toward promoting positive child and youth development.

It is clear that there is a lack of consensus about family policy, therefore there is an effort to look for a workable definition. Kamerman made a distinction between explicit and implicit family policies; this is also the case for families of children with disabilities.[8] Explicit policies perceive families as holistic units and aim to protect, promote and strengthen them.[9] Such policy consists of family income security policies, employment-related benefits for working parents, maternal and child health policies and childcare policies. Implicit policies are not aimed at families, nevertheless, they hold important consequences for children and their families. In such policies family characteristics may serve as a criterion for determining eligibility for benefits or services, that is, families are regarded as a means for achieving other policy goals or as an instrument to administer eligibility for benefits or specific provisions.[10]

A historical review of families of children with disabilities revealed that most of them experienced marginalization and segregation, similarly to members with disability in their household.[11] The turning point has been the civil rights movements; the disability rights movement demanded equality and social justice. The pioneering legislation of the Americans with Disabilities Act (ADA) brought significant change in the way government and society view people with disabilities.[12] Since the early 1990s there has been a paradigm shift in the perception of disability from a biomedical model to a social model of disability, which locates disability in the oppressing socio-cultural structure, rather than inside the person with the impairment.[13]

Szymanski argued that the ADA inspired the passage of many similar laws in various countries.[14] Approximately forty countries have enacted disability discrimination laws, and some of this legislation is based on the social model of disability.[15] This reflects a "dramatic worldwide

6 Ooms, T., "Families and government: Implementing a family perspective in public policy" (1990) Social Thought 16(2).

7 Ibid. 3. See also Longman, P., *The empty cradle: How falling birthrates threaten world prosperity and what to do about it* (Basic Books, 2004).

8 Kamerman, S. B., Special invited article families and family policies: Developing a holistic policy agenda. (2009) Hong Kong Journal of Pediatrics 14(2).

9 Strach, P., "All in the family: The private roots of American public policy" (2007) Stanford University Press.

10 Saraceno, C., "Family policies: Concepts, goals and instruments" in Carlo Alberto Notebooks 230 (2011).

11 Rimmerman, A., *Social inclusion of people with disabilities: National and international perspectives* (Cambridge University Press, 2014).

12 Blanck, P., Hill, E., Siegal, C., and Waterstone, M., *Disability, Civil Rights Law, and Policy* (Thomson/West, 2004).

13 Thomas, C., "How is disability understood? An examination of sociological approaches" (2004) Disability & Society 19(6) 569–583.

14 Szymanski, C., "The globalization of disability rights law – From the Americans with Disabilities Act to the UN Convention on The Rights of Persons with Disabilities" (2009) Baltic Journal of Law Politics 2(1).

15 Kanter, A. S., "Globalization of disability rights law" (2003) The Syracuse Journal of International Law and Commerce 30.

expansion of disability rights law . . . culminating in the recent adoption of the U.N. Convention of the Rights of Persons with Disabilities."[16] The United Nations Convention on the Rights of Persons with Disabilities (CRPD) – which the United Nations General Assembly adopted on December 13, 2006 and entered into force on May 3, 2008 – is therefore the epitome of the paradigm shift that began in the early 1990s. This pioneering and international piece of legislation aims, as stated in Article 1, "to promote, protect and ensure the full and equal enjoyment of all human rights and fundamental freedoms by all persons with disabilities, and to promote respect for their inherent dignity."[17]

The CRPD is a highly individualized legal document. Put differently, it centers on the individual, that is the person with the disability, while favoring the rights of persons with disabilities over those of their families.[18] Furthermore, the CRPD depicts family members with disabilities as having an instrumental role, rather than a dependent role, in their families. In other cases, the CRPD mandates States to assist families in realizing the human rights of the person with the disability.[19] Nonetheless, the person with the disability is perceived as an inherent part of a family, which is argued to be "the natural and fundamental group unit of society"[20] and therefore, the family:

> [I]s entitled to protection by society and the State, and that persons with disabilities and their family members should receive the necessary protection and assistance to enable families to contribute towards the full and equal enjoyment of the rights of persons with disabilities.

Article 4 of the CRPD lists the various obligations of States Parties, which have ratified the Convention. The beginning of the Article reads as follows:

> States Parties undertake to ensure and promote the full realization of all human rights and fundamental freedoms for all persons with disabilities without discrimination of any kind on the basis of disability. To this end, States Parties undertake:

> a. To adopt all appropriate legislative, administrative and other measures for the implementation of the rights recognized in the present Convention;
> b. To take all appropriate measures, including legislation, to modify or abolish existing laws, regulations, customs and practices that constitute discrimination against persons with disabilities;
> c. To take into account the protection and promotion of the human rights of persons with disabilities in all policies and programmes.

The focus of this chapter is an examination of family policies aimed at Israeli families of children with disabilities, therefore it is important to provide data concerning this population. Unfortunately, there is scant and non-systematic information about the prevalence and

---

16 Ibid. 14.
17 UN Convention for the Rights of Persons with Disabilities (2006).
18 Kayess, R., and French, P., "Out of darkness into light? Introducing the Convention on the Rights of Persons with Disabilities." (2008) Human Rights Law Review 1.
19 Ibid.
20 Ibid. see section x of the Preamble.

characteristics of children with disabilities.[21] The main source is a recent survey conducted by the National Insurance Institute of Israel and Myers–JDC-Brookdale between 1995 and 1997 of non-institutionalized children with disabilities under the age of 17. It is estimated that children with disabilities comprise 13.1% (321,000) of the disability population in Israel.[22] Children with severe disabilities, who have a permanent limitation or a chronic medical condition and have been defined as " in need of constant care" by the medical system, comprise 60% (189,000) of all children with disabilities.[23] According to *KESHER* ("the Home for Special Families," a non-profit organization), the number of children with disabilities and chronic illnesses was 322,000 in 2012, about two-thirds (about 214,667 children) are considered as having functional limitations.[24]

The chapter intends to review the current family policy related to households of children with disabilities, introduce proposed legislation in this regard and critically analyze it from the perspective of UN CRPD. The first section reviews implicit policies and explicit policies, focusing primarily on a prominent explicit policy, "Disabled Child Benefits," a family support policy that is provided to parents of children (minors) with disabilities in order to alleviate the "burden" that raising a child with a disability entails. The second section presents a new initiative for disability-related family policy in Israel – the *Families of Persons with Disabilities Bill*, which was introduced to the Israeli parliament in March 2014. This Bill sets out to "anchor, for the first time, the basic rights of special families in a way that aligns with the CRPD, which Israel has ratified."[25] Lastly, we critically analyze the current policy in Israel against the backdrop of the needs of families of children with disabilities in Israel, the CRPD – which Israel signed on March 2007 and ratified on September 10, 2012 – and central disability family policies in Israel.[26]

Implicit and explicit policies for families of children with disabilities in Israel: General family policies

Israel has been argued to maintain "an extensive system of laws designed to protect children's rights. It is a signatory to numerous international conventions and provides many health and welfare services to children."[27] There are basically two central policies for children in Israel – child allowance and tax benefits.

Child allowance

Child allowance is a monthly benefit that is paid by the National Insurance Institute to families who reside in Israel for children under the age of 18. "The allowance is aimed at helping the family with the expenses entailed in raising their children, and it is paid regardless of the amount of the family's income."[28]

21 Naon, D., Morginstin, B., Schimmel, M. and Rivlis, G., "Children with special needs: An assessment of needs and coverage by services" (2000) Myers–JDC-Brookdale Institute.
22 Ibid. See also Ben Moshe, E., Rofman, L, and Haber, Y., Persons with disabilities in Israel 2011: Disability and inclusion in Israeli society. A comparative and longitudinal perspective (Commission for Equal Rights of People with Disabilities, Ministry of Justice 2012).
23 Ibid.
24 Knesset, Labor, Welfare and Health Committee, *Protocol no. 654* (February 21, 2012).
25 Families of Persons with Disabilities Bill of 2014.
26 Association for Civil Rights in Israel. (September 11, 2012).
27 Library of Congress, Children's rights: Israel (February 28, 2014).
28 National Insurance Institute, *Children.*

Tax benefits

Tax benefits ('tax credit points') are given to families for each child who is under the age of 18. As of 2012, additional tax benefits are provided to: a) families with children under the age of 5 (in case of a married couple, these two benefits are provided to mothers), b) families with toddlers, that is children under the age of 4 (in case of a married couple, this benefit is provided to fathers).[29]

Brender and Strawczynski, who compared Israel's family support spending in comparison to countries, demonstrated that it has been considerably lower than most of the countries. Tax benefits have been lower, while child allowance is "significantly lower than in other developed countries."[30] Interestingly, unlike most of OECD countries, Israeli families are not eligible for specific tax benefits for child raising expenses, in addition to the universal tax benefits and child allowance.

Other implicit policies

It is beyond the scope of the current chapter to review the full array of implicit and explicit policies that concern families with children with disabilities. We note three important implicit policies – the *National Health Insurance Law 5754–1994*, the *Rehabilitative Day-Care Centers Law 5760–2000*, and the *Special Education Law 5748–1988*. According to the *National Health Insurance Law 5754–1994*, all Israeli residents are eligible for health services that are financed by the government. According to the *Rehabilitative Day-Care Centers Law 5760–2000*, toddlers with a disability between the ages of 1 and 3 are eligible for appropriate rehabilitative, therapeutic, and educational services that are financed by the government.[31]

The *Special Education Law 5748–1988* was "enacted to ensure education modified to accommodate students with disabilities aged between 3 to 21 years old."[32] Chapter 7 of the *Special Education Law 5748–1988* instructed school placement committees to favor placement in mainstream education with supports over placement in the special education system (Special Education Law 5748–1988).

Importantly, one of the central changes that are attributed to the *Special Education Law 5748–1988* was enhancing parents' involvement in their child's education. The law has anchored parents' rights to participate in decisions and discussions concerning their children's education as well as access to documents concerning their child.[33]

Nonetheless, in 2002 the State Comptroller and Ombudsman Report showed that government spending on children with special needs was primarily allocated to the special education system whereas only a small portion of the budget had been used for integrating students with disabilities into the mainstream education system. The concern raised was that parents who lacked assets to cover mainstreaming would find themselves enrolling their children in special education.

This policy was challenged by parents, in the case of *the Voluntary Association for Children and Adults with Down Syndrome v. the Ministry of Education*,[34] and in 2002 "the Inclusion Chapter –

29 All Rights, *Parents* (2014a).
30 Brender, A., and Strawczynski, M., *Government support for young families in Israel* (2014).
31 Ibid. 27.
32 Special Education Law 5748–1988. See also Feldman, D., "Human rights of children with disabilities in Israel – The vision and the reality" (2009) Disability Studies Quarterly 29(1).
33 Naon, D., Milstein, E., and Marom, M., "Including children with special needs in elementary school: Follow-up on inclusion subsequent to the Special Education Law" (2011) Myers-JDC-Brookdale Institute.
34 Rimmerman, A., Avrami, S., and Araten-Bergman, T., "Policy towards persons with Disabilities: From social legislation to rights legislation" in U. Aviram, J. Gal, and Y. Katan (eds.), *Formulating social policy in Israel – Issues and trends* (Taub Center for Social Policy Research, 2007).

D1" was added to the original law. This Chapter emphasizes the inclusion of children with disabilities in the "regular" school and preschool system. Nonetheless the "Inclusion Chapter" was not fully implemented and three additional cases were filed in court by parents and parents' organizations.[35]

In 2007, the Minister of Education, Professor Yuli Tamir, appointed a public committee headed by Justice (emeritus) Dalia Dorner. The "Committee for the Examination of the Special Education System in Israel," or the "Dorner Committee," emphasized the basic right of parents to be involved in their child's education and thus, to choose where, that is in which education system, he or she would be educated. The central recommendations of the Dorner Committee were to adopt a new model for placement and budgeting based on "parent choice."[36] In May 2013, the State Comptroller and Ombudsman Report concerning the year 2012 addressed the issue of inclusion of children with disabilities in mainstream education and generally concluded that although more than a decade has passed after the enactment of the "Inclusion Chapter," it has not been implemented.[37] Currently, families of children with disabilities and organizations for families of children with disabilities are pushing the implementation of the law. Parents' involvement and the right to choose were also catalysts in the Families of Persons with Disabilities Proposed Bill of 2014, which is discussed in this chapter.

Central explicit policies for families of children with disabilities

The vast majority of children with disabilities in Israel reside in the community. In 2011, the *Knesset's* Committee for Children's Rights requested from the *Knesset's* Information and Research Center to compile a report concerning the availability of community services for "children with special needs" in Israel.[38] The report cites the only study that was conducted in Israel by the National Insurance Institute of Israel and Myers-JDC-Brookdale, which as aforementioned was conducted between 1995 and 1997,[39] and found extensive disparities in service reception between different groups of populations, for example, between children from socio-economic disadvantaged regions versus children from more affluent regions (69% vs. 92%, respectively), and between Jewish and Arab (90% vs. 49%, respectively). The lack of services for families of Arab Israelis with disabilities and their inaccessibility was also evident in a later survey conducted by Sandler-Loeff and Shahak.[40] Similarly, Arab, Bedouin – but also Ultra-Orthodox – children and youth were argued to have unequal opportunities for inclusion in mainstream education.[41]

The central policy for families of children with disabilities in Israel is coined "Disabled Child Benefits."[42] The detailed list of what constitutes a child's "disability" is mentioned in the *National Insurance Institute Regulations (Disabled Child) of 2010*, and is a function of the type of the child's impairment and the extent to which the child is dependent on others.

Ample research has shown high direct costs for families with children with disabilities. Furthermore, out-of-pocket expenditures were found to be higher among families with children

35 Ibid. 33 for a comprehensive account of the events.
36 Committee for the Examination of the Special Education System in Israel, 2009.
37 State Comptroller and Ombudsman, *Annual Report 63C*, Jerusalem (2012).
38 Ibid. 24.
39 Ibid. 33.
40 Sandler-Loeff, A., and Shahak, Y., *People with disabilities in Arab society in Israel: An opportunity for social change* (The Unit for Disabilities and Rehabilitation, JDC Israel, 2006).
41 Ibid. 33.
42 National Insurance Institute, *Disabled child*.

with unique health care needs.[43] Therefore it is not surprising that the National Insurance Institute's website states that:

> The National Insurance Institute acknowledges the severe caring burden that is part of raising a handicapped child with a severe impairment and therefore it shares the family costs in order to assist with raising the child and in order to provide, as much as possible, a normal life for him/her, within the family and community.

According to Section 3 of the *National Insurance Institute Regulations (Disabled Child) of 2010*, additional benefits are given to "assist with caring and schooling," nevertheless, unlike the impression one receives from the website, these additional benefits do not attempt to cover all additional costs that are involved in raising a child with a disability.[44]

"Disabled Child Benefits" are provided until the child reaches the age of 18 years and 3 months of age.[45] Specifically, eligible children are one of the following[46] (National Insurance Institute of Israel, n.d.):

- A child (from the age of 91 days to 3 years) who is suffering from a severe developmental delay.
- A child (from the age of 3 to 18 years) who is far more dependent on the help of others than other children his age.
- A child (from the age of 91 days to 18 years) who requires the constant presence of another person.
- A child (from the age of 91 days to 18 years) who requires constant supervision.
- A child with a special disability: hearing disability (from birth to 18 years), Down Syndrome (from birth to 18 years), vision disability (from 91 days to 18 years), autism or a similar condition (from 91 days to 18 years).
- A child with a special disability in both limbs (from the age of 91 days to 18 years).
- A child who needs assistance in communicating (from age 3) due to a total lack of verbal communication.
- A child (from the age of 91 days to 18 years) who requires special medical treatment.

There are, however, "conditions of entitlement" as follows:[47]

a. The child is the child of an insured person who is an Israeli resident.
b. The child is located in Israel.
c. The child is not living with a foster family or in an institution.
d. The child is not receiving mobility allowance, except for a child who has been classified as being 80% mobility disabled, or requires and uses a wheelchair.

According to the National Insurance Institute of Israel and Myers-JDC-Brookdale survey, merely 80% of all children with disabilities in Israel have received Disabled Child Benefits between 1995 and 1997, while it has been argued that in light of the survey's results, 24% of children with

---

43 Stabile, M., and Allin, S. "The economic costs of childhood disability" (2012) *The Future of Children* 22(1).
44 Ibid. 42. See also Dagan, T., Rothler, R., Mishali, L., Rimmerman, A., and Soffer, M., *Employment, welfare and taxes and people with disabilities in Israel* (December 31, 2011).
45 Ibid.
46 Ibid. 42.
47 Ibid. 42.

disabilities should actually be entitled to these benefits.[48] Similarly, according to the National Council for the Child, in 2012, merely 10.1% of children with chronic illnesses and disabilities in Israel received Disabled Child Benefits.[49]

Dagan and colleagues (2011), who mapped all disability policies concerning welfare, taxes and employment in Israel, have argued that

> [W]e did not locate an official calculation that details the costs behind the rates of Disability Benefits and Disabled Child Benefits and their adjustment to the needs of persons disabilities or parents of children with disabilities.[50] It seems that these benefits are short of covering basic needs (housing, food, health) not to speak of the distinct health and accessibility needs of persons with disabilities.

As of today, "Disabled Child Benefits" in Israel range between 1,095 and 3,174 NIS.[51] For the sake of comparison and context, the minimum wage in Israel is 4,300.[52]

Other central benefits for families with children with a disability, that is children who were recognized by the National Insurance Institute of Israel as such, include various discounts on municipal taxes (which could be subjected to a means test and vary between different municipalities), water, electricity and phone bills,[53] as well as the tax benefits (income tax and property tax credit points).

It is clear that Israel's family disability policy is less progressive than the two leading European countries, Sweden and France. Israel relies primarily on monetary benefits and tax reductions. Sweden, for example, provides comprehensive and high-quality services for children with disability as well as for their families. In addition, decent monetary benefits are provided to parents of a child with a disability (a monthly childcare allowance; Attendance Allowance paid to those in need of personal assistance of more than 20 hours per week to cope with daily-life activities). Both benefits are non-means-tested and are provided based on medical and particularly functional assessment. Somewhat similarly, in France, cash benefits serve as supplements to comprehensive services that are available from early childhood.[54] However, Israel's family disability policy is favorable to that in the United States; unlike the case in Israel, in the United States monetary benefits (i.e. Supplemental Security Income [SSI]) are available only to low-income families. In both countries tax credits are provided to the middle and upper classes.

Families of Persons with Disabilities Proposed Bill of 2014

On March 18, 2014, the Families of Persons with Disabilities Bill of 2014 was submitted to the *Knesset*. The explanations section of the Bill argues that

> [H]undreds of families that have a family member with a disability as well as approximately 50 organizations formed a coalition to anchor, for the first time, the basic

---

48 Ibid. 42, 33, 21.
49 The Israel National Council for the Child, *Children in Israel* (2013).
50 Ibid. 44.
51 Ibid. 42.
52 All Rights, *Minimum wage (2014b)*.
53 Ibid. 44. See also All Rights, *Children with special needs* (2014c).
54 Tisdall, K., and Colver, A. F, "National contextual factors affecting the lives of disabled children in Denmark, France, Germany, Ireland, Italy, Sweden and UK" (University of Newcastle upon Tyne, Robinson Library, 2006).

rights of special families, in a way that aligns with the obligations of the CRPD which Israel has ratified.

The coalition was headed by *KESHER*. Other members were the legal clinic from Bar Ilan University and the legal clinic from the College of Law and Business, Ramat Gan.

The explanations section of the Bill further argues that Israel has failed to fully acknowledge the importance of families of person with disabilities.[55] The needs of families are neglected, their rights unacknowledged. The families of persons with disabilities, which the Bill coins "special families," are thus rendered invisible. The aim of the Bill as stated in the explanations section is therefore,

> [T]o anchor the rights of families of children and adults with disabilities while acknowledging their centrality, expertise and capabilities to care, support and empower the person with the disability, as well as to meet their special needs.[56]

The Bill consists of six chapters.[57] **Chapter A** (Purpose, Definitions and Basic Principals) deals with the following: **cultural and language adaptations** of services so that they reflect the person and family's preferences and are culturally sensitive; **determining eligibility** in a way that takes into consideration the person and family's natural life course; **the right to make decisions** – parents are entitled to make decisions concerning the life of their child, according to their will and preferences, to act on behalf of the child and represent him/her in order to realize the child's rights. Of note, children with disabilities who are capable of stating their opinions have a right to do so freely and his/her opinions are considered (according to age etc.); **the right to receive information** – family members are entitled to accessible information, in a number of languages, as well as information regarding the ways through which to realize these rights; **representation** (of family members and persons with disabilities) in public committees that deal with policy or programs for persons with disabilities or their families.

Chapter B (Family Centers) mandates the establishment of nationally spread one-stop family centers that will aim to "empower the family members of persons with disabilities."[58] The centers will be "operated by multidisciplinary teams who are experts in the needs of the families."[59] Nevertheless, families will be "active partners in running the centers." The chapter lists the following services for family members: "'mentoring and support services'"; "psychotherapy, family and marriage counseling"; "empowerment groups, advocacy, leadership and support"; "coordination of services, mediation as well as meeting between multi-professional staff members of service providers with families"; "assistance services, tutoring services and Para-professional services"; "vocational counseling"; and "counseling in decision making."[60] In addition, the centers will train volunteers who will assist families, "will provide counseling to employers of family members," "will initiate social and community activities for both persons with and without disabilities," will engage in activities to raise awareness and change attitudes towards persons with disabilities, "will provide accessible and current information to families and professionals, in various languages, on services and rights of persons with disabilities."

---

55 Ibid. 25.
56 Ibid. pp 10.
57 Chapter F entitled "Miscellaneous," will not be discussed.
58 Ibid. pp 4.
59 Ibid. pp 10.
60 Ibid. pp 5.

Chapter C (The Right to Family Life and Leisure) lists the various supports and services that families need in order to realize their rights for family life and leisure. These include, for example, "assistance during leisure time," that is tutoring services in the afternoon and on holidays, as well as "a short holiday." One way to realize this right would be via accessible and adjusted "holiday retreats" (*nofshonim*) for families, which will be established throughout Israel.

Chapter D (Employment) deals with initiating various programs for primary caretakers, such as vocational counseling and placement, incentives to employers, counseling and guidance services for employers of family members.

Chapter E (Decision Making) mandates that parents be fully informed before any decision concerning their child, be invited to any decision-making committee or activity and be heard.

Families of Persons with Disabilities Proposed Bill of 2014 and the CRPD: A Discussion

As was evident in our review, Israel relies primarily on non-means-tested monetary benefits for families with children with disabilities. Similar to most Western countries, eligibility is based on medical and functional assessments. As aforementioned, according to the National Insurance Institute, Disabled Child Benefits are geared towards alleviating additional costs that are a part and parcel of raising a child with a disability. Anecdotal evidence indicates that these benefits, however, fail to truly account for these additional costs. The limited available data also points to the fact that services are also lacking and neglect to cover parts of the population – often those who are most excluded and marginalized. Moreover, such evidence also implies that the medical and functional assessments that assist in determining eligibility are too strict, therefore, failing to cover many additional families. These faults clearly contrast with the CRPD's spirit in general, especially with the principals of equality and justice. Specifically, inadequate services and means contradict Article 28 – Adequate standard of living and social protection, in particular, which addresses the role of the state in providing adequate standards of living to families (section 1) and assistance to those living in situations of poverty (section 2c).[61]

Importantly and perhaps not less troubling is the National Insurance Institute's choice of terminology. While describing the nature of Disabled Child Benefits, the institute's website clearly depicts children with disabilities as a burden on families – financially and otherwise. This representation stands in sharp opposition to the CRPD where assistance to families is not due to burden but rather as a mean to enable families to promote the realization of the family member with the disability.[62]

Although the *Families of Persons with Disabilities Bill of 2014* carefully utilizes the rhetoric of rights in general and the CRPD in particular, a closer look at the Bill points out that it does not fully and truly align with a rights-based approach, the social model, and the Convention. A review of the initial periodic reports in the UN Refugee Agency's (UNHCR) website on the implementation of the CRPD, which were submitted by sixteen countries to the treaty's monitoring bodies (Argentina, Australia, Austria, Azerbaijan, Belgium, China, Costa Rica, Denmark, Hong Kong, Hungry, Macau, Mexico, Morocco, Paraguay, Peru and Sweden), shows that, unlike Israel, these countries regard the CRPD as the basis for change, rather than trying to modify existing policy with its historic shortcomings. As a whole, in terms of its terminology, the Bill is an

---

61 Ibid. 17.
62 Ibid. 18.

amalgam of biomedical, social welfare language and rights discourses. Specifically, the Bill is laden with references to needs. Welfare entails meeting basic needs.[63] Within a needs–based approach, needs are assessed and are met only when resources are available. Lang, Kett, Groce and Trani[64] argue that the CRPD 'goes beyond other theories of justice based on incomes and commodities, social primary goods or basic needs'. Rights, unlike needs, convey a legal and moral obligation.[65] Within a framework of rights, children with disability and their families are deserving citizens rather than mere recipients of social services. It is noteworthy that when the Bill does refer to rights, it actually intends to merely address social rights or entitlements at the very concrete level, that is whether families are aware of relevant services and know how to obtain them.

The reference to families in the *Families of Persons with Disabilities Bill of 2014* as "special families" is also problematic as it is reminiscent with the term "special needs" (a term which is unfortunately used as well in the Bill). The language of "special needs" was argued to be discriminatory, to evoke sentimentality, prejudice and fear.[66] Moreover, the language of "special needs" once again positions persons with disabilities and their families in the arena of meeting needs, rather than in a frame of realizing personhood.

The major content of the Bill refers to concrete future services for families. This is disappointing on various levels. It seems that the Bill in its current form is not, alas, intended to "anchor rights," as it claims, but rather to develop specific services in areas which were neglected in past policies, such as respite care. It is noteworthy that the Bill does not even attempt to modify existing policies, namely, Disabled Child Benefits, but merely to address wants. This does not reflect a paradigm shift but rather a continuation of past ideology, of welfare-oriented policies. The two central suggested programs, namely respite care and one-stop centers, focus on the family while largely neglecting the role of the environment, the socio-cultural and political structures that contribute to the oppression and disadvantage of persons with disabilities and their families. In other words, the Bill, unlike the CRPD, fails to "address issues such as discrimination, non-participation, social inequality, vulnerability and agency."[67] The one-stop family centers, in particular, primarily offer therapeutic services, that is, engage in person fixing. Once again, the arsenal of therapeutic services and the central role of paramedical and medical experts (as referred to in the Bill) align with a biomedical, rehabilitative model, rather than with a human rights approach. Another concern is that both the respite care program and the one-stop centers are highly segregated programs. It remains a question whether they will enable participation, or rather, unwittingly, contribute to the exclusion and stigmatization of persons with disabilities and their families.

Perhaps the most central critique of the Bill, apart from its terminology and specific content, lies in the answer to the following question: Does enacting a separate law for families align with the spirit and nature of the CRPD? It seems that the question to this question is negative. As was aforementioned, the CRPD gives preference to the rights of persons with disabilities over those of their families. Families are supported in order to promote the realization of the rights of the

63 Allardt, E., *To have, to Love, to be – About Welfare in the Nordic Countries* (Argos: Lund, 1975).
64 Lang, R., Kett, M., Groce, N., and Trani, J. F., "Implementing the United Nations Convention on the rights of persons with disabilities: principles, implications, practice and limitations." (2011, p. 216) ALTER-European Journal of Disability Research 5(3).
65 Jonsson, U., "A human rights-based approach to programming" (2005) Reinventing Development 47.
66 Corbett, J., *Bad mouthing: The language of special needs* (Cassell, 1995). Norwich, B., "The connotation of special education labels for professionals in the field" (1999) British Journal of Special Education 26(4).
67 Ibid. 64.

member with a disability. In other words, the beneficiary is the person, not the family,[68] which is not the case in the Bill. Furthermore, the CRPD acknowledges the complex and delicate relationships that persons with disabilities may have with their families. For example, Article 16 – Freedom from exploitation, violence and abuse – is formulated sensitively with respect to families, calling for examining these negative expressions within the home (section 1) and supporting families (section 2), avoiding situations where the family or family members are the source of exploitation or abuse. The Bill completely disregards such situations, reflecting a one-dimensional perception of the family institution.

In sum, the current central policy in Israel that addresses families with children with disabilities is rooted in the biomedical model and engages in practices that are alien to contemporary definitions of disability as a structural wrong. The CRPD is the epitome of these definitions. The *Families of Persons with Disabilities Bill of 2014*, although a recent initiative that attempts to address the needs of families, does not offer a paradigm shift. Israel, like other Western countries, is in the midst of a paradigm shift.[69] The ratification of the CRPD by Israel signifies a landmark in the framing of disability in Israeli society. We believe and hope that future legislation and policy initiatives in Israel will truly capture the essence and spirit of the CRPD.

Bibliography

Statutory instruments

All Rights, Children with special needs (2014c). http://www.kolzchut.org.il/en/Main_Page
All Rights, Minimum wage (2014b).
All Rights, Parents (2014a).
Families of Persons with Disabilities Bill (2014). https://knesset.gov.il/privatelaw/data/19/2348.rtf
Special Education Law 5748-1988.
UN Convention for the Rights of Persons with Disabilities (2006). http://www.un.org/disabilities/convention/conventionfull.shtml

Books

Allardt, E., *To have, to love, to be – about welfare in the Nordic countries* (Lund, 1975).
Ben Moshe, E., Rofman, L, and Haber, Y., *Persons with disabilities in Israel 2011: Disability and inclusion in Israeli society. A comparative and longitudinal perspective* (Commission for Equal Rights of People with Disabilities, Ministry of Justice, 2012).
Blanck, P., Hill, E., Siegal, C., and Waterstone, M., *Disability, civil rights law, and policy* (Thomson/West, 2004).
Bogenschneider, K., *Family policy matters: How policymaking affects families and what professionals can do* (Routledge, 2014).
Corbett, J., *Bad mouthing: The language of special needs* (Cassell, 1995).
Kamerman, S. B., and Kahn, A. J., "Families and the idea of family policy" in Kamerman, S. B., and Kahn, A. J., (eds.), *Government and families in fourteen countries* (Columbia University Press, 1978).
Longman, P., *The empty cradle: How falling birthrates threaten world prosperity and what to do about it* (Basic Books, 2004).
Rimmerman, A., *Social inclusion of people with disabilities: National and international perspectives* (Cambridge University Press, 2014).
Rimmerman, A., Avrami, S., and Araten-Bergman, T., "Policy towards persons with Disabilities: From social legislation to rights legislation" in Aviram, U., Gal, J., and Katan, Y., (eds.), *Formulating social policy in Israel – issues and trends* (Taub Center for Social Policy Research, 2007).
Strach, P., *All in the family: The private roots of American public policy* (Stanford University Press, 2007).

68 Ibid. 18.
69 Ibid. 12.

Journal articles

Aldous, J., and Dumon, W., "Family policy in the 1980s: Controversy and consensus" (1990) Journal of Marriage and the Family 52

Brender, A., and Strawczynski, M., "Government support for young families in Israel" (2014). Research Department, Bank of Israel, Jerusalem (in Hebrew).

Budgeon, S., and Roseneil, S., "Editors' introduction: Beyond the conventional family" (2004) Current Sociology 52(2).

Dagan, T., Rothler, R., Mishali, L., Rimmerman, A., and Soffer, M., "Employment, welfare and taxes and people with disabilities in Israel" (2011). Research report submitted to the National Insurance Institute, Jerusalem (in Hebrew).

Feldman, D., "Human rights of children with disabilities in Israel – The vision and the reality" (2009) Disability Studies Quarterly 29(1).

Furstenberg, F. F., "On a new schedule: Transitions to adulthood and family change" (2010) The future of children 20(1).

Jonsson, U., "A human rights-based approach to programming" (2005) Reinventing development 47.

Kamerman, S. B., "Special invited article families and family policies: Developing a holistic policy agenda" (2009) Hong Kong Journal of Pediatrics 14(2).

Kanter, A. S., "Globalization of disability rights law" (2003) The Syracuse Journal of International Law and Commerce 30.

Kayess, R., and French, P., "Out of darkness into light? Introducing the convention on the rights of persons with disabilities" (2008) Human Rights Law Review 1.

Lang, R., Kett, M., Groce, N., and Trani, J. F., "Implementing the United Nations Convention on the rights of persons with disabilities: Principles, implications, practice and limitations" (2011) ALTER-European Journal of Disability Research 5(3).

Naon, D., Milstein, E., and Marom, M., "Including children with special needs in elementary school: Follow-up on inclusion subsequent to the Special Education Law" (2011) Myers-JDC-Brookdale Institute.

Naon, D., Morginstin, B., Schimmel, M., and Rivlis, G., "Children with special needs: An assessment of needs and coverage by services" (2000) Myers-JDC-Brookdale Institute.

Norwich, B., "The connotation of special education labels for professionals in the Field" (1999) British Journal of Special Education 26(4).

Ooms, T., "Families and government: Implementing a family perspective in public policy" (1990) Social Thought 16(2).

Sandler-Loeff, A., and Shahak, Y., "People with disabilities in Arab society in Israel: An opportunity for social change" (2006) The Unit for Disabilities and Rehabilitation, JDC Israel.

Stabile, M., and Allin, S., "The economic costs of childhood disability" (2012) The Future of Children 22(1).

Szymanski, C., "The globalization of disability rights law-from the Americans with Disabilities Act to the UN Convention on The Rights of Persons with Disabilities" (2009) Baltic Journal of Law & Politics 2(1).

Thomas, C., "How is disability understood? An examination of sociological approaches" (2004) Disability & Society 19(6), 569–583.

Tisdall, K., and Colver, A. F., "National contextual factors affecting the lives of disabled children in Denmark, France, Germany, Ireland, Italy, Sweden and UK" (2006) University of Newcastle upon Tyne, Robinson Library.

Official publications

Association for Civil Rights in Israel (September 11, 2012). http://www.acri.org.il/en/

The Israel National Council for the Child, *Children in Israel* (in Hebrew) (2013).

Knesset, Labor, Welfare and Health Committee, *Protocol No. 654* (2012). (in Hebrew) see https://www.knesset.gov.il/protocols/heb/protocol_search.aspx?ComId=28

Library of Congress, *Children's Rights* (Israel, 2014).

National Insurance Institute, *Children.* https://www.btl.gov.il/English%20Homepage/Benefits/Children/Pages/default.aspx

National Insurance Institute, *Disabled Child.* https://www.btl.gov.il/English%20Homepage/Benefits/Disabledchild/Pages/default.aspx

State Comptroller and Ombudsman, *Annual Report 52B* (Jerusalem, 2002). (in Hebrew) http://www.mevaker.gov.il/En/Pages/default.aspx

State Comptroller and Ombudsman, *Annual Report 63C* (Jerusalem, 2012) (in Hebrew) http://www.mevaker.gov.il/En/Pages/default.aspx

The UN Refugee Agency, *States Parties Reports* (2013). http://www.refworld.org/type,STATEPARTIES-REP,CRPD,,,,0.html

Working papers

Saraceno, C., "Family policies. Concepts, goals and instruments" in Carlo Alberto Notebooks 230 (2011). http://www.carloalberto.org/assets/working-papers/no.230.pdf.

INDEX

Printed in Great Britain
by Amazon

56933149R00156